THE ART OF
Couture Sewing

THE ART OF
Couture Sewing

Second Edition

ZOYA NUDELMAN

CHICAGO, IL

Fairchild Books
An imprint of Bloomsbury Publishing Inc

BLOOMSBURY
NEW YORK · LONDON · OXFORD · NEW DELHI · SYDNEY

Fairchild Books

An imprint of Bloomsbury Publishing Inc

1385 Broadway	50 Bedford Square
New York	London
NY 10018	WC1B 3DP
USA	UK

www.bloomsbury.com

**FAIRCHILD BOOKS, BLOOMSBURY and the Diana logo
are trademarks of Bloomsbury Publishing Plc**

First edition published 2009

Library of Congress Cataloging-in-Publication Data
Nudelman, Zoya.
The art of couture sewing / Zoya Nudelman. -- Second [edition].
pages cm
Includes bibliographical references and index.
ISBN 978-1-60901-831-3 (paperback)
1. Sewing. 2. Tailoring (Women's) 3. Dressmaking. 4. Fashion design. I. Title.
TT515.N83 2016
646.4--dc23
2015023065

ISBN: HB: 978-1-60901-831-3
ePDF: 978-1-60901-921-1

Typeset by Lachina
Cover Art Credit: Giovanni Giannoni/WWD/© Conde Nast
Cover Design: Eleanor Rose
Illustrations: Zoya Nudelman
Printed and bound in China

This book is dedicated to my beautiful daughter, Julia.
I love you, you are my miracle, my inspiration, and my joy.
I believe you can make all your dreams come true.

CONTENTS

EXTENDED TABLE OF CONTENTS

PREFACE

The Art of Couture Sewing was written to offer designers and students the opportunity to be able to follow one book to create a couture garment. The book covers everything from seam variations, draping, and embellishment, to decorative design ideas.

This book was written to cover the following aspects of couture sewing:

- manipulating fabric
- seam and hem variations
- different types of closures
- basic draping techniques
- petticoats, trains, and hoops skirt construction
- decorative stitches and fabric embellishments with small detail in mind
- building a corset and designing a garment using a corset as a stay
- designing and constructing a suit jacket
- stimulating creativity in design and construction
- putting together a sample book and applying skills to making the samples of all the seams, hems, embellishments, and closures

Organization of the Text

This book is divided into chapters that cover techniques and skills needed to create a couture garment. The chapters are broken down into techniques, definitions, and step-by-step instructions.

Chapter 1 begins with an overview of couture history that began with Rose Bertin, a dressmaker for Marie Antoinette. It continues to describe the world of couture and offer ideas on how to become your own designer.

Chapter 2 discusses fibers and fabrics used in couture design. Photos of garments provide an example of the fabric drape and look.

Chapter 3 discusses and lists all the supplies needed for couture sewing. This chapter also covers proper pressing techniques.

Chapter 4 covers seams and stitches. These include temporary and permanent hand stitches, machine stitches, and ornamental decorative stitches.

Chapter 5 focuses on the concept of draping techniques beginning with the basic block and advancing to designs that are more complex. The chapter also discusses how to drape bias-cut slip dresses, bust twists, cowl necklines, asymmetrical designs, and details such as gathering, crunching, tucks, and pleats.

Chapter 6 (new to this edition) focuses on skirt variations, petticoats, trains, and even bustles.

Chapter 7 focuses entirely on corset history, design, structure, and construction.

Chapters 8 and 9 teach new techniques on fabric manipulation and garment embellishments. After studying these chapters, you should understand different smocking and shirring variations, quilting techniques, tuck and pleat manipulation, ruffles and flounces, embroidery stitch variations, and decorating with lace and beading, and you should be able to use cutwork and/or appliqué in your designs.

Chapter 10 is a guide to different closures. You will learn how to install zippers, buttons and buttonholes, hook and eyes, snaps, buttons, and even frogs.

Chapter 11 discusses different types of hem variations and offers step-by-step techniques on hemming garments, finishing garment edges, and designing garments with decorative hems.

Chapter 12 teaches the secrets of tailoring used in high-class dress making, pockets, waist stays, and the finishing touches that complete the garment.

New to This Edition

- Expanded coverage of the construction of facings, linings, underlinings, interlinings, and interfacings (Chapter 4)
- All-new chapter on constructing large skirts including trains, hoop skirts, and petticoats (Chapter 6)
- Chapter 8 features new fabric manipulation and embellishment techniques including couching, eyelet

stitching, ribbon embroidery, goldwork, beadwork arc stitching, motif beaded embroidery methods, and working with sequins, rhinestones, and crystals
- Over 185 updated fashion photographs and new illustrations throughout the book
- More than 850 color photos and illustrations throughout the text with over 20% new
- End-of-chapter biographies discussing notable designers and their couture techniques include new profiles of Alexander McQueen and Elie Saab
- Reorganized chapters to shift garment embellishment techniques to earlier in the book

Instructor's Resources

- Instructor's Guide provides suggestions for planning the course and using the text in the classroom, blank worksheets, assignment handouts, teaching suggestions for each chapter, and additional projects
- PowerPoint® presentations include images from the book and provide a framework for lecture and discussion

ACKNOWLEDGMENTS

Writing this book would have been an impossible task without help from my loving family. I would like to thank my parents, Dmitriy and Zhanna, and my parents-in-law, Svetlana and Anatoliy, for your dedicated love, help, and support. I would also like to give a loving thanks to my husband, Igor, and my daughter, Julia, for your love and belief in me. You told me everyday that I could do it. Thanks for all of your encouragement.

Also thanks to my grandfather, Yakov. Thank you for teaching me about the world of art. Without you, I may have never had the courage and patience to be the artist I strive to be.

I am also deeply grateful to Bloomsbury Publishing for taking on my challenging project and to the great staff who have helped me every step of the way in putting this book together.

I would also like to give my thanks to all my students whose enthusiasm and creativity have inspired me to write this book.

Finally, thank you to the reviewers who provided valuable feedback: Dr. Lalon Alexander, University of the Incarnate Word; Earl J. Battle, Mount Ida College; Lenda Jo Connell, Auburn University; Aleta Deyo, Mount Ida College; Joyce Greening, Columbia College Chicago; Theresa Ann Lopez, University of the Incarnate Word; Phyllis Misite, Mount Ida College; Cindy Roholt, North Dakota State University; Dr. Yukti Sancheti, West Virginia University; Mary Simpson, Baylor University; and Janie Stidham, University of North Texas.

1

Introduction to Couture

Objectives

- Review the background history behind the art of couture and fashion

- Learn about couture houses and how they work

- Learn about the couture houses today

- Learn the steps of becoming your own designer

- Learn about the life and work of Gabrielle Coco Chanel

Couture is magic. . . . Couture is art. . . . Couture is detail. But where does **couture** come from? Let's delve into fashion history and learn where couture originated.

Centuries ago, fashion in clothing was not very important; rather, wealth and status were indicated by the kind and amount of jewelry one wore. Most dresses were made by hand by the women who wore them; wealthier women had their dresses made by hired dressmakers. As time passed, however, clothing became a new marker of status. Style was set by kings and queens, and the fabric and detailing of clothing were signs of its wearer's wealth and social position. Beginning in the 1500s, dressmakers made miniature samples of their designs and displayed them on small handmade dolls. These dolls could be carried by traders from town to town, and so fashions popular in one place spread to others. In the eighteenth century, such dolls were sometimes even made life-size. Later, at the beginning of the nineteenth century, the first fashion magazines appeared, displaying sketches of the latest mode.

French dressmakers became known as the best needle workers in Europe, and as travel became easier, well-off women went to Paris to shop for fine clothing. They would consult with the **dressmaker**, ordering different styles and types of garments for morning, afternoon, and evening wear along with items such as tea gowns and nightgowns, which were only to be worn in the privacy of one's home.

Looking back into the 1700s, the first known French fashion designer was Rose Bertin. She was a milliner and a **designer** to Queen Marie Antoinette, who brought fashion and haute couture to the French culture. Marie Antoinette came to France with a taste for clothes. She hired Bertin to present her designs to the French court every week, sometimes even twice a week. Bertin was also her confidant and began designing Marie Antoinette's hairstyles. At this time women started to pouf their hair in a coiffure with pads to set proportion to their wide skirts. Marie Antoinette started to send dolls to her sisters and her mother back in Austria to show the latest fashion designs. These dolls, both small and large mannequin size, were used to show off Bertin's designs before the first catalog magazine came out. (Figure 1.1)

Figure 1.1 Painting of Marie Antoinette by Jean-Baptiste-André Gautier-Dagoty, 1775.

In 1850, an English designer living in Paris, Charles Frederick Worth, changed the way exclusive dressmakers conducted their business. Instead of working on just two or three custom-designed dresses at once for a few individual clients, he decided to design collections of dresses that were displayed on live models at his showroom.

Worth was born in England in 1825. As a young man, he worked for two textile firms in London; what he learned about fabrics during this stage would help him with his designs later in life. He also visited the National Gallery to study historical portraits, which he used as inspiration. Worth moved to Paris in 1845 and obtained work at the firm of Gagelin, which sold textile goods, shawls, and ready-made garments. Starting out as a salesman, Worth established a dressmaking department in the firm and created prize-winning designs that were displayed at London's 1851 Great Exhibition at the Crystal Palace and at the 1855 Exposition Universelle in Paris. He left in 1858 to open his own establishment. (Figure 1.2)

Worth's fortunes rose with those of Napoleon III, who became emperor of France in 1852 and revitalized France's economy, spurring the demand for luxury items.

Napoleon III's wife, Empress Eugénie, whose tastes led fashion all over Europe, favored Worth, ensuring his success. (Figure 1.3a)

Worth's design house became a huge enterprise during the last quarter of the nineteenth century. (Figure 1.3b) His

Figure 1.3a Evening dress. House of Worth, 1884.

Figure 1.2 Evening dress. House of Worth, 1861.

Figure 1.3b Detail of evening dress. House of Worth, 1884.

high standards were maintained by his sons, Gaston-Lucien and Jean-Philippe, after their father's death in 1895, and the design house continued to prosper through the 1950s, until the retirement of Worth's great-grandson, Jean-Charles.

Another prestigious designer, Jeanne Paquin, opened her own house in 1891. Paquin was known for her glamorous evening gowns. She was also the first designer to introduce a dress that was tailored for day wear but also elegant enough to wear in the evening to an informal event. She advertised her designs in a creative way, dressing up several models in exactly the same outfit and sending them to public places, where they attracted much attention. As her fame spread internationally, Paquin opened up branches of her design house. (Figure 1.4)

In 1907, the designer Paul Poiret changed the way women dressed, introducing a brand-new straight silhouette that did not require a **corset**. (Figure 1.5)

He was also known for a number of designs that made a brief splash, including the **hobble skirt**, so called because it was shaped like a mermaid tail and so tight at the knees that the wearer could not walk normally but was forced to hobble. (Figure 1.6)

Figure 1.5 Lepape, Madame Poiret's outfit, 1921.

Figure 1.4 Afternoon dress. Jeanne Paquin, 1910.

Figure 1.6 Sorbet evening dress. Paul Poiret, 1913. Made of silk satin chiffon, and glass beads.

Priorities changed in 1914, when World War I began, but after the war, as the world moved into the Roaring Twenties, women abandoned the corset, and hemlines rose to the knee. The locus of couture shifted, too, as many fashions were sold at department stores and boutiques instead of in the couturier's salon. Gabrielle Coco Chanel rose to prominence during this time, introducing jersey dresses and wool jackets. (Figure 1.7) In the same era, Jean Patou, who popularized V-neck sweaters and tennis skirts, brought a new casual style to women's clothing. (Figure 1.8)

In the late 1920s and 1930s, Elsa Schiaparelli brought elegance and a sense of drama back to women's fashion. Schiaparelli used artworks, including those of the Surrealists, as inspiration for her designs and fabrics. She was the first designer to use zippers in her dresses, and she introduced the long dinner suit and voluminous trousers. She originated the boxy, broad-shouldered look that dominated in the years prior to World War II. (Figure 1.9)

After the disruption of the war, Paris once again became the capital of couture, with Christian Dior introducing

Figure 1.8 Evening dress. Jean Patou Collection, 1922.

Figure 1.7 Coco Chanel, Paris, 1937.

Figure 1.9 Evening dress. Elsa Schiaparelli's butterflies, 1937.

a new look in 1947 (Figure 1.10), one with broad shoulders, a cinched waist, and a very full skirt. His innovations in silhouettes before his untimely death in 1957 helped establish the modern wardrobe for women. (Figure 1.11)

The couture house today is set up similar to the way it was in earlier eras, with the following roles:

1. The designer
2. The **première de l'atelier**
3. The **seconde de l'atelier**
4. The **tailleur**
5. The **flou**
6. The **atelier**
7. The **directrice**
8. The **vendeuse**

The designer or couturier takes full responsibility for the entire house, including designing the collections, overseeing the fit of the toiles (**muslin** samples), choosing the models, arranging fashion shows, and talking to the press.

A **toile** is known in the couture world as a mock-up garment of the design ready to be made. It could be

Figure 1.11 Christian Dior gown. Dior Studio, Paris, France, 1957.

patterned, draped, or both, sewn or pinned together to check accurate fit to the body or the form. In couture houses, toiles are made out of muslin or a light-colored cotton fabric. Muslin is cheaper than cotton and is very durable. It comes in variety of weights and colors. Most toiles are made in light-colored muslin to allow markings on the necessary changes that will have to be made to the pattern piece for a good fit and drape.

The première de l'atelier is the head of the tailoring workroom, one of two workrooms in the house. This person cuts the first pattern, makes and fits the toiles, prepares cuts and fits the garments, and oversees the garments' completion. The seconde de l'atelier is the second-in-command to the première de l'atelier. Tailleurs are responsible for the actual production of the garments.

The flou is in charge of the second workroom, where the soft pieces are made. In that workroom, the ateliers are the professional dressmakers.

The directrice role is to manage the entire couture house while the vendeuse oversees the whole experience of the client, from selection of styles to delivery of the finished garment. Vendeuse assists the client with advice on which collection pieces would suit the client and books fittings (there are three fittings before the garment is complete). She is there throughout the entire process, helping her clients. (Figure 1.12)

Figure 1.10 Christian Dior, 1947, New Look.

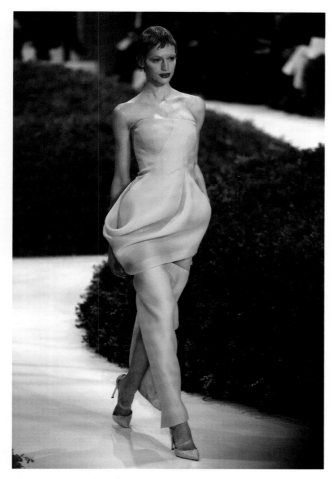

Figure 1.12 Christian Dior Haute Couture, Spring/Summer 2013.

The following couture houses are considered official members of the Chambre Syndicale: Adeline André, Anne Valérie Hash, Chanel, Christian Dior, Christian Lacroix, Dominique Sirop, Elie Saab, Emanuel Ungaro, Frank Sorbier, Giorgio Armani, Givenchy, Jean Paul Gaultier, Maison Martin Margiela, Maurizio Galante, and Valentino SpA.

What Is Haute Couture Today?

Today the center of couture is still in France, and each house spends millions each year to show its collections to the world twice a year. Each show is so grand it becomes almost a theatrical production. The shows attract important publicity on TV and in newspapers, magazines, and blogs on the Internet, helping the couture houses survive. The most popular designs from the shows are quickly copied into mass-produced clothing at all price levels.

Each collection is designed around a theme conceived by the designer. Inspiration for these themes can come from anywhere—current events, history, weather, or the work of another artist. (Figures 1.13a, b, and c)

The designer often begins by draping fabrics on a form to see how they drape on the cross grain, on the lengthwise grain, and on the bias. The designer then makes many sketches, superimposing possible styles over croquis (pre-drawn bodies). The best designs are chosen and then passed to the première de l'atelier, who constructs the toile. The entire design, including all details and the entoilage (the structure inside the garment, including interfacing, shoulder pads, boning, and so on), is constructed in muslin with exceptional craftsmanship, even though the design is still a work in progress, and fitted on a house model.

After the toile is finished, the designer checks it inside and out. When the toile is approved, it is then taken apart into pieces and pressed. These pieces serve as a pattern for the final garment.

The atelier de tailleur, or tailoring workroom, usually makes all the clothes that have more structure, use heavier fabric, and incorporate more tailoring details, such as wool suits and coats. Some couture houses have two ateliers de tailleur, one for men's suits in heavy fabrics and another for lighter-weight suits and women's suits.

In couture, designs are enhanced by great fabrics, fine trims, hand beadwork, and more. Only the finest luxury fabrics are used in couture; many are designed specifically for a garment by the couturier and can cost hundreds to thousands of dollars a yard. Today, Paris continues to be the center of couture, and there is a very strong support structure of skilled workers in many specialties. There are two associations in Paris that support couture designers: the **Fédération Française de la Couture**, in which membership is based on high standards of excellence, and the **Chambre Syndicale** de la Haute Couture Parisienne. To become a member of the Chambre Syndicale, a couture house is required to have at least one atelier in Paris with a minimum of fifteen staff members and present a collection of at least fifty designs, both day and evening garments, in January and July. Most couture houses and boutiques are located in the avenue Montaigne and the rue du Faubourg Saint-Honoré in Paris.

Figure 1.13a, b, and c Couture collection by Valentino, Spring/ Summer 2014.

If the garment being prepared is a gown, dress, blouse, or similar soft item, it is sewn in the atelier de flou, or dressmaking atelier, where silk is often the predominant fabric. In this workroom, garments are often sewn right on the form, with the folds stitched into place until the garment is fully sewn, so that the folds are kept in the right place. In this workroom, garments can be made with or without entoilage. Some dresses—those that are very soft and fluid—have no structure inside, so the use of a form during construction helps shape the garment to a woman's body.

In either process, the garment can be fitted two or three times, or even more, during development to ensure that it fits correctly. (Figure 1.14)

Figure 1.14 Fashion designer Nicolas Ghesquière and Cate Blanchett wearing a Balenciaga gown.

Figure 1.15 Designer boards. From the top down: inspirational photos, inspiration board, color story board with fabric swatches.

Becoming a Designer

Becoming a designer in the fashion industry means that you don't just design individual garments. Rather, you create entire collections in which the individual pieces work together to create a great look. To achieve this unified style, collections depend on an inspiration that links each piece with all the others.

In order to develop your inspiration, pull images that appeal to you from magazines, the Internet, and catalogs. You can also start looking through fabrics in your closet or stores and collect swatches for this collection. Mount the fabrics and images together on an "inspiration board." (Figure 1.15)

When you have your inspiration, you can begin to work on your color story. Pull together fabric swatches, trims, and buttons, and try different combinations. When you have your color story, mount those colors on a board as well. These two boards will help you as you sketch your garment ideas.

COCO CHANEL

Coco Chanel was born in the small city of Saumur, France, in 1883, as Gabrielle Bonheur Chanel. Her mother died when she was six, and shortly afterward her father abandoned her and her four siblings. The Chanel children were placed in the care of relatives and spent some time in an orphanage, where she was always known as being very creative.

Later in life, she met a wealthy Englishman who helped her open her first shop in Paris in 1909 selling hats. Within a year she moved the business to the fashionable rue Cambon. It wasn't long before Coco Chanel became an icon in the fashion industry.

Coco Chanel wearing one of her designs, early 1950s.

Two of her most famous creations are Chanel No. 5 perfume, which was launched in 1923, and the influential Chanel suit, an elegant suit comprising a knee-length skirt and trim, boxy jacket traditionally made of woven wool with black trim and gold buttons and worn with large costume-pearl necklaces. She also popularized the little black dress, whose blank-slate versatility allowed it to be worn for both day and evening, depending on how it was accessorized. Although unassuming black dresses existed before Chanel, the ones she designed were considered the haute couture standard. In 1923, she told *Harper's Bazaar* that "simplicity is the keynote of all true elegance."

Gloria Swanson (actress) wearing an orchid chiffon velvet gown with diamonds and steel beads by Chanel, 1931.

With the arrival of World War II, Chanel closed her boutiques. Her affair with a Nazi officer during the war brought her disgrace, but she returned to design in the mid-1950s. By then things had changed, and Dior's "New Look" was in ascendance. This angered Chanel, so she set out to rework many of her older designs. In a testament to her natural eye for style and grace, her designs once again became very popular, especially in the United States.

Chanel died in 1971, and for a time several of her assistants continued the line. In 1983 Karl Lagerfeld took over and has kept the name going by using

Chanel Fashion House, 1933.

a mix of Coco's traditional styling cues and those of more modern times.

When you have some ideas, take out your sketchbook and begin sketching thumbnail ideas or, using your pre-made croquis (body templates), sketch quick ideas of your designs. When you get many done, you can begin designing further by thinking of the fit and all the techniques you will use to finish these garments.

When you know exactly what steps you will need to perform in order to construct your garment, you can start to work the patterns on paper or by draping. Patterns are very important to get a good fit. Make sure you have patterns for all the facings, linings, and other trimming.

In order to sew your garments correctly, you can now make up an order-of-construction list. This list is a step-by-step guide that will help you construct the garments.

Then you can begin to sew.

Chapter Review

This chapter briefly reviewed the history of couture and fashion by going back in time to the beginning of couture. Way back then, Marie Antoinette hired Rose Bertin to be her personal designer and seamstress. France became the center of all fashion, and Charles Worth opened the first couture house. Since then many designers opened their own couture houses, and couture clothing became very popular. With designers such as Paul Poiret, who brought the embroidered loose coat and the hobble skirt to the couture world, and Gabrielle Coco Chanel, who designed the little black dress, fashion took on a new look. Today the center of couture is still in France, and each house spends millions each year to show its collections to the world twice a year in order to keep its membership at the Chambre Syndicale. Each collection is designed around a theme conceived by the designer. Inspiration for these themes can come from anywhere—current events, history, weather, or the work of another artist. To become your own designer, you can get inspired by anything.

Projects

1. Collect pictures of designer designs from magazines and/or the Internet. Use these pictures and photographs to build an inspiration scrapbook for yourself. Use your creativity to make it very colorful and inspirational for yourself, because this is going to be a book that will inspire you to design your designs.

2. Visit a museum or a gallery showing different collections going back in history. Take a sketchbook with you and sketch ten different garment details of famous designer garments. You can use these details to get inspired to design your own five-outfit collection that will fit our lifestyle today.

3. Research a three-page paper on the famous designer Elsa Schiaparelli. Include five pictures of her work and describe what you like about her designs and what would inspire you. List all your resources in a bibliography.

4. Design a four-outfit collection inspired by Charles Worth's designs. Build an inspiration board, color storyboard, an illustration board, and a flat sketch board for your collection. You can make your own croquis models and use them for the illustration board.

Key Terms

Atelier	Dressmaker	Seconde de l'atelier
Chambre Syndicale	Fédération Française de la Couture	Tailleur
Corset	Flou	Toile
Couture	Hobble skirt	Vendeuse
Designer	Muslin	
Directrice	Première de l'atelier	

2

The Art of Textiles

Objectives

- Learn about natural fibers and natural fabrics

- Learn about man-made fibers

- Learn about specialty fabrics

- Learn about lace

- Learn about the needles and threads needed for the types of fabrics

- Learn about the life and work of Paul Poiret

Textiles

Textiles are used by designers as their primary creative medium. For the designer, choosing the right fabrics for a particular design is one of the most important aspects of designing. Often the fabric itself can inspire the design; for example, soft, drapey fabric can inspire the designer to focus on gathers and ruffles. Most experienced designers can picture their designs completely finished and ready to go before the garments are done, and each and every one understands the importance of matching fabric to a particular style. (Figures 2.1 and 2.2)

Figure 2.2 Stephane Rolland gown.

Figure 2.1 Jean Louis Sabaji gown.

"Textiles" is a term referring to fabrics made from **fibers** (threadlike strands spun into yarns that in turn are woven or knitted) or from animal skins. There are two types of fabrics: natural and man-made. Natural fabrics are derived from animals or plants and have been used for millennia. Some of the best-known natural fabrics are **cotton**, flax, **wool**, **silk**, and leather. The history of man-made fabrics goes back to 1855, when chemists started experimenting with synthetic fibers. In 1884 a French chemist named Hilaire Bernigaud, comte de Chardonnet, patented a fiber he called "Chardonnet silk," which now is called rayon.

Today natural and man-made fibers are blended together for better wear. For example, cotton can be blended with rayon for extra softness or with Spandex for extra stretch.

Natural Fibers

SILK

Silk is a natural fiber used to make soft, drapable woven or knitted fabrics. Silk comes in different thicknesses and textures; it can be soft and shiny, or soft and rough like Dupioni. Silk fiber comes from a cocoon of the silkworm. The silkworm produces the natural glue sericin, which is removed during the silk manufacturing. It serves as a natural sizing when brought out in the warm wash. (Figures 2.3a and b)

Figure 2.3b Silk.

Silk is one of the fabrics that is very nice to wear in any season. It is warm in the cold season, yet cool enough when it is 100 degrees. Silk is soft enough to resist wrinkling and very moisture absorbent.

Silk Uses and Directions
1. While sewing, most of the time hand basting or pin basting is necessary.
2. Prewashing silk with shampoo or mild soap is recommended to remove all of the leftover dyes and prevent shrinking. Rinse the shampoo at least two to three times to remove all of the soap. Air dry or use a hairdryer to speed up the process.
3. Before pressing, test-press a small piece to make sure the iron is not too hot because silks can be damaged by heat.
4. Always use sharp scissors to cut silk in order to avoid snags.

Figure 2.3a Silk.

5. Pin tissue paper on one or both sides of slippery silks when cutting. The paper will hold the silk from shifting.

6. Needles used for silk can be sharp hand needles for hand sewing or machine sewing; Sharps/Microtex needles that are used for finely woven fabrics are perfect. These needles range in size from 60/8 to 90/14 and feature a narrow shaft and sharper point to pierce the threads of woven fabrics.

7. Use a new needle for a new silk garment. This will ensure that your needle is still sharp.

8. Good quality cotton or polyester thread works well. Silk thread is not recommended, as it is not strong enough to hold the garment together and begins to fray or break.

9. Pin tissue paper to one or both sides of your silk seam allowance when sewing slippery or sheer silks to avoid stretching and shifting them under the pressing foot. Use a flat-bottom presser foot and a straight stitch needle plate.

10. Test your seams and adjust the settings on your sewing machine. A stitch length of 2mm or 8–12 spi works best and offers the least amount of puckering. There is no need to pull the silk through; just guide and slightly help it under the foot.

11. For notches, make small clips into the fabric that are not too far apart to avoid fraying. Do not notch on loose woven silk fabrics (for example, chiffon or organza). Use tailor's tacks.

SILK FABRIC VARIATIONS

Dupioni Silk. Sometimes called shantung; has an irregular weave that looks like ribs. It is. It is one of the most commonly used silks in couture, especially bridal wear. This fabric frays, wrinkles, and needs care with the iron. (Figure 2.4)

While sewing it would be ideal to hand baste the fabric because of its delicate nature. Start sewing with a new needle, and try not to make mistakes on the seams, as that will leave holes in the fabric. Adding organza as underlining can make Dupioni more structured and crisp. Adding cotton can make it heavier and help it drape down (as in circular skirts). Canvas makes it much heavier and can help tailor it better to a 3-D architectural design. Garments fit better with a lining. Press with a warm (not hot) iron through a press cloth. Dry clean only to avoid shrinkage and stains.

Figure 2.4 Dupioni silk.

China Silk. Good quality, more expensive silk. It is offered in two thicknesses, 1 ply and 2 ply. It frays easily; therefore, watch the edges. (Figure 2.5)

Brocade Silk. Woven on a jacquard loom with a pattern on the face and long floats on the back. Brocade is used for evening wear, suits, and bridal wear due to its beautiful shine and pattern. Match up your prints when cutting out your patterns. (Figure 2.6) Bind the edges or serge right away to avoid fraying, and always use new needles. Use a lining for brocade garments to avoid snagging of the long floats in the back. Dry clean only. Test-press before pressing. Use a pressing cloth, especially if the brocade is woven with metallic threads.

Jacquard Silk. A type of a weave used with different fibers and one of the more expensive silks. This weave has a design relief on the underside and is often confused with brocade silk. Jacquard silk is offered in variety of

Figure 2.5 China silk.

Figure 2.7 Jacquard silk.

Figure 2.6 Brocade silk.

designs/colors. It is tough to pleat and crease due to its weave and delicacy to high heat pressing. (Figure 2.7 and 2.8) It is best to dry clean.

Silk Satin. Has a shiny, smooth face and either a smooth or a matte back. Satins fray, snag, wrinkle, and are

Figure 2.8 Jacquard silk.

vulnerable to the iron as well as water spots. (Figures 2.9 and 2.10a, b, and c) Before sewing, pin or baste so the fabric does not travel. You can even baste by hand. For sewing, set the machine to ten to twelve stitches per inch. Use lining and underlining for a better fit. It must be dry cleaned. Satin works well for draping and bias-cut garments.

Figure 2.10b Silk satin.

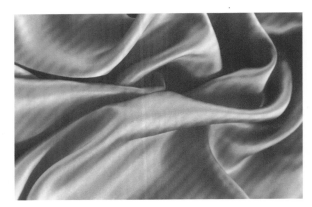

Figure 2.9 Silk satin.

Figure 2.10a Silk satin.

Figure 2.10c Silk satin.

Silk Taffeta. A crisp fabric. Taffeta is very vulnerable to heat, pin marks, and water, which causes stains. It is good for gathered and pleated designs. During sewing, pin or baste it because it has a slippery face. (Figure 2.11a and b) Taffeta works well for designs with corsets or evening gowns and underlining. Use caution when pressing, as it can melt or burn, and water from the iron can leave stains. Try to steam it with a pressing cloth. It must be dry cleaned.

Habotai Silk. Very thin and mostly used for lining. It is offered in a variety of colors. Surface designers use Habotai for silk painting. (Figure 2.12)

Silk Charmeuse. A light, soft fabric with a satin front and dull back known as a luxury and lingerie fabric. It is great for draping, however, it frays, snags easily, and stains very quickly. Charmeuse is used for clothing, lingerie, bias binding, bias hems, and garment linings.

Figure 2.11a Silk taffeta.

Figure 2.11b Silk taffeta.

Figure 2.12 Habotai silk.

Figure 2.13a Silk charmeuse.

Figure 2.13b Silk charmeuse.

(Figure 2.13a and b) During sewing, hand baste prior to machine sewing. Use caution, as needles can leave holes in the fabric. Begin sewing using a new Sharps (Microtex) needle sizes 8/60 to 14/90 with a 12 spi (2mm) setting on your sewing machine. Try to use steam when pressing to avoid burning, and use dry iron with a cloth. Dry clean or wash depending on the finish.

Silk Chiffon. A transparent, fluid, soft fabric made of finely twisted silk yarns. It is great for draping with a feminine touch but can be damaged quickly with a hot iron. (Figures 2.14 and 2.15) When cutting, pin the pattern outside the seam, as pins leave holes.

Hand baste before sewing, and use silk or cotton thread. Chiffon can be underlined with itself; this can add more weight and body while letting it keep some of its sheer quality. Usual lining fabrics also work well. To add crispiness and volume structure, you can even use organza as an underlining to keep it sheer. Darts need to be trimmed and turned under. Neatness is necessary due to chiffon's transparency.

Silk Crepe de Chine. A very delicate fabric that can snag easily, rip, burn under the iron, and suffer from water spots. Hand baste before sewing. It is offered in many different weights and thicknesses, from sheer to almost opaque, and is great for draping. (Figure 2.16a and b) Silk crepe de chine is vulnerable to heat, so it should only be steamed; it must only be dry cleaned. To mark, use a needle and thread; avoid marking pens and chalk. Try not to sew seams straight on the grain; move the patterns a bit diagonally.

Silk Georgette. A sheer fabric that frays and wrinkles. Be careful pressing georgette, as it can burn. (Figure 2.17a and b) Hand baste it because it will shift.

Figure 2.14 Silk chiffon.

Figure 2.16b Silk crepe de chine.

Figure 2.15 Silk chiffon. Design by Zoya Nudelman, author.

Figure 2.16a Silk crepe de chine.

Figure 2.17a Silk georgette.

Figure 2.17b Silk georgette.

Figure 2.18a Silk organza.

Too many stitches or tight stitches will rip the fabric. Do not backstitch. Tie off the threads inside the garment, and try to get the seams right the first time, as taking out seams can cause the fabric to rip.

Silk Organza. A light, transparent fabric that is similar to chiffon but much stiffer; it feels almost starched. Organza wrinkles quickly and frays a lot. It is often used as underlining to weaker and thinner fabrics. (Figure 2.18a and b) Organza requires hand basting before sewing. Neatness is necessary due to its transparency. French seams and flat-fell seams work nicely. When sewing, use a sharp needle size 8/60 to 10/70 for the best seams. Organza is easy to press, but you may still need to test it.

Silk Velvet. A pile fabric woven with extra warp yarns. Because of its nap, pressing it is not recommended, as the hot iron will press down the nap; instead, use a needle board to press velvet facedown without ruining the pile. (Figure 2.19) Velvet is tricky to sew, as it tends to creep, so you need to pin every inch or hand baste it. Alternatively, use a walking foot for your sewing machine to help you when your velvet starts to creep. Velvet is durable and can be used in couture for evening wear and corset bustiers.

Figure 2.18b Silk organza.

Figure 2.19 Silk velvet.

Figure 2.20a Wool.

Figure 2.20b Wool.

WOOL

Wool is a natural fiber that comes from sheep and was used widely up until the Industrial Revolution. Wool comes in variety of different types, and it varies by the breed of sheep. Australia produces 43 percent of the world's merino wool, which is considered to be the highest quality wools. In the United States, there are four breeds of sheep that produce very fine wool, and there are another fifteen breeds of sheep raised for food that produce medium-grade and coarse wool. (Figure 2.20a and b)

Wool dyes easily and is absorbent, so make sure to follow directions on the wool type and the fabric dye to the exact detail and measurement to avoid ruining your fabric.

Figure 2.21 Alpaca wool.

Alpaca Wool. A very silky and rich wool. It is more expensive and has a great luster. This wool comes from the alpaca. (Figure 2.21)

Angora Wool. A hairy, fuzzy wool that is used very often to achieve a soft feel to the skin. This wool comes from the angora rabbit. (Figure 2.22)

Mohair Wool. A hairy and fuzzy wool that is valued for its luster. Mohair comes from the angora goat and is very durable. (Figure 2.23)

Cashmere Wool. A very expensive wool because of the production process and the long separation of soft fibers from coarse fibers. This wool can also be blended with silk, cotton, and even other types of wool. It comes from the down of the Kashmir goat. (Figure 2.24)

Camel Hair Wool. Known to be very soft, this wool comes from the fine fur of the camel's undercoat. It can be used alone or blended with other fibers. Camel hair wool has a beautiful natural color that usually is not dyed. (Figure 2.25)

Figure 2.23 Mohair wool.

Figure 2.22 Angora wool.

Wool is durable and flexible. It is a great insulator and is known for its water resistance. Therefore, it keeps the body dry and cool when it's hot. Wool does not spot as easily as other fabrics and therefore does not need to be washed often. Most wool must be dry cleaned to keep its quality and shine; however, there are wools that are washable.

Even though wool is a natural flame retardant, use cheesecloth when pressing to avoid burning the top layer fibers and causing shine. You can also use steam to shape wool.

COTTON

Cotton is a soft, comfortable, and easy-to-use fabric. It is the most commonly used fabric in the world and has been used for centuries. It comes from the cotton plant's seed pod. The fiber appears to be hollow inside; however, when you look at it under a microscope, you can see that it is a small, twisted piece of yarn, almost like a ribbon. Cotton can absorb up to twenty-five times its own weight in water and is stronger wet than dry. (Figure 2.26a)

Figure 2.24 Cashmere wool.

Figure 2.25 Camel hair.

Figure 2.26a Cotton.

The most common cotton characteristic of cotton is that it allows our skin to breathe so we do not feel hot or cold wearing it. It is easy to care for, very easy to dye, and can be pressed at relatively high temperatures.

Today it is often blended with man-made fibers such as polyester to reduce wrinkle effects. However, many designers still like to use 100 percent cotton because they believe that polyester takes away the quality of the cotton and its ability to allow our skin to breathe. (Figure 2.26b)

Today, cotton can have a permanent finish that allows for easy care and helps prevent it from shrinking. Cotton can be deteriorated by mildew and weakened by sunlight. Be sure to prewash your cotton before use.

Commonly used cottons:

Dimity Cotton. Thin, sheer cotton in white or printed patterns with lengthwise stripes, checks, or cords. (Figure 2.27) When cutting dimity, match up your prints;

Figure 2.27 Dimity cotton.

Figure 2.26b Cotton.

Figure 2.28 Cotton drill.

when sewing it, use a size 8/60 or 9/65 needle and mercerized cotton, cotton/polyester blend, or polyester thread. Press with a medium to hot iron and test it.

Drill. Twill cotton fabric commonly used in slacks for its strong and durable nature. (Figure 2.28) When working with drill, use all-purpose thread, cotton/polyester blend thread, or plain cotton thread. Use universal needles sizes 8/60 to 19/120.

Gingham. A lightweight, easy-to-use, washable fabric that is woven with a plaid or stripe print. (Figure 2.29) The plaid print size and stripe print

Figure 2.30 Cotton gauze.

Figure 2.29 Gingham cotton.

size come in many different sizes. (See dimity cotton directions.)

Gauze. Woven in a sheer, cheesecloth weave (Figure 2.30). Always use sharp scissors to cut gauze in order to avoid snags, and pin outside the seam to avoid holes. Hand baste because this fabric is so fine and thin. Use cotton thread when sewing. A French seam, double zigzag seam, and flat-felled seam or hairline seam are best. Underline it with itself to add more weight and body while retaining its sheer quality. You can also use lining fabrics to add a different color and to close the sheer areas if needed. To add crispiness and volume structure, you can even use silk organza as an underlining to keep it sheer. Darts need to be trimmed and turned under.

Organdy Cotton. A very thin and transparent cotton. It looks very much like silk organza and has a

Figure 2.31 Organdy cotton.

crisp finish. (Figure 2.31) Use sharp scissors to cut to avoid snags, and use tissue paper on one or both sides pinned together before cutting. The paper will hold it from shifting. Hand baste before sewing. When sewing, use a sharp needle size 8/60 or 10/70 for the best seams. Organdy is easy to press, but you may still need to test it first. Neatness is necessary due to its transparency.

Figure 2.33 Polished cotton.

Figure 2.32 Pima cotton.

Figure 2.34 Sateen cotton.

Pima Cotton. Comes from Egypt and is known to be the highest quality cotton. Pima cotton is woven with the most threads and has a very soft and shiny finish. (Figure 2.32) (See dimity cotton directions.)

Polished Cotton. Woven with a satin weave, which gives it a shiny appearance. Polished cotton is finished with chemicals to add more shine and sometimes woven in a plain weave as well. (Figure 2.33) (See Sateen cotton directions.)

Sateen Cotton. Satin weave woven out of cotton threads, which makes it very shiny and silky to the touch. Some sateen is treated with special wrinkle-resistant finishes. (Figure 2.34) Hand baste before sewing. When sewing sateen, set your machine to ten to twelve stitches per inch. Use polyester and cotton threads. Use lining and underlining for a better fit, or do not line.

Swiss Cotton. A very fine, sheer cotton. It is commonly printed with designs and dots. (Figure 2.35) (See gauze cotton directions.)

Figure 2.36 Velveteen cotton.

Figure 2.35 Swiss cotton.

Velveteen. A cotton velvet weave pile fabric woven with extra warp yarns. Because of its nap, velveteen cannot be pressed in the usual way, as the hot iron will press down the nap; instead, use a needle board to press velvet facedown without ruining the pile. It resembles silk velvet and frays easily. (See silk velvet instructions) (Figure 2.36). Velveteen is durable and can be used in beautiful couture evening wear.

LINEN

Linen is the second oldest natural fiber used in clothing. It comes from the flax plant, which has a natural luster due to its wax content. Linen is naturally light in color and comes in white or cream; it is easy to dye. Linen fiber is also smooth and lint free. It is a durable luxury fabric that is three times stronger than cotton. However, it wrinkles more than cotton does. Linen can be pressed easily and boiled without damage. (Figure 2.37)

Be careful pressing linen because its creases can be permanent; pressing can break the linen threads, which causes the fabric to keep the crease.

Figure 2.37 Linen.

Figure 2.39 Venise linen.

Figure 2.38 Damask linen.

Figure 2.40 Leather.

Figure 2.41 Suede.

Commonly Used Linens

Butcher's Linen. A very sturdy linen used in interfacing.

Damask Linen. Linen woven with a jacquard weave that has a reversible pattern. It can also be woven in a satin or plain weave. (Figure 2.38)

Venise Linen. Linen woven similar to damask with a floral pattern. (Figure 2.39)

LEATHER AND SUEDE

Leather and **suede** leather are attractive, smooth, soft, tear-resistant materials. (Figures 2.40 and 2.41) Leather protects against heat, cold, and wind, and it repels moisture. Garments made of leather mold to the body and retain their shape. Leather cannot be pressed. Use a beater to flatten the seams; trimming the seams can also help reduce bulk. Use leather needles or very sharp, durable needles, switching them between garments because they get dull quickly. Use care, as stitching needles and pins can leave permanent holes. Use 8–12 spi (2.5mm) all purpose, polyester/cotton blend thread. The best seams

Figure 2.42 Man-made fabric.

to use with leather are butted seams, lapped seams, and topstitching.

Man-Made Fibers

Man-made fabrics consist of filaments extruded in a liquid form into various fibers. These fibers are usually colored and dyed while they are in the liquid form before the fibers become filaments. (Figure 2.42)

Commonly used **man-made fibers** include the following:

Acetate. Manufactured cellulose fiber. Acetate has high luster, drapes very well, and has good moisture absorbency, although it can melt under the iron if left for too long. It is a chemical fiber and is shrink-, moth-, and mildew-resistant. Acetate is used for evening gowns and lining for garments made of different fabrics. Some fabrics made

Figure 2.43 Acetate.

Figure 2.44 Acrylic.

from acetate include satin, taffeta, crepe, brocade, faille, **lace**, jersey, satin, tricot, and a variety of double knits. When sewing, it is best to avoid seams on the straight grain; it usually helps to cut the patterns a bit off the grain. Acetate garments should only be dry-cleaned. (Figure 2.43)

Acrylic. A synthetic fiber derived from coal or oil known for its warmth. Many times it takes the place of wool. It is woven or knitted, quick-drying, resilient, and resistant to sunlight, wrinkling, chemicals, moths, and mildew. Acrylic does shrink, retains static, and absorbs very little moisture, which is the reason it dries fast and holds perspiration odors. It can be damaged easily by hot irons, steam, and dryers. Use sharp needles and switch often because they get dull quickly. (Figure 2.44)

Nylon. A manufactured fiber used in hosiery and netting in bridal dresses and veils. Nylon is strong and weighs less than any other man-made fiber. It is resilient to heat and is known to be elastic (stretchy), smooth, non-absorbent, and dry very quickly. Nylon does not get weak from chemicals, and dirt does not stick to it. When washing and drying nylon, be careful not to use too much

Figure 2.45 Nylon.

heat to avoid piling, and make sure you separate the colors, especially with the white nylons. Nylon will melt at high temperatures; therefore, always iron at low temperatures with a press cloth. (Figure 2.45)

Polyester. A very strong fiber that is used on its own or blended with other fibers to add crease resistance. It has low absorbency and holds in body heat. Polyester resists mildew, shrinking, wrinkling, and moths. When washing, use warm water; you can either tumble or drip dry. It melts at high temperatures, so be careful when ironing. Thread spun with polyester becomes strong and can be used for extensive sewing. (Figure 2.46)

Rayon. A man-made cellulose fiber that is very similar to cotton. Rayon is very strong and can be woven in many different weaves to resemble natural fiber fabrics. It is absorbent and does not melt at high temperatures. Rayon is great for draping and can be soft, smooth, and even silky, depending on the weave. It wrinkles easily and may shrink in the wash. You may want to prewash rayon before use. (Figure 2.47)

Commonly used man-made fabrics include the following:

Satin. Made from several fibers, including polyester, acetate, and rayon. (Figure 2.48)

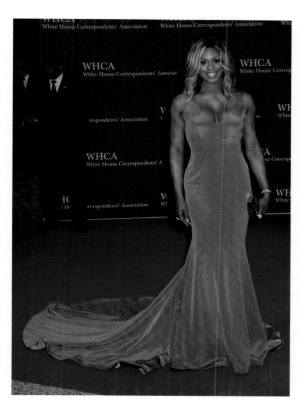
Figure 2.47 Rayon.

Figure 2.46 Polyester.

Figure 2.48 Satin.

Charmeuse. Woven out of rayon and polyester. (Figure 2.49)

Chiffon. A transparent, fluid, soft fabric made of fine twisted polyester yarns that looks similar to silk chiffon and exhibits similar characteristics. (Figure 2.50) (See the silk chiffon section.)

Taffeta. A fabric woven out of many different fibers, including rayon, acetate, and polyester. (Figure 2.51)

Georgette. A sheer fabric woven out of rayon or polyester. (Figure 2.52)

Organza. A fabric made of polyester. (Figure 2.53) Unlike silk organza, polyester organza is very hard to work with because it melts with heat. It is best to use this polyester for large prom dress skirts or ball gowns, where many seams are not necessary, since you cannot press out your seams well, causing it to look puckered at times.

Polyester organza cannot be used as underlining like the silk organza can because of its delicacy to heat.

Velvet. Can be made of many different fibers, including polyester, rayon, or acetate. (See the silk velvet section.) (Figure 2.54)

Figure 2.50 Chiffon.

Figure 2.49 Charmeuse.

Figure 2.51 Taffeta.

Lamé. Fabric that is woven or knit using metallic yarns (incorporating either metal or plastic). It frays and can easily snag. (Figure 2.55) Use a new needle, and change it often. Lining a lamé garment may keep it from rubbing against the skin. Try not to press or steam lamé,

Figure 2.52 Georgette.

Figure 2.54 Velvet.

Figure 2.53 Organza.

Figure 2.55 Lamé.

Figure 2.56 Crinoline.

be ripped if it is stressed too much. (Figure 2.57) Pins and seams leave holes; therefore, pin outside the seams. Use a roller foot to keep the fabric from sticking to the metal plate. Clip darts open to take out the bulk. Add ventilation areas or vents when necessary for the body to breathe. Faux leather should be dry-cleaned.

Faux Suede. A man-made suede that is also called ultra suede. Like its sister, ultra leather, it does not fray and has no grainline. Most faux suedes are machine washable but cannot be put in the dryer. While sewing, stick to the same rules as for faux leather. Faux suede resists moisture, which is the very reason it dries fast and holds perspiration odors. It can be damaged by hot irons and steam. Be careful with pins and stitches. Topstitch seam

Figure 2.57 Faux leather.

as it may melt. Test-press first. Use a Sharps (Microtex) needle to avoid pulling the threads out and skipping stitches.

Crinoline. A stiff tulle. This net fabric is used for slips or petticoats in skirts and sleeve heads, bows, and bustles to add shape to fabric. Most of the time it is made of polyester or nylon, though sometimes you will see tulle made of cotton or silk. (Figure 2. 56) The fabric is easy to work with because it has no grainline and does not fray. Be careful with the iron, as crinoline will melt. To avoid scratchy edges, finish your seams with a serge or a soft binding. It is used for wedding veils and skirts. Crinoline tears easily and is not best for bodices or fitted sleeves.

Specialty Fabrics

Faux Leather. A man-made leather also called pleather and ultra leather. Like real leather, faux leather does not have a grainline or fray like other woven fabrics do. Faux leather can be melted or burned by the iron; it can also

Figure 2.58 Faux suede.

allowance down to keep in place. Most faux suede garments are lined for a better fit. (Figure 2.58)

Faux Fur. A manufactured fur made from synthetic fibers that have been processed, dyed, and cut to match a specific fur texture and color. Faux fur is easily dyed with animallike colors and highly resistant to heat, sunlight, soot, and smoke; is strong and resilient; and shows good stability during laundering. (Figure 2.59)

Lace

Lace. A fabric that dates far back into fashion history, when laces were crocheted and embroidered by hand. Most laces show floral motifs, although sometimes you can find a geometric motif with circles and triangles. Some laces come pre-beaded and embroidered over again with different color thread. Lace is a great fabric to use in entire yardage or cut out appliqué pieces. When sewing your seams, try to overlap similar motifs to hide the existence

of the seams. Underline to avoid the sheer look, or choose to keep the sheer. Laces usually do not need any prewashing and shrinking, unless you are using cotton eyelet fabric. Some laces allow you to machine-wash; however, dry cleaning or hand washing is best. Pressing may damage lace, so use a press cloth. Place the lace right side down to avoid burning the motif. Use low temperature.

LACE TYPES

Alençon. A fine lace with filled-in motifs outlined with a heavy silk cord, called cordonette, that creates a raised outer edge on a sheer net background. True alençon is made in France and characterized by a fine fringe of threads along the edges of the scallops. The fringe of threads is called a beard. Domestic reembroidered lace does not have the fringe, so you can tell if it is the real French fabric or not. Alençon can be used on tightly fitted garments, sleeves, back dress designs, handbags, and shoes. (Figure 2.60) Use an 11/75 machine needle; when

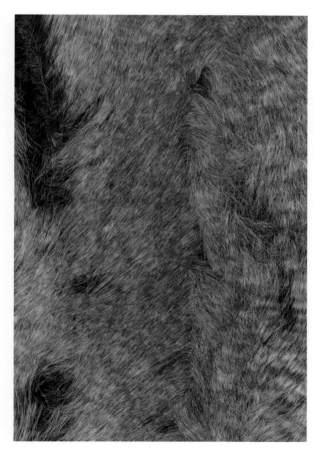

Figure 2.59 Faux fur.

Figure 2.60 Alençon lace.

hand sewing, use a size 7 needle or Betweens and cotton, cotton/polyester blend, or all-purpose thread. Machine stitching can be done with 10–12 spi (2.5mm).

Chantilly Lace. Made in France and named after the city where it came from. Chantilly lace features delicate floral and swirl designs outlined with silk threads that define the motif on a fine net background. It is best used on tight and long A-line or circular skirts, long sleeves, back dress designs, or trim on cuffs or hems. (Figure 2.61) Use an 8/60 to 9/65 size machine needle; when hand sewing, use a size 7 needle or Betweens. Thread options are cotton, extra fine, silk, or Sulky embroidery thread. Machine stitching can be done with 12–16 spi (2mm).

Venice Lace. One of the oldest of laces. It is also known as needle lace by Venetian designers and 3-D Guipure, as a type of openwork embroidery because it is made from unique crochet stitches and wrapped satin stitch embroidery over the crochet forming a 3-D motif. Unlike other laces, Venice lace has a crochet net

background or no net, just creative crochet stitches. (Figure 2.62) Use an 11/75 machine needle; when hand sewing, use size 7 needle or Betweens. Thread options are cotton, cotton/polyester blend, or all-purpose thread. Machine stitching can be done with 10–12 spi (2.5mm).

Guipure Lace. Similar to Venice lace, it is one of the most beautiful laces. It features close stitches that create a heavy, raised design. This embroidery is stitched on a cloth that disintegrates in the finishing process, leaving the motifs to stand alone. This lace has no net behind the motifs. (Figure 2.63) Follow the instructions for Venice lace.

Schiffli Lace. A sheer net fabric lace that is embroidered and decorated on a Schiffli machine. A Schiffli machine is used when embroidery that looks like it is done by hand is needed. Use a 9/65 to 11/75 size machine needle; when hand sewing, use a size 7 needle or Betweens. Thread options are cotton, cotton/polyester blend, or all-purpose thread. Machine stitching can be done with 10–12 spi (2.5mm). (Figure 2.64)

Eyelet Lace. Cotton lace that began to be used in underclothing and bedding decorations back in medieval

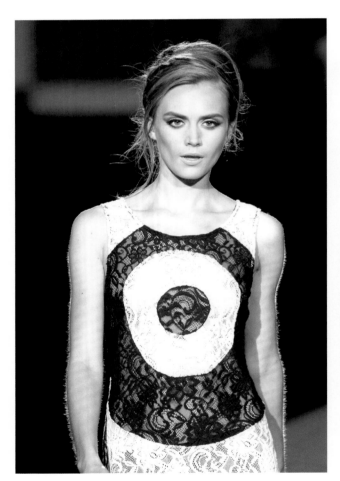

Figure 2.61 Chantilly lace.

Figure 2.62 Venice lace.

Figure 2.63 Guipure lace.

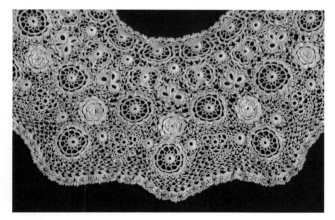

Figure 2.64 Schiffli lace.

Figure 2.65 Eyelet lace.

times and earlier in Byzantine times. This lace is embroidered over cotton either as a trim or as full yardage. The motifs are always different, but all include small cutout embroidered circles or drops. The lace is called eyelet

due to the small embroidered eyelet holes. Treat it like a lace. For sewing, apply cotton sewing and Schiffli lace directions. (Figure 2.65)

Table 2.1 NEEDLES AND THREAD

Fabric Type	Hand Needle	Thread	Machine Needls	Machine SPI
Very fine fabrics—e.g., lace, organdy, organza, chiffon, net	Sharps sizes 10, 11 Embroidery size 9	Mercerized cotton #70, 100 silk, synthetic	Fine size 9/65	16–18
Fine fabrics—e.g., silk, batiste	Sharps size 9 Embroidery size 8	Mercerized cotton #60, 70 silk, synthetic	Fine sizes 9/65 to 11/75	14, 15, 16
Light fabrics—e.g., gingham, jersey, tricot, wool crepe	Sharps sizes 8, 9 Embroidery sizes 7, 8	Mercerized cotton #60, 70 silk, synthetic	Fine sizes 9/65 to 11/85	12, 13, 14
Medium fabrics—e.g., crepe, flannel, linen, velvet, corduroy, broadcloth	Sharps size 7, 8 Embroidery size 6, 7	Mercerized cotton #50, 60 silk, synthetic	Medium sizes 11/75 to 14/90	10, 11, 12, 13, 14
Medium/heavy fabrics —e.g., denim, fake fur, felt, terry cloth, brocade	Sharps sizes 6, 7 Embroidery size 6	Mercerized cotton #40, silk, synthetic	Medium sizes 14/90 to 16/100	10, 11, 12, 13, 14
Heavy fabric—e.g., double-faced wools, heavy denim, heavy corduroy	Sharps sizes 4, 5 Embroidery sizes 4, 5	Mercerized cotton heavy-duty #24, 30 silk, nylon	Coarse sizes 16/100 to 18/110	8, 9, 10
Very heavy fabrics—e.g., canvas, leather, suede, upholstery fabric	Sharps sizes 1, 2, 3 Betweens size 3 Embroidery sizes 3, 4, 5	Mercerized cotton heavy-duty #8, 16, 20	Coarse sizes 16/100 to 18/110	6, 7, 8

A BRIEF LOOK INTO THE LIFE OF
PAUL POIRET

Paul Poiret (1879–1944) was a French costume designer, dress designer, and painter. He introduced free-flowing dresses, eliminated corsets, and added an artistic look to fashion.

Dress with train, 1925.

Poiret's father worked as a cloth merchant, and Poiret became interested in fashion at an early age. His father wanted him to take over the family trade; however, Poiret wanted to go into fashion. In 1898, he was hired as an apprentice draftsman by the fashion designer Jacques Doucet. Poiret's first design at Doucet's, a red cloak, sold four hundred copies, and customers demanded the design in other colors.

After leaving Doucet, Poiret went into the military for a year, and when he returned he started working for the House of Worth as an apprentice. In 1904, Poiret opened up his own fashion house, where he introduced his revolutionary style.

Headdress from Les Robes de Paul Poiret, engraving by Georges Lepape, 1911.

His shop was modest; however, Poiret designed very colorful window displays that attracted customers. His shop became popular in a month for its innovative kimono coat and highly colored dresses made of rich materials that were influenced by the Ballets Russes. He was also famous for his oriental and art deco gowns and for the hobble skirt. Of this skirt,

Poiret wrote in his autobiography, *My First Fifty Years*, "It was in the name of Liberty that I proclaimed the fall of the corset and the adoption of the brassiere which, since then, has won the day. Yes, I freed the bust, but I shackled the legs." Poiret also designed the first sheath and sack dresses and was the first couturier to launch his own perfume, which he named after his oldest daughter, Rosine.

Paul Poiret, 1925.

Poiret's logo was a rose, which was designed by graphic artist Paul Iribe. Poiret was also known for designing costumes for the theater in Paris. He was joined by another designer, Erté, who worked with him until Maison Poiret closed.

Chapter Review

This chapter discussed different textiles and their uses. *Textiles* is a broad term referring to fabrics made from fibers (threadlike strands spun into yarns that in turn are woven or knitted) or from animal skins. There are two types of fabrics: natural and man-made. **Natural fibers** include silk, cotton, wool, and **linen**, and man-made fabrics include acrylic, polyester, nylon, acetate, and rayon. Before designing, make sure you research your fabric and learn how to work with it.

Projects

1. Visit your local fabric store, and research all the different types of fabrics. Purchase small amounts of different fabrics. Use your pinking sheers to cut square shapes out of every type of fabric you buy. Build a scrapbook filled with different fabrics. Label all the fabrics, and make sure you put in all the information about the uses, care, and pressing instructions of each type of fabric.

2. Choose one of the natural fiber fabrics, and design a five-outfit collection using this type of fabric in every part of the garments. Build an illustration board and a flat sketch board for this collection. Make sure you show the fabric you are using for this collection on the boards.

3. Choose one of the man-made fiber fabrics, and design a five-outfit collection using this type of fabric in every part of the garments. Build an illustration board and a flat sketch board for this collection. Make sure you show the fabric you are using for this collection on the boards.

Key Terms

Cotton	Linen	Suede
Fibers	Man-made fibers	Textiles
Lace	Natural fibers	Wool
Leather	Silk	

3

Uses of Tools and Supplies

Objectives

- Review uses of tools and supplies

- Review needle types and thread

- Learn proper pressing methods

- Learn how to tailor tack and thread trace your patterns

- Learn about the life and work of Christian Dior

Needles

There are many different kinds of **needles** made for all kinds of sewing purposes. Needles vary in size, shape, and eye. The best choice for a specific job is a needle that is fine enough to slip easily through the fabric and strong enough not to break or bend. Needles will help you succeed in your sewing. Remember to change needles regularly. It is suggested that every new garment should have a needle change, especially silk garments. Needle sizes in the United States are numbered from 8 to 19. The higher the number, the heavier and thicker the needle. You may also see a size that looks like this: 14/90. This is associated with machines used worldwide. The first number, 14, reflects the US needle number, and the second number, 90, is the European sizing. European needle sizes range from 60 to 120. See Tables 3.1 and 3.2.

Thread

Thread comes in a variety of fibers and sizes. (Figure 3.1) Choose thread that is strong and durable enough for the fabric you are using. See Table 3.3 for thread types and usage.

Thread is labeled according to weight and number of plies. In 50/3 thread, for example, the 50 refers to the weight (the higher the number, the finer the thread), and the 3 refers to the number of plies twisted together. However, sometimes thread is labeled by letter, with A being the finest. Other labeling systems exist as well.

Remember when you are sewing permanent stitches by hand that it is important to pull the thread through a piece of beeswax and press it for strength.

Figure 3.1 Thread spools.

Table 3.1 GENERAL HAND SEWING, NEEDLECRAFT, AND MACHINE NEEDLES AND USAGE

General Hand Sewing and Needlecraft Needles		
Needle Type	**Description**	**Usage**
Sharps	Medium long needles with round eyes (sizes 1–12)	Used for general sewing; have a size range to accommodate most weights of fabric
Betweens	Shorter in length with round eyes (sizes 3–9)	Also known as quilting needles; are able to make fine stitches in heavier fabrics
Ball-points	Medium long needles with round points (sizes 5–10)	Used to sew knit fabrics; resemble Sharps but have rounder points to penetrate between knit yarns
Milliner's	Long needles with round eyes (sizes 1–10)	Used to make long basting stitches and stab stitches
Embroidery	Medium long needles with oval eyes (sizes 1–10)	Also known as crewels; used for embroidery, and the long oval eye helps several embroidery threads be threaded at the same time
Chenille	Sharp and heavy needles with oval eyes (sizes 13–24)	Used for embroidery and hand-worked buttonholes
Beading	Long thin needles with round eyes and fine points (sizes 10–13)	Used to make long stitches on fine fabrics and made thin for beading narrow beads and sequins
Tapestry	Short thick needles with blunt points and oval eyes (sizes 14–26)	Used for needlework and as a substitute for bodkin
Cotton darners	Long needles with oval eyes (sizes 1–9)	Used to make long basting stitches and stab stitches to darn with fine cotton or wool
Yarn darners	Long and heavy needles (sizes 14–18)	Used for sewing together knit garment pieces and patterns with yarn
Glovers	Short needles with sharp points to pierce tough fabrics (sizes 1–8)	Used to sew leather, vinyl, fur, suede, and plastic without tearing
Sailmakers	Look like glovers, except their sharp points extend up the shaft (sizes 14–17)	Used for sewing canvas and heavy leather
Sack/curved	Packing needles with curved wedge points	Used for weaving, upholstery, and sewing burlap
Upholstery/curved	Fine round-eye needles shaped in half circles (sizes 5–20)	Used for upholstery and ramp shades where a curved needle would be needed

General Sewing Machine Needles		
Needle Type	**Description**	**Usage**
Universal	Sizes 8/60 to 19/120	Can be used on most fabrics as well as knits due to its slightly rounded point; can be used on woven fabrics as well because they are usually sharp enough, unless you are sewing sheers or silk-like fabrics similar to silk charmeuse
Sharps (Microtex)	Needles with narrow long shafts and sharper points (sizes 8/60 to 14/90)	These needles have a size range to accommodate most weights of fabric: sizes 8/60 to 10/70 are used with sheers, silk, and silklike fabric; also great for topstitching and edge stitching due to the sharp point that can penetrate through many layers of fabric; sizes 10/70 to 14/90 are used for fine woven fabric sewing and universal sewing purposes
Quilting	Needles with sharp, tapered points (sizes 11/75 to 14/90)	Used to make fine stitches in heavier fabrics; thicker than Sharps needles to sew thick layers of fabric or many layers of fabric and won't break as often as regular Sharps needles
Ball-points	Needles with rounder medium-size points than Sharps (sizes 10/70 to 16/100)	Used to sew knit fabrics; resemble Sharps but have rounder points to penetrate between knit yarns; are best to make even stitches without pulling and puckering your knits; can also be very fragile and will not leave permanent holes and break knit threads or the spandex threads in knit fabric
Double	Needles range in slightly different sizes, with the first number representing the distance between the needles in millimeters and the second representing the size of the needle in European sizes; each needle is made of two needles that are attached to a shaft above (sizes 1.6/70 to 4.0/100)	Used to make two parallel stitches and rows of stitches in one seam; can only be used on machines that can accommodate these specific stitches as well as overlock or serger machines; the smaller the distance between the needles, the finer the fabric you can sew on, but make sure you get the right double needle, because they come in different uses (Sharps, Ball-point [knits], embroidery, hemming, and special ones for metallic thread)
Triple	Needles made of three needles that are attached to a shaft above; they range in slightly different sizes, with the first number representing the distance between the needles in millimeters and the second representing the size of the needle in European sizes (sizes 2.5/80 to 3.0/80)	Used the same as double needles, but only come in one universal size; used to topstitch a row of three parallel stitched lines in one seam or topstitch

Table 3.1 GENERAL HAND SEWING, NEEDLECRAFT, AND MACHINE NEEDLES AND USAGE (*continued*)

General Sewing Machine Needles		
Needle Type	**Description**	**Usage**
Hemstitch (wing)	Needles that look like double needle, but the shaft holding the two needles is flared and the needles are different; one needle is a wing needle, and the other one is a universal needle (sizes 16/100 to 19/120)	Great to use for hemstitching, decorative topstitching, heirloom stitching, and freehand embroidery stitching; because the needles are mostly universal, they can be used on most fabrics; try a test stitch before you begin working with your fabric to make sure the needle does not pull the weaves out and snag the fabric
Machine embroidery	Needles with larger eyes and a protective designed edge in the eyes and shafts to protect thread from breaking while stitching tightly embroidered designs (sizes 10/70 to 14/90)	Meant to offer easier, stronger embroidery decorative stitches without breaking the thread; work great with nylon, acrylic, metallic, and even rayon threads
Metallic	Needles with a protective edge in the eyes similar to embroidery needles but with even larger eyes (size 12/80)	Specialty needles used for metallic thread embroidery, monofilament thread, and decorative topstitching; made with special protection around the hole and sharp points to keep the thread from breaking because metallic thread is easily broken; work even better with metallic thread than embroidery needles do
Denim (jeans)	Needles that are stronger and thicker in the shaft and sharp point because they need to work on stronger, thicker fabric (sizes 10/70 to 18/110)	Strong needles used to sew fabrics such as denim, thick wool, canvas, horsehair, buckrum, duck, and starched fabrics; have a sharp point and a thicker shaft; do not use on fine woven fabrics, silky fabrics, or leathers; the shaft is very thick and starts getting thicker as it gets higher up the needle; if used on delicate fabrics or leather, it may penetrate a larger hole in the fabric than you are hoping for, leaving a permanent hole and even snags in the weaves in loosely woven fabrics; the strong shaft and sharp point can penetrate through various layers of thick fabric
Leather	Needles that are extra sharp and thicker for strong fabrics with points that have a wedge edge to help cut through thick layers of fabric and leather; they act like a three-edge knife point to cut through leather and vinyl (sizes 12/80 to 18/110)	Great to use with leather, thicker non-woven fabrics, high-tech fabrics, suede, faux leather, and vinyl fabrics; can easily penetrate fabrics with the wedge sharp point without breaking or ripping them Note: the needle is very sharp and leaves a permanent hole in the fabric, so make sure that your seams and stitches are always perfect. You may end up with permanent holes in your project if you need to remove a not-so-perfect seam; therefore, you cannot backstitch your start and ends. Use the old-fashioned technique of tying the ends on the backside to avoid making extra holes and breaking a large hole in your fabrics or leather.

Table 3.2 THREAD TYPES AND USAGE

Thread Type	Description	Usage
Cotton wrapped polyester	All-purpose strong thread; can take the hot iron pressing for cotton fabrics	Can be used on all fabric types except fine fabrics for multi-seam sewing (regular seams, hems, buttons, buttonholes, machine sewing, etc.)
Glazed cotton	Strong thread with a starch glaze that is easy to use because of its slick, easy pull; when pressing, it can leave an impression	Is used often to ease and baste pattern pieces while gathering the fabrics
Mercerized cotton	All-purpose thread with a slight sheen that can fade or crack with time	Used for machine sewing for all-purpose sewing; can be used to sew cotton and linen fabrics; some sewing techniques such as hems, seams, zippers, and pad stitching are done well with this type of thread
DMC cotton	All-purpose thread for fine fabrics that also has a sheen like Mercerized cotton thread but is not as strong	Can be used to perform the same seams and stitches as Mercerized cotton but on finer fabrics
Spun polyester	Strong synthetic thread that has give and is used to sew fabrics and wool fabrics	Used to sew all types of seams on knit fabrics, stretch fabrics, and wool
Silk line stitch or silk embroidery	Medium strength thread made of silk	Used for sewing on fine or medium fabrics; also used for buttonholes, machine topstitching, and embroidery on fine fabrics and medium fabrics
Buttonhole twist	Made of silk or polyester, this thread is strong and heavy	Used for topstitching, hand stitching buttonholes, and sewing on buttons with stems

Pressing Tools

Iron. Steam and dry irons provide us with a wide range of temperature controls that enable us to control the heat for pressing many different varieties of fabrics. You cannot sew without an iron. Keep the iron warm so that you can press each seam after you stitch. (Figure 3.2a)

Sleeve Board. A smaller ironing board with different size ends meant to fit through different size sleeves and small tubular seam areas. This board rests on the original large ironing board. (Figure 3.2b)

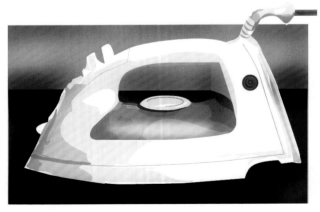

Figure 3.2a Iron.

Figure 3.2b Sleeve board.

Table 3.3 PRESSING TECHNIQUES

Fabric Type	Technique
Beaded fabrics	For fabrics that are beaded, have beaded embroidery, or are covered in sequins, press with a lower heat setting on your iron. However, make sure that you press with a dry iron because the steam and high heat can melt the beads and/or remove their shiny finish.
Brocade fabrics	When pressing brocades or fabrics with a relief embroidery, you need to use a soft pressing cloth or a towel over the relief. This prevents the iron and the heat from flattening and keeps the material shiny. Make sure you do not press on the right side of the fabric. When using steam—only through a towel on low steam—be careful. It is best to press with a dry iron.
Blend fabrics	When pressing blended fabrics, use a small sample to test before pressing your garment. Start testing with a low setting and work your way up. Also test for moisture spots from spray or steam.
Crepe fabrics	When pressing crepe, press lightly on the wrong side of the fabric without moisture. If you need some moisture, use a pressing cloth.
Dark color fabrics with dull finish	When pressing dark colors, press from the wrong side of the fabric. If you absolutely need to press from the right side, use a press cloth. This will prevent the iron from burning the shine.
Durable press fabrics	Begin by checking the fiber content and the pressing directions on the tag of the fabric. On these fabrics, folds and creases may stay permanently after pressing; therefore, use lower to medium temperatures and press seams you are very sure about. Begin by pressing with the point of your iron; then place a pressing cloth over the fabric, and use a higher temperature to crease a permanent fold.
Fake fur	When pressing fake fur, remember that it can melt, and the pile can flatten. Stay away from the iron if you can. Most of the time you can press down with your fingers. However, if you absolutely must press with an iron, use a dry iron with no steam and press on the wrong side of the fabric.
Glossy fabrics	When pressing glossy fabrics, press on the wrong side of the fabric and try not to use steam/moisture.
Knit fabrics	When pressing knits or stretchy fabrics, make sure you use very low pressure because heat combined with pressure can stretch the fabric. When you press, press on the wrong side of the fabric along the lengthwise grain. Steam should be used with caution.
Lace	When pressing lace, use the same caution you use on embroidered fabrics. Press through a soft press cloth in order not to flatten the relief. Very little steam should be used over a cloth.
Laminated fabrics	Laminated fabrics are plastic covered and melt in high heat. When pressing them, make sure you press them inside out on the fabric side over a cloth. Do not let the iron touch the laminated side.
Leather	Leather should not be pressed. If it is absolutely necessary, use a low heat setting on a dry iron and brown paper in between to protect the leather from burn, stretch, and discoloration.
Pile fabrics	To press pile fabrics, use a needle board or a Turkish towel under the right side of the fabric. Press on the wrong side of the fabric with the face in the needle board, and make sure you keep the pressure light so that the pile does not flatten. When pressing delicate pile fabrics, use another pressing cloth over it and steam instead of press.
Satin	When pressing satin fabrics, press on the wrong side of the fabric and try not to use steam or moisture.
Sheer fabrics	When pressing sheers, use a dry iron and low heat setting. Try to stay away from too much steam, as it may pucker your fabric.
Vinyls	Do not press vinyl; it will melt.
Wool	When pressing wool, use moisture with heat and a wool press cloth. Place the cloth on the right side of the fabric, place another cotton press cloth, and cover with a damp cheese cloth. Do not slide the iron all over to press. You will need to lift the iron up and down over the specific areas. When you press, you will need to lift the press cloth off the fabric to let the steam out from the wool. Do not press until the wool dries and cools from the previous press in order not to distort the fabric. Wool is the easiest fabric to mold and shape with heat and pressure.

Clapper (Pounding Block). A smooth, hard, wooden block used to press seams that are meant to keep their shape, such as creases on pants, hems, and pleats. After you press, place this block on the crease until it cools. A clapper is often used on woolens and synthetic fabrics that cannot be pressed with high heat. (Figure 3.3a)

Tailor's Board. A wooden tool that ends in a point. It is used to press hard-to-reach places in collars, lapels, and other pointed corners. This board has multiple padded surfaces. The largest curve is the best for pressing armscye seams on tailored garments. (Figure 3.3b)

Tailor's Ham. A small, ham-shaped cushion that is firmly padded and covered with cotton on one side to press many different fabrics and wool on the other to press wool fabrics. Hold the ham in one hand and press with the other to press seams, darts, princess seams, collars, and so on. (Figure 3.4)

Silicone Mitt. A heat-resistant mitt used while pressing to protect hands from the hot iron. It is heat resistant and is a good tool to have as you guide fabric and small seams under the iron. (Figure 3.5a)

Pressing Mitt. A flexible, heat-resistant mitt used to press seams such as sleeve caps and other areas that need to be held in place and pressed flat. (Figure 3.5b)

Needle Board. A rectangular board made of thousands of small needles on one side and a flat surface on the other. This board is used to press napped fabrics such as velvet and corduroy. The needles keep the nap from pressing flat. (Figure 3.6)

Figure 3.4 Tailor's ham.

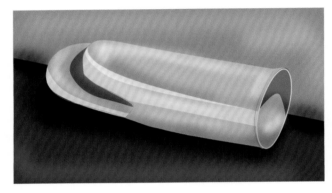

Figure 3.5a Silicone mitt.

Figure 3.5b Pressing mitt.

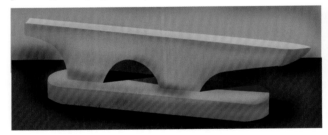

Figure 3.3a Clapper.

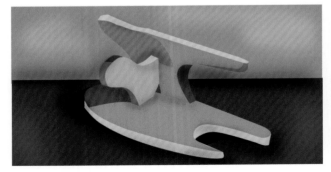

Figure 3.3b Tailor's board.

Figure 3.6 Needle board.

Pressing Techniques

Good-quality pressing is the key to constructing a high-quality garment. It requires time, practice, and techniques to keep from ruining the fabric. The most important thing to remember is that pressing is not ironing. When you iron, you push the iron from one spot to another to remove wrinkles. However, when you press, you lift the iron from one spot to another to flatten or shape small areas in the seams. Make sure you do not slide the iron while pressing down; it will stretch your fabric. Good pressing should not make the fabric shine, flatten the pile, or distort the pattern.

Higher or lower heat is used in different ranges, depending on the fabric being pressed. Fabrics also react differently to moisture and pressure. Make sure that you test a small piece of the fabric before pressing. When you are testing it, check to see if you get any imprints on the right side of the fabric from seam allowances or darts. If you see an imprint, place a piece of heavy paper under the seam edge so that the imprint does not show through to the other side. Try to press on the wrong side of the fabric when possible to avoid shine and fabric flattening. Also, after pressing, let the fabric cool down before moving it to avoid any stretching and distorting of the fabric.

Most fabrics being pressed need moisture. Many irons come with a great steam function that may provide enough moisture for most fabrics. However, moisture can give some fabrics a shiny look. Therefore, use a press cloth over the fabric. If you don't have a steam iron, try two press cloths, with the top being damp.

When you are finished constructing your garment, also use a press cloth on the right side of the garment.

PRESSING TIP #1

When pressing, make sure to read instructions for your iron in order to determine the right settings for your fabrics.

- When pressing man-made fibers such as polyester, use lower heat.
- When pressing natural fibers such as cotton, use higher heat settings.

- When pressing a mix of different fibers, use the heat setting that is required for the fiber more likely to burn. Some synthetic fibers cannot be pressed at all.

PRESSING TIP #2

Certain fabrics need moisture while others cannot come in contact with it at all because it causes stains. Moisture can also cause fabrics to look over pressed and shiny.

- Use a damp pressing cloth over a dry cloth before ironing to avoid these issues. Avoid spraying the fabric with water.

PRESSING TIP #3

When pressing seams, press them flat to one side first, in the same direction in which you stitched the seam. This technique allows the thread to settle and press into the fabric. (Figure 3.7a)

- Press the seams as soon as you sew them to avoid waves and ripples.
- If you want to press the seam open, press along the opened seam with the tip of the iron first. This allows you to press the seam open really close to the seam. Next, you can apply moisture or a cloth over the

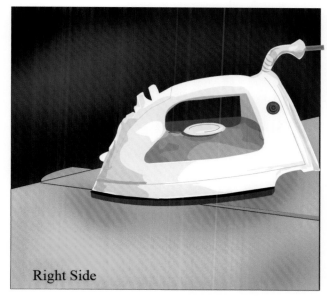

Right Side

Figure 3.7a Pressing seams.

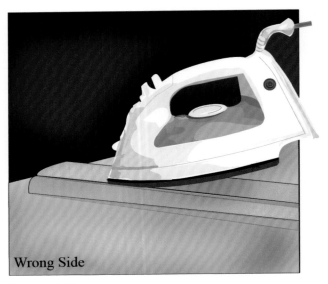

Wrong Side

Figure 3.7b Pressing seams.

Figure 3.7c Pressing gathers.

fabric and apply more heat to press it firmly open. (Figure 3.7b)

Remember, if the seam leaves an imprint on the right side when pressing, insert the heavy-weight paper between the fabric and the seam allowance before pressing.

- When working with waistline stitches that connect to a lower body section, the seam allowances are usually turned up.

PRESSING TIP #4

When pressing, support the weight of the iron with your hand. This keeps the iron light over the fabric and helps avoid pressing down the pile of the fabric.

- When using firmly woven heavy-weight fabric, use a little more pressure.

PRESSING TIP #5

When pressing gathers and shirring, it is very important not to flatten the gathers too much, which will make them look like pleats.
- Pressing should be done on the wrong side of the fabric.
- Before pressing, make sure you secure the gathers along the stitch line with one of your hands.
- Press toward the gathers by sliding the iron point into the gathers, toward your hand holding the seam.
- Slide the iron into and out of the gathers. Do not slide the iron side to side. (Figure 3.7c)

PRESSING TIP #6

When pressing darts, press them over a tailor's ham or another curved surface.

- Press the dart flat before pressing it to one side using a ham.
- Press the dart only within the stitching area; do not go beyond the seam.
- To avoid imprints, follow the same technique used for regular seams.
- Vertical darts are pressed toward the center. Horizontal darts are pressed down.
- When working with very bulky darts, slash them and press them open to reduce the bulk.

PRESSING TIP #7

When pressing curved seams, use a curved area on your ironing board or a tailor's ham.

- Bust, armhole, and crotch seams are curved seams.
- Begin pressing the curved seam flat on the ironing board. To press the seam open, clip your seam allowances first. Then press open using a tailor's ham. (Figure 3.7d)

Curved seams in the armhole are usually pressed toward the sleeve. Seam allowances around the crotch seam only press open for the waist down along the center front/back opening right up to the start of the curved crotch.

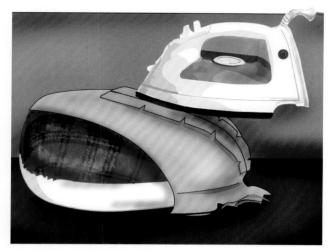

Figure 3.7d Pressing curved seams.

PRESSING TIP #8

When pressing hems, press them up from the bottom edge. Mark the hem, and baste or ease at the top for easier pressing.

- Afterward, shrink the fullness of the hem by using a strip of heavyweight paper between the hem and garment using steam.

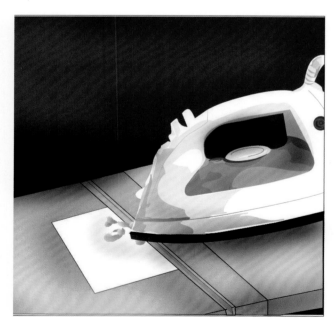

Figure 3.7e Pressing hems.

- Keep the iron light over the fabric. Steam while you slip the point of the iron into the fullness. (Figure 3.7e)

Sewing Tools

Pincushions. Keep pins organized in a very convenient way. The most popular one is a red tomato with an emery-filled strawberry, which sharpens and cleans pins and needles. (Figure 3.8)

Seam Ripper. A curved metal cutting blade used to rip stitches. One end of the curved blade has a sharp point, and the other has a small plastic ball that prevents the ripper from slipping. (Figure 3.9)

Clamp and Bird Set. This tool is sometimes called the "third hand" because it attaches itself to

Figure 3.8 Pincushion.

Figure 3.9 Seam ripper.

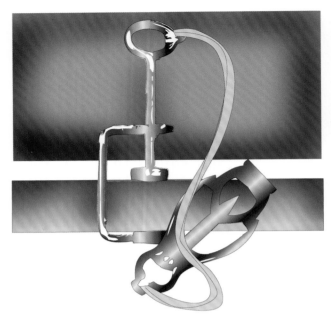

Figure 3.10 Clamp and bird set.

Figure 3.12 Chalk.

your sewing table and holds the fabric so you can use both hands to sew and trim seams and hems. (Figure 3.10)

Thimble. A small cover, made of metal, rubber, leather, or plastic, that slips over the index or middle finger, protecting the fingertip from pinpricks and helping to push the needle through thick fabric while hand sewing. (Figure 3.11)

Chalk. One of many marking tools used on fabric. Chalk makes a fine line on fabric that stays long enough to sew but brushes away easily when no longer needed. It comes in many forms: chalk pencils, disappearing-ink pens, wax pencils, and rollers with chalk powder are very common. In Europe, where chalk is not as common, home

sewers use a small piece of hard soap, which marks well and washes off easily. (Figure 3.12)

Straight Pins. Stainless steel or brass pins with sharp, smooth, rustproof ends. These pins can bend without breaking and are safe to use on any fabrics. They come in a variety of types, lengths, and widths. (Figure 3.13)

Point Turner. A handheld plastic or wood pointed tool used to poke into tight corners. When you sew corners, use this tool to push out the corners of collars and cuffs before pressing. The opposite end is flat and

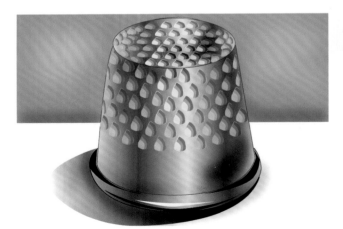

Figure 3.11 Thimble.

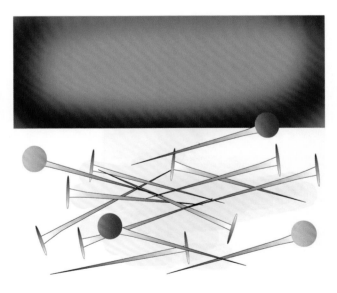

Figure 3.13 Straight pins.

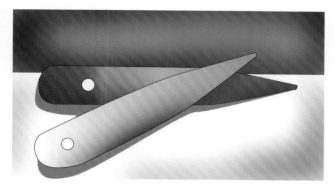

Figure 3.14 Point turner.

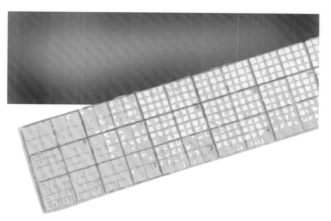

Figure 3.16 18-inch clear plastic ruler.

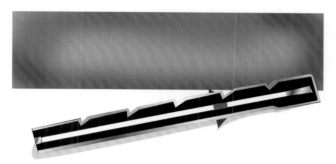

Figure 3.17 Seam gauge.

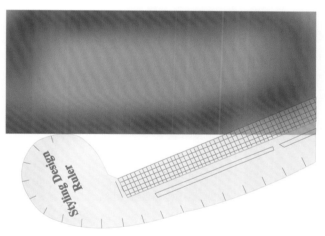

Figure 3.18 French curve/hip curve ruler.

rounded and is used to hold open seam allowances while pressing. (Figure 3.14)

Loop Turner. A handheld metal wire with a latch hook on one end and a circular loop on the other. When you need to flip narrow straps, bias strips, and more, you can use this tool. Attach the latch tip on one end of the strap, and wiggle back and forth a bit with your fingers until you can pull the wire loop on the other end and begin pulling the fabric through, in order to flip the strip inside out.

Tracing Wheel. This serrated-edge wheel connected to a handle is used with or without tracing paper to transfer markings from patterns to fabric. The wheel comes with sharp points that leave a good impression on the fabric without making holes. (Figure 3.15)

18-inch Clear Plastic Ruler. A two-inch-wide ruler divided into ⅛-inch increments. This ruler is used for pattern drafting and measuring grainlines and alteration lines. It is also great to mark seam allowances. (Figure 3.16)

Seam Gauge. This is a small adjustable guide used to determine the length of stitches, seams, hems, and even buttonholes. (Figure 3.17)

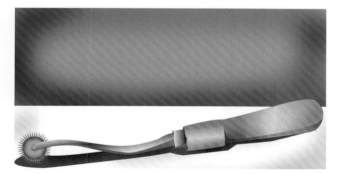

Figure 3.15 Tracing wheel.

French Curve, Hip Curve Ruler. These rulers have a variety of curves to mimic the body's curves and are used to create patterns. Depending on how you turn the ruler and what segment you use, one ruler can give you all the curves necessary to complete pattern lines when altering or drafting patterns. (Figure 3.18)

Hem Maker. Used to measure the distance from the floor to the bottom of the garment. (Figure 3.19)

T-Square Ruler. Used for altering patterns, squaring off fabric edges, and locating cross grains on fabric. (Figure 3.20)

Pattern Notcher. Used like a regular hole punch during pattern drafting to mark notches in matching areas, armholes, darts, sleeves, and so on. Instead of circular holes, this tool cuts a small V-shaped notch. (Figure 3.21)

Figure 3.21 Pattern notcher.

Figure 3.22 Tape measure.

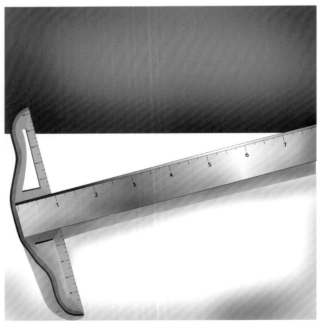

Figure 3.19 Hem maker.

Tape Measure. Flexible 60-inch fiberglass or fabric measuring tape that is ideal for taking body measurements, measuring patterns and layouts, and general measuring. (Figure 3.22)

Hem Gauge. This tool is used to speed up the marking of hems by turning up the hem and pressing in one step. (Figure 3.23)

Cutting Tools

What is the difference between **scissors** and **shears**? You may have heard people use both of these words when describing cutting tools. Scissors that have handles of equal size are called scissors. Scissors with one handle larger than the other, for comfortable cutting, are referred to as shears. When you buy scissors or shears for your fabric, make sure they are fabric, not paper, scissors or shears. Look at the quality of the pair. Are they made of steel? Steel shears are stronger. Do they have a strong screw to allow stronger pressure when you cut your fabric?

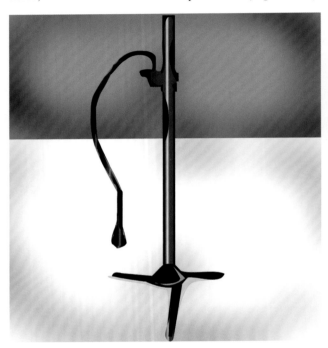

Figure 3.20 T-square ruler.

Figure 3.23 Hem gauge.

Are the blades sharp enough? Once you buy brand-new, strong, sharp scissors or shears, make sure you never use them to cut other materials besides fabric. If you need to cut paper or other items in your house or school, use a different pair. If you use the fabric shears on other materials, you can dull the blades, making them unable to cut fabric.

Bent Sewing Shears. Used for general sewing, fabric cutting, and thread clipping for all fabrics, natural and synthetic. These shears are forged and so stay very sharp for a longer period of time. They are bent for easier cutting on a table. When buying, look for the brands Gingher, Dovo, or Wiss. (Figure 3.24a)

Pinking Shears. Sharp scissors with scalloped blades that cut a zigzag edge on your fabric to prevent it from fraying. These scissors come in many different shapes of scalloped edges and are used for various types of fabric. The deeper the scalloped edge, the better the fray resistance. Before you begin cutting out your patterns, cut a small piece of fabric and check how much the fabric frays to determine which pair of scissors you may need to use. (Figure 3.24b)

Tailor's Shears. Tailor's shears are much longer and wider than regular sewing shears are. These shears are also referred to as heavy-duty shears and are used for cutting heavy fabrics and layered fabrics. These shears come bent or straight. The bent shears make it easier to cut fabric on a tabletop. When buying these shears, make sure they are steel and have a large, strong screw holding the blades together. (Figure 3.24c)

Gold Stork Scissors. These scissors are high-quality embroidery scissors. They are shaped like a stork and are often very detailed in design. The wings

are gold-plated, and the beak and the screw are chrome-plated. These scissors can be bought in sets with sewing scissors by Gingher or Wasa. These scissors are great for embroidery because they have very fine blade points that help to pierce the fabric when cutting it for embroidery relief. They are very sharp and are forged, so they stay sharp for a while. (Figure 3.24d)

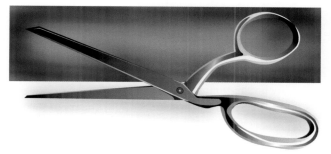

Figure 3.24a Bent sewing shears.

Figure 3.24b Pinking shears.

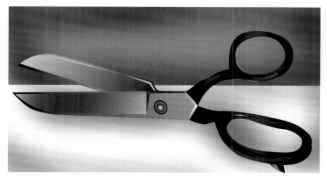

Figure 3.24c Tailor's shears.

Figure 3.24d Gold stork scissors.

Thread Clippers. Thread clippers have a spring-action blade. You can use these to clip thread while sewing after you finish your seam on a sewing machine and/or by hand. You can also use these instead of a seam ripper; they may actually be a better choice to rip apart the seam without making holes in the fabric. (Figure 3.24e)

Appliqué Scissors. These very sharp scissors are forged to stay sharp longer and are double-chrome-plated for strength. You can use these scissors to cut around appliqué designs and to cut out negative fabric inside the appliqué. **Appliqué scissors** can also be used for close trimming and buttonholes. (Figure 3.24f and g)

Straight Sewing Shears. Straight shears are made for fabrics of all weight and thickness and are used for general sewing, fabric cutting, and thread clipping.

They are forged to stay strong and sharp for a longer period of time. These sewing scissors have one fine point and one round point. When buying these shears, look for the following brands: Gingher, Dovo, and Wiss. (Figure 3.24h)

Buttonhole Scissors. Buttonhole scissors are specially shaped for cutting buttonholes. They are forged for stronger cuts and to stay sharp longer. When buying, look for forged, nickel-plated ones from Wasa or Gingher. Gingher also makes a double-chrome-plated pair. (Figure 3.24i)

Fiskars Razor-Edged Scissors. These can be used in the same way as sewing scissors. They are very sharp and strong and can cut well through many layers of fabric. They are a good choice for quilts, wool, corduroy, denim, and other heavy materials. (Figure 3.24j)

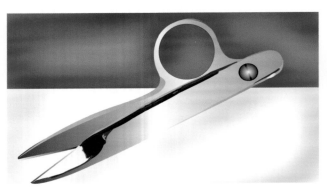

Figure 3.24e Thread clippers.

Figure 3.24g Appliqué scissors.

Figure 3.24f Appliqué scissors.

Figure 3.24h Straight sewing shears.

Figure 3.24i Buttonhole scissors.

Figure 3.24j Fiskars razor-edged scissors.

Garment Marking

Couture garments are usually marked with thread using **tailor's tacks** and **thread tracing**. This type of marking is important for couture garments because the marked tacks show through on both sides of the fabric and are strong enough to stay in place during the fabric manipulation of the construction process.

TAILOR'S TACKS

Tailor's tacks are used to mark patterns, darts, pleats, and tucks on double layers of fabric when you do not wish to mark fabric with chalk (for example, to avoid stains on delicate fabrics). Use tailor's tacks during tailoring of thicker fabrics such as wool and denim. Thinner fabrics tend to come loose during construction, and tailor's tacks would not be the best choice. Tailor's tacks are often used on soft, sheer fabrics and in tailoring.

1. Pin the pattern to the fabric; begin to tack. Make sure you do not remove the pins and the pattern until you are done with all the tacks.
2. Then thread the needle with doubled, unknotted thread, and sew a small stitch through all the layers of the fabric.

1. Make another stitch at the same point.
2. Leave approximately one to two inches of the thread loose in every stitch. (Figure 3.25)
3. As soon as you finish marking every line, dart, and symbol on your pattern, take the pattern off the fabric.

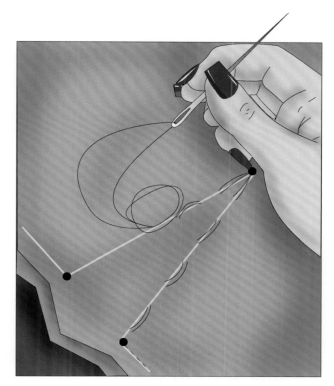

Figure 3.25 Tailor's tacks leaving loose thread.

4. Be careful not to pull out the thread. Pull up one layer of the fabric to the full length of the tacks you made, and cut them right in the center between the two layers of fabric. (Figure 3.26)
5. The remaining threads stay in the fabric and are used as marks. Pull them out after the garment is finished.

Hint: Tailor's tacks can also be done in one single running stitch to mark fold lines for pleats and tucks. Make a loose running stitch along the lines you wish to fold, sewing them through both the paper pattern and the fabric. Leave approximately one inch of loose thread between each stitch. Cut the stitches in half and take the pattern off carefully, leaving the thread tacks in the fabric. (Figure 3.27a and b)

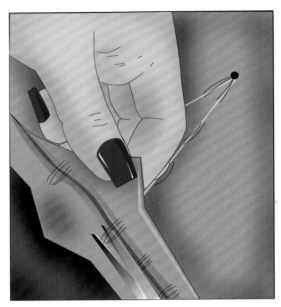

Figure 3.26 Tailor's tacks—cut in the center between the two layers of fabric.

Figure 3.27a and b Tailor's tacks—one single running stitch.

THREAD TRACING

Tread tracing is used to mark couture fabrics made of thinner fabrics and muslin samples (toiles). To begin marking, use your chalk to mark all of the seams, darts, pockets, and so on.

1. To start tracing with thread, secure your thread with a backstitch on one side of the seam line, preferably the right side if you are right-handed and the left side if you are left-handed.

2. Begin sewing a basting stitch along the chalk line you have marked around the entire pattern piece. (Figure 3.28a, b, and c)

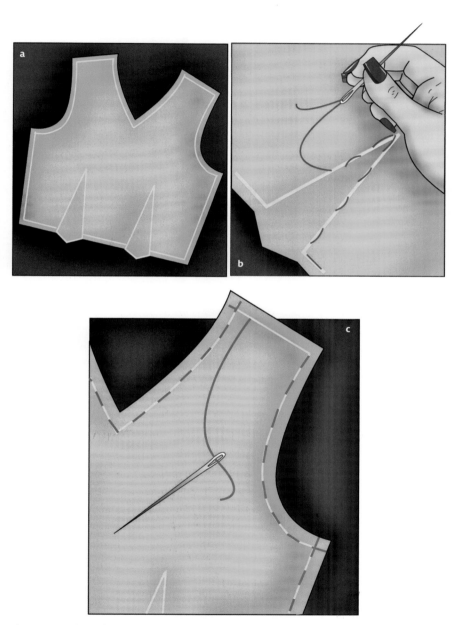

Figure 3.28a, b, and c Thread tracing.

A BRIEF LOOK INTO THE LIFE OF
CHRISTIAN DIOR

Christian Dior was born in 1905 in Granville, a city on the Normandy coast. His father, Maurice Dior, was a fertilizer and chemical manufacturer. Dior was the second of five children in his family. They moved to Paris in 1910. Dior always wanted to become an architect; however, his father sent him to the Ecole des Sciences Politiques in Paris to obtain a degree in politics.

After finishing school, Dior wanted to pursue the arts. He opened up a gallery in 1928, although his father forbade him to use the family name in the business. Unfortunately, the Dior family business collapsed, and Dior had to close the gallery and scramble for money. He began to sell his fashion illustrations to designers and in 1938 landed a job as an assistant to the couturier Robert Piguet.

Models wearing dress designs from Christian Dior, 1957.

Christian Dior, 1954.

When World War II began, Dior became an officer for a year; after his military service, he worked for the fashion house of Lucien Lelong as one of its two primary designers. Backed by Marcel Boussac, Dior was able to open his own house in 1946. He presented his first fashion show a year later. He introduced the "New Look," which featured soft shoulders, a wasp waist, and full, flowing skirts. This silhouette made women look elegant and beautiful. The New Look became immensely popular,

helping to bring France back into the forefront of fashion, and the House of Dior flourished with orders from media stars and royalty.

By the 1950s, Dior was the biggest and best-run couture house in Paris. Dior hired very talented assistants, including Pierre Cardin and Yves Saint Laurent.

Dior died suddenly in 1957, but his couture house carried on. Yves Saint Laurent was named as Dior's successor and unveiled his first collection in January 1958.

Chapter Review

This chapter was about the uses of tools and supplies. There are different needles used for different types of fabrics that are fine enough to slip easily through the fabrics yet strong enough not to break or bend. Thread used for that same fabric comes in a variety of fibers and sizes. Choose thread that is strong and durable enough for the fabric you are using. After choosing the right needle and the best thread for your garment, you can begin to sew. Now, for the most important part: pressing. Good-quality pressing is the key to constructing a high-quality garment. You cannot sew a perfect garment without knowing the different types of sewing tools available to you, such as the scissors or shears you should use to cut your fabric. You can read this chapter to review everything available to you so you can sew that perfect garment.

Projects

1. Start a samples book for yourself so that you can collect all of the practice samples you will make. You can use plastic page protectors to insert your samples.
2. Practice garment markings by making a sample for both tailor's tacks and thread tracing. Write down your steps, and insert them into one of your plastic cover sheets.
3. Practice the pressing techniques covered in this chapter.

Key Terms

Appliqué scissors	Needles	Tailor's tacks
Buttonhole scissors	Scissors	Thread
Loop turner	Shears	Thread tracing

4

The Skill of Hand and Machine Stitching

Objectives

- Learn temporary and permanent hand and machine stitches

- Learn how to apply lining to your garment

- Learn proper facing techniques

- Learn how to apply interlining to your garment

- Learn underlining applications

- Learn stay stitching

- Learn about life and work of Gianni Versace

The Art of Hand Sewing

Couture technicians use hand stitches to control the entire construction of the designed garment. Sewing by hand enables you to sew on the right side of the garment as well as areas that a sewing machine can never reach, such as small corners of designed pockets, fabric overlays, and much more. Hand stitching is sometimes best with thin, soft fabrics because it does not leave marks, and if there's a mistake, it allows you to take out the seams without ruining the fabric.

Hand sewing is very important in couture ateliers. Most of the ateliers have technicians working on garments by hand on tables with no sewing machines. In part, this is a reflection of tradition in Europe, where many of the most famous couture houses are located. My family is from a small European country, Moldova, and when I was five years old, my mother started to teach me how to sew by hand. This was done all around Europe and the rest of the world by many mothers.

Hand Seams

- To start hand sewing, you need a needle and a spool of thread that matches the color of your garment.
- Cut the thread at a diagonal angle (to help keep the thread from untwisting). When you bite or break the thread, the thread then has a messy edge that is hard to thread into the needle and also starts untwisting and tangles faster.
- Using a very long piece of thread risks getting it tangled.

- For permanent sewing, use a piece of thread between 18 and 24 inches long. If you are using the thread to baste, then you can make it longer.
- Choose a needle that is suitable for the fabric being used. Use a short needle if you are planning on making short stitches; use a long needle for long stitches.
- To thread the needle, hold the needle with the eye up in the air. Pull one end of the thread through the eye of the needle. (Figure 4.1)
- Tie a knot at the longest end of the thread. (There are very few exceptions when a knot is not used, such as in tailor's tacks.)
- If basting, don't worry about the knot being big and visible, since you will be pulling it out at the end. If sewing permanent stitches, make a very small knot, and place it very deep inside the layer of fabric to hide bulk.

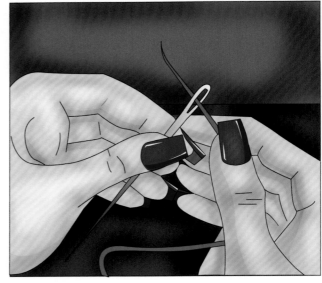

Figure 4.1 Threading the needle.

Starting Knot Techniques

EUROPEAN KNOT

This knot is commonly used in the European countries. If you get a large, tangled, messy knot at first, just keep trying.

1. Using one of the cut ends of your thread, wrap loops twice around your index finger, tightly holding them with your thumb (but not too tightly or you won't be able to roll them off your finger). (Figure 4.2a, b, c, and d)

2. Roll these thread loops off your index finger with your thumb by pushing and sliding your thumb against the loops and your index finger, forward and back, five to ten times until the twisted loops begin to roll closer to the end of your finger. With the help of your thumb, continue sliding your fingers until the loops roll off. Pull the gathered thread down with your thumb and index finger to make it into a knot.

Figure 4.2 European knot.

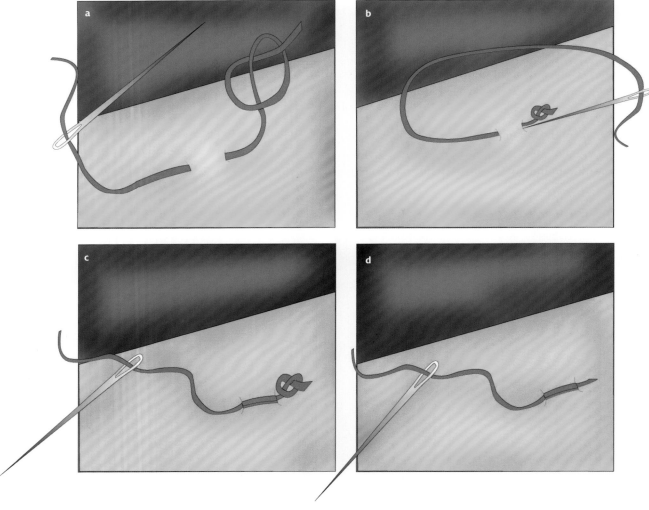

Figure 4.3 Simple knot.

SIMPLE KNOT

A **simple knot**, also called the waste knot, is very common because of its simplicity. This knot temporarily holds the thread in the fabric until you can secure it with backstitches; then you can trim off the knot.

1. Tie a **European knot**, and take one basting stitch forward.
2. Guide the needle back through the same holes already made from the last stitch.
3. Continue these backstitched wraps several times to secure the thread. Trim off the knot and keep sewing. (Figure 4.3a, b, c, and d)

Temporary Stitches

The most common term for temporary stitching is basting. Temporary stitches are removed during construction or after the garment is finished. Basting usually consists of stitches that are larger and farther apart than permanent stitches, often in a color of thread that contrasts with the fabric of the garment.

Temporary stitches are used for fittings, marking of the garment, and holding layers of fabric together during the construction of the garment instead of using pins.

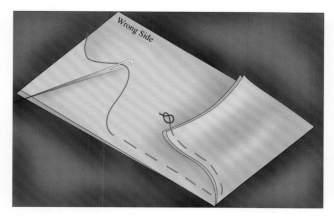

Figure 4.4a Even basting.

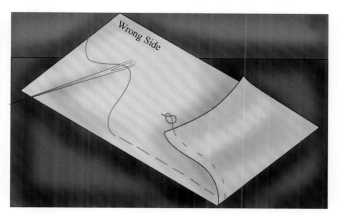

Figure 4.4b Uneven basting.

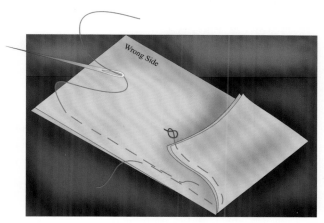

Figure 4.5 Lap basting.

EVEN BASTING

Even basting uses a series of stitches even in length with a ⅜-inch pickup. Even basting is commonly used during garment construction, easing and gathering fabric.

1. Line up two fabric pieces together along the edge, right sides together.
2. Secure your thread at one end of your piece.
3. Begin stitching in and out through both layers, picking up evenly spaced ⅜-inch stitches.
4. Leave the end loose, or secure the thread with an end knot. (Figure 4.4a)

UNEVEN BASTING

Uneven basting is a series of stitches uneven in length (long and short). It is used for control during permanent stitching, temporary hold for hems, ease, and marking. (Figure 4.4b)

1. Line up two fabric pieces right sides together, and secure the thread at one end.
2. Begin stitching in and out through both layers by alternating long and short stitches.
3. Leave the end loose, or secure the thread with an end knot.

LAP BASTING

Lap basting is helpful when working with bias-cut fabric during seam construction. This stitch helps to keep it from stretching.

1. Secure your thread at one end.
2. Stitch one row of even basting stitches. Trim off your thread, leaving a small tail of thread, or backstitch once or twice in place.
3. Beginning at one of the basted end sides, stitch another row of even stitches through first row using the same holes in the fabric and alternating the in and out, filling in the opposites (for every in, you will make an out stitch). (Figure 4.5)
4. Finish with a couple of backstitches. Trim the thread.

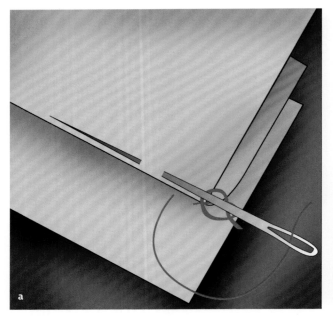

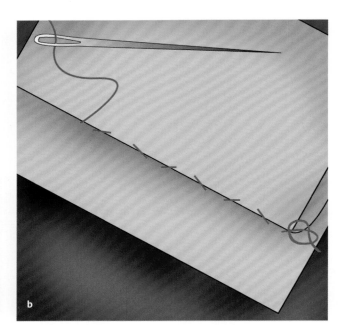

Figure 4.6a and b Slip basting.

SLIP BASTING

Slip basting is used for precise matching of plaids and prints, curved sections, securing draped pieces in place on a dress form, as well as securing fit adjustments during fittings. Stitched on the right side and worked from right to left.

1. Fold one piece, and overlap another piece. (Fold the seam allowances along the seam line, pattern, or fitting changes.)
2. Secure your thread at one end.
3. Make a small stitch pickup along the bottom piece close to the fold line of the overlapping piece, and pull the needle and thread out tightening the stitch.
4. Make another stitch of the same length through the top piece of fabric.
5. Continue steps 3 and 4. Finish with a couple of backstitches. (Figure 4.6a and b)

PLAIN-STITCH BASTING

Plain-stitch basting is commonly used to hold facing flat to the garment after construction. Work from right to left. If you are left-handed, follow the same directions with opposite sides. (Figure 4.7)

1. Sew the facing to the garment, right sides together, with a straight seam.
2. Press and fold the facing back (wrong sides together). You will need to understitch the facing side.
3. With the backside facing up, fold back the facing bottom edge half way, and pin it in place temporarily.
4. Secure your thread against the back of the facing.
5. Make a small ⅛-inch to ¼-inch pickup stitch along the facing fold line.
6. Make another stitch pickup similar in length through the top garment fabric.
7. If your garment has an interfacing or underlining, attach your stitches to that layer. If not, color match the thread, and pick up only one to two woven threads on the garment fabric side. Make long in-between basting stitches.
8. Continue with steps 5 and 6, catching only one layer at a time.

DIAGONAL BASTING

Diagonal basting is used to hold fabric layers together during garment construction. It is often used in suit tailoring and couture garments to hold down interfacing.

1. Secure the thread, and insert the needle horizontally from right to left, holding the fabric with your

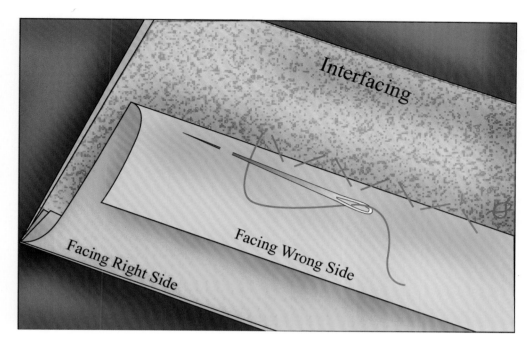

Figure 4.7 Plain-stitch basting.

left hand. (If you are left-handed, flip the opposite direction.)

2. Pull the thread until it is tight and flat along the fabric.

3. Then start another stitch right to left about ½ inch above or below the previous stitch, making diagonal stitches outside and a column of horizontal stitches on the underside formed by the needle going through the fabric right to left. (Figure 4.8)

Permanent Stitches

Permanent stitches are used for garment construction, hems, edges, tucks, and pleats and are meant to stay, unlike the temporary stitches, which are usually taken out.

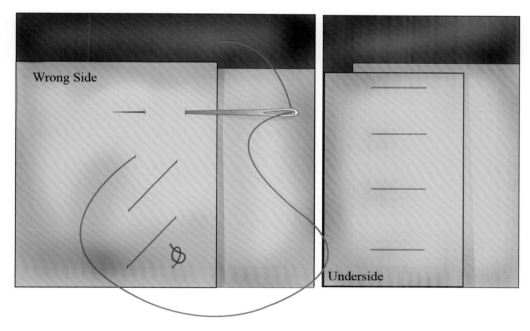

Figure 4.8 Diagonal basting.

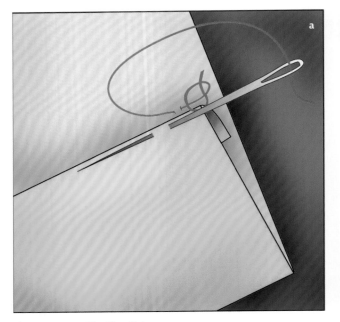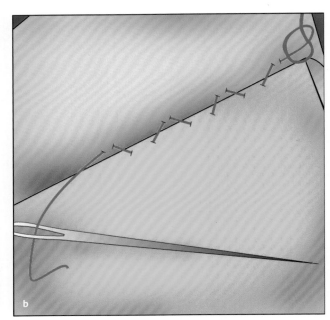

Figure 4.9a and b Slip stitch.

SLIP STITCH

A slip stitch is very similar to slip basting and is used for hemming and basting. It is commonly used to join two pieces together from the right side of the fabric. Secure the thread with a knot.

1. Start by catching a couple of threads on each side—a couple on the folded side and a couple on the garment.
2. Keep alternating stitches up and down, catching only a couple of threads each time. (Figure 4.9a and b)

SELF-BOUND EDGE

A self-bound edge is used to neatly finish the inside seam allowance without serging inside a sheer garment or a double-sided fabric.

1. Make a straight seam, right sides together.
2. Trim one seam allowance to ⅛ inch.
3. Turn in the edge of the wider (nontrimmed) seam allowance, and fold it over the trimmed edge.
4. Stitch a slip stitch seam above the straight seam stitching in order to secure the fold down. (Figure 4.10)

BACKSTITCH

Backstitch, which is the strongest permanent hand stitch, has been used to make clothing for centuries, long before the invention of the sewing machine. There are two kinds of backstitches: full backstitch and half backstitch. The full backstitch looks like a sewing machine straight stitch.

1. Secure the thread, make one basting stitch through the underside and bringing the thread back out to the face side.

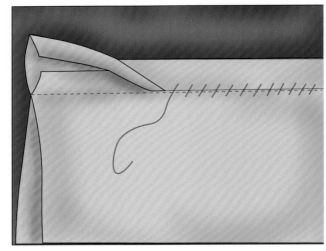

Figure 4.10 Self-bound edge.

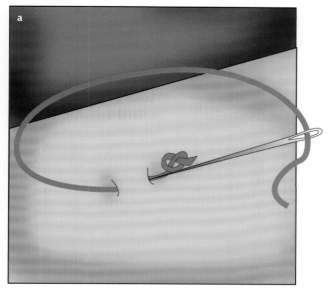

Figure 4.11a and b Backstitch.

2. After the thread is pulled out, take the needle back through the beginning of the last stitch where you secured your thread.
3. While the needle is still under the fabric, count two stitches of space, and bring the needle point back up to the right side of the fabric.
4. Take one stitch back and then two stitches forward under the fabric once more.
5. Continue the same sequence. (Figure 4.11a and b)
6. For a half backstitch, follow steps 1–4; however, for every time there is a stitch backward, instead of making a backstitch all the way to the last stitch, take a backstitch half the distance to the last stitch, leaving a small unstitched space in between the stitches.

CATCH STITCH

A **catch stitch** is used for both hems and catching garment pieces. This stitch also allows for the stretch in knit fabrics and bias-cut fabrics. Work from left to right.

1. Secure the thread on the left side, pick up a couple of threads, and close to the edge, with the needle going right to left.
2. Cross over diagonally to the front section, picking up a couple of threads. (Figure 4.12a and b)
3. Repeat steps 2 and 3 until the end of the seam.

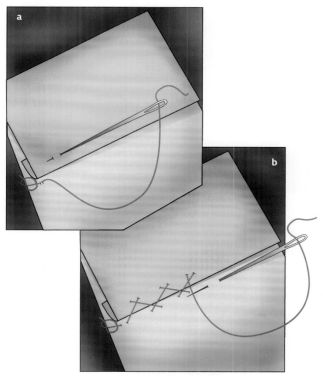

Figure 4.12a and b Catch stitch.

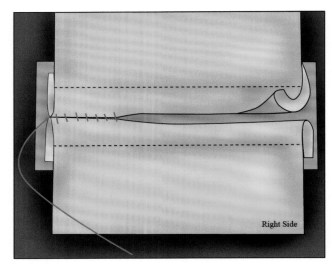

Figure 4.13 Slot seam.

SLOT SEAM

A slot seam is a decorative, permanent tucked seam that adds embellishment. Use ribbon, lace, brightly colored fabric, or silk organza for the backing.

1. Baste a plain seam, and press it open.
2. Cut a strip of bias fabric or ribbon an inch longer than the seam and ¼-inch wider than the sum of both seam allowances. Center it under the seam allowances, and pin.
3. Topstitch anywhere from ⅛ inch to ½ inch on both sides of the center seam. The stitch is stronger closer to the center. However, the wider spaces show more ribbon.
4. Trim off the excess ribbon. (Figure 4.13)

STAB STITCH

A stab stitch is used when sewing pockets, buttonholes, zippers, and shoulder pads. You make this from the right side of the fabric. It is similar to a basting stitch except it is used as a permanent and decorative stitch.

1. Secure your thread underside all the layers.
2. Make in and out stitches, stabbing all the layers.
3. Do not pull too tight, as that will leave marks on the right side of the fabric. (Figure 4.14a and b)

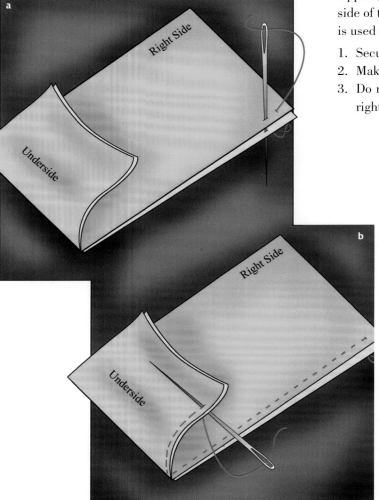

Figure 4.14a and b Stab stitch.

BLANKET STITCH

A blanket stitch is used to finish an edge, cover hooks, eyes, or thread chains, as well as buttonholes when stitches are small.

1. Secure the thread, and insert the needle into the fabric about ¼-inch from the edge.
2. Loop the thread under the needle's point; pull the needle through to the other side. Now loop the thread before you insert the needle, but not too tight or it will roll the fabric edge. (Figure 4.15a and b)
3. Continue until you reach the end of the seam.

OVERCASTING STITCH

An overcasting stitch is used for finishing a raw edge of the fabric. It is similar to a serge seam done by hand. The seam is sewn one direction to the end of the seam and then coming back in the opposite direction, forming small X shapes at the edge of the fabric.

1. Secure the thread, insert the needle through the fabric ⅛ inch from the edge, and pull it out.
2. Bring the needle around to the back, keeping the thread taut, and insert the needle into the fabric again about ⅛ inch from the previous stitch.
3. Repeat.
4. If you need to make a stronger stitch, sew in the opposite direction, crossing the previous stitches and inserting the needle in the same holes as the previous stitches. (Figure 4.16a and b)

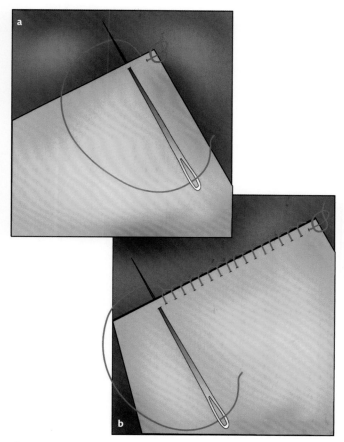

Figure 4.15a and b Blanket stitch.

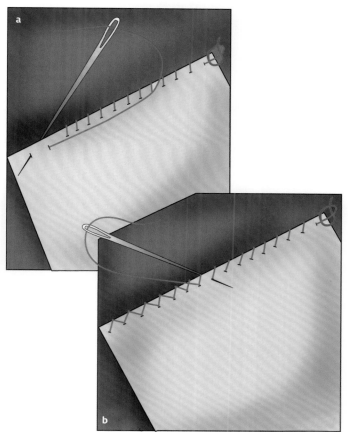

Figure 4.16a and b Overcasting stitch.

BASEBALL STITCH

A baseball stitch is used on facings and interfacings. It joins two parallel straight or curved edges without seam allowance.

1. Secure the thread. Place the needle and thread in between the fabric edges.
2. Insert the needle from the underside into one of the pieces of fabric ⅛ to ¼ inch from the edge.
3. Do the same on the other side, passing the needle under the other piece of fabric and inserting the needle from the underside. (Figure 4.17a and b)
4. Repeat steps 2 and 3 until you get to the end of the seam.

WHIPSTITCH

A whipstitch is used for seaming and hemming, not for finishing a raw edge. This seam can be sewn either with right sides together or with wrong sides together.

1. Stab the needle through the layers of fabric, and leave a little tail hanging so that the next stitches will secure it.
2. Bring the needle around to the back, and insert it into the layers of fabric again about ⅛ inch to the side of the previous stitch.
3. Repeat step 2. (Figure 4.18a and b)
4. To finish, make a couple of whipstitches in the same spot.

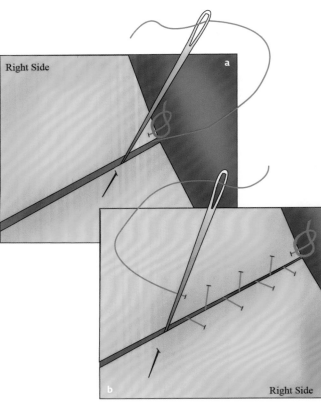

Figure 4.17a and b Baseball stitch.

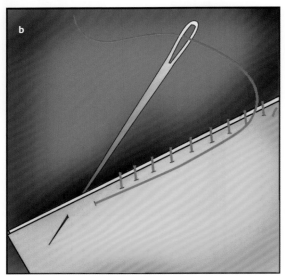

Figure 4.18a and b Whipstitch.

Ornamental Stitches

Ornamental stitches are used to sew garments together, in embroidery, or to finish hems and topstitch in a decorative way. These stitches use sewing stitches and variations to make beautiful decorative embroidery and can be used to edge finish or decorate a hem.

ARROW STITCH

An arrow stitch is used as a decorative topstitch in couture clothing, to create design elements while tacking garment pieces, and for embroidery. The arrow stitch consists of diagonal stitches sewn at right angles to one another. It is also used for ribbon embroidery with a ribbon instead of thread.

1. Secure your thread and start at one end about ¼ inch from the edge, bringing your needle to the right side of the fabric.
2. Make diagonal stitches running in the same direction.
3. Start from the opposite end and make diagonal stitches going the opposite direction forming angles. (Figure 4.19a and b)

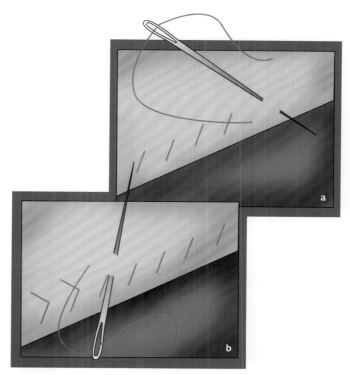

Figure 4.19a and b Arrow stitch.

THREADED ARROW STITCH

This stitch is more decorative than the regular arrow stitch but is usually stitched horizontally, forming a zigzag line. Thread it to create a decorative look.

1. Secure your thread and start at one end about ¼ inch from the edge, bringing your needle to the right side of the fabric.
2. Start by making arrow stitches along a horizontal line to look like a zigzag.
3. Start another thread in a contrasting color. Secure it, and bring it up to the right side of the fabric on either side of the stitch.
4. Begin threading by taking the needle and thread under both threads of the peak, then around the peak, and back under the peak to continue threading the next peak. Make sure you are only threading the seam, not catching the fabric. (Figure 4.20a and b).

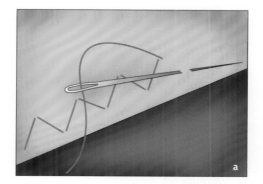

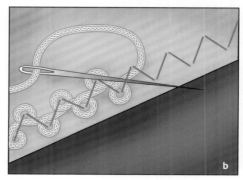

Figure 4.20a and b Threaded arrow stitch.

BACKSTITCH

A backstitch, as mentioned earlier in this chapter, is used to make permanent hand stitches. However, this stitch can also be decorative if sewn in a pattern (Figure 4.21a, b, and c). You can use it to finish decorative edges and to make permanent embroidered patterns on your garments. This stitch is good for following intricate curves. You can draw the pattern or design with a marking tool first to make it easier to follow. (See backstitch steps in Permanent Stitches.)

THREADED BACKSTITCH

Add more decoration by threading the backstitch.

1. Start by working a plain backstitch.
2. Using a different color thread, trim, or ribbon, secure it and bring it up to the right side of the fabric on either side.
3. Begin threading the thread by taking your needle tip upward under the first stitch and then downward under the second stitch (up, down, up, down).
4. Make sure not to catch the fabric; thread only. (Figure 4.22a and b)
5. Secure your thread/ribbon on the backside. Trim.

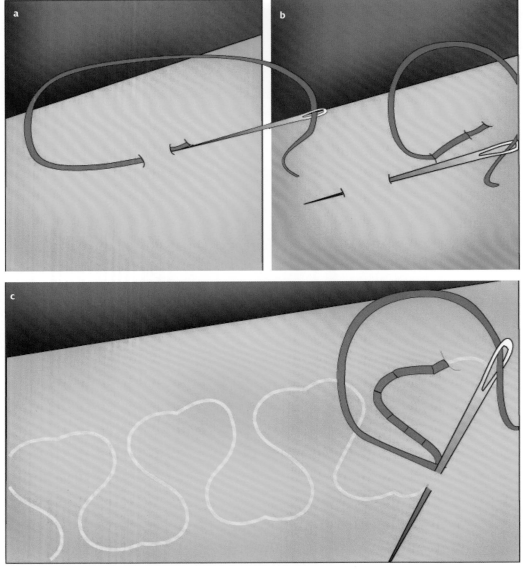

Figure 4.21a, b, and c Ornamental backstitch.

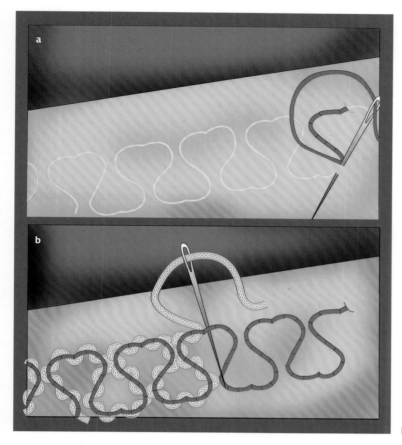

Figure 4.22a and b Threaded backstitch.

WHIPPED BACKSTITCH

Add more decoration by threading the backstitch.

1. Start by working a plain backstitch.
2. Using a different color thread, trim, or ribbon, secure it and bring it up to the right side of the fabric on either side.
3. Begin weaving the thread under the first backstitch with your needle tip facing upward, wrapping around to make the next wrap.
4. Make sure not to catch the fabric; thread only. (Figure 4.23a and b)
5. Continue wrapping stitches. Secure your thread/ribbon on the backside. Trim.

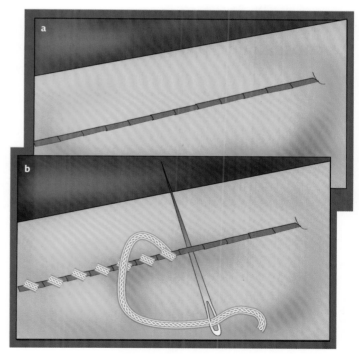

Figure 4.23a and b Whipped backstitch.

DECORATIVE BUTTONHOLE STITCHES

A buttonhole stitch is sometimes called a blanked stitch. When this stitch was first introduced, it was only used for buttonholes; only later was it used for stitching embroidery.

CLOSED BUTTONHOLE STITCH

Use a closed buttonhole stitch to decorate and fill in rows to create a netlike effect. Sew from left to right. Mark two guidelines for this seam: one line for the top of the stitch and another for the bottom of the stitch.

1. Secure the thread; bring your needle out along the bottom line at mark #1.
2. Holding the needle diagonally pointing downward and left, insert the needle through mark #2 and back out at mark #3. Make sure the thread wraps under the needle point.
3. Hold the thread with your thumb along the bottom guideline.
4. Holding the needle diagonally once more facing the opposite direction and pointing downward right, insert the needle through mark #2 and back out at mark #4. Make sure the thread wraps under the needle point at mark #4. Pull the needle through.
5. The stitch will begin looking triangular. (Figure 4.24a and b) Repeat steps 3–5.

CROSSED BUTTONHOLE STITCH

This is another variation of the buttonhole stitch used for edging, stitching, decorative patterns, and embroidery. To begin, mark parallel lines.

1. Secure the thread; bring your needle out along the bottom line at mark #1.
2. Holding the needle diagonally pointing downward and left, insert the needle through mark #2 and back out at mark #3. Make sure the thread wraps under the needle point.
3. Holding the needle diagonally facing the opposite direction and pointing downward right, insert the needle through mark #2 (⅛ inch from the top point of the last stitch) and back out at mark #4. Make sure the thread wraps under the needle point at mark #4.
4. Repeat steps 3–5. (Figure 4.25a and b)

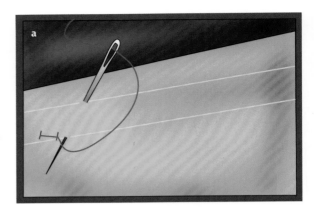

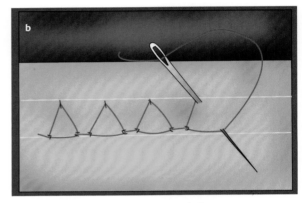

Figure 4.24a and b Closed buttonhole stitch.

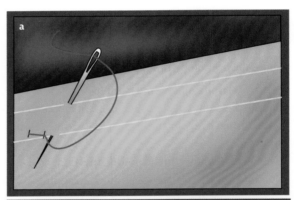

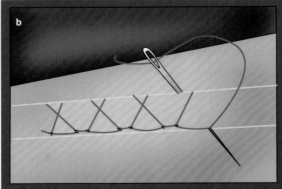

Figure 4.25a and b Crossed buttonhole stitch.

BUTTONHOLE WHEEL STITCH

A buttonhole wheel stitch is worked in a circular pattern. It can be used to create motifs of small floral sprays. Mark a circle on the fabric and the center.

1. Secure the thread.
2. Bring the needle out at mark #1.
3. With your needle facing toward the outer guideline, insert your needle into the center at mark #2 and back out at mark #3 along the outer guideline once more slightly over from mark #1.
4. Make sure the loop of thread from the previous stitch is behind the needle; once it is, pull the needle and tighten the thread, but not too tight, as that will flip up the stitches.
5. Repeat the stitch by inserting the needle through the center once more at mark #2 and back out at mark #4 with the loop under the needle point. You will start to form a wheel. Repeat.
6. When you reach the starting point, secure the thread behind the fabric. (Figure 4.26a and b)

BUTTONHOLE ROSETTE OF THORNS STITCH

This stitch is worked in a half-circle pattern and used as decoration, topstitching, or sewing around appliqués. Work it in a straight line or curved. Work from left to right, and mark the guidelines.

1. Secure the thread and bring the needle to the right side of the fabric in the center of the half circle at mark #1.
2. Holding the needle diagonally, insert the needle through mark #2 along the top guideline and back into the center at mark #1. Make sure the thread wraps under the needle point.
3. Holding the needle diagonally, insert the needle through mark #3 (⅛ inch from the top point of the last stitch) and back out at the center at mark #1. Make sure the thread wraps under the needle point.
4. Repeat steps 3 and 4 to make a half circle.
5. Start a new half circle. Insert the needle into the center of that new half circle and repeat steps 2 and 3. (Figure 4.27a and b)

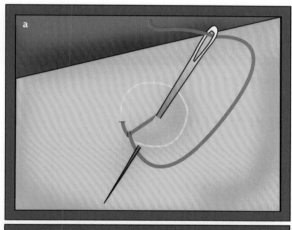

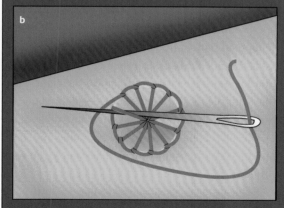

Figure 4.26a and b Buttonhole wheel stitch.

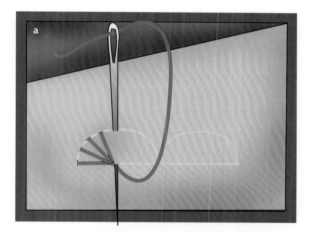

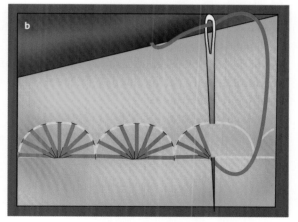

Figure 4.27a and b Buttonhole rosette of thorns stitch.

Chain Stitches

CHAIN STITCH

A chain stitch is one of the oldest decorative stitches and is used as a base for many other stitches. It is believed to have originated in Persia or India and is used in embroidery or to draw patterns on clothing and as a filling stitch.

1. Secure the thread behind the fabric, and insert the needle up to the right side at mark #1.
2. Hold the thread with your left thumb, and insert the needle back into the same mark #1 with the needle point facing left and back out at mark #2. Make sure to check that the loop of thread held by the thumb is under the needle tip before the needle is pulled out.
3. Tighten the stitch. The loop gets caught and held by the thread at mark #2.
4. The next chain loop follows the same steps 2 and 3. (Figure 4.28a and b)
5. Continue the chain stitches.

Hint: Work the chain stitches in rows to fill space.

DETACHED CHAIN STITCH (LAZY DAISY)

This stitch is used as a decoration for couture garments and worked in the shape of a circle forming a daisy flower. Bead the middle. Work this stitch in a half circle or narrow down to three chains.

1. Mark a circle guideline and a center point.
2. Secure the thread, and insert the needle up into the fabric at mark #1 (center).
3. Hold the thread with your left thumb. Then insert the needle back into mark #1 with the needle point facing toward the outer guideline.
4. Bring the needle back out at mark #2 along the outer guideline. Make sure that the loop of thread held by the thumb is under the needle tip.
5. Secure the loop by fastening another stitch down into the fabric directly outside the loop along the guideline. (Figure 4.29a and b)
6. Bring the needle back out in the center point.
7. Repeat steps 3–6, making chain stitches all around the circle.

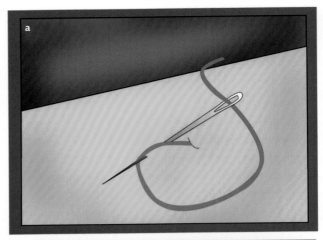

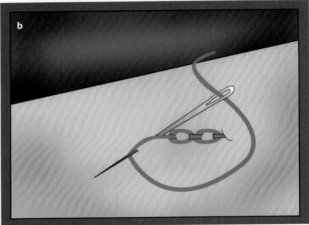

Figure 4.28a and b Chain stitch.

FEATHERED CHAIN STITCH

This chain stitch forms a zigzag type of line used to make decorative topstitches and in embroidery with or without beads. Mark two parallel lines on the fabric to use as guidelines. Worked from left to right.

1. Secure your thread, and insert your needle up at mark #1.
2. Hold the thread with your left thumb halfway between the top and bottom lines.
3. Insert the needle back into mark #1 with the needle point facing diagonally down and to the right, pulling it out with the loop under the needle point at mark #2.
4. Work one straight stitch along the same diagonal line down into the fabric at mark #3 along the bottom guideline, and bring the needle back out again next to it at mark #4.

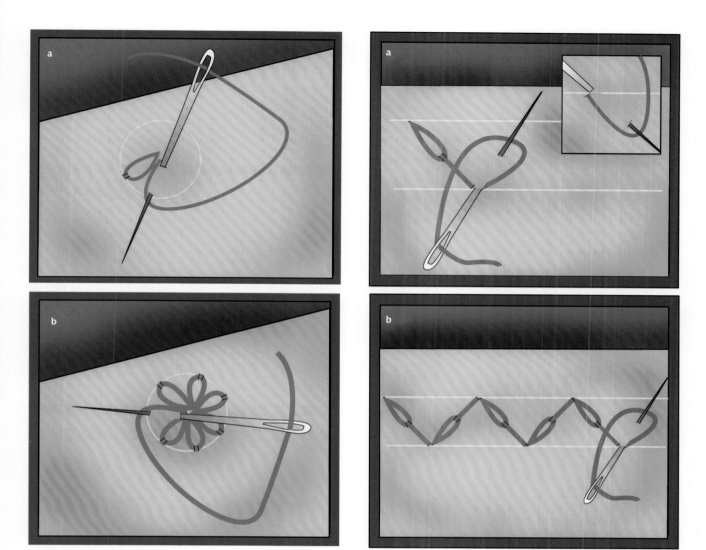

Figure 4.29a and b Detached chain stitch.

Figure 4.30a and b Feathered chain stitch.

5. Hold the thread with your left thumb halfway between the top and bottom lines.
6. Insert the needle back into mark #4 with the needle point facing diagonally upward and to the right, pulling it out with the loop under the needle point at mark #5.

7. Next, work a straight stitch along the same diagonal line down into the fabric at mark #6 along the top guideline, and bring the needle back out again directly next to it at mark #7. (Figure 4.30a and b)
8. Repeat steps 2–7 going up and down making a zigzag.

OPEN CHAIN STITCH

An open chain stitch resembles large open chain circles used for embroidery or as topstitch during garment construction. Work this stitch from top to bottom.

1. Mark vertical parallel guidelines.
2. Secure the thread, and insert the needle upward to the face side along the left guideline at mark #1. Hold the thread with your left thumb.
3. Then insert the needle along the right guideline at mark #2 without letting go of the thread loop with your left thumb.
4. With the needle point facing left, bring it behind the fabric toward the left guideline at mark #3. With the loop under the needle point, pull the needle out and tighten.
5. Hold the thread with your left thumb to form a loop, and insert the needle along the right guideline at mark #4 without letting go of the thread loop.
6. With the needle point facing left, bring it behind the fabric toward the left guideline at mark #5 with the loop under the needle point. Pull the needle out, and tighten your stitch. (Figure 4.31a and b)
7. Repeat steps 3–6.

CRETAN STITCH

This stitch is centuries old and looks like a feather used to decorate clothing on the island of Crete, hence its name. It originated in Persia and is sometimes called the Persian stitch; it is used to stitch leaves or feathers. Mark a guideline shape on the fabric to help, and add a center line.

1. Secure the thread. Make a straight stitch down along your guideline. Then pull the needle out a bit past the middle of the leaf while letting the thread loop under the needle point.
2. Stitch a straight stitch upward along the top guideline. Then pull the needle back out a bit past the middle,

pointing downward. Loop the thread under the needle point, and pull the needle out. (Figure 4.32a and b)

3. Repeat these steps until you finish the desired pattern.

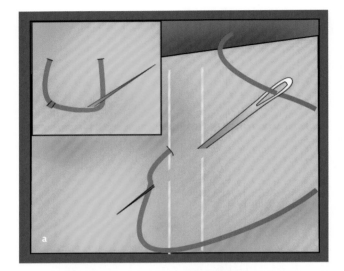

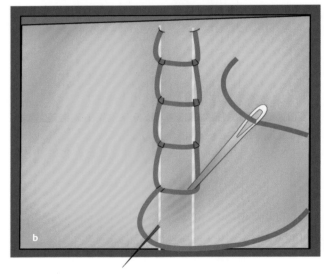

Figure 4.31a and b Open chain stitch.

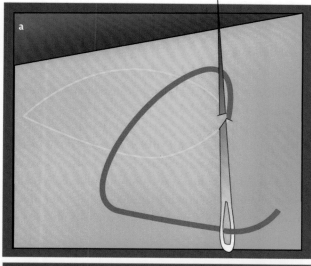

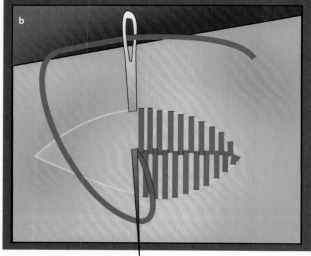

Figure 4.32a and b Cretan stitch.

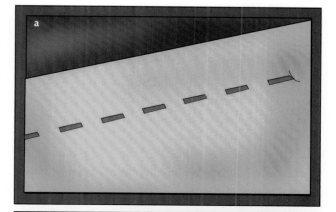

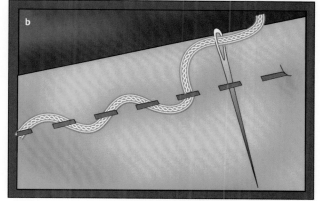

Figure 4.33a and b Threaded running stitch.

THREADED RUNNING STITCH

This attractive stitch line, a variation of a running stitch (basting), can draw motifs and follows curves well.

1. Secure the thread, and bring the needle up.
2. Begin stitching in-and-out running stitches to create a line. Secure the thread.
3. Use a different thread/ribbon, and lace it through the running stitches in an up-and-down motion, stitching only through the stitches without catching the fabric. (Figure 4.33a and b)

Hint: Make a double-threaded running stitch by using two rows of running stitches ¼ inch apart and threading another ribbon through both rows. (Figure 4.34a and b)

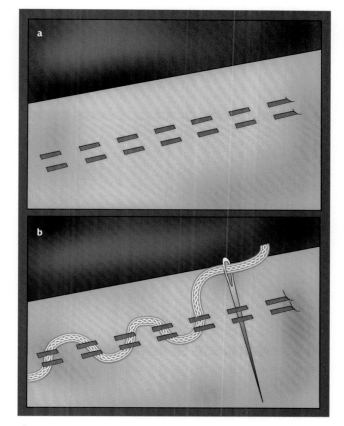

Figure 4.34a and b Double-threaded running stitch.

INTERLACED RUNNING STITCH

This attractive stitch line, a variation of a running stitch (basting), can draw motifs, follows curves well, and can be laced in a different ways.

1. Secure the thread, and bring the needle up.
2. Begin stitching in-and-out running stitches to create a line. Secure the thread.
3. Use a different thread/ribbon, and lace it through the running stitches in an up-and-down motion, stitching only through the stitches without catching the fabric. This forms the first half of the loops.
4. At the end of the line, turn and lace the same way back, alternating stitches so that they catch the stitches that were not laced. (Figure 4.35a and b)

Hint: Make a double-interlaced running stitch by using two rows of running stitches ¼ inch apart and interlacing another ribbon through both rows. (Figure 4.36a and b)

LOOPED DOUBLE RUNNING STITCH

The looped double running stitch creates an attractive line of thin loops.

1. Secure the thread, and bring the needle up.
2. Begin stitching in-and-out running stitches to create a line. Secure the thread.
3. Make another running stitch ¼ inch below.
4. Using a different thread/ribbon, insert the needle upward into the bottom stitch, overlap the topstitch, and then insert the needle downward through both of the stitches. The stitch looks like a loop, and due to the overlap of the topstitch, it stays a loop and does not roll. (Figure 4.37a and b)

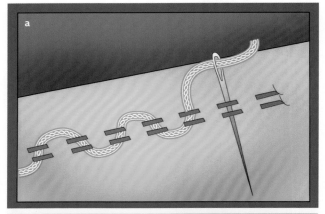

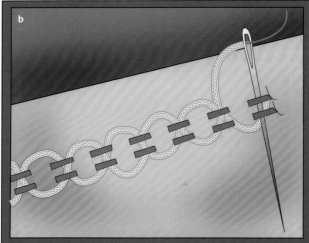

Figure 4.36a and b Double interlaced running stitch.

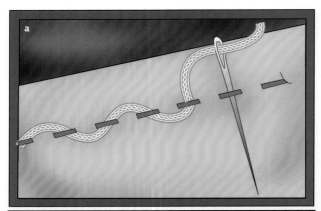

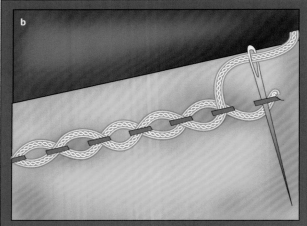

Figure 4.35a and b Interlaced running stitch.

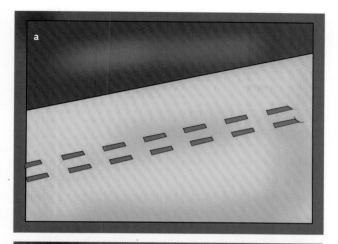

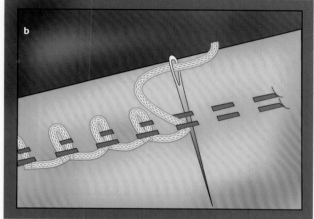

Figure 4.37a and b Looped double running stitch.

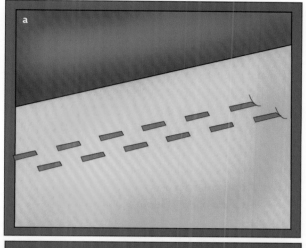

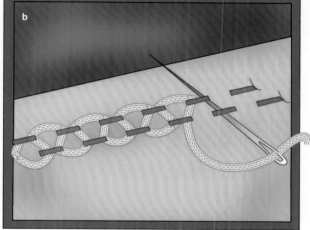

Figure 4.38a and b Stepped threaded running stitch.

STEPPED THREADED RUNNING STITCH

The stepped threaded running stitch, another variation of the running stitch, has a braid-like appearance.

1. Secure the thread, and bring the needle up.
2. Begin stitching in-and-out running stitches to create a line. Secure the thread.

3. Make another running stitch ¼ inch below; however, make sure you alternate the stitches. (Figure 4.38a and b)
4. Use a different thread or ribbon to lace in and out of the running stitches without catching the fabric. You will be lacing diagonally upward with your needle, over to the next stitch, then downward, and over again.

Machine Seams

FLAT SEAM

A flat seam is an easy way of joining two pieces of fabric together, and is also known as the regular straight stitch. This stitch can be used anywhere on the garment with almost any fabric and serves as a foundation for other seams.

1. Place two pieces of fabric together face-to-face, and make a straight seam.
2. Press the seam open. (Figure 4.39a and b)

FRENCH SEAM

A **French seam** is a commonly used seam for joining sheer and silky fabrics. It does not show raw edges. In France, it is called an English seam, and in English-speaking countries, a French seam.

1. With the wrong sides together, make a flat single seam near the edge. Press the seam to flatten the stitch.

2. Trim the seam allowances close to the seam.
3. Refold the fabric with right sides together. Press.
4. Stitch another seam with a seam allowance that hides the trimmed seam allowance on the inside. Press. (Figure 4.40a–d)

MOCK FRENCH SEAM

A **Mock French seam** is used the same way as the French seam when you are unsure of the fit of the garment or need more assurance to get a perfect French seam. Since it is very difficult sometimes to get a nice French seam on a curved edge, you can use this method.

1. Fit the garment with the seams basted in the usual way, and then stitch a plain seam. Press.
2. Fold both seam allowances to the inside, press, and stitch together close to the folds. (Figure 4.41a and b)

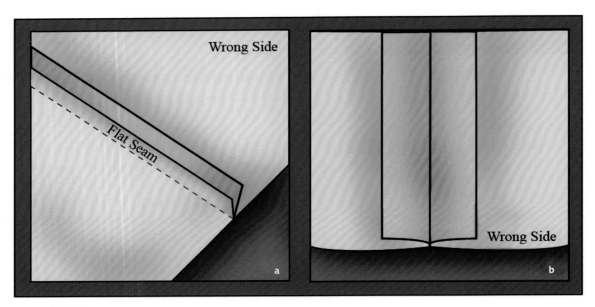

Figure 4.39a and b Flat seam.

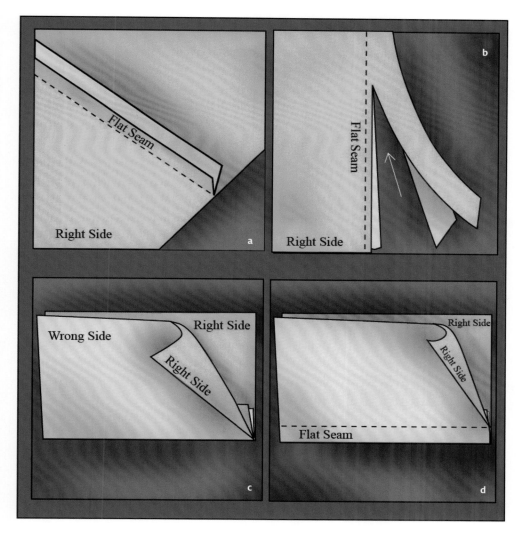

Figure 4.40a-d French seam.

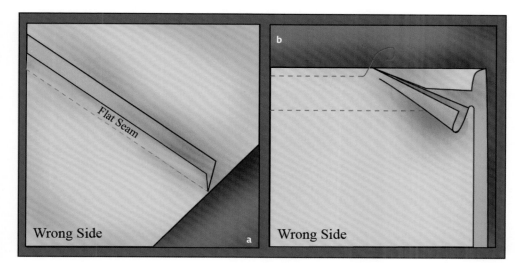

Figure 4.41a and b Mock French seam.

TOPSTITCHED SEAM

A topstitched seam is used in sportswear and on leather, suede, faux leather, and faux suede.

Method #1

1. Make a flat seam, and press the seam open flat.
2. Topstitch on both sides of the seam, ⅛ inch to ¼ inch away from the seam, stitching through all of the layers. (Figure 4.42a)

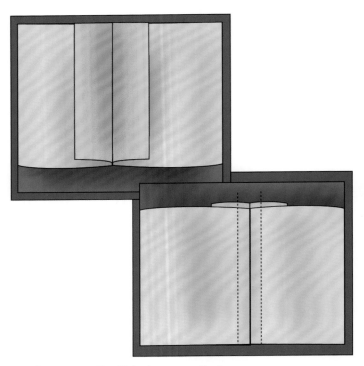

Figure 4.42a Topstitched seam—method 1.

Method #2

1. First, stitch a plain seam.
2. Press the seam open, and then press the seam to the side on which you will topstitch.
3. Along the side all the layers were pressed toward, topstitch through all of the layers ⅛ inch to ¼ inch away from original seam. (Figure 4.42b)

Hint: Make a method #2 double-stitched seam by adding another topstitched seam ⅛ inch to ¼ inch from the first edge seam. You can also use a double needle for your machine and make the seam only once properly parallel. (Figure 4.43a and b) Alternatively, use a Zigzag (double zigzag seam) stitch for a decorative effect and with bias or stretchy fabrics.

FLAT-FELL SEAM

A flat-felled seam is used to finish raw edges in men's dress shirts and in jeans. It offers a clean seam finish on both sides of the garment. Sometimes it serves as a decorative seam.

1. With the right sides of the fabric together, make a flat single seam near the edge. Press.
2. Trim one side of the seam allowance close to the seam.
3. Fold over the longer side of seam allowance, press, and topstitch.
4. You can stitch one side or both sides. (Figure 4.44a, b, and c)

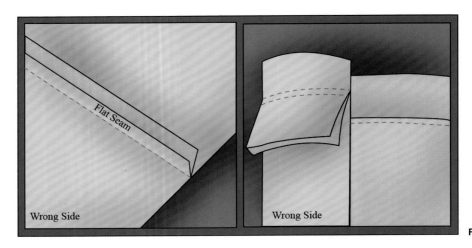

Figure 4.42b Topstitched seam—method 2.

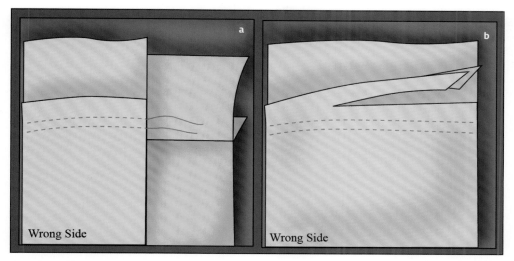

Figure 4.43a and b Double-stitched seam.

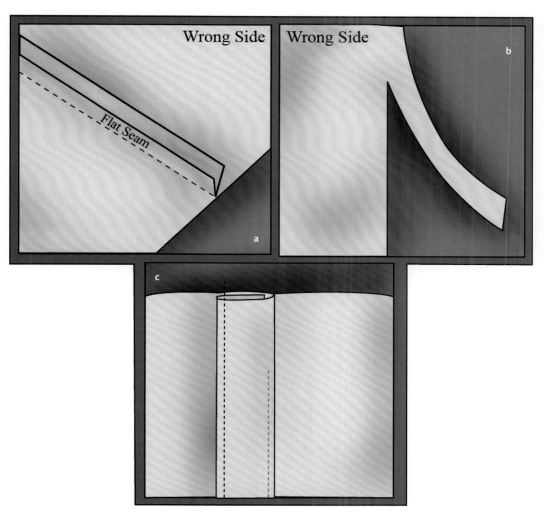

Figure 4.44a, b, and c Flat-fell seam.

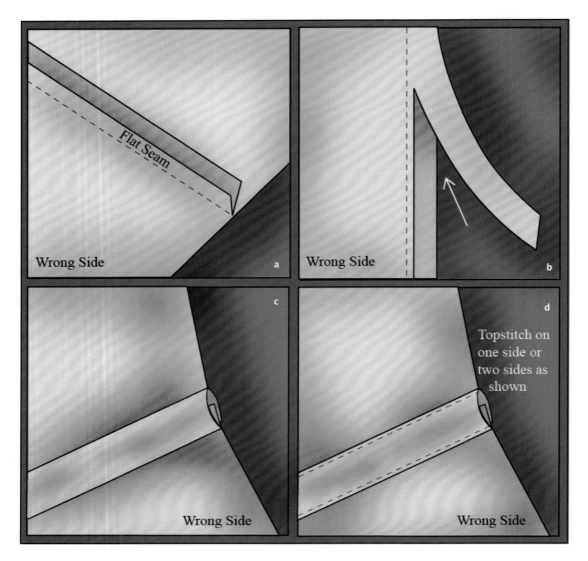

Figure 4.45a–d Hairline seam.

Hint: Make this stitch narrower for a **hairline seam**. It is mostly used to finish seams on sheer and lightweight fabrics instead of using binding or a serger. (Figure 4.45a–d)

RIBBON SEAM

This seam is used inside a garment on a seam or outside a garment as a decorative design element. Use it to cover the seam with a ribbon topstitched over it to get a finished look on the inside and a beautifully decorated look on the outside. (Figure 4.46a and b)

1. Make a flat seam, and press it open.
2. Place the ribbon evenly over the pressed open seam, and topstitch through all the layers. Press again.

LAPPED SEAM

A lapped seam is used for yokes and applied pieces such as gussets, appliqués, pockets, exposed zippers, and more.

1. Fold the seam allowance under on one piece of fabric, right side up. Press the crease.

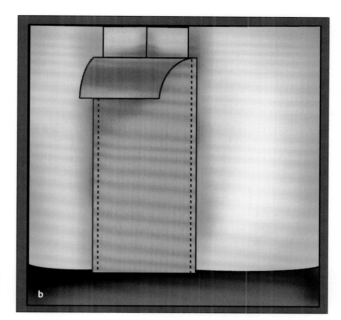

Figure 4.46a and b Ribbon seam.

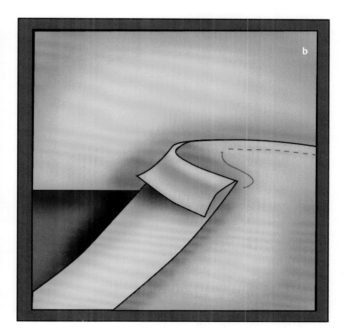

Figure 4.47a and b Lapped seam.

2. Lap it over the seam allowance of another piece of fabric, also right side up.

3. Pin/baste the lapped section in place so that the folded edge meets the seam line of the corresponding section.

4. Topstitch through all of the layers close to the folded edge. Press. (Figure 4.47a and b)

Garment Facings and Construction

Facings are used to finish edges on necklines, armholes, hems, pockets, zipper flaps, collars, cuffs, and so on. Facings take care of strengthening the edge so that they do not stretch when the garment is worn or washed.

FACTS ABOUT FACINGS

- Facings are cut using the same fabric as the outer shell of the garment and traced from the same pattern and the same shape at the edges.
- To make a facing, place the garment pattern on the table. Trace the pattern on a separate piece of paper. Measure 1.5–2 inches plus seam allowance from the edge of either the neckline or the armhole to make a facing pattern.
- Cut the facing along the same grainline as the garment to prevent stretching in the wrong direction and distortion of the garment.
- When facings are sewn, interfacing is required that is cut the same shape as the facing and sandwiched in between the facing and the garment. Use iron-on (fusible) interfacing as an alternative.
- Facings can be either neckline alone or extended along the neckline and the center front opening. (Figure 4.48)

FACING CONSTRUCTION

1. Join the facing pieces together at the seam lines by attaching the seam allowances. Press all seams open.
2. Make sure to leave the zipper placket open so that you can attach the facing to the zipper on the garment.
3. If the facing will not be attached to a lining, finish the bottom edge of the facing by either serging or pinking it.

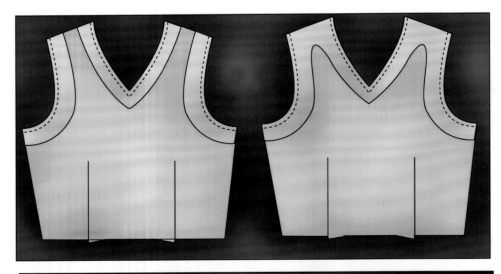

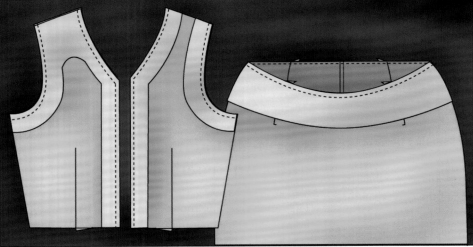

Figure 4.48 Facings.

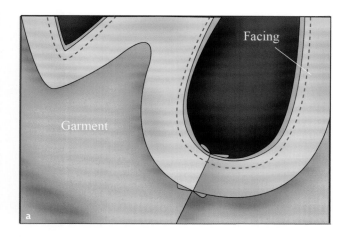

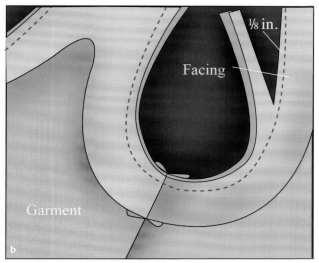

Figure 4.49a and b Facing construction.

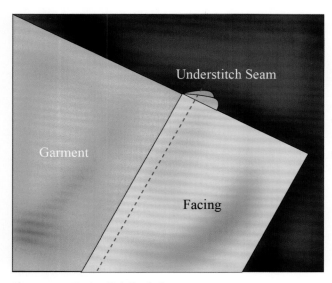

Figure 4.50 Understitch the facing.

4. If the facing edge is attached to a lining, stitch them together face-to-face, matching up the seams.
5. Make sure to attach the zipper to the outer shell layer of the garment before the facing.
6. Line up the facing edge to the sewn garment, right sides together, pin, and stitch the edge seam line with a regular machine stitch.
7. Trim off the seam allowance to ⅛ inch from the seam, and clip into it to flatten the curved edge. (Figure 4.49a and b)
8. Flip the garment right side out, and press.
9. Either topstitch around the neckline or understitch to flatten the seam allowance and help the facing stay rolled on the inside of the garment without coming out. (Figure 4.50)
10. Make a small tack by hand in between the layers, and attach the shoulder seams allowances to keep the facing in place.

Garment Lining and Construction

LINING

Lining is used to finish the inside of a garment to hide the garment's inner construction and raw seams. Lining offers better wear and easier dressing and adds luxury and quality to garments.

Lining can match the garment color or not. If it is transparent, for example, sometimes silk brocade garments are lined with silk organza, and the seams are bound with a bias tape. Brocade is decorative on the backside; therefore, the sheer lining makes the garment look and feel expensive.

It is important to match the care instructions for the lining fabric to those for the rest of the garment. Choose lining fabric that accommodates your garment. See Table 4.1.

Lining can be sewn by machine or by hand and uses a different drafted pattern than that used for the outer garment layer. The pieces of lining patterns have to fit together just like the outer garment patterns. Many times the regular garment patterns have both separate lining patterns and facings patterns.

Complete the outer shell of your garment first before working on the lining in order to be able to attach the lining to the outer shell.

Table 4.1 LINING TYPES AND USES

Types	Weight	Uses	Care
Polyester or acetate satin	Medium-weight lining	Used often in garments that need to hold shape such as corsets and evening dresses	Polyester satin is machine washable, and acetate satin needs to be dry-cleaned.
Cotton	Light-weight lining	Used often in tailored garments such as suits, skirts, pants, and coats; ravels easily	Cotton is machine washable; however, depending on the garment, dry cleaning may also be a good option.
Acetate	Light-weight lining	Used in tailored garments, dresses, skirts, and pants; has a slippery, smooth finish and can ravel easily	Acetate needs to be dry-cleaned.
Polyester/rayon/acetate	Light-weight lining	Has a slippery and smooth finish and is used for tailored garments, dresses, skirts, pants, etc.	This lining is machine washable.
Crepe polyester	Light-weight lining	Used on jackets, coats, and many different tailored garments; is stronger and more durable then other lining options.	This crepe lining is machine washable. Be careful when pressing. Use low heat.

LINING CONSTRUCTION

1. Cut lining fabric patterns. Make sure to transfer all of the lines, darts, and other markings to the lining patterns.
2. Attach the entire lining layer together.
3. If your garment has sleeves, attach them into the armholes with a double seam.
4. Press all seams open, and clip the seam allowance in the armhole to reduce tension and bulk. Leave the lining inside out. (Figure 4.51)

When sewing princess seams or rounder edges, clip seam allowances every inch or two to reduce tension. To reduce bulk for your darts, press them in the opposite direction to the direction they are pressed on the outer shell of your garment.

1. Cut and connect your **facing** pieces together at the shoulders. Press the seams open. (Figure 4.52)
2. Starting in the center back and moving down, with right sides together, baste/pin the facing layer to the

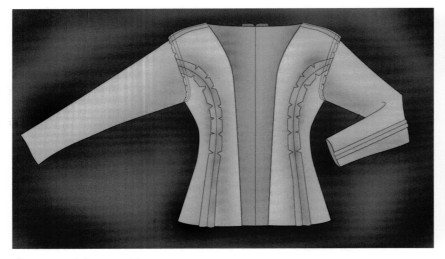

Figure 4.51 Lining assembly.

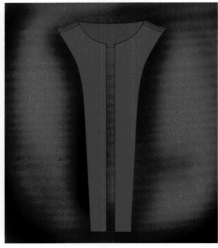

Figure 4.52 Facing assembly.

lining layer, matching up the seam allowances. Clip the curved edges to reduce tension. (Figure 4.53a)

3. Start stitching in the center back, and then work your way down toward the front bottom. Repeat on the other side.

4. If you have a zipper in the front of a jacket, apply it before connecting the lining/facing layer.

5. When both the lining and the outer shell of the garment are finished and pressed, turn the garment outer shell right side out. Keep the lining layer wrong side out.

6. Place the garment outer shell into the lining. This should line up the layers face-to-face and match up all of the seams and notches.

7. Pin/baste all the way around, starting at the center back and working your way around the neck down the center front. Then repeat on the other side.

8. Now you can stitch your seam the same way, working from the center back around the neck and down in the front. (Figure 4.53b)

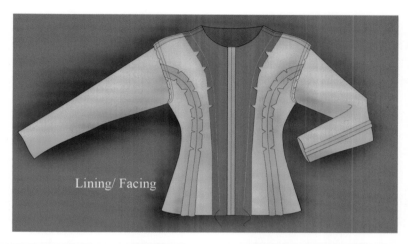

Figure 4.53a and b Lining/facing assembly.

9. If you are looking for a quick finished hem for your facing piece, you can continue to sew down and around the facing hem, stopping at the lining start, where you will clip the seam allowance close to the hemline.

10. Or continue stitching the hem all the way to the center back to finish the hem faster. However, since the only open side to flip the garment right side out is now closed, you will have to rip open one side seam in the lining layer in order to flip the garment. When you are done, you can hand stitch the opening closed with a slipstitch.

Underlining and Construction

Underlining is used for support and reinforcement of delicate, stretch, sheer, lace, and loosely woven fabrics. (Figure 4.54)

Underlining adds stability and strength to lightweight fabrics, reduces wrinkling, reduces transparency in sheer or light-colored fabrics, and provides a great layer of fabric to connect the hems.

UNDERLINING FACTS

- Underlining is cut from the same pattern pieces as the face fabric and stays stitched to the wrong side of the outer shell fabric before the garment is constructed. This keeps the two fabric layers together while the garment is sewn, at which point it will be treated as one layer.
- When selecting an underlining, make sure you choose a fabric that has fiber contents similar to your outer shell fabric as well as the same care instructions.
- For knits, choose a knit underlining fabric.
- For soft drape garments, select a similar soft fabric with the same drape qualities for the underlining.

UNDERLINING CONSTRUCTION

To begin, make sure you preshrink both fabrics. Press. Any small wrinkle can cause a bubble while sewing the underlining to the face fabric.

1. To make underlining patterns, trace your outer shell garment pattern, and remove the hem seam allowance to reduce bulk at the hem. Use these patterns to cut the fabric underlining pieces. (Figure 4.55a and b)

2. Match up the underlining piece under the outer shell fabric, with both layers facing up.

3. With the underlining backside facing up, pin the layers together along the edges.

4. Starting from the center of the pattern, baste your way up, down, right, and left a couple of times to smooth out the fabric bubbles and gathers from the center of the pattern.

5. Then stitch diagonal basting stitches up and down along the side sections of the still-open darts to keep the face and underlining together. Pin.

6. After basting the patterns, treat them as one layer, and stay stitch the seams along the outer piece seam allowance through both of the layers.

7. Fold the darts lining up the dart sides, and baste darts closed through all of the layers.

Figure 4.54 Lace dress with underlining.

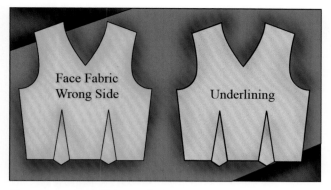

Figure 4.55a Underlining method.

Figure 4.56a Underlining method.

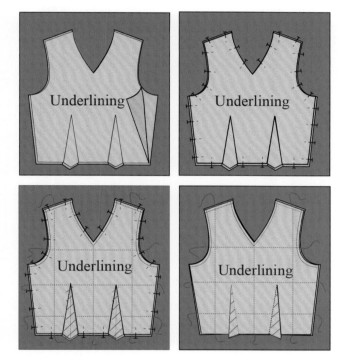

Figure 4.55b Underlining method assembly.

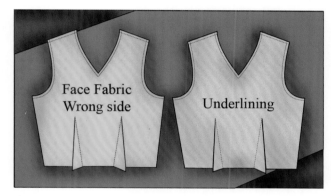

Figure 4.56b Underlining method darts.

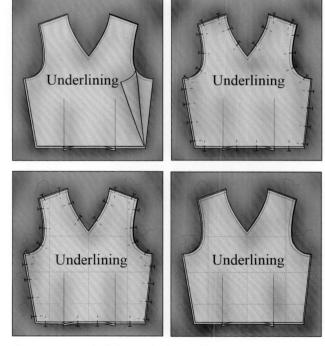

Figure 4.56c Underlining method assembly.

8. Machine stitch the darts closed along the basting stitch.
9. Since both layers are treated as one, only sew the darts once through both layers at the same time. (Figure 4.56a, b, and c)
10. The piece is ready to be attached to another pattern piece. Underline all of the pieces.

Hint: Sometimes only the front piece of a garment bodice needs underlining.

Interlining and Construction

Interlining is very similar to underlining. (Figure 4.57) The only difference is its purpose. Underlining is intended to strengthen the face fabric, but interlining's main purpose is to effectively add warmth to your garment without adding too much bulk.

Interlining is applied with the same steps as underlining. However, it can be applied to either the face fabric's wrong side or the wrong side of the lining. Both techniques will sandwich the interlining and hide it in between layers. If you are making a tightly fitted or semi-fitted garment, apply the interlining to the face fabric.

You can also quilt the interlining onto the lining layer or the outer garment layer against the wrong sides of either one of the layers.

Different fibers provide different levels of warmth when used in interlining fabric.

INTERLINING FACTS

- When making the pattern for the garment, make sure you add enough ease to allow for the thickness of the interlining; you do not want the finished garment to be too small for the wearer.
- Cut interlining using lining pattern pieces minus the hem seam allowance.
- If quilting the interlining to any of the two layers, quilt without seam allowance by lining the interlining edges up to the seams. Pin and baste to keep it from moving while you quilt.
- Make sure the interlining fibers have the same care instructions as the rest of the garment; however, interlined garments are usually dry cleaned.

Interfacing and Construction

Interfacing is a fabric added for support in between the facing and garment fabrics and is a very critical part of the garment construction. It is most commonly used to increase the life of a garment, stabilize, and prevent stretching in necklines, buttonholes, waistbands, and pocket edges. It also adds shape to collars, cuffs, waistbands, lapels, and plackets while reducing the need to press the garment too often. See Table 4.2 for interfacing variations.

Figure 4.57 Interlining.

INTERFACING FACTS

- Interfacings can be made from natural and manufactured fibers and different thicknesses and can be woven or nonwoven, sew-in or iron-on (fusible).
- Fusible interfacing has a layer of fabric glue that melts with heat and sticks itself to the fabric using heat.
- Fusible interfacing is quick and easy to use. Fusible interfacing needs to be soaked in warm water for fifteen to twenty minutes with a small amount of dishwashing liquid, rinsed, towel blotted, and left flat to air dry.
- Do not preshrink fusible interfacing in washing machines or dryers. Do not use any steam, as it will melt the glue.
- On the negative side, fusible interfacing can get too firm after the glue melts and add some discoloration to light-colored fabrics. It is also a bad choice for fabrics that cannot be pressed, such as napped fabrics and highly textured fabrics, because it will flatten them. It cannot be used with fabrics that cannot tolerate steam as well because steam is used during the fusing process.

Table 4.2 INTERFACING TYPES AND USES

Interfacing Type	Purpose	Color	Care Requirements
Batiste	Used on thin fabrics and light-weight garments	White	Sew-in; needs preshrinking before use; washable
Canvas	Used in heavy-weight garments such as jackets, coat collars, lapels, and more	Beige or white	Sew-in; needs preshrinking before use; washable.
Fusible polyester/rayon blend	Used in women's jackets, coats, and heavier dresses and shirts	White or black	Iron-on; no pre-shrinking nessesary unless the garment will be washable
Fusible polyester/nylon blend all-purpose	Used for almost all fabrics and gives garments a tailored look	White or black	Iron-on; no preshrinking necessary unless the garment will be washable
Fusible nylon tricot	Used in knit fabrics and has a great drape to it for draped garments	White or black	Iron-on; no preshrinking necessary
Fusible polyester tricot	Used with sheer fabrics and light-weight fabrics	White or black	Iron-on; no preshrinking necessary
Fusible cotton (muslin)	Used in light-weight to medium-weight fabrics; not used with synthetic fabrics	White or black	Iron-on; washable
Unbleached muslin	Used in jackets, suits, and coats; adds body without making garments too stiff	Natural	Sew-in; needs preshrinking before use; washable

- Woven interfacings should be preshrunk before use if the garment will be washable, as should the face fabric. You would not want the interfacing to shrink inside your garment and wrinkle or bubble the outer layer.
- Cut woven interfacing straight on the grain to match the garment grain.

- Sew-in interfacing can be preshrunk like regular fabric and stay stitched to the garment by hand or by machine before sewing. (Figure 4.58)
- Sew-in interfacing gives soft shaping to both woven and knit garments.

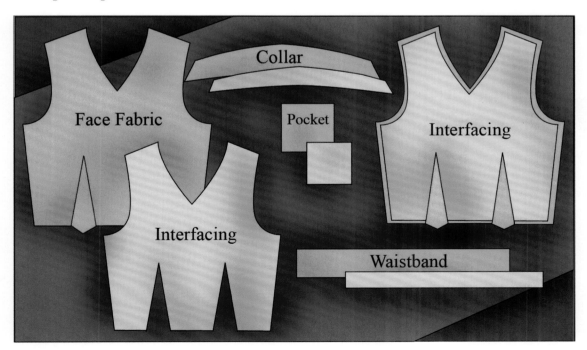

Figure 4.58 Interfacing.

- Nonwoven interfacing has no grain and can be cut in either direction.
- You can use bias interfacing, which stretches in all directions, on knits and bias-cut garments.
- Choose interfacing that will complement and reinforce your garment fabric and not overwhelm it by adding too much stiffness, air bubbles, or bulk.
- It is okay to use more than one kind of interfacing in the same garment, as different interfacings serve different purposes.

ATTACHING INTERFACING

Catch Stitch

Use a catch stitch with very thick interfacing. In order to reduce bulk, remove seam allowances and darts and catch stitch the interfacing to the garment fabric.

1. Align the interfacing patterns with the garment patterns at the seam lines, and pin in place.

2. Using matching color thread, catch stitch the edge all around, catching the raw edge of the interfacing on one end and only a couple of threads of the garment fabric right outside of the seam line in the seam allowance area. (Figure 4.59a and b)

Lapped Stitch

A lapped stitch is used for lightweight to medium-weight interfacings. The seam allowance on one side is overlapped over the pattern of another side so that they meet at the seam line. Very often the seam is a zigzag stitch. (Figure 4.60a and b)

1. Cut the interfacing pattern pieces with seam allowances.
2. Overlap the seams, and stitch a zigzag seam along the seam line.
3. Trim the seam allowance along the seam on both sides ⅛ inch from the seam.
4. Repeat steps 2–3.

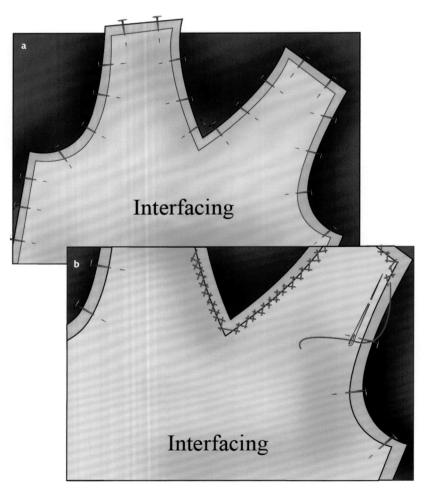

Figure 4.59a and b Catch stitch.

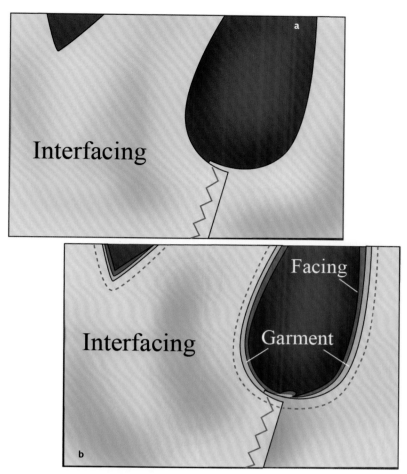

Figure 4.60a and b Lapped stitch.

5. Line up the interfacing neckline and armholes with the garment and the facing layers. Sandwich pieces in the following order before stitching: facing and garment right sides together and interfacing on the garment side back to back. Stitch all of the layers together.

6. Clip off the seam allowances close to the seam line. Turn the garment right side out. Understitch, and press.

Iron-On (Fusible)

This type of interfacing is cut to match the piece that needs interfacing, using the same pattern pieces without seam allowances.

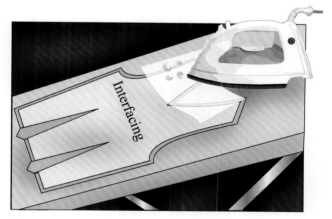

Figure 4.61 Iron-on interfacing.

1. Line up the interfacing with the seam lines of the garment edges, and steam with your iron over it. Use a pressing cloth so you can steam it well. (Figure 4.61)

2. Continue with garment construction.

A BRIEF LOOK INTO THE LIFE OF
GIANNI VERSACE

Gianni Versace was born in Reggio Calabria, Italy, on December 2, 1946. His mother, Francesca, was a dressmaker and encouraged her son to help in her workshop. Versace was very creative and interested in all kinds of arts. He studied architecture for a while before moving to Milan in 1972 to work in fashion design. Later he was hired to create ready-to-wear collections for Genny and Callaghan. He also designed an all-leather collection for Complice. Working with his brother, Santo, and his sister, Donatella, Versace created his own label, and he presented his first women's collection in March 1978. A men's collection followed in September of the same year.

Versace was known for his use of unconventional materials, brilliant colors, and vibrant prints that drew on Baroque and classical inspirations. His 1982–83 fall/winter collection featured metal mesh dresses inspired by punk styles in London. Later collections used the metal mesh again, this time in bright colors. Versace also worked on a technique to bond leather to rubber, and in the early 1990s he brought out a line of what became known as "bondage dresses," which provoked much controversy.

Haute couture Spring/Summer collection, 1994.

Versace was always interested in the theater, and over the years he collaborated with major performing arts companies to produce costumes for operas, ballets, modern dance performances, and rock concerts. This influenced his women's and men's ready-to-wear collections as well; they displayed a certain sense of theatricality that was both admired and criticized. He brought together the visual arts, fashion, and music in new ways, hiring fashion photographers such as Richard Avedon, Helmut Newton, and Bruce Weber for his advertising campaigns and commissioning the musician Prince to write music for his fashion shows. He had already received many awards and had been the subject of a number of retrospectives when he designed his first couture collection in 1989. He also branched out into accessories, fragrances, and home products and had boutiques in major cities around the world. Versace died in 1997 when he was shot in front of his home in Miami, Florida. After his death, his sister, Donatella, took over the job of designing for the company.

Gianni Versace, 1993.

Haute couture Fall/Winter collection, 1993/1994.

Chapter Review

This chapter reviewed all of the important hand sewing and machine sewing stitches and seams. It is very important to know hand sewing in garment construction because, in couture houses, many garments are carefully hand sewn to perfection. By learning the temporary and permanent stitches in this chapter, you can begin garment construction.

Learning the steps to proper underlining, interlining, and interfacing will help the garment construction and enable the best quality in the sewing process.

Finish your garment with a nice faced lining layer hiding all the unpleasant insides while offering better wear of the garment.

Projects

1. Make temporary stitch samples for your book. Write down your steps, and insert them into one of your plastic cover sheets.
2. Make permanent stitch samples for your book. Write down your steps, and insert them into one of your plastic cover sheets.
3. Make machine stitch samples for your book. Write down your steps, and insert them into one of your plastic cover sheets.
4. Make a lining/facing sample for your book; use muslin. Write down your steps, and insert them into one of your plastic cover sheets.
5. Make interfacing samples for your book. Write down your steps, and insert them into one of your plastic cover sheets.
6. Make underlining samples for your book. Write down your steps, and insert them into one of your plastic cover sheets.

Key Terms

Backstitch

Buttonhole stitch

Catch stitch

European knot

Facing

French seam

Hairline seam

Interfacing

Interlining

Lining

Mock French seam

Simple knot

Underlining

5

The Skill of Couture Draping

Objectives

- Learn the concept of draping

- Learn the importance of grainline

- Learn how to drape ½ torso block using one dart, princess block,
bias-cut garments, a cowl neckline, and a bust twist

- Learn how to turn the block into a halter neckline, princess block into a corset,
darts into gathers, pleats, tucks, or yokes

- Learn how to use a princess seam block as a lining

- Learn how to drape with texture and asymmetrically

- Learn how to sew bias-cut fabrics

- Learn about the life and work of Madeleine Vionnet

Draping is a technique used commonly in couture. In draping, fabric is directly draped over a dress form, which makes it easier to see the design while the pattern is made up. Draping is mostly done using **muslin** or cheaper cotton; however, muslin does not always match the thickness and the drape of the garment fabric you will be using. Make sure you keep this in mind when draping, and remember the kind of fabric you will end up using. (Figure 5.1)

Sometimes the garment fabric can be draped directly on the form if it is unique and its specific features are needed for the design. Be careful—this should only be done if you have draping experience, as you would not want to waste expensive fabrics.

When you drape, it allows you the freedom to design something out of the ordinary and get really creative. You can drape asymmetrically, make **pleats** in different spots, make gathers and twists, and drape on the **bias** to get a very snug fit. Draping is sometimes the easiest way to get your design to come to life because it may be too hard or even impossible to get there with a flat pattern.

Figure 5.1 Keep the fabric in mind when draping.

Establishing the Grainline

Grainline refers to the orientation of the yarns in a woven fabric. The **lengthwise grains** run along the length of the fabric and are called the warp yarns. The yarns that are woven in and out perpendicular to the warp yarns are called the weft yarns. These run side to side forming the **cross grain** of the fabric. The weft yarns are woven to form selvage on both sides of the fabric. The selvage is a finished edge that is formed by the weft yarns being woven, rotating side to side. (Figure 5.2)

The warp yarns get stretched while the fabric is being woven, and that is why the lengthwise grain does not stretch anymore. It is best to cut your patterns to line up perpendicular to the grainline at the hem level so that the hem does not stretch with wear and tear.

The cross grain is known to have a better give and stretch than the lengthwise grain. That is why it is usually cut to wrap around the body side to side for better fit.

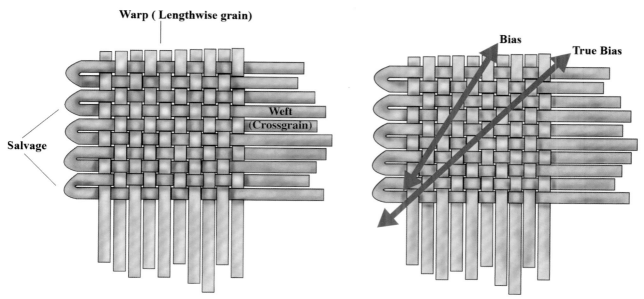

Figure 5.2 Woven fabric close up showing the warp and the weft yarns. Bias and true bias is cut along the diagonal pull of the woven fabric.

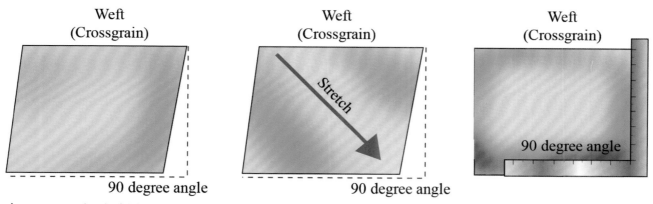

Figure 5.3 Squaring the fabric.

The bias of the fabric refers to the diagonal pull. If you pull on the fabric diagonally, you will notice that the fabric stretches. Because of its stretch, the garment cut on the bias has a closer fit to the body. It also offers a great drape to the fabric when draping skirts, ruffles, and so on. To find a true bias, which is known to have the greatest stretch, find the 45-degree angle to any of the straight grainlines.

Keep in mind that sometimes when the fabric is worked and rolled in production for manufacturing purposes, it is stretched out of straight grain. To check if the fabric is on grain, use your L-shaped ruler or the corner of your table. Line up the corner of the fabric with the corner of the ruler or table and check if your edges line up to form a perfect 90-degree angle. If they line up, then you are set to begin; if not, you can stretch the fabric back into shape by pulling the bias with both hands to form a 90-degree angle. This process is called **squaring the fabric**. Make sure you check the grain before you cut your patterns or your garment will be off grain and may get distorted. (Figure 5.3)

As soon as you get the grainline to line up perfectly with your L-shaped ruler, you can begin draping.

Draping a One-Dart Block

DRAPING THE FRONT BLOCK

1. Measure the distance from the shoulder neck point down to the waist. Add 4 inches to the length, clip the muslin, and tear along the grainline.
2. Then, at the **chest level**, measure from the center front to the side seam. Add 4 inches to the width, clip, and tear along the grainline. You now have a muslin piece ready to drape the front pattern. Press the piece. (Figure 5.4)
3. Mark the muslin piece.
   a. You will be draping on the left side of the front of the dress form; therefore, on the right side of the muslin piece, measure 1 inch, and draw a line with your marking tool along the length of the muslin. This will be your center front line.
   b. Fold the muslin along this line, and press down.
   c. Fold the muslin in half along the width of the piece, and mark the halfway point. Add a pencil marked line along the halfway point, perpendicular to the center front. This line will be the bust level.
   d. On the dress form, measure the distance from the center front and the apex along the bust level. On your muslin, measure the same distance along the bustline, and mark with an X. This will be your apex point.
   e. Now you can also measure the same way for the distance from the center front to the side seam and mark it on your muslin.
4. To begin draping, pin the apex point at the princess line apex of your form with two pins. (Figure 5.5a) The two pins should be in a cross to keep the muslin from moving in any direction.
5. Smooth the muslin with your left hand toward the center front, and start pinning the center fold along the center front line on the dress form. This is your lengthwise grain; you line up along the center front. Pin at the neckline and waist while holding one finger under the fabric at the chest level. You want to leave some fabric to give at the chest level between the two sides of the bust. Pin as you see in Figure 5.5b, with pins facing left to avoid shifting.
6. Smooth the muslin up toward the neckline and shoulder. With your scissors, at the neckline, clip off a corner 1 inch above the neckline point at the center front. Cut a 1-inch square into the corner. Clip into the muslin to smooth out the neckline. Pin at the shoulder neckline mark to avoid shifting.
7. Use your left hand to smooth the muslin from the pin at the neck/shoulder point to the shoulder point. Make sure that the muslin lies smooth and flat along the shoulder line. Pin at the shoulder point downward.
8. With your left hand, smooth all the muslin down around the armhole, and pin at the armhole side seam point. Pin toward the center front.
9. As you have pinned at the armhole already, smooth all of the fabric down, and pin at the side seam/waist point.
10. You now have a bulk of fabric at the bottom of the waistline that will become a dart. To form the dart, smooth the muslin with your left hand from the side waist point to the princess line. Pin toward the side seam at the princess line.
11. With your left hand, smooth the fabric from the center front waist to the princess line, and pin at the princess line with the pin facing the center front. You have just made the dart.

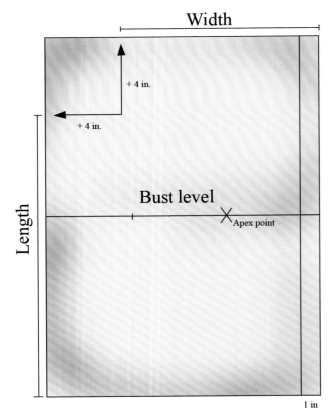

Figure 5.4 Prepare and measure the muslin to begin draping the front block.

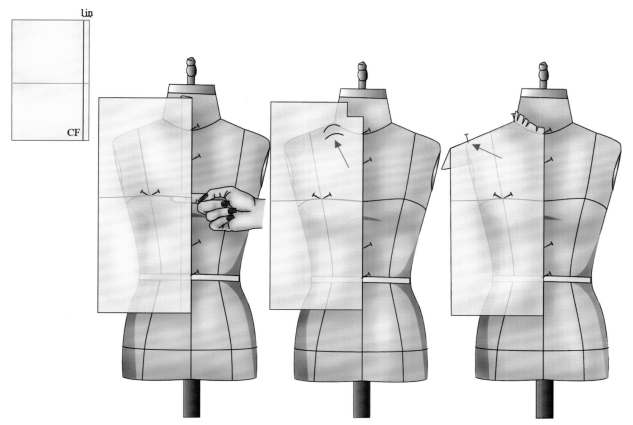

Figure 5.5a Pin the muslin to the apex and the center front, clip the neckline, and smooth the muslin along the shoulder.

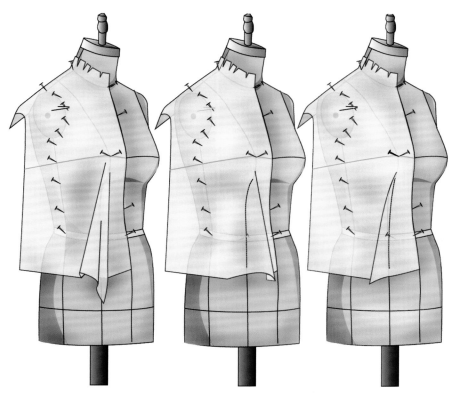

Figure 5.5b Pin the muslin down around the armhole and down the side seam, and make your dart along the princess line.

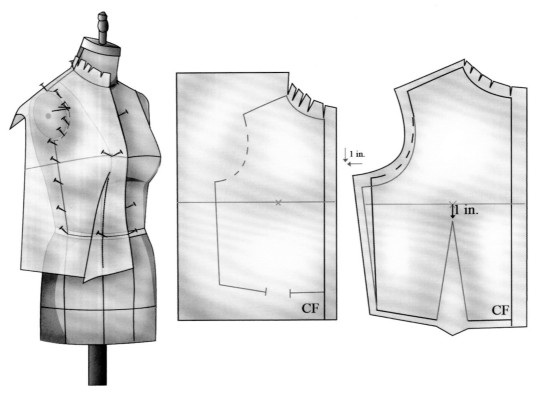

Figure 5.5c Mark the seam lines on your muslin with a marking tool, take it off the form, true the pattern, and add seam allowances.

12. Use your marking tool to mark the entire pattern. (Figure 5.5c) Using your finger to feel every seam line through the muslin, mark the fabric beginning at the neckline point, then up the neckline to the shoulder/neck point, to the shoulder point, around the armhole, down the side seam, and to the waistline through the center of the tape originally placed on the dress form.

13. Mark both of the dart legs at the princess line/waistline. When marking the armhole, instead of making line marks, make dot marks. Unpin the muslin to see the pattern.

14. Now you can start truing the pattern. Truing is a method that helps you fix all of your lines and show the exact measurements you need on the pattern.
    • To begin truing, use a ruler to fix all of the lines.
    • Use a French curve to fix the neckline and armhole curves.
    • Lower the armhole point 1 inch down and 1 inch out to add ease in the armhole for better arm movement.

• When truing the dart, lower the dart drill hole 1 inch from the apex point to avoid a sharp point at the apex. Using the ruler, attach the lines from the drill hole down to each one of the marked dart legs at the waistline. Make sure the dart legs are the same length, so that when they are sewn together they match at all ends.

• Mark the seam allowances around the pattern, and cut off the extra fabric. The neckline should have a ½-inch seam allowance, and the armhole should have 1½ inches from the armhole line for the seam allowance.

• Pin the dart together by folding the leg on the side closer to the center front and overlapping it over the second dart leg.

• Pin, with the pins pointing toward the center front. Now place the muslin back on the form and check every part to make sure everything lines up correctly and the fit looks good, without any gathers or pulls.

DRAPING THE BACK BLOCK

1. Measure the distance from the neck point down to the waist along the **center back**. Add 4 inches to the length. You can clip the muslin to this distance and tear along the lengthwise grainline. Then at the widest point of the back at the **shoulder blade level**, measure from the center back to the side seam. Add 4 inches to the width, clip, and tear along the crosswise grainline. You now have a muslin piece ready to drape the front pattern. Press the piece. (Figure 5.6)

2. Mark the muslin piece.

   a. You will be draping on the right side of the back of the dress form to match the front pattern you have already draped. From the left side of the muslin, measure 1 inch, and draw a line with your marking tool along the length of the muslin. This will be the center back line.

   b. Fold the muslin under along this line, and press down.

   c. Measure 3 inches from the top of your muslin piece at the center back fold line. This will be your neckline point.

   d. On the dress form, measure the distance from the center back neck point to the waist. Measure the same distance from your neckline point on the muslin, and mark the waistline point.

   e. On your muslin, divide the distance from the neckline to the waist into four sections. The first section from the top will be the shoulder blade level. Draw a line along this level perpendicular to the center back line.

   f. On the dress form, measure the length of the shoulder blade level ending at the arm plate, and mark it on your muslin shoulder blade line. Then add 1/8 inch.

   g. From the new mark, measure 1¼ inches toward the center back, and mark. This will be your grainline mark, from which you need to draw a line going downward along the muslin.

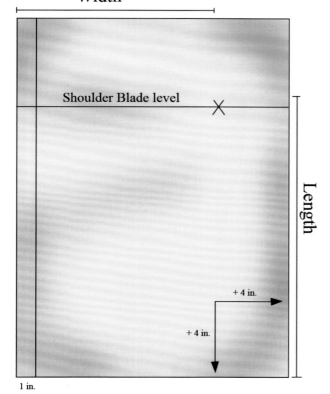

Figure 5.6 Prepare and measure the muslin to begin draping the back block.

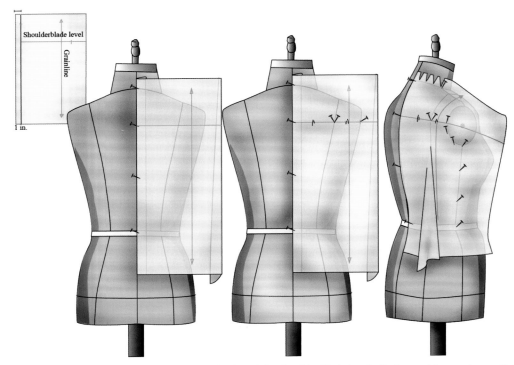

Figure 5.7a Pin the muslin along the center back and the shoulder blade level, clip the neckline, and smooth the muslin along the shoulder, down around the armhole, and down the side seam.

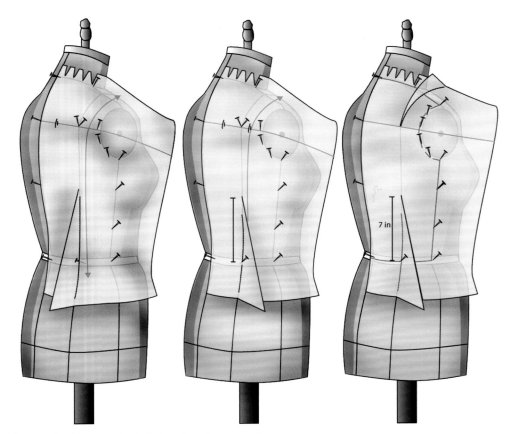

Figure 5.7b Shape your back dart, and mark your muslin.

3. To begin draping, pin the center back fold along the center back. (Figure 5.7a)

4. With your left hand, smooth the muslin toward the side at the shoulder blade level. Pin at the shoulder blade level at the arm plate. The shoulder blade level line should be parallel to the floor along the cross grain of the fabric piece. Ease the shoulder blade, and pin along every inch.

5. Use your left hand to smooth the grainline down to the waist, and pin with your right hand.

6. Smooth down around the arm plate, and pin. Then pin at the armhole side seam point. Pin toward the center back.

7. As you have pinned at the armhole already, smooth all of the fabric down, and pin at the side seam/waist point.

8. Notice there is a bulk of fabric at the bottom of the waistline. This will become a dart. To form the dart, smooth the muslin with your left hand from the side waist point to the princess line. Pin toward the side seam at the princess line. (Figure 5.7b)

9. With your left hand, smooth the fabric from the center back waist to the princess line. Pin at the princess line with the pin facing the center back.

10. In order to find the drill hole, measure 7 inches up at the middle of the dart along the fold of the bulk you have just gathered. You have just made the dart.

11. Now you will need to drape above the shoulder blade level. First, smooth the muslin up toward the neckline and shoulder at the center back. With your scissors, clip off a corner at the neckline, 1 inch above the neckline point at the center back. Cut a 1-inch square into the corner. Clip into the muslin to smooth out the neckline. Pin at the shoulder neckline mark to avoid shifting.

12. With your left hand, smooth the muslin toward the princess line, and pin at the seam.

13. Smooth the muslin from the arm plate at the shoulder to the princess line, and pin. You have just created a small shoulder dart.

14. Take your marking tool and mark the entire pattern. Using your finger to feel every seam line through the muslin, mark the fabric beginning at the neckline point and then up the neckline to the shoulder/

neck point. Mark your shoulder dart legs, the shoulder point, and around the armhole. Mark down the side seam to the waistline through the center of the tape originally placed on the dress form. Mark both of the dart legs at the princess line/waistline. When marking the armhole, instead of making line marks, make dot marks. Unpin the entire muslin. You have just patterned a front **block**.

15. Now you can start truing your pattern.

   a. Use a ruler to fix all of your lines. Use a French curve to fix the neckline and armhole curves. However, before you begin truing the armhole, pin the back block side seam to the front block side seam to see where the armhole begins. Figure 5.7c shows how you can use a French curve to make a continued curve in the armhole.

   b. Using a ruler, attach the lines from the drill hole down to each one of the marked dart legs at the waistline. Make sure the dart legs are the same length, so that when they are sewn together they match at all ends.

   c. Mark the seam allowances around the pattern, and cut off the extra fabric. The neckline should have a ½-inch seam allowance, and the armhole should have 1½ inches from the armhole line for the seam allowance.

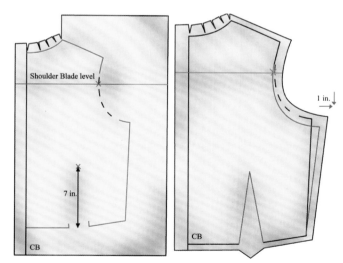

Figure 5.7c Take the muslin off the dress form, true your patterns, and add seam allowance.

d. Pin the dart together by folding the leg on the side closer to the center back and overlapping it over the second dart leg. Pin, with the pins pointing toward the center front. Pin the front and back together at the side seams and the shoulders. Now place the muslin back on the form, and check every part to make sure everything lines up correctly and the fit looks good, without any **gathers** or pulls. (Figure 5.7d)

You have just created a one-dart pattern block. You can now turn this block into any design you want. You can also drape a block with two darts using the same technique, or even one dart in a different spot, like a French dart or a side dart. (Figure 5.8)

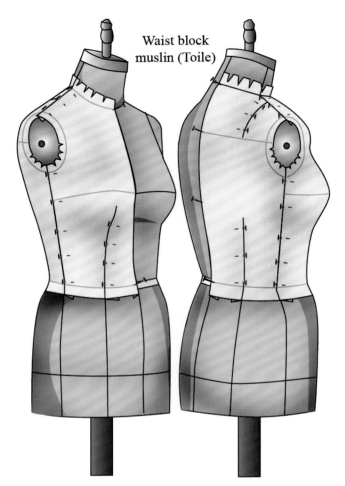

Waist block muslin (Toile)

Figure 5.7d Pin and check front and back waist blocks for fit.

Figure 5.8 Dart placement examples.

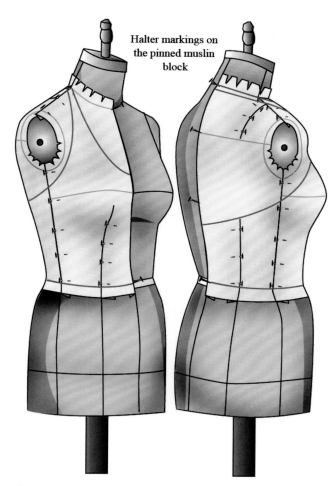

Halter markings on the pinned muslin block

Figure 5.9a Mark your style lines on your pinned muslin blocks.

Turn This Block into a Halter

In couture, a halter top is very common in dresses. You can drape the halter separately from scratch, or you can drape a complete front and back dart block and turn it into a halter top.

1. To begin, drape the front and back blocks. It will be your choice which darts you choose to use in your design.
2. The front and back blocks need to be pinned together on the dress form to continue.
3. Mark the style lines with your marking tool. Mark the halter line at the neckline and shoulder/armhole, and take the style line to the back of the pattern by continuing the line to the back. (Figure 5.9a) Take the fabric off the form, and true all of your lines with a ruler. Add seam allowance, and clip off the extra fabric. Pin the pattern pieces back together, and place on the dress form to check for fit. (Figure 5.9b)

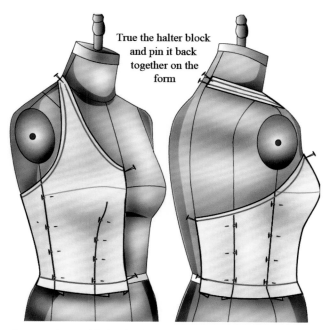

True the halter block and pin it back together on the form

Figure 5.9b Trued halter block.

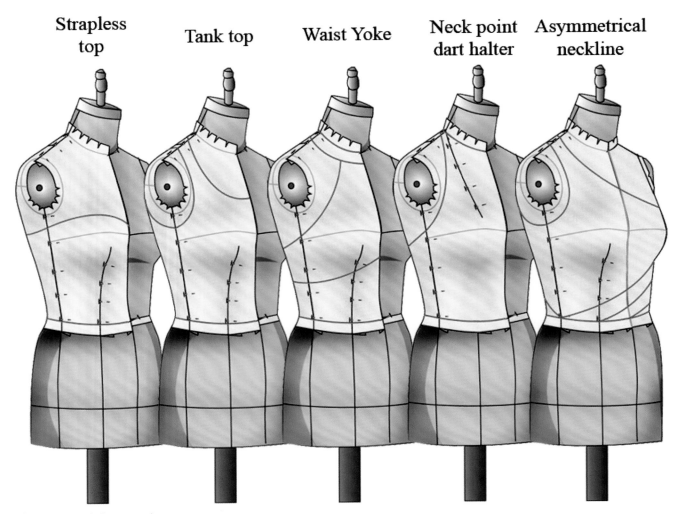

Strapless top **Tank top** **Waist Yoke** **Neck point dart halter** **Asymmetrical neckline**

Figure 5.9c Style line examples.

You can use this same technique to design many different designs just by drawing style lines on your pattern blocks. (Figure 5.9c)

How to Turn a Dart into Pleats, Gathers, Tucks, or a Yoke

A great way to eliminate darts is to turn the bulk of fabric of the dart into gathers, pleats, **tucks**, or a **yoke**.

- When you work with pleats, you do not need to press them down. Let them drape on their own. You can use pleats instead of darts 360 degrees around the **apex**, in any area you have placed a dart. (Figure 5.10a)

- When you work with tucks, pin them closed to check the fit of the garment on the form first. Then you can stitch them closed. You can use tucks instead of darts 360 degrees around the apex, in any area you have placed the dart. (Figure 5.10b)

- When gathering the dart, baste and gather it on the form so you can see how it fits the body. This way you have power to control the gathers on the dress form. (Figure 5.10c) You can come up with many different

Figure 5.10a Dart elimination—pleat examples.

Figure 5.10b Dart elimination—tuck examples.

Figure 5.10c Dart elimination—gathering examples.

variations for gathering the darts 360 degrees around the apex. (Figure 5.11)

- When you would like to completely take out your darts, you have the option of adding a yoke.
  a. Lay the pattern block flat on the table.
  b. Trace the muslin pattern to paper.
  c. Cut the pattern out with your dart cut open. Draw a line anywhere across the pattern, dividing the pattern into two parts. You can eliminate darts by gathering into the yoke.
  d. Cut along that line, and separate the patterns. You should now be holding two pieces of the pattern.
  e. Add seam allowance around both pieces so that you will be able to reattach the pieces.
  f. Trace the pattern to muslin.
  g. Cut, pin together, and place on the dress form to check the fit.
- There are so many different variations you can design with the use of a yoke, which works in any type of garment—dress, shirt, skirt, jacket, or pants. (Figure 5.12)

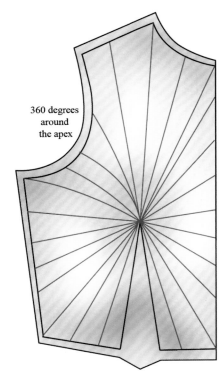

360 degrees around the apex

Figure 5.11 Pattern layout—rotating the dart 360 degrees around the apex.

Figure 5.12 Dart elimination—yoke examples.

Draping a Princess Seam Block

DRAPING THE FRONT

1. To begin, measure the distance from the shoulder neck point down to the waist. Add 4 inches to the length. Clip the muslin to this distance, and tear along the grainline. (Figure 5.13a) Then at the chest level, measure from the center front to the side seam. Add 8 inches to the width, clip, and tear along the grainline. Divide this width in half, clip, and tear. You now have two muslin pieces ready to drape the front princess panels. Press the pieces. (Figure 5.13b)
2. Mark your muslin pieces.
   a. You will be draping on the left side of the front of the dress form, so on your muslin, from the right side of one of the panels, measure 1 inch, and draw a line with your marking tool along the length of the muslin. This will be your center front line.
   b. Fold the muslin under along this line, and press down.
   c. On the side panel, draw a line going through the center of the panel lengthwise for your grainline.
   d. Fold the muslin panels in half along the width, and mark the halfway point. Sketch a line along the halfway point perpendicular to the center front. This line will be the bust level.
   e. On the dress form, measure the distance from the center front and the apex along the bust level. On your muslin center panel, measure the same distance along the bustline, and mark with an X. This will be your apex point.

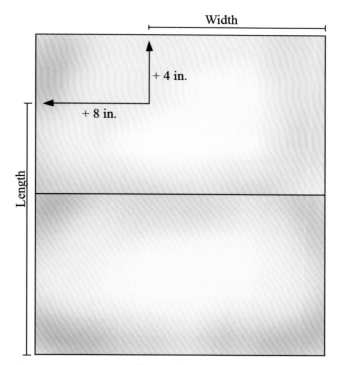

Figure 5.13a Measure muslin to begin draping the front princess block.

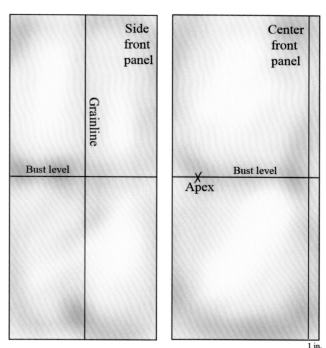

Figure 5.13b Prepare muslin to begin draping the front princess block.

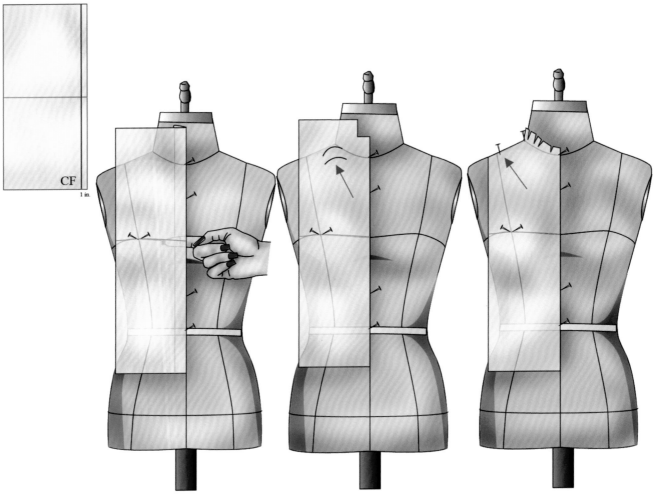

Figure 5.14a Line up one panel of the muslin to the apex and the center front; clip the neckline, smooth along the shoulder.

3. To begin draping, pin the apex point at the princess seam apex of your form with two pins. The two pins should form a cross to keep the muslin from moving in any direction. (Figure 5.14a)

4. With your left hand, smooth the muslin toward the center front, and start pinning the center fold along the center front line on the dress form. Pin at the neckline and waist while holding one finger under the fabric at the chest level. You want to leave some fabric to give at the chest level between the two sides of the bust. Pin as you see in Figure 5.14b, with pins facing left to avoid shifting.

5. Smooth the muslin up toward the neckline and shoulder. With your scissors, clip off a corner at the neckline 1 inch above the neckline point at the center front. Cut a 1-inch square into the corner. Clip into the

muslin to smooth out the neckline. Pin at the shoulder neckline mark to avoid shifting.

6. Use your left hand to smooth the muslin from the pin at the neck/shoulder point to the princess line. Make sure that the muslin lies smooth and flat along the shoulder line. Pin at the princess line downward.

7. With your left hand, smooth the fabric from the center front line to the princess line and along the princess line downward to the apex. (Figure 5.14b)

8. With your left hand, smooth the muslin panel from the center front waistline to the princess waistline. Pin at the waistline with your pins facing the center front.

9. With your left hand, smooth the fabric from the center front line to the princess line up from the waist to the apex.

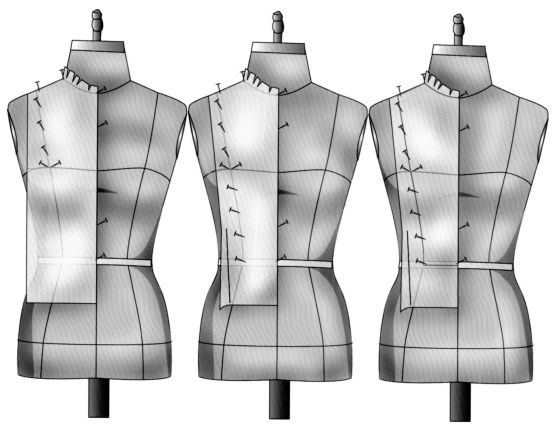

Figure 5.14b Pin down the princess line toward the apex, pin down toward the waistline, and mark the seam lines on your muslin.

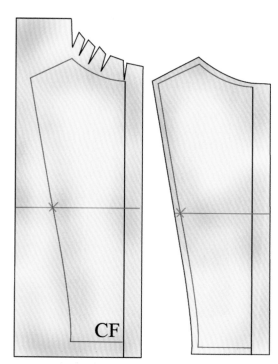

Figure 5.14c Take the center panel off the dress form, true the pattern, and add seam allowances.

10. Take your marking tool, and mark the entire panel. Using your finger to feel every seam line through the muslin, beginning at the neckline point, then up the neckline to the shoulder/neck point, to the princess line point at the shoulder, and down the princess line all the way to the waist, you can mark the waistline through the center of the tape originally placed on the dress form.

11. Unpin the panel. You have just patterned a center front panel block.

12. Now you can start truing your pattern.
    a. To begin truing, use a ruler to fix all of the lines. (Figure 5.14c) Use a French curve to fix the neckline.
    b. Mark the seam allowances around the pattern, and cut off the extra fabric. The neckline should have a ½-inch seam allowance. The rest can be wider.
    c. Now place the muslin back on the form, and check every part to make sure everything lines up correctly and the fit looks good, without any gathers or pulls.

13. To start draping the side panel, mark 1 inch from the right end of your panel along the bust level line. This is the apex point for the side panel. Pin the apex point marked on the muslin along the apex point on your dress form by lining up the bust level line with your center panel. Make sure that the line lies parallel to the floor to keep the correct grainline. (Figure 5.15a) Smooth the muslin along the bust level, and pin at the side seam.

14. Smooth the muslin downward along the side seam, and pin at the waist.

15. Smooth all of the muslin from the waist at the side seam toward the princess line, and pin at the princess line with your pin facing the side seam. Smooth under the bustline all of the muslin from the side seam, and pin along the princess line up to the apex.

16. Smooth all of the muslin up from the side seam bust level, and pin at the arm plate.

17. Keep smoothing the muslin upward along the armhole and shoulder toward the princess line. Pin at the princess line with the pin facing downward. Smooth all of the muslin above the bust level, and pin downward along the princess line up to the apex.

18. Now mark the lines along the princess line, shoulder line, armhole, side seam, and waistline. (Figure 5.15b)
    a. Pull the muslin off the dress form, true the lines, and add seam allowances.
    b. Lower the armhole point 1 inch down and 1 inch out to add ease in the armhole and allow better arm movement.
    c. Make sure the armhole seam allowance will be 1½ inches wide. Cut off all extra fabric.
    d. Pin the center front to the side front by folding under the seam allowance on the princess line on the center panel and overlapping it on the princess side panel.
    e. Make sure you line up the bust level lines when pinning. Your pins should face the center front. (Figure 5.15c)

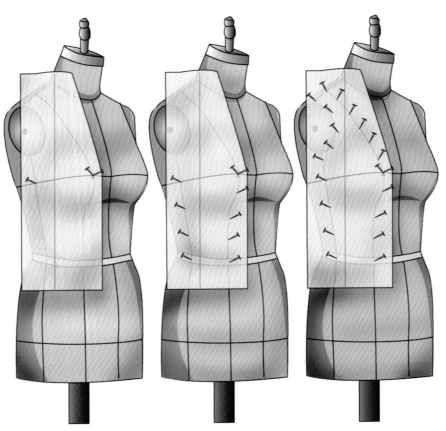

Figure 5.15a Line up the side panel muslin piece to the apex, pin down the princess line toward the waist, pin the side seam, and then pin above the chest level along both the armhole and the princess line.

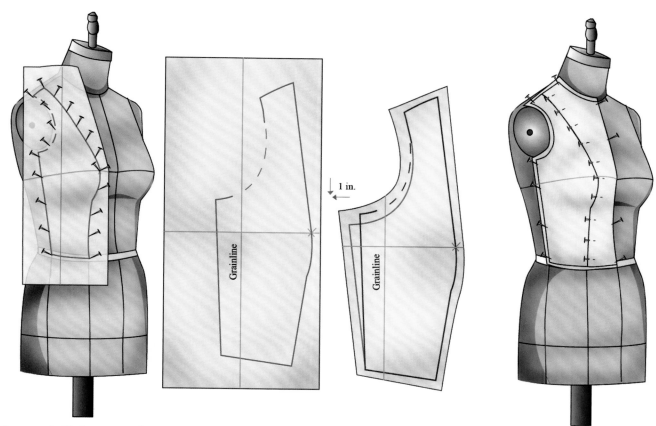

Figure 5.15b Mark your seam lines on your muslin, take it off the dress form, true your pattern, and add seam allowances.

Figure 5.15c Pin both princess panels together, and place them back on the form to check the fit.

DRAPING THE BACK

1. To begin, measure the distance from the neck point down to the waist along the center back. Add 4 inches to the length. Clip the muslin to this distance, and tear along the lengthwise grainline. Then, at the widest point of the back at the shoulder blade level, measure from the center back to the side seam. Add 8 inches to the width, clip, and tear along the crosswise grainline. You now have a muslin piece ready to drape the front pattern. Press the piece. (Figure 5.16a)

2. Before you start draping, you need to mark the muslin piece.

   a. You will be draping on the right side of the back of the dress form to match the front pattern you have already draped.

   b. Measure 3 inches from the top of the muslin piece at the center back fold line. This will be your neck-line point.

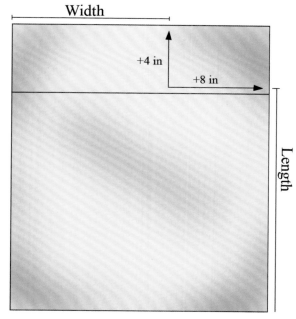

Figure 5.16a Measure muslin to begin draping the back princess block.

c. On the dress form, measure the distance from the center back neck point to the waist. Measure the same distance from the neckline point on the muslin, and mark the waistline point.

d. Divide the distance from the neckline to the waist on your muslin into four sections. The first section mark from the top will be the shoulder blade level. Draw a line along this level perpendicular to the center back line.

e. Next, mark the center of the cross grain width, clip, and tear along the center of the muslin piece. You now have two panels you can drape with.

f. On the muslin center panel, measure 1 inch from the left side, and draw a line with your marking tool along the length of the muslin. This will be the center back line. (Figure 5.16b)

g. Fold the muslin under along this line, and press down. Make sure you copy the marking you have made to the fold.

h. On the side panel, draw a line going through the center of the panel lengthwise for the grainline.

3. To begin draping, pin the center back fold along the center back. Pin the neck point and the waist to get the correct shoulder blade level. (Figure 5.17a)

4. With your left hand, smooth the muslin toward the princess line at the shoulder blade level, and pin along the line. Make sure the shoulder blade line is parallel to the floor.

5. Smooth the muslin up toward the neckline and shoulder at the center back. With your scissors, clip off a corner at the neckline 1 inch above the neckline point at the center back. Cut a 1-inch square into the corner. Clip into the muslin to smooth out the neckline. (Figure 5.17b) Pin at the shoulder neckline mark to avoid shifting.

6. Use your left hand to smooth the muslin from the pin at the neck/shoulder point to the princess line. Make sure that the muslin lies smooth and flat along the shoulder line. Pin downward at the princess line.

7. With your left hand, smooth the fabric from the center back line to the princess line and then along the princess line downward to the shoulder blade level.

8. With your left hand, smooth the muslin panel from the center back waistline to the princess line at the waist level. Pin at the princess line with your pin facing the center back.

9. With your left hand, smooth the fabric from the center back line to the princess line up from the waist to the shoulder blade.

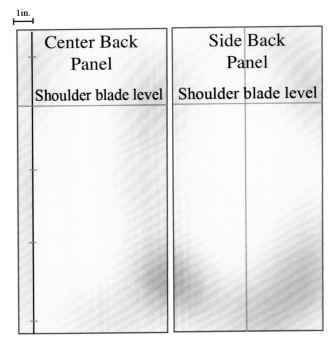

Figure 5.16b Prepare muslin to begin draping the back princess block.

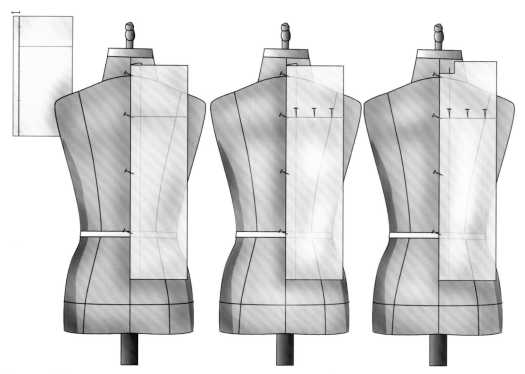

Figure 5.17a Line up and pin the center back panel to the center back and the shoulder blade level, and then trim off a corner at the neckline.

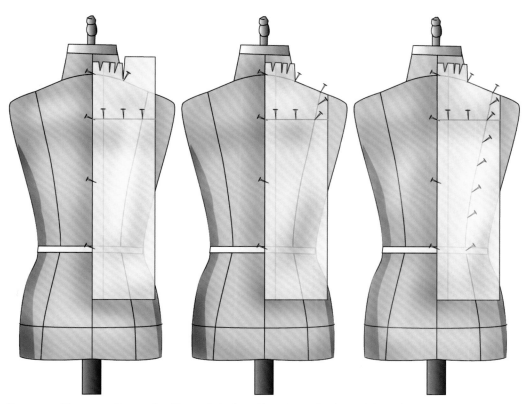

Figure 5.17b Clip your neckline, smooth your shoulder, and pin down the princess line toward the waist.

10. Take your marking tool, and mark the entire panel. Using your finger to feel every seam line through the muslin beginning at the neckline point, then up the neckline to the shoulder/neck point, to the princess line point at the shoulder, and down the princess line all the way to the waist, you can mark the waistline through the center of the tape originally placed on the dress form. (Figure 5.17c)

11. Unpin the panel. You have just patterned a center back panel block with your markings.

12. Now you can start truing your pattern.

    a. To begin truing, use a ruler to fix all of the lines. Use your French curve to fix the neckline.

    b. Mark seam allowances around the pattern, and cut off the extra fabric. The neckline should have a ½-inch seam allowance. The rest can be wider. Place the muslin back on the form, and check every part to make sure everything lines up correctly and the fit looks good, without any gathers or pulls.

13. To start draping the side panel, mark 1 inch from the right end of your panel along the shoulder blade level line. Pin the point along the princess line on your form by lining up the shoulder blade level line with your center back panel. Make sure that the line lies parallel to the floor to keep the same grainline. (Figure 5.17d) Smooth the muslin along the shoulder blade level, and pin at the side seam.

14. Smooth the muslin downward around the armhole, and pin. Then smooth along the side seam, and pin at the waist.

15. Smooth all of the muslin from the waist at the side seam toward the princess line. Pin at the princess line with your pins facing the side seam. Smooth under the bust-line all of the muslin from the side seam, and pin along the princess line up to the shoulder blade line.

16. Smooth all of the muslin up from the shoulder blade level, and pin at the shoulder point.

17. Keep smoothing the muslin upward along the arm-hole and shoulder toward the princess line. Pin at the princess line with your pin facing downward. Smooth all of the muslin above the shoulder blade level, and pin downward along the princess line up to the shoulder blade line. (Figure 5.17e)

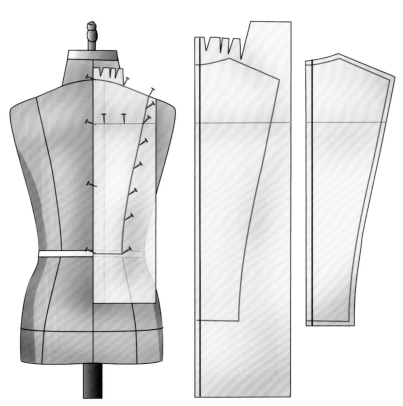

Figure 5.17c Mark your seam lines on your muslin, take it off the form, true your pattern, and add seam allowances.

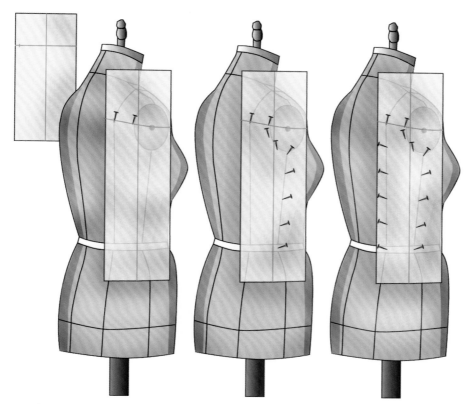

Figure 5.17d Line up your side back panel to the shoulder blade level, pin down the armhole and down the side seam, smooth the muslin toward the center back, and pin down the princess line from the shoulder blade.

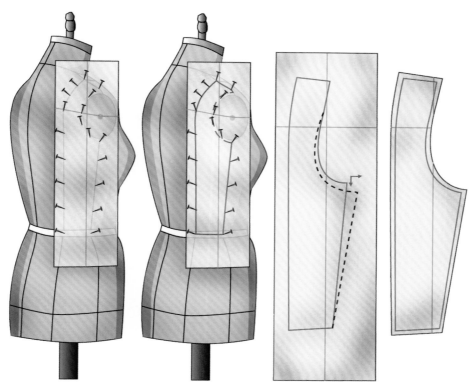

Figure 5.17e Pin above the shoulder blade level along the shoulder and the princess line. Mark the seam lines on your muslin. Take the muslin off the dress form, true your pattern, and add seam allowances.

18. Mark your lines along the princess line, shoulder line, armhole, side seam, and waistline.

19. Pull the muslin off the dress form, true your lines, and add seam allowances.

    a. Before you true the armhole, pin the back and front side seams together to match up the armhole. Use your French curve to make a continuous curved line at the bottom of the armhole.

    b. Make sure your armhole seam allowance will be 1½ inches wide. Cut off all extra fabric.

    c. Pin the center back to the side back by folding under the seam allowance on the princess line on the center panel and overlapping it on the princess side panel.

    d. Make sure you line up the shoulder blade level lines when pinning. Your pins should face the center back. (Figure 5.17f)

    e. Pin the front to the back at the shoulders and the side seam. Make sure the princess lines align at the shoulder seam.

    f. Place back on the form, and check for fit. (Figure 5.17g)

How to Turn a Princess Seam Block into a Corset Pattern

A **corset** is commonly used in couture, not just for a corset garment but also as the structure for the lining inside a dress or a shirt. You can drape the corset separately from scratch or piece by piece, or you can drape front and back princess blocks and turn them into a corset top.

1. Drape the front and back princess blocks.

2. Pin the front and back blocks together on the dress form.

3. Mark the style lines with your marking tool.

    a. Mark the corset lines for the top of the corset, and continue the line to the back of the pattern. (Figure 5.18a) There are many, many ways to do the corset neckline. It is much easier to mark it on a full princess block, as this way you can control how high the neckline of the corset goes.

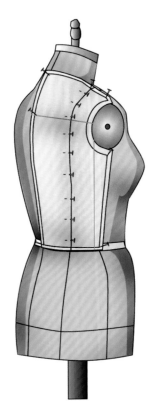

Figure 5.17f Pin the center and side panels together, and place back on the dress form to check the fit.

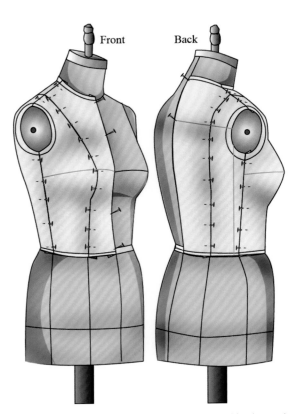

Front   Back

Figure 5.17g Check the fit by pinning both front and back together and placing it back on the dress form.

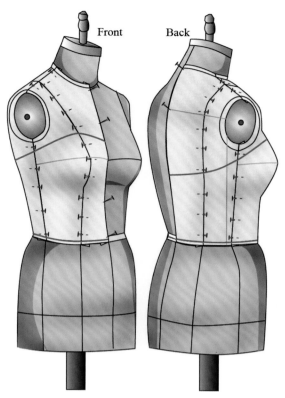

Figure 5.18a Using your pinned waist princess block, mark your corset style lines.

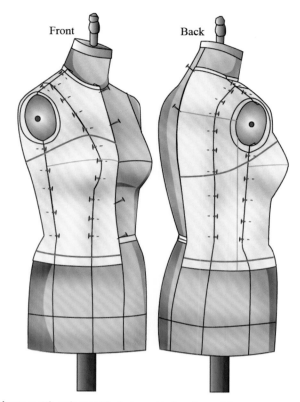

Figure 5.18b Princess block draped below the waist.

b. Some corsets drape below the waist. For this style, instead of stopping at the waist when draping, continue below the waist to the hip. (Figure 5.18b)

c. When you are done marking, take it off the form and true all of the lines with a ruler.

d. Add your seam allowance, and clip off the extra fabric.

4. Pin the pattern pieces back together, and place on the dress form to check for fit. (Figure 5.18c)

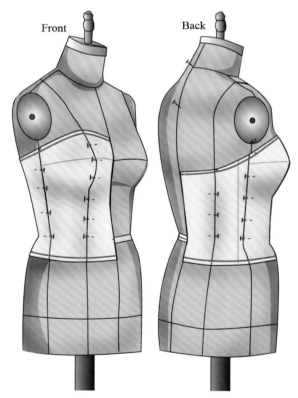

Figure 5.18c True the corset pattern, and pin it back on the dress form to check the fit.

Figure 5.19 Corset style lines examples.

For more examples of different designs you can come up with, see Figure 5.19.

Princess Seam Block as a Structured Dress/Shirt Lining

When working with a couture gown, you will most likely be using a structure on the inside of the lining. The structure is very important to hold up the gown and give it stiffness and sometimes to help give the body shape. If the gown does not have proper structure, in many cases the fabric starts stretching and gathering around the waist, under the chest, and even around the neckline. Using a structure avoids this error. A boned lining can hold up strapless gowns, asymmetrical gowns, and even halter gowns.

When making up the structure, you will be sewing boning into the seam allowances in between the princess panels. (Figure 5.20) While in the past, a corset used to be boned with wood, hard metal, or even ivory, boning is now made mostly out of plastic or flat wire coils, which will allow the garment to be more flexible. Boning can be used in any spot on the corset where support is needed—for example, the center front, front **princess seams**, side seam, and back princess seams. Sometimes boning is also inserted under the cup and through the apex to give the bust support.

These structured bodices are very often made as a lining piece and then sewn inside the garment. Sometimes these boned bodices are made to be invisible and are inserted as an underlining/interfacing between the garment and the lining. And occasionally they are used on the outside of the garment as part of the design.

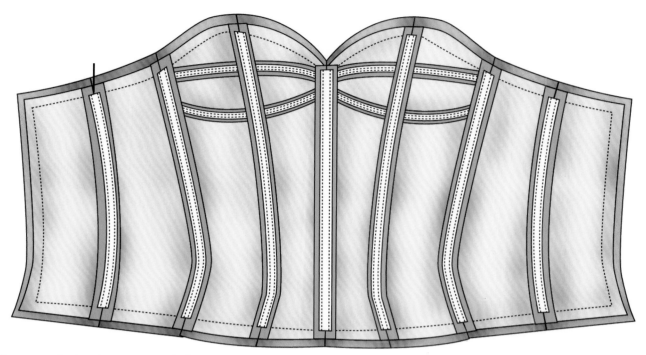

Figure 5.20 Boning placement example, lined up to the seam allowances of the princess seams.

If you are using this bodice as a structure to hold up a certain design, you will need to make sure you finish the corset first so that you can pin it on the form before you begin draping the garment. Then you can drape the garment fabric over it and attach the garment fabric in any spot directly to the corset by hand sewing it. That way, when you remove it from the form, the garment will keep its shape. (Figure 5.21)

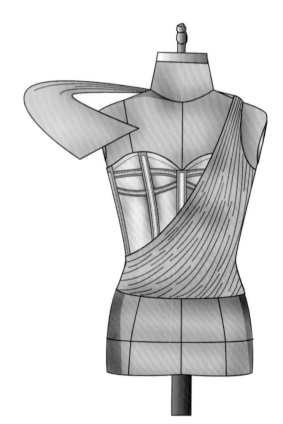

Figure 5.21 Using your corset as a stay during intricate detail draping.

The Bust Twist

A bust **twist** comes in very handy when you would like to eliminate a bust dart. It is also a very elegant look to add to a gown, shirt, and even a swimsuit. The bust twist is draped with one piece of fabric. The twist works best when you use soft fabrics. Make sure you use a double-sided fabric, because you would not want one side to show the backside of the fabric. (Figure 5.22) To begin, you will need to get your fabric ready.

1. To work on a bust twist, you need to cut a square of fabric, preferably no smaller than 30 × 30 inches. Then fold the square diagonally in half to find the bias, or measure a 45-degree angle from one corner and mark a bias line and then fold. (Figure 5.23a)

2. Find the center of the bias line you have marked, and measure 3 inches both ways from the center point. Mark this point. (Figure 5.23b)
3. With your fabric scissors, cut into this line, and stop when you get to the 3-inch mark on both sides. (Figure 5.24a)
4. To begin draping, fold 1 inch on both sides of the cut on one side, which will give you enough for the seam allowance at the neck.
5. With one hand, gather the center of the square between the 3-inch marks and with another hand, help twist the corners. This way you will get a twist in the center. (Figure 5.24b)

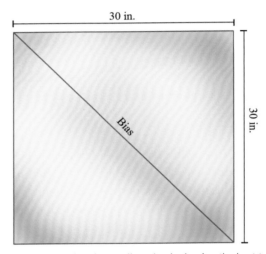

Figure 5.23a Preparing the muslin to begin draping the bust twist.

Figure 5.22 Bust twist.

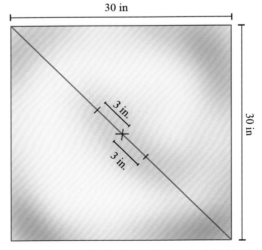

Figure 5.23b Measure 3 inches from the center of the bias line.

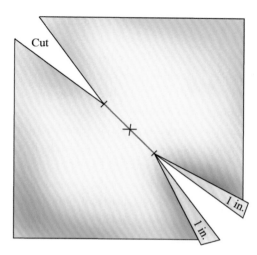

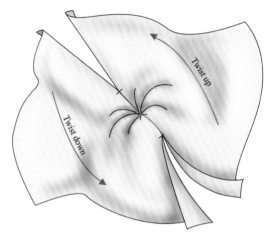

Figure 5.24a Cut into the bias line, stopping at the 3-inch mark on both sides of the muslin.

Figure 5.24b Gather in the center and twist.

6. Now you can make different types of twist looks. You can drape on the form over the bust and pin on the sides for a strapless look or for a halter look. (Figure 5.25a)

7. To achieve the halter look, smooth the sides up, and pin at the neckline. Then smooth down, and pin at the waist. (Figure 5.25b)

8. When you are ready, mark all of your lines, seams, pleats, or gathers and take it off the form. Keep all of

your pleats pinned when taking fabric off the form. (Figure 5.25c)

9. True all of your markings on one side, and then trace them to the other side if you desire a symmetrical look. If you stretched asymmetrically, then you can true each side separately. Place back on the form to check fit. (Figure 5.25d)

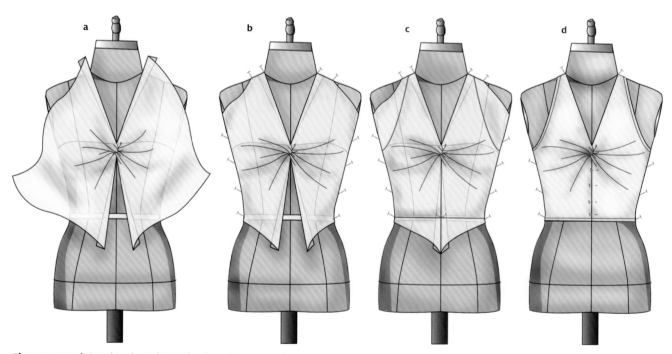

Figure 5.25a–d Draping the twist on the dress form example.

Examples of Twist Variations

Examples of bust twist variations (Figure 5.26)

TWO-PIECE TWIST

This twist consists of two pieces of fabric twisted together. You can design any garment with this type of twist. You can design a swimsuit, a blouse, a dress, and so on. And you can place the twist wherever you desire on the dress form.

1. To begin, you will need to use your style tape to mark your style lines on the dress form.
2. Then you will need to get your fabric ready. To do so, first measure the distance of your twist sides. Multiply the distance by two, and then add 6 to 8 inches, depending on where the twist will be placed. If it is in the bust, then add more than 6 inches.

   a. Then measure the distance of the width for your twist.
   b. Keep in mind that if you are only draping a twist to connect to another part of the shirt, then you will only need fabric for the twist. However, if you are draping a twist and the rest of the shirt with the same pieces as the twist, then the fabric needs to be wide enough to cover the rest of the body.
   c. Cut your fabric pieces.
3. To start draping, fold one of the pieces in half, then take the other piece of fabric and pull it through the loop of the first piece of folded fabric. Now fold the second piece. You should get a twist knot in the center. (Figure 5.27a)
4. Now you can drape on the dress form. (Figure 5.27b)

Two-piece twist examples are shown in Figure 5.28.

Figure 5.26 Bust twist examples from left to right: tank top neckline, strapless neckline, and halter neckline.

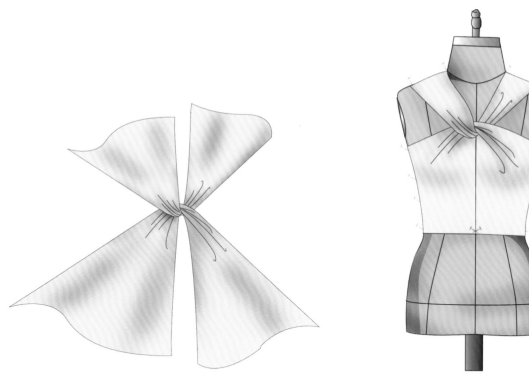

Figure 5.27a Prepare the muslin, and fold the two pieces.

Figure 5.27b Drape the two pieces on the dress form, and pin.

Figure 5.28 Two-piece twist variations. From left to right: halter neckline, one-shoulder twist, and waist twist.

Draping with Texture

In couture, draping is not only done with the fabric draping down; you can also be more creative. The following draping techniques will help you be more creative with your designs.

GATHERING TECHNIQUE

While draping, you can gather in any area of the design. See examples below.

To begin gathering, baste a stitch along the edge of the fabric on the dress form, and begin gathering while shaping the fabric and the gathers around the body. (Figure 5.29a) You can use this technique together with other gathered pieces or with a draped nongathered piece.

PLEATING TECHNIQUE

Pleating is done similar to gathering. (Figure 5.29b)

To begin pleating, make sure you use a piece of fabric long enough to be pleated—you don't want it to be too short for your garment. You can pleat directly on the form to make sure your pleats are shaped around the body and positioned in the right place. When you are done, mark your pleats so that you can take it off the form and true a pattern.

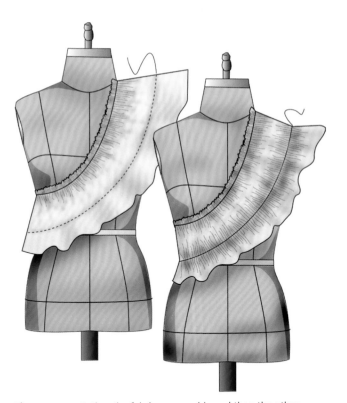

Figure 5.29a Gather the fabric on one side and then the other, shaping around the dress.

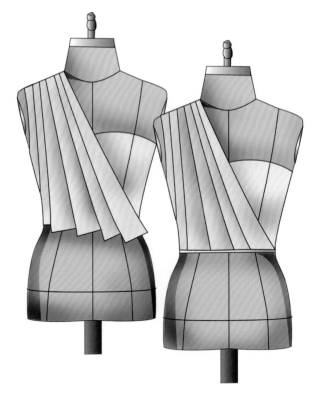

Figure 5.29b Pleating example.

CRUNCH TECHNIQUE

This technique is done by hand on a form and is hand sewn to a stay. The stay can be a simple piece of muslin, or if you are crunching transparent fabric, use another fabric to show through.

The stay is a pre-draped pattern that was already stitched and pressed. This stay is pinned back on the form before you begin crunching. The stay should be shaped like your design, with the correct length, neckline, and armholes. (Figure 5.30a)

1. Place another piece of fabric over your stay, and begin crunching small amounts of fabric in one area. Pin to the stay to hold the crunch in place. (Figure 5.30b)

2. Next, use a needle and thread to sew a small stitch and to backstitch a couple of times in the pinned area. This will secure the crunch to the stay.

3. Next you can make another crunch and pin it to the stay.

4. Then repeat step 2.

5. Keep crunching the garment to get the effect you designed. Be creative. (Figure 5.30c)

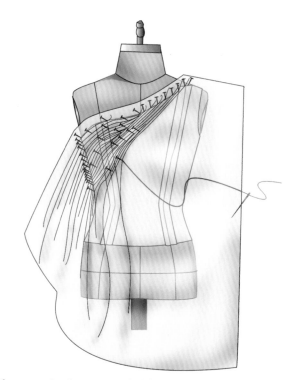

Figure 5.30b Pin your crunched fabric to the stay, and then hand stitch it in place.

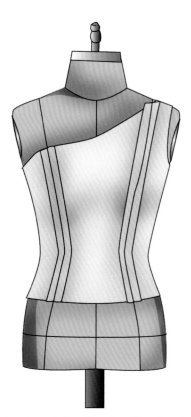

Figure 5.30a Pre-draped stay pinned and fitted on the dress form.

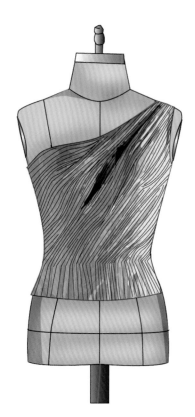

Figure 5.30c Finished effect of the crunching technique.

6. The stay does not act like a lining for this type of a garment. You still need to make a lining to hide the stitches you made to connect the crunches on the stay.

Draping Asymmetrically

When draping asymmetrical garments, you have to decide whether you will be draping on the bias of the fabric for all of the layers of the garment or just on the outside. Draping on the bias just means that you will still structure an inside lining on grain to hold the garment in place on the body. When you are thinking of your design, look at the fabric you will be using. You can even play with it on the form to get some ideas and to see how the fabric drapes. (Figure 5.31a–c)

USING INTERFACING TO HOLD ASYMMETRICAL PATTERNS AND DRAPERY

For structure, you can use a boned bodice. Or you can use a softer version for lighter garments and softer fabrics: interfacing.

Use sew-on interfacing fabric, preferably a stiff fabric or muslin. This way, you can make a complete pattern of your garment out of the interfacing and place it on the form before you begin draping. Just like using a boned bodice as a stay, you can use the interfacing on the form as a stay. You can drape, swirl, roll, and even bubble the fabric and then attach it to the interfacing on the dress form by hand sewing. (Figure 5.32)

Figure 5.31a–c Examples of asymmetrical designs.

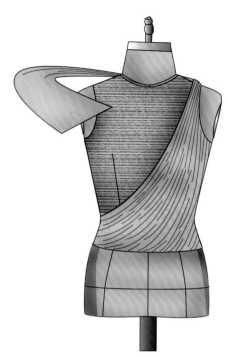

Figure 5.32 Using interfacing as a stay.

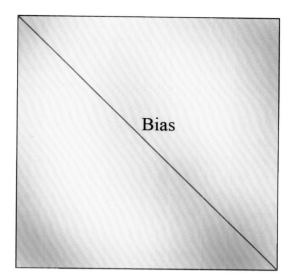

Figure 5.33a Preparing muslin to drape on the bias.

Bias Draping

Bias draping is another type of draping where the garment is draped on the bias of the fabric. You can get even more creative by adding a bias into your design. Bias draping gives you an opportunity to add a softer drape or a closer fit.

1. To begin, you will first need to mark a bias on your piece of fabric. To do this, you will need to draw a line perpendicular to the lengthwise grain of the fabric.
   a. Now find the 45-degree angle from this lengthwise grain. Fold your fabric along the 45-degree angle, and pat down on the fold to create a crease.
   b. When you open up the fold you should see a crease line. You can use it as is, or you can use a marking tool to outline it. (Figure 5.33a)
2. When you work with bias fabric, you need to remember to add to your seam allowances to equal at least 1.5 inches so that you will have enough fabric in the seam allowances to fix and adjust during the stretch of your fabric.
   a. Also, when you cut your fabric along the bias line, you need to remember to move the stitch line seam farther away from that edge because the edge seems to stretch after cutting and is longer than the needed edge.
   b. By doing this, you will save yourself from stressful rippled seams.
3. To begin cutting your bias patterns, lay a piece of paper underneath the fabric on the cutting table.
   a. Pin your fabric to the paper before you line up the patterns on it. This way you will keep the fabric from stretching while you are lining up the patterns and cutting them out. Then line up your pattern pieces, and cut them out. (Figure 5.33b)
   b. Mark all your stitch lines. Make sure you keep the paper pinned to the bias fabric until you are ready to stay stitch your edge.

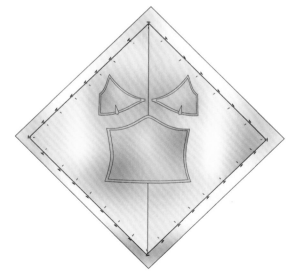

Figure 5.33b Lining up and cutting the patterns on the bias.

DRAPING A BIAS SLIP DRESS WITH NO CENTER FRONT/BACK SEAM

This type of slip dress is done in one piece of bias fabric for the front of the dress and another for the back of the dress. (Figure 5.34) To begin, you will need to get your fabric ready and mark your **true bias** line at a 45-degree angle. This will assure you the best fit and the best stretch. Make sure you cut a square of fabric wide enough to cover the length of the desired dress. It's best to use fabric 60 inches wide for a longer dress. You will be draping both sides at the same time to get the best fit.

DRAPING THE FRONT

1. When you are ready with your fabric and you have marked your bias line, use your style tape to mark the desired style of the dress neckline.
2. Now line up your bias line with the center front line on the dress form. Make sure that your fabric covers the style line plus seam allowances.
   a. Pin the bias line fabric all the way down along the center front. (Figure 5.35a)
   b. Make sure you place two pins in an X in each spot so that when the fabric is stretched to the right and left, the pins won't come out and the dress won't shift.
3. When you are done pinning, smooth your fabric toward the side seam at the waist on both sides of the body so that you keep everything in place in the center front.
   a. You will notice that it is very hard to stretch all the way to the side seam; therefore you will need to release some of the tension from the fabric.
   b. To do so, clip into the fabric until you get to at least ⅛ inch away from the side seam. Be careful not to cut in too much or you will cut into the garment. Cut little by little, and keep testing by smoothing the fabric toward the side seam after every clip.
4. When you are done clipping, pin at the side seam waistline and start smoothing along the hip level side seam on both sides to keep the center front from shifting. Keep stretching to get a snug fit, if desired.

Figure 5.34 Bias slip dress examples with no center seam.

5. When you are ready, continue stretching to both sides above the waistline and then the chest. (Figure 5.35b) If the chest is not large, you may be able to stretch out the darts and eliminate the bulk altogether.
   a. If the chest is a bit larger, then you will have some bulk for the dart.
   b. You can make a side chest dart, or you can gather, pleat, or tuck the dart into the straps to get a more creative design.
6. If you desire a tight gown below the hip, continue stretching the fabric until you get to the bottom of the dress form.
7. If you desire an A-line below the hipline, you can mark the wider style line along the side seam of the bottom of the dress. You can also cut the bias dress at the hip and add seam allowance, and then you can connect a circle skirt to the hipline to get another desired look.
8. Mark your seams and darts. Take the pattern off the form. True your seam allowances, and then pin it back on the form to drape the back pattern. (Figure 5.35c)

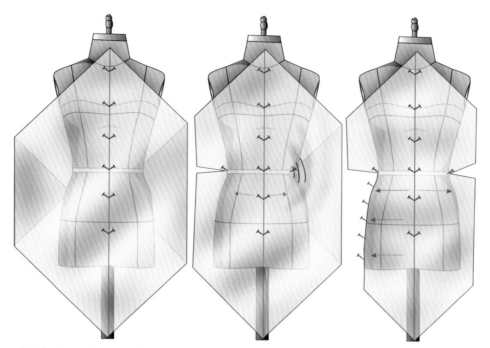

Figure 5.35a Line up the bias line to the center front of the dress form, stretch toward the side seam at the waist, and clip the tension then pin down the side seam while stretching the fabric.

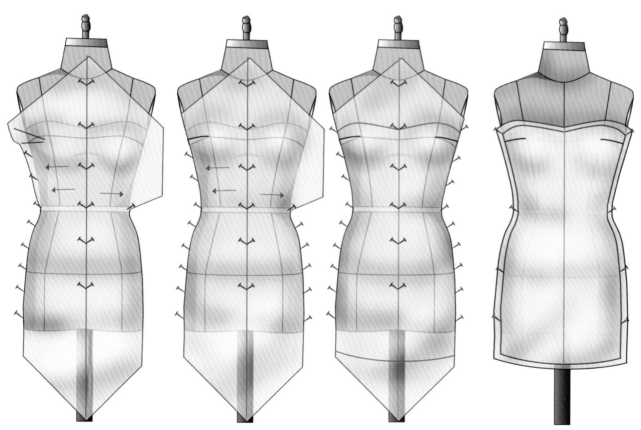

Figure 5.35b Pin up the side seam while stretching the fabric, and form a side dart. Stretch the muslin toward the other side seam at the waist, clip the tension, and then pin down and up the side seam, forming another side dart.

Figure 5.35c After you true your bias pattern, place it back on the dress form to check the fit.

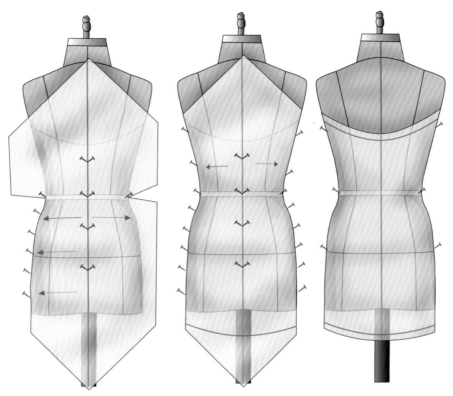

Figure 5.35d Line up the bias line along the center back of the dress form. Stretch the muslin sideways, clip at the waist to reduce tension, and pin up and down the side seams while stretching the muslin. When you're done truing the pattern, check the fit.

DRAPING THE BACK

1. When you begin draping the back, you will first need to get your fabric ready. Mark your bias line at a 45-degree angle.

2. To drape, you will repeat the same steps you did for the front pattern, except instead of the bias lining up with the center front, you line it with center back. You should not have any darts in the dress unless you are draping all the way up to the shoulder line. Sometimes when the shoulders have a larger shoulder muscle, you may need to add a dart. (Figure 5.35d)

3. As you smooth and stretch the fabric toward the side seam, you can line the side seams up with the front pattern and mark your lines to match up correctly.

4. When you are done, take the back pattern off the form, true your seam allowances, and pin both patterns together on the dress form to check the fit. (Figure 5.35e)

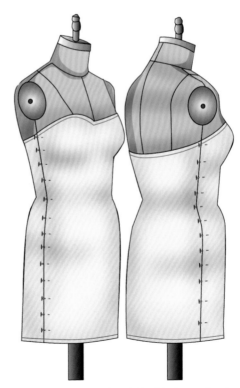

Figure 5.35e Pin both front and back bias blocks together to check the fit.

DRAPING A BIAS SLIP DRESS WITH A CENTER FRONT SEAM

Bias slip dresses with a center seam take very careful draping and sewing. (Figure 5.36) You need to make sure you do not stretch the center seam because it will wrinkle.

These dresses can offer you even more creative ideas for your desired look. In the 1930s these dresses were very popular.

1. To start draping, you will first need to get your fabric ready again. Mark your bias line 45 degrees from the straight grain. Now mark a line 1 inch away on both sides of the marked bias line.

2. Then stay stitch along those lines to keep the bias from stretching. Once you are done stay stitching, cut along the center bias line you first marked. This will give you two even bias-cut fabric pieces. (Figure 5.37)

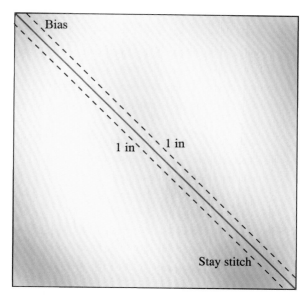

Figure 5.37 Preparing the muslin to drape bias slip dress with center seam.

Figure 5.36 Bias slip dress examples with center front seam.

3. Your stay stitched line should be lined up with the center front line on your dress form. Pin it all the way down, with your pins facing toward the side seam on the side you are working. (Figure 5.38a)

4. Now you can work the same steps as a regular bias slip dress by smoothing your fabric toward the side seam at the waist.

   a. You will notice that it is very hard to stretch all the way to the side seam; therefore you will need to release some of the tension from the fabric.

   b. To do so, clip into the fabric until you get to at least ⅛ inch away from the side seam.

   c. Be careful not to cut in too much or you will cut into the garment. Cut little by little, and keep testing by smoothing the fabric toward the side seam after every clip.

5. When you are done clipping, pin at the side seam waistline, and start smoothing along the hip level side seam. Keep stretching to get a snug fit, if desired.

6. Now continue stretching to the side seam above the waistline and then the chest. If the chest is not large, you may be able to stretch out the darts and eliminate the bulk. Or you can gather the bulk into the straps. (Figure 5.38b)

7. To work below the hip line, you can either stretch to the side or make it fit tight, or you can let it hang loose.

8. Mark your seams and darts. Take the pattern off the form. True your seam allowances, and then pin it back on the form to drape the back pattern.

9. Repeat steps 4–8 for the other side of the dress. Now you can pin or baste two front pieces together.

10. To work on the back pattern, follow the same draping steps as you followed for the front piece. Then pin and baste everything together. Place it back on the form, and check the fit. (Figure 5.38c)

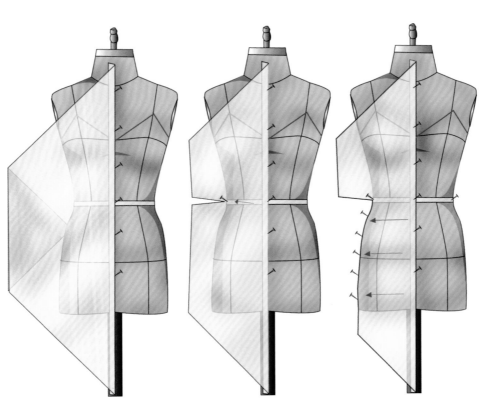

Figure 5.38a Line up one of the pieces to the center front of your dress form, pin and clip at the side seam waistline, and then pin down the side seam.

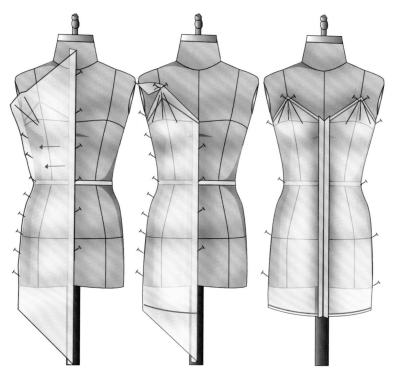

Figure 5.38b Pin up the side seam, and form a dart or a gather. Drape the other side of the block, using the second piece of fabric the same way, and then pin them together to check the fit.

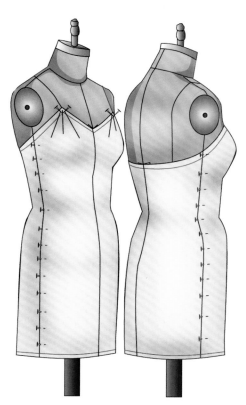

Figure 5.38c When you finish draping the back, pin both front and back together, and check the fit.

MORE BIAS DRESS VARIATIONS

Example of a bias dress variation (Figure 5.39)

BIAS SEWING TIPS

1. To begin sewing, you will need to sew and work with the stretch of your bias fabric.
   a. If you work against it, it will stretch your fabric.
   b. You will need to stay stitch around your edges, especially all of your necklines, waistlines, armholes, and any other seams that are diagonal or concave. (Figure 5.40)
2. Pin all of your seams before sewing to reduce any ripples and stretching. Some designers like to let the garment hang pinned together on a hanger for a day before sewing to allow the fabric to stretch.
   a. You can even hand baste them together instead of pinning.
   b. You will need to pin and/or baste on a table surface.

3. To baste two bias pieces together, you will need to leave a couple of inches of thread hanging at the edge and then baste for a couple of inches.
   a. After that, leave a small loop of thread loose, and baste a couple more inches. At the end, do not knot the thread. (Figure 5.41a)
   b. This loop and an unknotted thread hanging at the beginning and the end of the seam line will allow the bias to stretch.
4. If you are joining the bias edge to a straight grain fabric, you will need to put your bias piece on a hanger and let it hang for at least two hours.
   a. This would help stretch the bias edge a bit so that it does not stretch as much while you sew. It will also help you get the ripple out.

Figure 5.39 Bias dress example.

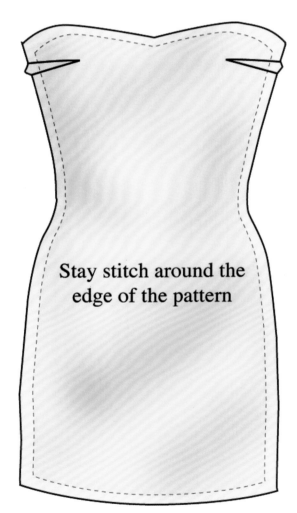

Stay stitch around the edge of the pattern

Figure 5.40 Stay stitching the bias pattern.

b. When you are ready, pin the bias edge to the straight grain edge, then re-mark the new length of the pattern piece before you baste.

5. When you are ready to sew your seams together to make permanent stitches, you will need to follow the same steps if hand sewing.

   a. Work on a flat surface so that the fabric does not stretch over your knee. If you are machine sewing, you will need to lower the presser foot first before you lower your needle into the fabric.

   b. Then stitch a couple of inches. Leave the needle in the fabric, and raise the presser foot. Release some of the fabric tension, and lower the foot again.

   c. While you sew, make sure you keep one hand in front of the feeding fabric and one behind to control the movement. Keep doing this until you are done with your seam. This will reduce the wrinkles and the ripples. (Figure 5.41b)

   d. Also, if you stitch along the basted seam, you will keep the bias edge from stretching even more.

6. When you are done stitching, press all of your seams.

   a. Make sure you press in the same direction you stitched to keep the fabric from wrinkling. Also, avoid pressing a lot of weight on the fabric to keep the bias from stretching.

   b. Now you can trim your seam allowances to ⅝ inch.

7. When you are ready to hem the garment and/or the sleeves, piece it on a hanger or the dress form for at least twenty-four hours to allow it to stretch down, and then work on a rolled hem.

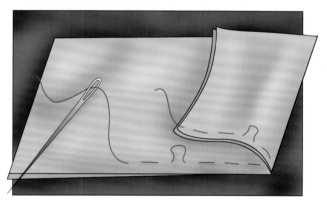

Figure 5.41a Basting bias patterns.

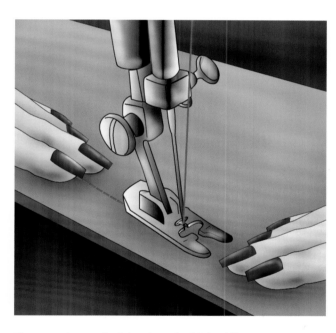

Figure 5.41b Keep both hands on the fabric while you are sewing to keep the fabric moving instead of stretching the fabric.

Cowl Draping

Cowls have been around for centuries. (Figure 5.42a) A cowl can be added at the neckline, armhole, and hips. It can also be placed in both the front and the back of the body. (Figure 5.42b) If you desire to add a cowl to your garment, make sure you choose a softer fabric so that it drapes well.

You can use the fabric to drape, not the muslin, so that you can see how it will drape and be able to control it. With muslin, you may not be able to get the same drape because it is very stiff. If you desire to add a cowl to both the front and back of the garment, you need to use a strap on either side to hold the cowl from sliding off your shoulders.

A cowl can be draped as one piece with the bodice, or it can be sewn onto the cut open neckline. To drape the one-piece **cowl neckline**, you will need to get your fabric ready.

1. Cut a square of fabric the length you desire to work with. You will need to find a bias at a 45-degree angle by folding the fabric on the bias line. Pat down on the fold with your hands to mark the bias.

2. Mark the depth of your cowl drape. Place a pin in the dress form to mark it. Then place two pins along the shoulder line to mark the width of the cowl.

3. Fold the top corner to the inside of the fabric.

4. Make sure the fold line is wide enough to drape from one mark on the shoulder to the other side mark while draping around the depth mark. (Figure 5.43)

5. Also, make sure you have at least 2 extra inches for the folds and seam allowances as well. If you are planning to have a lot of folds, make sure you leave even more extra fabric.

6. The folded fabric will serve as a facing for your cowl.

7. To begin draping, pin the muslin at the shoulders so that the center bias line you marked earlier lines up with your depth mark and the **center front** line. (Figure 5.44a)

8. You will be draping it on the bias of the fabric.

Figure 5.42a Cowl neckline.

Figure 5.42b Cowl neckline on the back of the dress.

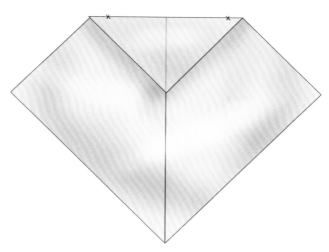

Figure 5.43 Preparing your muslin to drape your cowl neckline.

9. Allow your fabric to drop and drape around the depth mark pin. If you pull too tight, you will lose your cowl.

10. Now you can begin adding folds or small pleats at the shoulder.

11. Make sure your folds are similar and equal on both sides of the body. This way you will get even cowl drapes.

12. The distance between the pleated folds will cause wider drapes. If you want softer, smaller drapes, gather at the shoulder instead of pleating.

13. When you get the desired drape look, you can begin working on the lower piece of the garment.

14. To start, pin the bias line all the way down under the cowl along the center front line. If you have a deep cowl, you can drape the rest of the garment like a bias slip dress, stretching the fabric both ways with no darts.

15. If your cowl is small and high up near the neck, you may have some extra bulk, and a dart may be needed on the straight grain, forming a French dart.

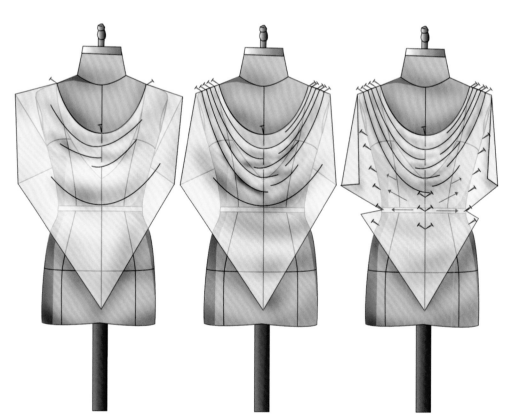

Figure 5.44a Pin the muslin at the shoulders, begin pleating and/or gathering along the shoulder seam line, smooth below your drapery to the waist and pin, smooth toward your side seams, clip into the waist, and pin up and around the armholes.

16. When you are done draping, mark all of your pleats on one of the shoulders. Then take the pattern off the form, keeping the folds pinned.
   a. True one side of the cowl at the shoulder, and then fold along the bias center line and trace the markings to the other side. (Figure 5.44b) Now both of your sides are equal.
   b. Add seam allowances, and attach to the back pattern.
   c. Place it back on the form and fit. If the facing seems to pull, trim it shorter, cutting off the corner. Make sure not to trim off too much or you will cut off the facing. (Figure 5.44c)
   d. If you decide to add the cowl to the back of the body, follow the same steps you followed for the front cowl.

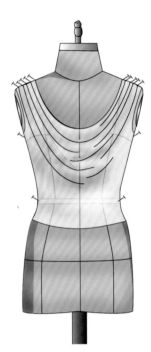

Figure 5.44c Pin the cowl back on the dress form to check the drape and the fit.

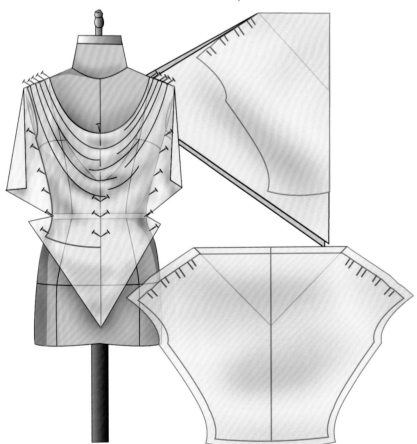

Figure 5.44b Mark only one side of the muslin along the side seams, and mark all of your pleats in place. Take the muslin off the dress form; fold the muslin in half along the bias line, and then true the pattern while folded to make both sides of the pattern symmetrical.

Cowl Variations

Examples of cowl variations (Figure 5.45a and b)

LINING

No matter how your outside piece was draped and structured, your lining should always be cut and sewn on the grain if the garment is on the grain. This is very important to hold the garment on the body and to keep it from stretching, shifting, and puckering.

When you are making an asymmetrical garment on the bias and would like to keep the entire garment on the bias, you will need to cut and sew the lining on the same bias so that it will not pull the garment in a different direction from the top layer. Sometimes you may be able to make a bias dress that will line itself with the same fabric, and you can cut the main garment and lining together on the same bias of the fabric.

Figure 5.45a and b Cowl examples.

MADELEINE VIONNET

Madeleine Vionnet was born in 1876. When she was twelve years old, she became an apprentice to a dressmaker in Paris. By the age of fifteen, she worked in London for dressmaker Kate Reilly. Reilly bought designs from couture houses in Paris, and Vionnet helped her copy them for clients.

Evening dress, 1938.

In her late teens, she became an apprentice for the Callot sisters in Paris, and in five years she was hired by Jacques Doucet. Here Vionnet was able to design novel ideas for new clients on her own.

By the time she was thirty-six in 1912, she opened her own fashion house in Paris. Her house did well until World War I, when she had to close it down, She reopened it after the war. Once this house was successful, she opened another one in New York in 1925, which was the first house to create prêt-a-porter designs for the US market. Every actress and royal lady wanted a Vionnet gown.

Vionnet was again forced to close her house during World War II. She retired in 1939.

Vionnet liberated women from uncomfortable corsets and designed gowns that were free, feminine, and graceful and allowed women to breathe. She was the first to introduce exposed arms, backs, and even some cleavage on her own gowns. These gowns were all cut on the bias of the fabric, and Vionnet became known as an expert of bias-cut fabric because she knew exactly how the textiles had to be cut on the bias to match every curve of the body.

Her designs were inspired by Greek art. Her styles were the result of a very long process of draping and pinning fabrics to miniature dolls; the designs were then re-created in life-size. When Vionnet ordered her fabric, she always ordered two extra yards to give her enough fabric for her designs. She enjoyed designing dresses that could be slipped over the head with ease and worn comfortably. Many of her designs did not even have closures because the bias she created stretched enough to be slipped on without a zipper. Vionnet loved to replace darts in the bust with twists and gathers. When she sewed garments, she liked to use overcast seams, and she clipped all of the curved seams so they would lie flat. Vionnet also liked to make very narrow seams to reduce bulk and wrinkles or eliminate side seams altogether if the design allowed for it.

Evening dress, 1938.

Vionnet used to cut her circular skirts and then hang them on a dress form for forty-eight hours so that the bias could stretch before the hem was sewn.

To this day, Vionnet is known for changing the way couturiers use bias fabric, and she inspires new and upcoming designers every day.

Madeleine Vionnet died in 1975 at age ninety-nine, and she is still a couture legend.

Chapter Review

Draping is a technique used commonly in couture. In draping, fabric is directly draped over a dress form, which makes it easier to see the design while the pattern is made up.

When you drape, it allows you the freedom to design something out of the ordinary and get really creative. You can drape with asymmetry, make pleats in different spots, add gathers and twists, and drape on the bias to get a very snug fit. Draping is sometimes the easiest way to get your design to come to life because it may be too hard or impossible to get there with a flat pattern. In this chapter, you learned the concept of draping and the importance of the grainline. You practiced draping blocks for your garments and reviewed the details of draping by adding pleats, tucks, gathers, and twists. Draping blocks can also help you turn them into other patterns like halters and corsets, the same way you would turn a block flat pattern into another pattern.

In this chapter, you read about bias draping, which is another type of draping where the garment is draped on the bias of the fabric. You can get even more creative by adding a bias into your design. Bias draping gives you an opportunity to add a softer drape or make a closer fit.

Projects

1. Drape a bias-cut slip dress. Choose one of the two types covered in this chapter. Make sure you true your pattern and pin it together to check fit. Then sew this dress out of a fashion fabric of your choice.
2. Drape a cowl neckline top with a style of your own design. Include one texture covered in this chapter (tucks, crunching, pleats, or gathers).
3. Drape an outfit of your design using five of the techniques you learned in this chapter.
4. Drape a corset top and decorate it with tucks, pleats, crunching, or gathers.
5. Use Madeleine Vionnet as an inspiration. Find a picture of one of Vionnet's dresses. Design and drape a garment influenced by the Vionnet dress.

Key Terms

Apex	Cowl neckline	Pleats
Bias	Cross grain	Princess seams
Block	Draping	Shoulder blade level
Center back	Gathers	Squaring the fabric
Center front	Grainline	True bias
Chest level	Lengthwise grain	Tucks
Corset	Muslin	Twist

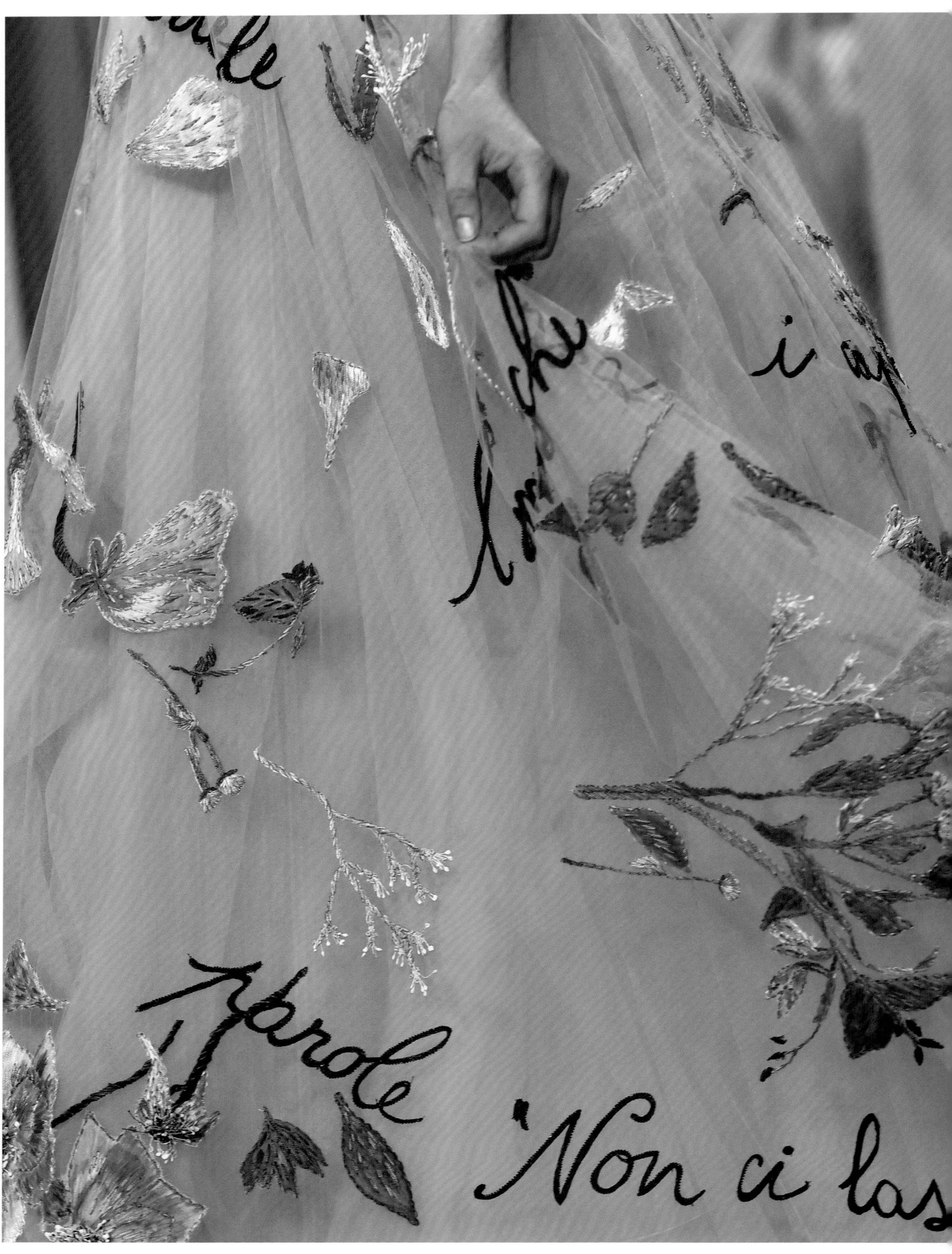
parole
'Non ci las

6

The Art of Skirts

Objectives

• **Learn the concept of draping and drafting skirts**

• **Learn the concept of yokes, darts, and waistbands**

• **Learn how to work with crinolline and hooped petticoats**

• **Learn how to work with bustles**

• **Learn about the life and work of Cristobal Balenciaga**

Skirts

In the past, during the large petticoat and long train years, a skirt was draped on a woman ordering a dress. The skirt was made to fit over her hips, and the maker checked the customer's walking ability while wearing the toile sample. This helped save time and added perfection to the pattern as well as customer satisfaction and comfort.

Skirts are a very important part of women's dress and have always been a symbol of a feminine look. A skirt completes an entire dressed up look and comes in many shapes, lengths, and fullnesses. To be a great designer, you must think of the entire silhouette of the garment and use all of the different ways you can change the shape of the skirt, such as dart rotation, adding flare, fullness, pleats, or gathers. (Figure 6.1)

Skirt Draping

FRONT SLOPER

1. Measure the distance from the waist down to the hem of your skirt; add 4 inches. Clip the muslin, and tear along the grainline. Then at the **hip level** (7 to 9 inches below the waist), measure from the center front to the side seam; add 4 inches, clip, and tear. Press the piece. Your muslin piece is ready to drape. (Figure 6.2)
2. Mark your muslin.
   a. Begin draping on the left side of the dress form front. On your muslin, measure 1 inch from the right side; draw a line with your marking tool along the

Figure 6.1 A unique full skirt silhouette.

length of the muslin marking the front line. Fold the muslin under along this line, and press down.
   b. Measure down 2 inches from the top of the muslin for the waist level, and mark.
   c. Measure 7 to 9 inches down from the waist, marking the hip level.

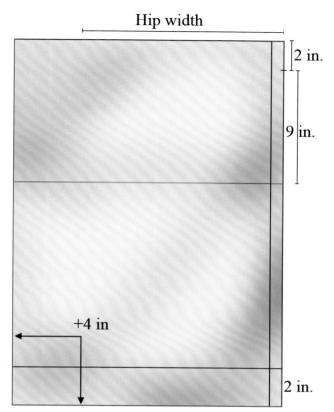

Figure 6.2 Preparing muslin.

Hip width

2 in.

9 in.

+4 in

2 in.

Hint: Hip level varies. Curvier women have a shorter hip length from the waist to the widest hip level. Less curvy women have a longer length between the waist and the widest hip level.

    d. Draft a line along the hip level perpendicular to the Center Front (CF).

    e. Two inches from the bottom of the muslin, mark the hem level, drafting a line perpendicular to the Center Front (CF).

3. Begin draping. Pin the waist point at the center front, with the sharp pin side facing the side seam.

4. Pin downward along the Center Front (CF) all the way to the bottom of the dress form. (Figure 6.3a, b, and c)

5. With your left hand, smooth the muslin along the hip level toward the side seam, and pin at the side seam, with the pin facing the center front. Keep the hip level parallel to the floor to keep the correct grainline.

6. Smooth the muslin down along the side seam, and pin downward toward the bottom of the dress form, with the pins facing the Center Front (CF).

7. To fit the hip and the dart, smooth the fabric up along the side seam from the hip level, and pin at the waist.

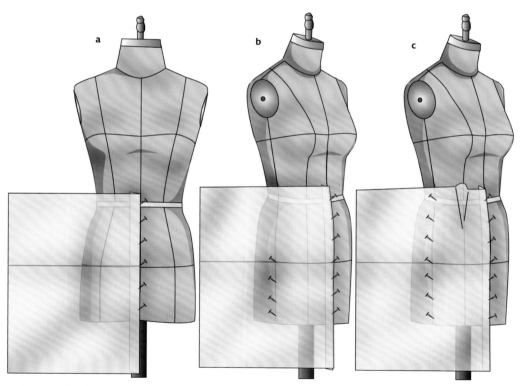

Figure 6.3a, b, and c Front draping.

8. The bulk of fabric at the waistline will become a dart. To form the dart, smooth the muslin from the side waist point to the princess line, and pin down. Then smooth the fabric from the center front waist to the princess line, and pin.

   a. Depending on how curvy the dress form is, the dart sometimes ends with the drill hole at the hip level line; however, sometimes it may end above the hip level.

   b. Keep in mind that the drill hole should not be more than 6 inches below the waistline and does not always fall on the princess line.

9. Mark the entire pattern, using your finger to feel every seam line through the muslin. Mark the waistline through the center of the tape originally placed on the dress form. Mark the side seam and dart. The end of the fabric bulk is the drill hole; Mark it with an X.

10. Unpin the entire muslin of your front bodice block.

11. True the pattern using a ruler.

   a. Use a French curve to fix the hip line and the waistline if it curves down toward the center front from the side.

   b. Make sure the dart legs are the same length. If they are not, move the drill hole a bit and connect your dart legs. You can curve them inward ⅛ inch to offer a better fit on a curvier body.

   c. Add seam allowances. Cut.

   d. Pin the dart together, and check the fit. (Figure 6.4a–e)

Hint: You can divide the bulk of one dart into two darts for a closer fit.

BACK SLOPER

1. Measure the distance from the waist down to the hem of skirt; add 4 inches, matching your front pattern. Clip and tear.

2. At the hip level (7 to 9 inches below the waist), measure from the center front to the side seam; add 4 inches, clip, and tear. Make sure the hip line matches the front pattern. Press.

3. You will be draping on the right side of the back of the dress form.

   a. On your muslin, measure 1 inch from the left side, and draft a Center Back (CB) line along the length of the muslin. Fold under and press.

   b. Measure down 2 inches from the top of the muslin, and mark the Center Back (CB) waist level.

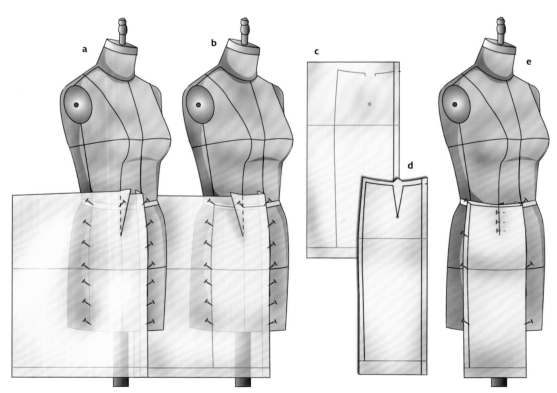

Figure 6.4 a–e Front draping continued.

c. Measure 7 to 9 inches down from this waist, marking the hip level. Draft a line along the hip level perpendicular to the Center Back (CB).

d. Mark the hem level 2 inches from the bottom of the muslin. (Figure 6.5)

4. Pin the waist at the Center Back (CB) of the form, with the pin facing toward the side seam. Continue pinning down the Center Back (CB) to the bottom.

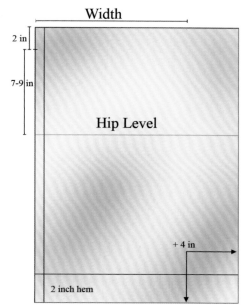

Figure 6.5 Preparing muslin.

5. With your left hand, smooth the muslin along the hip level toward the side seam, and pin at the side seam. Make sure the hip level is parallel to the floor and matches the hip level of the front pattern. You can measure to the floor from the hip level to be sure.

6. Smooth the muslin down along the side seam, and pin down at the side seam all the way to the bottom of the dress form.

7. To form the hip and the dart, smooth the fabric up along the side seam from the hip level, and pin at the waist.

8. The bulk of fabric at the waistline will become a dart. To form the dart, smooth the muslin with your left hand from the side waist point to the princess seam, and pin. Now with your left hand, smooth the fabric from the center back waist to the princess line, and pin at the princess line.

9. You have just made a dart. Depending on how curvy the dress form is, the dart sometimes ends with the drill hole at the hip level line; however, sometimes it may end above or below the hip level. (Figure 6.6a–d)

10. Mark the pattern using your finger to feel every seam line through the muslin. Mark the waistline through the center of the tape originally placed on the dress form, and then mark the side seam and the dart legs. Try to see where the dart seams end. Mark the end of the fold with an X. This will be your drill hole.

11. Unpin the entire muslin.

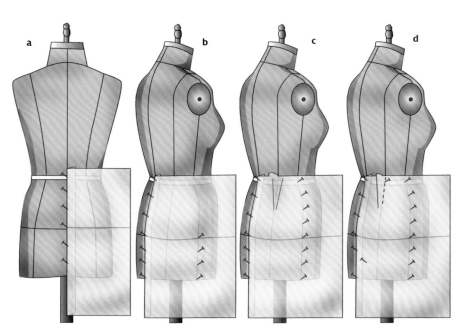

Figure 6.6 a–d Back draping.

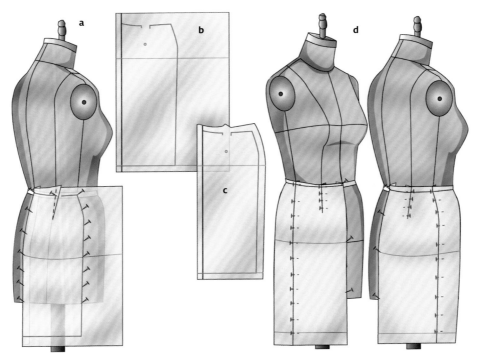

Figure 6.7a–d Back draping continued.

12. True the pattern, add seam allowances, and pin the dart closed.
13. Check the fit. (Figure 6.7a–d)

Hint: To make the skirt flare out a little, you can add some width to the bottom of the skirt while truing the pattern.

Darts

Skirt waist **Darts** are added to allow a great fit around the waistline because they allow a wider cylinder around the hips to fit tighter around the waist. By folding up the darts, the cylinder gets narrower. In pattern drafting, darts offer a great opportunity for designers to add details by moving darts, rotating darts, or using style lines. This gives us infinite design possibilities.

When we describe darts, we refer to a triangular shape along the waistline that points down. In patterns, the dart sides, called dart legs, should always be equal in length. The dart point, called the drill hole, is marked with a small dot inside a circle. Making a smooth dart point without leaving a small gather is important; you would not want to have two or more puckers directly over the lower abdomen and stomach area.

SEWING DARTS

1. Mark the dart legs ½ inch above the drill hole.
2. Using your marked dart notches, fold the dart with the fabric face-to-face, and pin along the marked dart legs.
3. Start stitching your folded triangle along the marked line. Stop stitching at your mark ½ inch away from the drill hole.
4. Slowly stitch down to the point of your triangle.
5. As you reach the point and stitch toward the end point of the dart, stop stitching, lift the presser foot, and pull some thread out of the needle and bobbin. Cut your thread, leaving long enough tails to tie a knot by hand. (Figure 6.8a and b)
6. Tie a couple of knots for more strength. Make sure your knot is at the dart point. Leaving it loose will make the far tip open up. (Also make sure you are not pulling the thread too tight when you make the knots, as it can gather up at the seam.)

PRESSING DARTS

1. First press the dart flat down over the ironing surface.
2. Then press the dart to one side toward the center of the body. It is always best to use a piece of cardstock

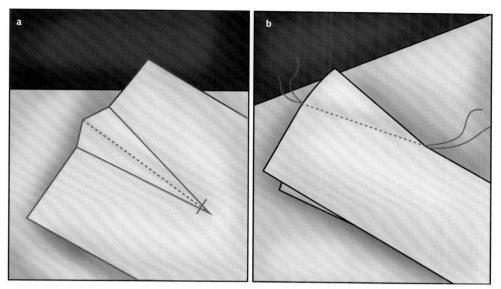

Figure 6.8a and b Sewing darts.

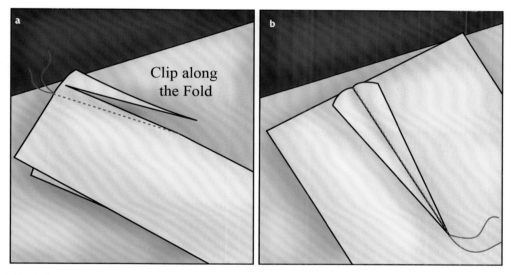

Figure 6.9a and b Bulky darts.

paper with a straight edge underneath the dart when you fold it over to the side to prevent the dart from engraving a dart outline on the right side of your garment.

BULKY DARTS

Bulky darts? No problem. Follow these steps to reduce bulk.
1. First press the dart flat down over the ironing surface.
2. Clip off the dart fold, and leave a ¼-inch seam allowance away from the seam of your dart.
3. If nessesary to remove more bulk, clip into the corner of the dart point seam allowance. Be careful not to cut too far; stop your scissor point ¹⁄₁₆ inch away from the dart point seam.
4. Press seam open using a piece of cardstock paper with a straight edge underneath both of the dart seam allowances to avoid the seam allowance edges engraving an outline on the right side of your garment. (Figure 6.9a and b)

CREATING BALANCED DARTS

When sewing a dart and pressing it to one side, your garment may sometimes pull your fabric unevenly or make it roll down on the opposite side. This may force extra attention to your darts when the garment is worn, and darts are usually the least pleasing details in the entire garment design. For better quality and a tailored look, sometimes its best to make your regular darts into balanced darts.

A balanced dart helps you distribute the weight of your dart evenly to both sides while keeping the outside face of your garment flat and smooth around the dart area.

Making a balanced dart requires your garment and one strip of the same fabric to offer equal weight and thickness. Cut the strip to be a bit longer and at least three times wider than your dart when folded closed. Mark the center of the strip using your chalk.

1. Before you sew your dart, pin it closed, lining up your dart notches with your fabric face-to-face. Alternatively, you can baste it ⅛ inch away from your marked seam line.

2. To begin sewing, place your fabric strip under the dart so that the strip is low enough that the center line of the strip aligns with your dart fold. Pin through your layers to hold them together.

3. Stitch the dart through all of the layers the same way you would do a regular dart, leaving the thread tails at the dart point and making a well-secured knot. Then, using the edge of your dart fold as a guide, fold up both layers of your strip fabric, and cut off the excess fabric. You want both sides of the dart to be the same shape, width, and weight. (Figure 6.10a–e)

4. Press your dart to one side of your garment and the strip to the opposite side. Use a pressing ham to help you press, especially when you have a curved dart or a fish-eye dart (2-point dart).

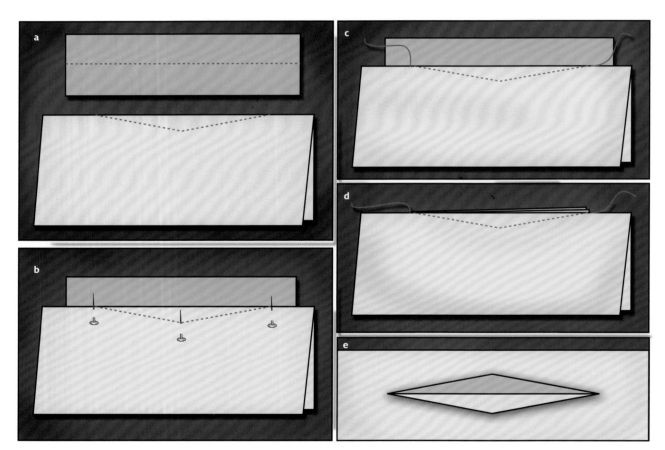

Figure 6.10a–e Balanced dart.

Yokes

A **Yoke** is another way to be able to add a nice fit at a skirt waist without using darts. A yoke can be made in many shapes, and is similar to a style line. (Figure 6.11)

1. In order to eliminate darts, the style lineneeds to go through the drill holes. (Figure 6.14) Then the pattern can be divided into two parts, A and B.

2. Part A is then be taped shut at the dart openings (legs).

3. Now it is one pattern piece and a yoke. This piece can be a different color, fabric, or texture. You can do some fabric manipulations, such as pleats, tucks, gathers, crunching, quilting, and so much more. (Figure 6.13)

A yoke can also be used to eliminate both the front and the back darts, although there is one problem with this technique. The darts on the back pattern are longer than

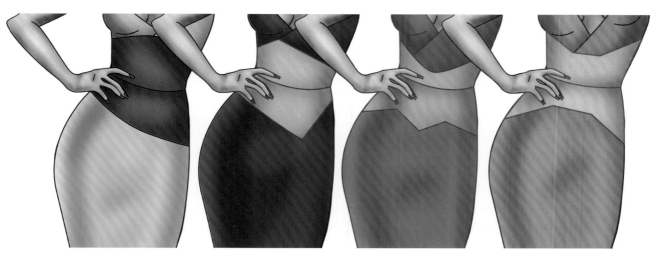

Figure 6.11 Yokes.

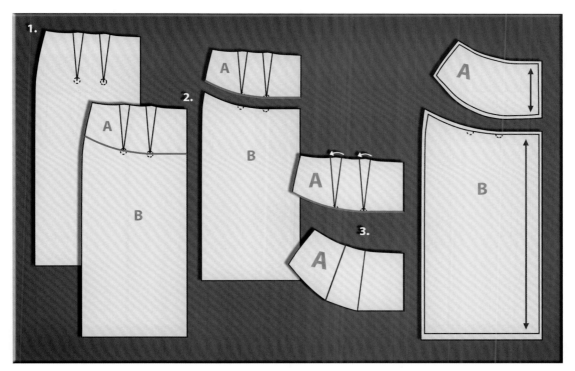

Figure 6.12 Drafting yokes.

the front darts. When you make a front yoke and take the style line to the side seams, the back yoke needs to continue in a smooth line connecting at the side seam. In other words, the yoke seams need to match and line up during construction. However, the back darts are longer.

1. Cut into the back darts. This will leave a small dart below the yoke. Stitch the little dart closed before connecting the yoke to the lower section of the skirt. If the darts are tiny, try to ease them into the seam. Darts can also be taken out when the lower section of the skirt is turned into a full, flared, or pleated skirt.

2. Try to use creative ideas with the style line of the yoke. Asymmetry and diagonal lines can add interesting details to your yoke and completely eliminate the dart. (Figure 6.13)

YOKE ASSEMBLY

Yokes are often patterned with a sharp corner or curve. It is essential to know the steps it takes to correctly attach both the yoke and the rest of the skirt to avoid seam puckering. The seam needs to be smooth and flat to complement the short silhouette. If the yoke has a sharp corner, whether it's an inside corner or outer pointed corner, it is important to perfect the skirt patterns with the proper notches to help you line the pieces back together.

1. Begin by cutting out the fabric pieces. Pay close attention to the grainlines. Mark all notches, especially the Center Front (CF) and Center Back (CB) notches, and all corner points. (Figure 6.14a–f)

2. Before you begin sewing, reinforce the pieces to prevent the stretching of the fabric along the bias areas of the seams. Stay stitch around the patterns, or fuse a small strip of fusible interfacing inside the seam allowances.

3. Use your small clippers or shears to clip your seam allowances.
   a. For corners, clip straight into the corner, stopping close to the corner point mark. Clipping allows the inner corner piece to open and bend backward to match with the other pattern piece pointed outward.
   b. If you are sewing a curved yoke seam, clip into the inner curve piece to allow it to open up and be flexible enough to shape a seam similar to the curve bent outward on the second pattern piece.

4. Line up your pieces by pinning your fabric face-to-face along the seams. Begin by matching up your Center Front and Center Back notches first to make sure that the yokes are centered.

5. If the skirt has a Center Back (CB) closure, then first attach the yoke to the front. Then complete both back pieces separately with the yokes attached to the lower pieces of the skirt.

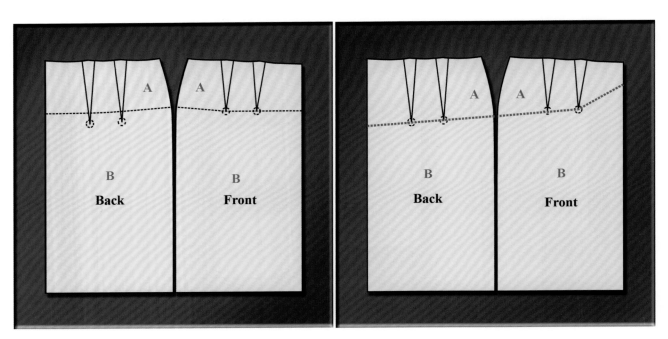

Figure 6.13 Yoke front to back.

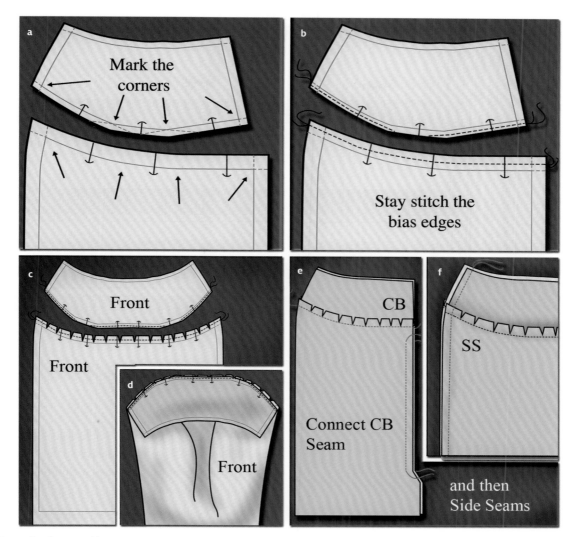

Figure 6.14a–f Yoke assembly.

6. Press the seam allowances upward toward the waist area. Add the zipper, and finish the kick pleat.
7. Next, close the side seams.

Hint: It is very helpful to work away from the center point in both directions when sewing, especially on diagonal and curved seam lines, as well as stitch away in both directions from the corner points. This will help you avoid puckers in the corners.

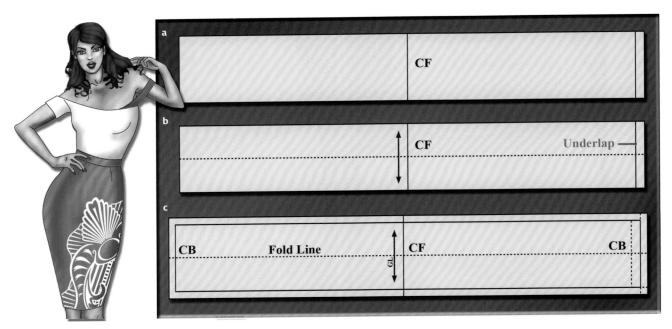

Figure 6.15 Waistband.

Waistbands

Waistbands add strength to our skirts and pants during wear and help them stay up along our waistlines. Waistbands are also a great way to add detail to our designs.

ABOVE THE WAIST

A straight waistband placed above the waistline at all times can stay straight if kept within 2 inches above the waist. Anything higher than 2 inches will begin cutting into the curved area of a woman's body shape and will need to follow different shaping rules. (Figure 6.15)

1. Make a regular rectangle shape matching the length of the waistline plus the underlap or the overlap on one side. The overlap/underlap can be between 1 and 3 inches depending on the design desired and the clasp.
2. The width of the rectangle should be double the width desired.
3. Mark the center line dividing two long sides of the rectangle in half. This will be your fold line. Add seam allowances.

POINTED WAISTBAND

The bottom of the band is a straight line along the waist, and the top of the band is pointed up in the center front or back. You can also use the same technique pointing the waistband downward.

1. Make a regular rectangle shape matching to the length of the waistline. The width of the rectangle should be a single width. Decide on the placement of your zipper, side or center back.
2. If the zipper is in the center back and the desired point is in the center front, then you can divide the rectangle in half and mark the line. This is your Center Front (CF).
3. Now you can add a pointed corner extending above the waistband. Use a French curve or a hip curve ruler to get a smooth curve. The curve down from the corner should not extend more than 3 inches wide. It helps to mark a 3-inch notch away from the Center Front (CF). (Figure 6.16)
4. When one side is complete, you can fold the belt along the Center Front (CF) line and trace the point curve to the opposite side. Add seam allowances.
5. This will be your outer waistband. Trace another to use as an under waistband (facing).

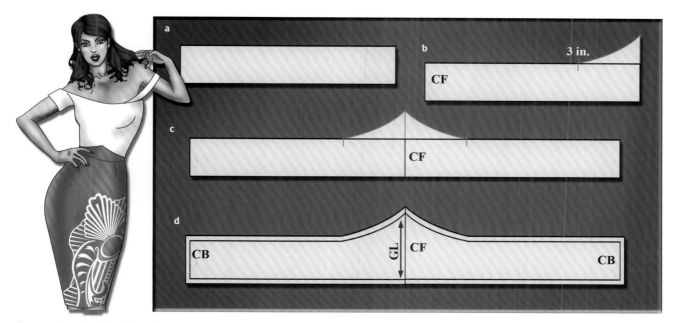

Figure 6.16 Pointed waistband.

HIGH WAISTBAND

When the waistband is designed higher than 2 inches above the waistline, it has to be treated like a yoke; therefore the pattern will be shaped and curved using the upper body slopers.

1. To begin, use your front or back bodice slopers, and trace the lower portion below the darts to use for the waistband.
2. Draw your desired shape on the pattern piece. Cut out the pattern. (Figure 6.17a–e)
3. Tape the darts closed. Add a back under/overlap.
4. When one side is complete, fold the belt along the Center Front (CF) line and trace the point curve to the opposite side. Add seam allowances.
5. This will be your outer waistband. Trace another to use as an under waistband (facing).

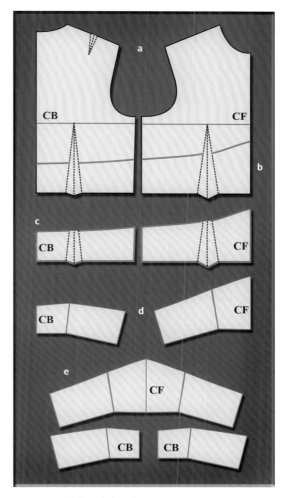

Figure 6.17a–e High waistband.

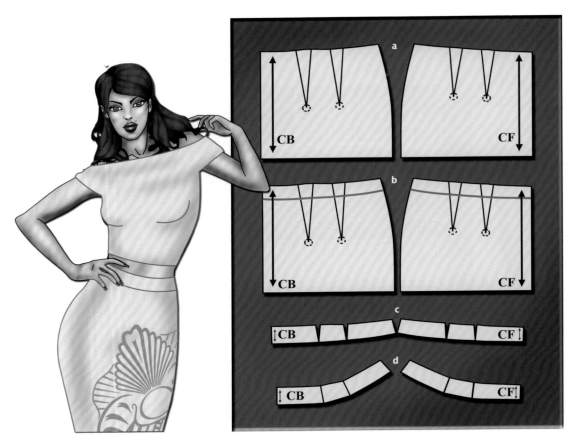

Figure 6.18 Contour waistband.

CONTOUR WAISTBAND

1. To begin, trace front or back skirt slopers. Draw your desired shape on the pattern piece, similar to a yoke but narrower. Mark the same width from the waistband for both front and back pattern pieces.

2. Cut along the style line marked to separate the waistband from the skirt on both the front and back.

3. For the waistband area, tape the darts closed. This will turn it into one single pattern piece.

4. Continue with two separate pieces for the waistband front and back. This will add a seam down the side seam of the waistband. This also helps with the proper grainline. The Center Front is parallel to the grainline, as well as the Center Back (CB).

5. Add a Back under/overlap if you desire a back zipper closure or a side overlap for a side seam closure. If desired, sew the zipper though the waistband without a flap.

6. When one side is complete, you can fold the belt along the Center Front line and trace the point curve to the opposite side. Add seam allowances.

7. Do the same for the Center Back if you are adding a side closure.

8. If you are adding a back closure, you will need to add seam allowances to your one side waistband piece and then cut two during fabric cutting. This will be your outer waistband. Trace another to use as an under waistband (facing). (Figure 6.18)

SEWING WAISTLINES

We move around daily, and the clothes we wear move with us. Waistbands need to help us move comfortably but at the same time must be strong enough to allow us to go about our everyday lives.

You can add a waist stay made of grosgrain ribbon to the waistband inner structrure. Stitch a seam attaching it to the facing layer of the waistband directly above the waistline seam. See the section in Chapter 12 on waist stays.

Fusible Interfacing

1. Fusing the waistband is best with ArmoWeft interfacing. This interfacing can move with the fabric because it is loosely woven and is more flexible while offering more stability to the fabric.
2. Cut one side of your pattern using the interfacing fabric and no seam allowances if you are making a two-layer waistband with a separate facing piece.
3. If you are making a waistband with a top fold, you will need to cut the interfacing to be only one side of the waistband in width but the same length and with no seam allowances. (Figure 6.19a)
4. Line up your interfacing piece to the top and bottom seam lines along the outer side of the waistband.
5. Make sure that the waistband wrong side is facing up and the fusible strip is facing down with the glue side.
6. Press the interfacing piece to your fabric using a pressing cloth to protect your iron and the fusible. Before taking the waistband off the ironing board, check to make sure that the fusible is well attached to the fabric and cooled. Removing it in hot form may loosen the

fusible glue and cause it to separate from your fabric, creating air bubbles.

Sew-In Interfacing

You can also use sew-in interfacing. This could be a piece of cotton or a stiffer fabric such as canvas or horsehair interfacing.

1. Cut one side of your pattern using the interfacing fabric and no seam allowances if you are making a two-layer waistband with a separate facing piece.
2. Follow the same steps 3–5 from the Fusible Interfacing method.
3. You will need to attach the interfacing to the outer side of the waistband; therefore, make sure that the wrong side of the waistband fabric is facing up when you line up the interfacing strip. Use your pins to secure the strip in place.
4. Use a needle and thread to hand baste a temporary seam down the center of the interfacing strip attaching it to the waistband fabric side.
5. Now, you can run a catch stitch seam attaching the interfacing to the waistband along the seam allowances on the bottom and sides.
6. When you are making this stitch, make sure to catch only threads of the interfacing when catching the interfacing side and only the threads of the waistband fabric when catching on the fabric side. (Figure 6.19b)

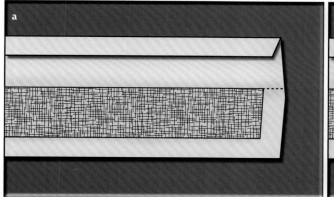 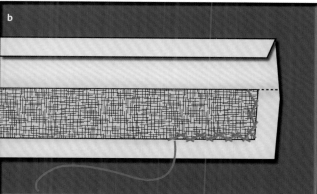

Figure 6.19a Fusible interfacing.

Figure 6.19b Sew-in interfacing.

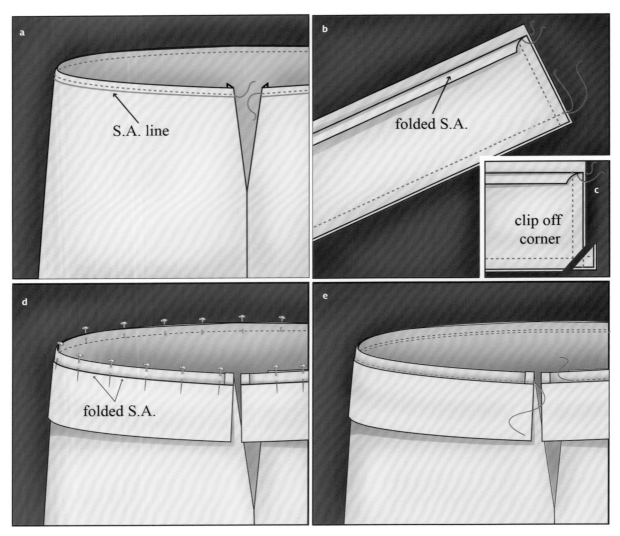

Figure 6.20a–e Waistband assembly.

ATTACHING YOUR WAISTBAND

There are two commonly used methods, both very similar except for the last couple of steps. The first method finishes the waistband by hand, and the second by machine.

1. Secure your waistline with a stay stitch along your skirt waist. Example shows ½ inch seam allowance therefore we are stay-stitching at 3/8 inch away from the edge.

2. If you are sewing a two-piece waistband, attach both the waistband side and its facing side together face-to-face along the top seam line of the waistband. Press seam allowances in toward the inside (wrong side).

3. Fold back your waistband sides face-to-face, keeping one side still pressed back at the seam allowance area.

4. Begin stitching from the fold line of the shorter side down toward the waistband fold.

5. To complete your corner and flip it, you need to first clip off your corner on both ends and then clip off some of your seam allowances close to your corner to at least ¹⁄₁₆ inch from the seam line.

6. Flip your corners and use a sharp edge to help you make a nice, sharp, 90-degree corner. Press your corners and fold.

7. Match up your waistband facing edge seam allowance to your skirt face-to-face using your notches at the Center Front and the side seams.

8. To secure it in place, use pins or a basting stitch to hold the pieces together.
9. Make sure that the zipper side aligns with the edge of the waistband on both ends.
10. Stitch a straight stitch, attaching the waistband to the skirt. (Figure 6.20a–e)

1. Press your seam flat, and then press the seam allowances upward away from the skirt in order to remove bulk from the skirt.
2. Match up the fold of your waistband over your seam, and stitch it closed. Make sure your seam allowances are still pressed up into the waistband.

3. To attach the inside waistband, you can use the slip stitch hand sewing method with a single strand of thread. Attach the fold line of the waistband to the skirt. (Figure 6.21a and b)
4. Another method is called "Stitch in the ditch":
   a. Pin the inside waistband with the fold covering the seam line, and pass it slightly about ⅛ inch. Baste the waistband to secure it in place (or pin).
   b. Turn your skirt right side up, and stitch a straight seam in the grove of your seam line. Work slowly; to avoid a slanted seam, it is important to hide it from view on the right side. (Figure 6.21c and d)

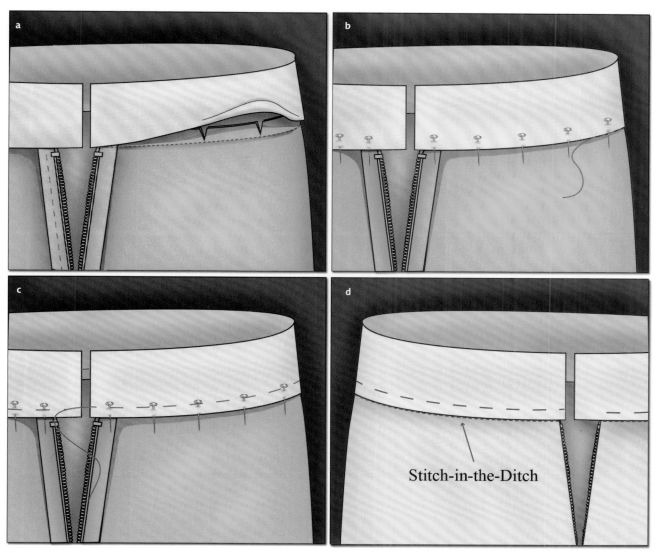

Stitch-in-the-Ditch

Figure 6.21a–d Waistband assembly continued.

SEWING A CURVED WAISTBAND

1. To sew the curved waistbands, the method requires two waistbands, the outer and the under waistband (facing).
2. Connect the waistband outer patterns face-to-face at the side seams. Then connect the waistband facing patterns face-to-face at the side seams. Press open.
3. Match up both the outer side and the facing face-to-face along the upper seam allowance. Pin.
4. Stitch a regular seam along the pinned seam line. Press flat first, and then press toward the facing side to get it ready for understitching.
5. Understitch the facing side through all the layers. Press the facing folded right side out.
6. Match up the waistband and skirt waist edge face-to-face using your notches and side seams. Clip into the seam allowance along the waistline to help the edge curve without any tension along the curve of the waistband. Pin.
7. Stitch a regular seam along the pinned seam line. Press flat first, and then press up toward the waistband.
8. Lower the facing side down over the seam allowance to help you fold it up. (Figure 6.22a–e)
9. Follow steps 13 and 14 from the previous section.

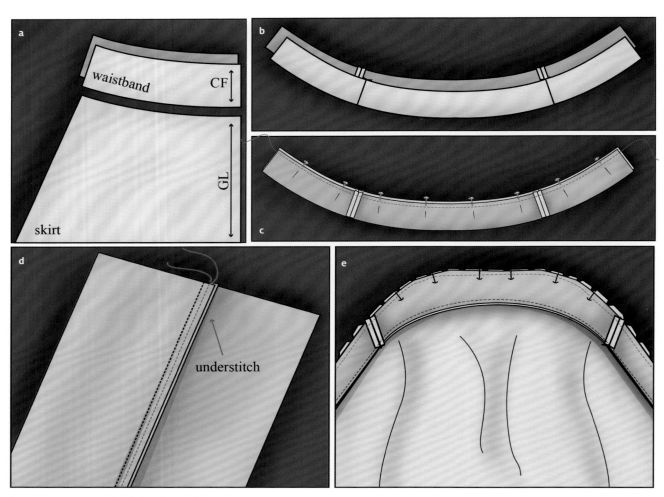

Figure 6.22a–e Curved waistband assembly.

Vents, Slits, or Kick Pleats

A vent is an extension to the seam allowance along the Center Back (CB), side seam, and sometimes the Center Front (CF) seam to allow more ease during movement. In skirts, vents, slits, and kick pleats help us take a step and walk in a tight skirt, long jacket, shirt, or coat. Our lower bodies get wider during sitting, and our clothes need to get wider as well without popping the garment seams and allow for a tailored look with the ease for movement. (Figure 6.23)

Figure 6.23 Vent.

VENT METHOD

1. To begin, trace your back skirt sloper.
2. Add a 1¼-inch wide extension to the Center Back (CB) from the hem up to the vent top edge.
3. Along the top of the extension, add a slanted angle up toward the Center Back (CB) line. Make it a bias angle of 45 degrees.
4. Add seam allowances, notch your zipper and vent, and cut it out.
5. Match up both sides of your skirt face-to-face (right sides).
6. Stitch from the zipper notch to the vent notch with a regular straight stitch.
7. Continue stitching down the same seam line to the hem fold using a basting larger stitch.
8. Clip the vent corner along the top vent notch. Press the vent sides open. Press the hem up along the hemline. You should now see vent corners on both sides of the vent.
9. Miter your corners. (Figure 6.24a–f)

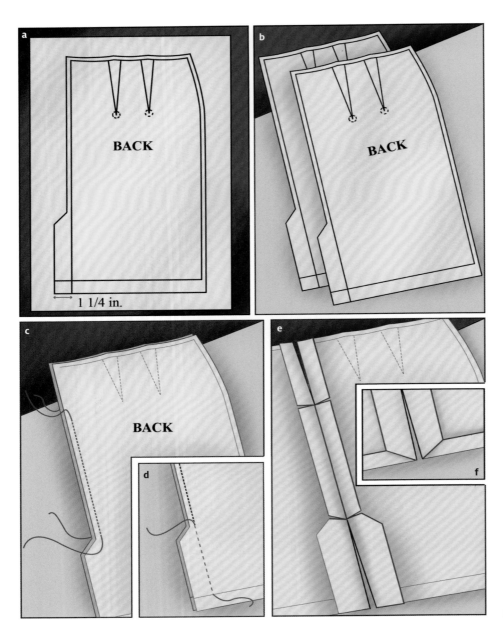

Figure 6.24a–f Vent assembly.

KICK OPEN VENT METHOD

1. To begin, trace the back skirt sloper and add a 1½- to 2-inch wide extension to the Center Back (CB) from the hem up to the vent top edge.
2. Along the top of the extension, add a slanted angle up toward the Center Back (CB) line. Make it a bias angle of 45 degrees.
3. Add seam allowances, notch your zipper and extension top corner, and cut it out.
4. Match up both sides of your skirt face-to-face (right sides)
5. To add more strength to the Center Back (CB) seam and the vent, add a strip of silk organza cut on grain to the seam allowance area along the Center Back (CB) seam line. Pin in place. (The silk organza adds an interfacing and stability to the seam and keeps it from stretching during the wear and sitting.)
6. Stitch from the zipper notch to the extension notch with a straight stitch. Insert your Center Back (CB) zipper.
7. Clip the corner along the top extension notch on one side. Press the extension sides to one side while pressing the back seam open. (Figure 6.25a–f)

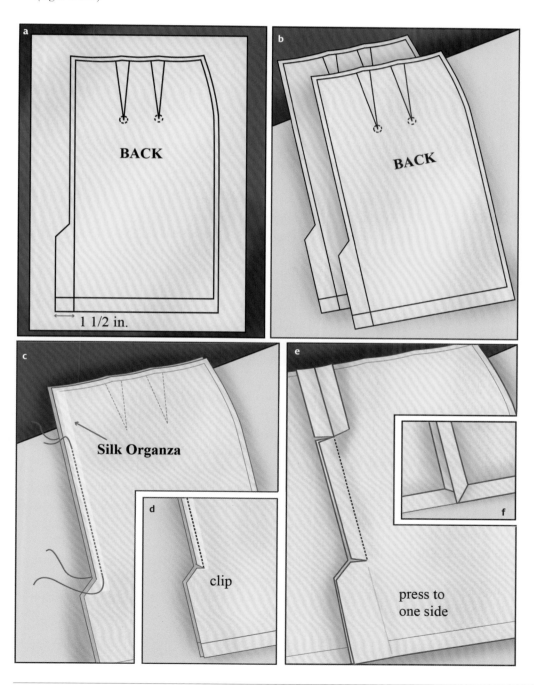

Figure 6.25a–f Kick open vent assembly.

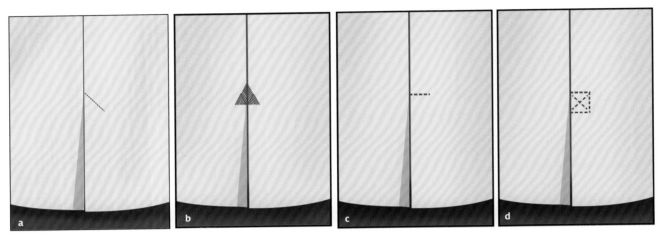

Figure 6.26a–d Vent stitches.

1. Press the hem up along the hemline. You should now see a corner on the side close to the ironing board. Miter that corner.
2. Pin down the top edge of the extension, which is now pressed to one side. Pin at the top, securing all layers of the skirt.
3. Make a small stitch across the extension top line ¼ inch below the top edge. Stitch through all of the layers. You can stitch a straight line, a diagonal line, or an embroidery stitch (arrowhead). (Figure 6.26a–d)

KICK PLEAT METHOD

1. To begin, trace the back skirt sloper.
2. Add your **kick pleat** extension to the Center Back (CB) in the following order:
   a. Add an underfold extension (A). This extension should be ¾ inch to 1 inch in width.
   b. Add another extension, which will fold out to make the back under pleat (B). This extension should be ¾ inch to 1 inch in width.
   c. Mark the line in between A and B with a dotted line. This will be a fold line.
   d. Mark the side edge line along the outer edge of the (B) extension as your new Center Back (CB) line for the kick pleat. This new Center Back (CB) is in addition to the skirt Center Back (CB) line above the kick pleat.
   e. Trace a mirror image of this entire skirt pattern, and attach it to the Center Back (CB) of the kick pleat.
   f. Add seam allowances and notch. Cut it out.

3. Match up both sides of your skirt face-to-face (right sides) from the waistline to your kick pleat corners.
4. If you are adding a Center Back (CB) zipper, you will be matching and pinning the skirt from the zipper notch down to the kick pleat corners only.
5. Stitch from the zipper notch to the extension corner with a regular stitch.
6. Clip the kick pleat corner, and press the Center Back (CB) seam above the pleat open.
7. Insert your Center Back zipper if you are adding one.
8. Press the kick pleat flat so that the Center Back (CB) of the kick pleat will line up along the Center Back (CB) seam of the skirt. In other words, flip the skirt right side up, and using fold notches along the bottom edge of the kick pleat match them up so that the side notch and the Center Back (CB) notch line up on both sides of the center back of the kick pleat. The Center Back (CB) seam of the skirt should also align with both folds of the pleat fold lines.
9. Flip the skirt back to the wrong side, and fold back the top seam allowances of your pleat. Pick up two layers of the pleat without catching the outer layer of the skirt. Pin to secure.
10. Stitch on both sides of the Center Back (CB). Often you can sew one seam along the top from one side of the Center Back (CB) to the other.
11. Press the skirt, and check your kick pleat. (Figure 6.27a–g)

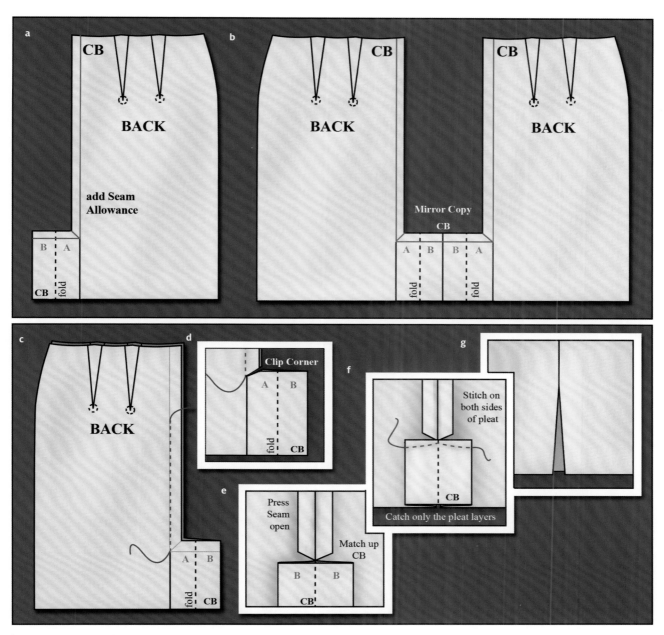

Figure 6.27a–g Kick pleat.

Gored and Mermaid Skirts

Gored skirts allow the skirt to follow the Grainline for a proper fit using panels without the use of darts. You can design a skirt with princess lines extended down from the waist and accomplish a skirt pattern split into gores. The gore panels are devided through the dart drill holes to eliminate the darts.

Gored skirts also allow designers more options to add flare to a skirt without wasting too much fabric as well as freedom to change the shape of a skirt at a certain level. It is important to understand how to add flare to your gores to achieve the correct drape and effect.

The **Mermaid (Trumpet) skirt** got its name for the silhouette shape it takes when the straight gored skirt begins to flare out toward the bottom hem, turning into a mermaid tail shape.

DRAFTING A GORED SKIRT

1. Trace your one dart skirt sloper, front and back. Draw a perpendicular line down from the drill hole to the hem for both front and back. This should devide the slopers into two panels for both sides. Label the pieces.
2. Add all the design features, length, waistline, and pocket placement.
3. This will make an eight-gore skirt, a six-gore skirt if the center front and center back panels are cut on a fold, or seven-gore skirt if the center front is cut on a fold and the center back panels are cut apart to form a center back seam for the closure.
4. Cut along the gore lines through the dart drill hole, and cut the dart out to separate the panels.

5. Add a hem and seam allowance around every panel, lining, and facing. Notch your patterns. (Figure 6.28a–e)

ADDING FLARE

Helpful Tips

1. Balanced Flare is an equal space in between the slashed panels. This will allow the skirt to drape with similar vertical drapes. A balanced flare drapes evenly and centered, draping outward away from the body without overlapping.
2. If you add a very wide flare to both sides, the skirt bottom will flare out dramatically. (Figure 6.29)

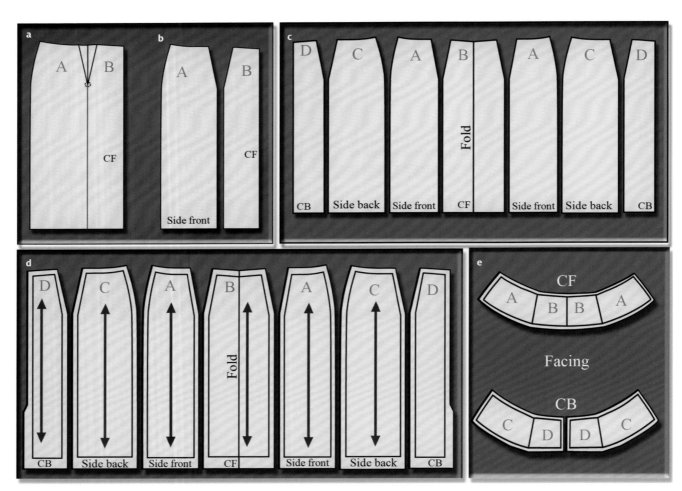

Figure 6.28a–e Drafting the gored skirt.

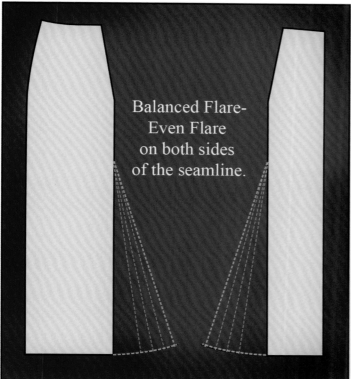

Figure 6.29 Balanced flare.

1. If you add a flare only to one side of the gore panel but not the other, the flared side will overlap the non-flared side of the next panel and will stay in place. Add a flare to the Center Back (CB) seam for a decorative option to make a longer sweep or a small train as well as more walking room.

2. Before you begin, decide on your flares and how much flare to add to each of the panels (for the example, 120 inches is added).

3. Count the total number of flare sides you will be adding along your panels. Don't forget, you are working on only half the body pattern when drafting; therefore, you will need to double the flare amount when counting. (The example shows a total of fourteen flare sides.)

4. Measure the sum of the panel widths along the hem level only. (The example hem is 39½ inches). The equation used to figure out the flare side widths is simple: Take 120 inches, and subtract 39½ inches. The total of 80½ inches is the total amount we need to add to the circumference of our skirt.

5. Take the 80½ inches and divide by fourteen flare sides. We get 5¾ inches added to each side of our panels along the hemline.

$$\frac{120 - 39}{14} = 5$$

6. Trace your gore skirt panels on a large piece of paper. Make sure you trace the panels with good amount of space in between them. If a longer skirt is desired, extend the length of the skirt panels straight down

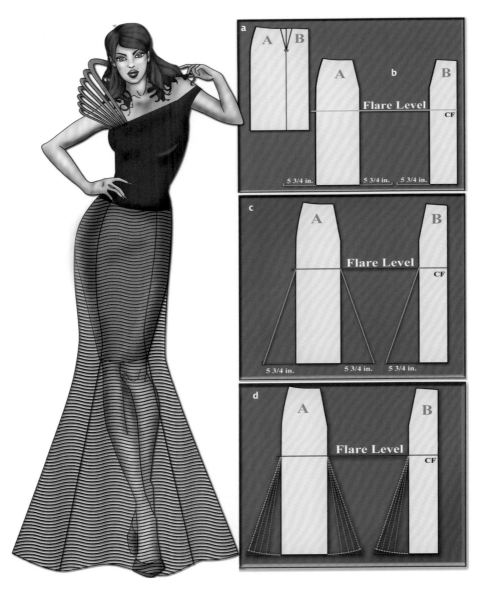

Figure 6.30a–d Adding flare.

using your L ruler to make sure the lines are parallel. (Figure 6.30a)

7. Decide on the placement of the flares along your panels. Would you like them to begin flaring above the knee or mid-thigh? Mark a point along all of your panel sides to make sure that the starting point will be the same level upward from the hemline. (If desired, this can be at different levels front to back or side to side. For example, a high low has a higher level in the front and a lower level in the center back. On the other hand, an assymetrical look can be created with a higher level on one side of the body and lower level on the other.)

8. Add a flare to each of the seam edges along the bottom of the hemline. You will be adding the flares to the sides according to your skirt design.

9. According to the equation above, add 5¾ inches to each side of the panels along the hemline. (Figure 6.30b)

10. The example shows a flare added to the front section along the princess seam only, both sides of the front side panel, both sides of the backside panel, and both sides of the Center Back (CB) panel. The Center Front (CF) panel cuts on a fold. (Figure 6.30c)

11. The flare width along the bottom hem needs to connect to the points you have already marked above the knee or mid-thigh level.

12. Make sure the flares will curve properly along the hemline of the skirt. First measure the distance along the side panel lines from the hem up to the flare top marked point.

13. Use this measurement to measure down from the top flare mark along the new flare line. You will notice that the flare line will be longer; your goal is to shorten it to the same distance. Mark a new level point along the outer line. Measure again along the center of the flare, and mark the new level. You can make more measurements in between as well if you would like help with the curve. Use your French curve ruler. (Figure 6.30d)

14. Repeat steps 12–13, adding the curve hem to all of the flare sides.

15. Add seam allowances and notches to your panels. It helps to notch the flare top points to help the sewing process. It also helps to line up the panels properly and match them up correctly. Label all panels; color coding helps.

MERMAID TWO-PIECE

1. The skirt pattern is divided into part A and part B. (Figure 6.31a)

2. Part B will get slashed into vertical panels. This step, the "slash and spread" method, is a common technique used in pattern drafting to add flares and width to pattern pieces.

3. If the panels are even in widths, you can achieve an even flare, especially if you spread the flares out with an even space in between each panel. (Figure 6.31b)

4. Make sure that the top corners of the panels touch when you tape them down to another piece of pattern paper to hold them in place. (Figure 6.31c)

5. Trace around the outer lines of the pattern pieces at the side, Center Front (CF), and top knee curved line.

6. To get the bottom hem line, you will need to use a ruler to measure an even length. To do so, measure down from the knee to the hem along the knee curve. The measurement should be equal. It is best to measure and make one or two small point marks in between each panel. The more marks you make, the smoother a curve you will get.

7. Connect your points using a hip curve or a French curve. (Figure 6.31d)

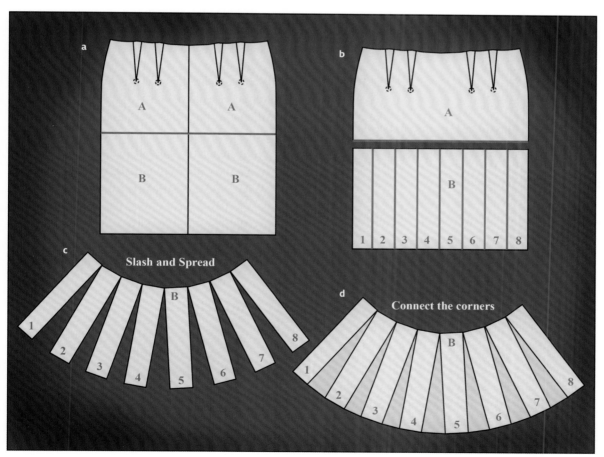

Figure 6.31a–d Mermaid skirt.

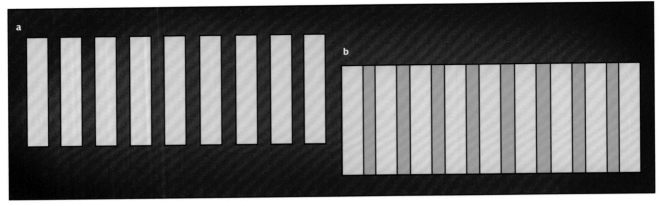

Figure 6.32a and b Mermaid skirt gathered method.

1. Add seam allowances and notches to both pieces. Attach A and B together.

Hint: To get a gathered flounce, spread the slashed strips of your part B width. By spreading sideways, you make a wider rectangle. Gather it up on top of the section before attaching it to part A. You can achieve a mermaid skirt with more volume because of the gathering. (Figure 6.32a and b)

Godets

A godet is a triangular pattern piece inserted in between the seams or to the edges of cutout areas. A godet creates walking space and allows the skirt hem to flare. The godet gets attached to the skirt individually, for example at the Center Back (CB) seam, instead of a kick pleat; or a group of godets can be inserted either in-between skirt panels (gores) or into cutout openings.

Godets can be added to add flare or a cut-out opening in a regular skirt pattern, or they can be used for any garment type, such as flared shirts, peplums, sleeves, and even collars.

To begin making your godet pattern, measure the length of the godet from the placement point down to the hem.

1. Start by making a straight line on your paper. Then square off a perpendicular line in both directions along the bottom of your straight line. (Figure 6.33a)

2. Measure the flare width on each side of the straight line. According to the gored skirt equation, we will add 5¾ inches to each side along the hemline. (Figure 6.33b)

3. The flare width along the bottom hem needs to connect to the top of the straight line, forming a triangle.

4. Make sure the flares will curve properly along the hemline of the skirt. Measure the straight line in the center and the sides of your flares on either side. The distance along the side should equal the center straight line. (Figure 6.33c)

5. You will notice that the flare lines will be longer; your goal is to shorten them to match. Mark a new level point along the bottom of the flare. Measure again along the center of the flare, and mark the new level. Make more measurements in between as well, if you would like a nicer curve. Use your curve ruler. (Figure 6.33d)

6. When you finish the godet pattern, test it by making a muslin version to check the flare of your godet.

GODET VARIATIONS

Godets can be triangular, or they can take on a different shape. A godet can be made with the slash and spread method to create a non-triangular godet. (Figure 6.34)

1. To begin making the godet pattern, you will need to trace the skirt pattern slopers.

Figure 6.33a–d Godet skirt.

In the diagrams:
- a: 5¾ in. 5¾ in.
- b: 5¾ in. 5¾ in.
- c: *godet length* 5¾ in. 5¾ in.
- d

Figure 6.34 Godet variations.

2. Draw a style line godet placement and shape directly on the skirt sloper. Cut the skirt and godet pieces out and separate.

3. Slash the godet pieces into separate strips, and spread them out to add a flounced flare. Keep the top corners connected at all times, even when the bottom strips are spread widely apart.

4. Connect the bottom of the strips with your curved ruler.

5. Trace the pattern; add seam allowances to the godet and the skirt sloper. Attach the godet to the skirt. (Figure 6.35a–d)

LINING A FLARED SKIRT

Mermaid skirts or circle skirts can be very difficult to line and can easily use too much fabric, be too flouncy, and or be too bouncy and pull in different directions on the bias of the fabric.

Hints

- Too much fabric creates bulk; therefore, add a lining that is narrower than the outer full skirt, such as an A-line–shaped lining or a straight skirt lining with an open slit in the back or a kick pleat, to add movement space.

- If your skirt also has a tail or a train, cut the lining without the tail or train to reduce bulk and weight.

- Because of the differences in hem circumferences, the skirt lining needs a free-hanging lining hem. Add thread tacks or thread chains 1 to 1½ inches in length along the seams to keep the lining from twisting inside the skirt and around the legs.

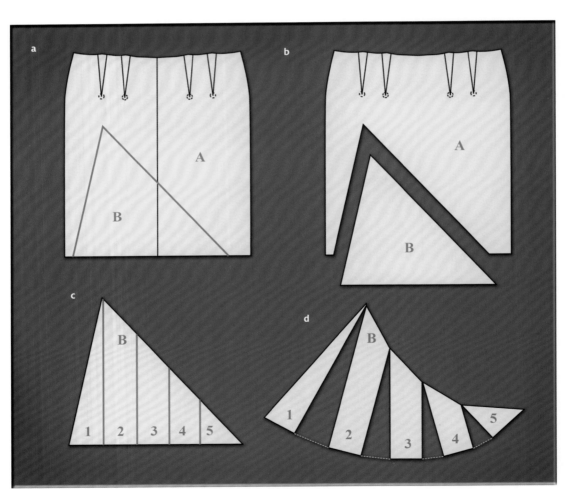

Figure 6.35a–d Drafting variations.

Flared Skirts

DRAFTING AN A-LINE FLARE

1. To begin, trace your front skirt sloper, and draw a straight line down from the point of the dart to the hem.
2. Cut along the line and along one of the sides of the dart to separate the skirt block into two parts.
3. Line up the dart legs to close the dart and tape it down. Doing this flares out your hem and creates a flare.

4. To close the open flare, tape it down on top of another piece of pattern paper.
5. Measure the flare length, and mark the hem level at the center of the flare. Add more in between the center and the sides of the flare. This will give you a nicely curved hemline. (Figure 6.36a–d)
6. Measure half the width of the slashed flare, and add it to the side seam along the hem. Connect it to the hip level.

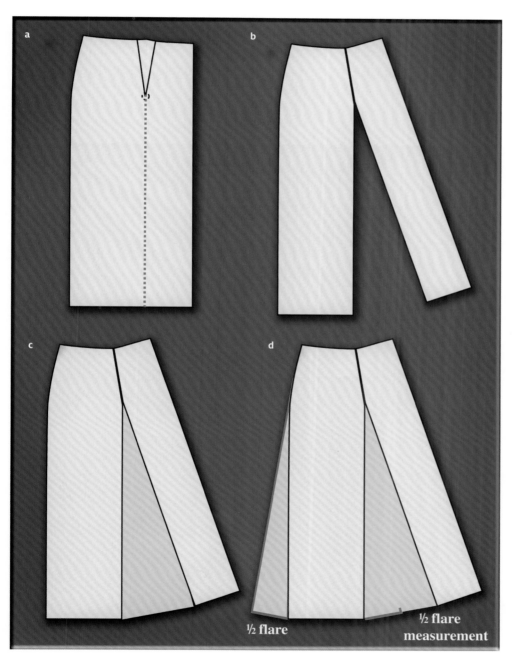

½ flare

½ flare measurement

Figure 6.36a–d Flared skirt.

7. Measure the flare length, and mark the hem level along the outer line and also in between to easily curve a nice hem. Add seam allowances.

8. Repeat steps 1–7 for the back pattern.

FULLER FLARE (SLASH AND SPREAD METHOD)

1. Trace your skirt slopers, and begin marking vertical slash lines along the pattern piece by first taking the slash line through your dart drill hole(s). To achieve an even flare, make the panels even in width. Number all the pieces.

2. Cut along the slash lines, leaving the tip $\frac{1}{16}$ of an inch uncut on top of the pattern to keep them attached. When slashing the dart line, cut the dart out completely.

3. Spread out the pieces on top of another piece of paper, and tape them down to hold them in place. Evenly spread out the flares.

4. When the pieces are secure, trace around the outer lines of the pattern pieces at the side, Center Front (CF), and waistline.

5. To get the bottom hem line, use a ruler to measure an even length inside the flares. Measure down from the flare corner to the hem along the slash lines. The measurement should be equal inside the flares as well. The more marks, the smoother your curve will be.

6. Use a curved ruler to connect your points when done for a curved hem.

7. Add seam allowances, the grainline parallel to the Center Front (CF) and Center Back (CB), and notches. (Figure 6.37a–e)

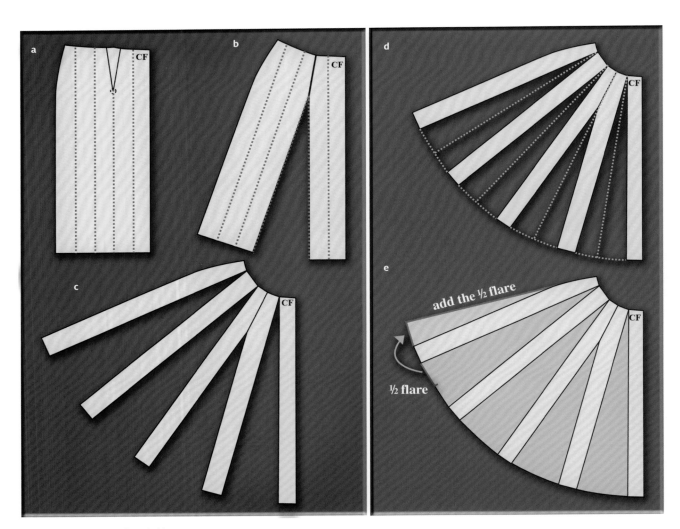

Figure 6.37a–e Fuller flared skirt.

Full Skirts

The Full (Circle) Skirt was easily adopted into the North American wardrobe in 1947 with Christian Dior's New Look and the 1950s with the Poodle Skirt. It is a very flattering, feminine look, especially when worn with a very narrow waistline, which gives a woman a minimized waistline and nice curves. (Figure 6.38)

DRAFTING A FULL SKIRT

1. To begin, use a large sheet of pattern paper.
2. With your L-ruler, draft a right angle along one of the corners of the paper.
3. Use the following formula to calculate the correct waist arc length:

$$\frac{\text{Waist measurement} - 2 \text{ inches (Bias stretch)}}{4 \text{ (Quarters)}}$$

4. To determine the radius of your waist opening, see Table 6.1.

Figure 6.38 Dior full skirt.

Table 6.1 Suggested Radius Measurement for Full Circle Skirt Waistlines

Waist Measurement in Inches (or Flounce Opening)	Waist Radius in Inches (or Flounce Opening Radius)
22	3.18
24	3.50
26	3.82
28	4.14
30	4.46
32	4.78
34	5.10
36	5.41
38	5.73
40	6.05
42	6.37
44	6.69
46	7.01
48	7.32
50	7.64
52	7.96
54	8.28

1. Using the known radius, from your corner, measure along both of the sides of the angle and mark. Do the same thing at 45-degree angle.
2. Continue marking the radius in between the sides and the 45-degree mark, curving the waistline into a perfect fourth of a circle.
3. Measure the lengths of the line you have connected; it should be close to your measurement from step 3. If not, try adjusting the radius of the waistline closer to the corner for a shorter line, or trying to slightly extend the outer lines of the corner.
4. For the hem, the example shows red lines indicating the hem measurement from the waist, forming another arc at the hem.
5. Add hem allowance and mark the Grainline along one of the side lines along either the X-axis or the

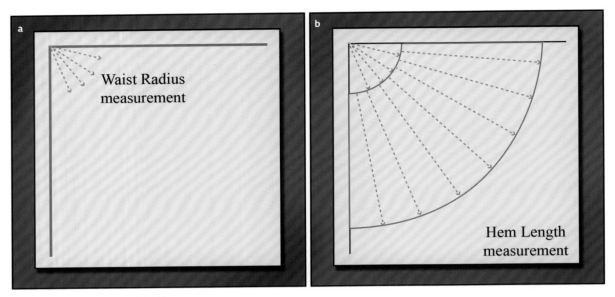

Figure 6.39a and b Drafting the full skirt.

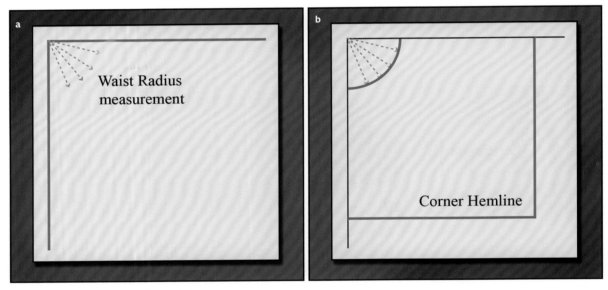

Figure 6.40a and b Handkerchief skirt variation.

Y-axis, which will serve as a fold line for your skirt. Add seam allowance to the side opposite the fold line. (Figure 6.39a and b)

Hint: Hankerchief skirts can be drafted using the same steps as for Full skirts; however, leave the bottom hem as a corner instead of curving it. (Figure 6.40a and b)

Peplums

Historically, the **peplum** dates back to as early as the nineteenth century and was worn as an overskirt and attached to the skirt at the waist or the jacket. We also see the dramatic influence of the peplum in Dior's New Look of 1947, when women began wearing cinched waist silhouettes along with full or pencil skirts. Peplums also made comebacks in the 1980s, 1990s, and 2000s.

Peplums are a wonderful feminine waist detail that can be added to a dress, a skirt, a blouse, a tank top, or a jacket. Peplums help a woman look and feel confident while hiding certain body shape imperfections, adding hips, hiding large hips, and narrowing the waist. Keep the legth of the peplum 2–3 inches below the waist

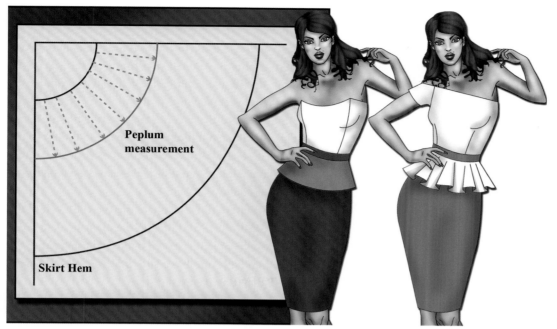

Peplum
measurement

Skirt Hem

Figure 6.41 Peplums.

to help keep the body looking slim. Use a flared skirt pattern, A-line gored skirt, circle skirt, pleated ruffle, flounce, or gathered ruffle pattern to draft a peplum. (Figure 6.41)

Understructure

CRINOLINE PETTICOATS

Crinoline petticoats are made of crinoline netting, nylon netting, or many layers of tulle and are made to hold a dress away from the body and keep it from falling in. It helps the skirt from becoming tangled between legs during wear. Crinoline **petticoats** are softer, fluffier, and more comfortable to wear than hoop skirts are. (Figure 6.42)

- It is always best to use a rotary cutter to cut netting to get a smooth, straight cut.
- When sewing on a sewing machine, use a piece of clear tape along the stitch line. Place the tape on the side facing down toward the teeth. This will prevent the netting bunching under the teeth.
- When done stitching, remove the tape.
- Crinoline will not fray. When you are working with stiffer crinoline, bind the edges with either cotton or satin ribbon to avoid snagging.

Figure 6.42 Crinoline petticoat.

1. To begin the petticoat, you will need to get lining fabric such as cotton or even taffeta. Get 6–10 yards of netting to create a good full skirt.

2. Petticoat will have three tiers of netting; therefore, use an A-line skirt pattern. Cut it out; sew up the side seams, not the back.

3. Divide the length of your lining into three horizontal parts minus at least 3–4 inches from the waist top or the yoke. This will reduce the bulk around the waistline and reduce the exaggerated roundness of the hip at the waistline.

4. It is usually best to make the top part be the widest for an A-line ball gown.

5. Mark the levels on your skirt with chalk or a basting stitch.

6. Measure the width of all three of your skirt parts and the length. Write it down.

7. Usually, you can use the entire 5 yards around one skirt at each of the ruffles. Therefore, you can cut these crinoline ruffle strips along the length of the netting, using the width of your measured skirt parts. (You can make them strips 1–2 inches wider for the top and the middle section only.)

8. To create the crinoline ruffles, begin sewing two parallel straight stitches down the edge of the net strips. For extra poof, use two layers of netting for each strip, and stitch both of them when making the parallel edge stitches.

9. Pull on the threads to gather it long enough to attach to the bottom section of your lining skirt.

10. Line up the gathered edge of the netting along the marked lower section, and pin it in place. Stitch through all of the layers using a straight stitch or a zigzag stitch, attaching the ruffle to the lining.

11. Repeat steps 7–9 to create another gathered ruffle, and attach it to the middle section and the top section marked lines.

12. When you are finished attaching the ruffles, fold the skirt face-to-face and line up the open sides in order to close the opening. Stitch it closed or just surge the opening; however, make sure that you are not catching the netting inside the skirt.

13. Add a waistband or a ribbon you can tie along the waistline. (Figure 6.43a-f)

Hint: Use this same technique to make different types of petticoats. See Figure 6.44 to see many varieties of petticoats. Only the ruffle levels change. You can also use fabric such as cotton instead of netting to make a petticoat. (Figure 6.44)

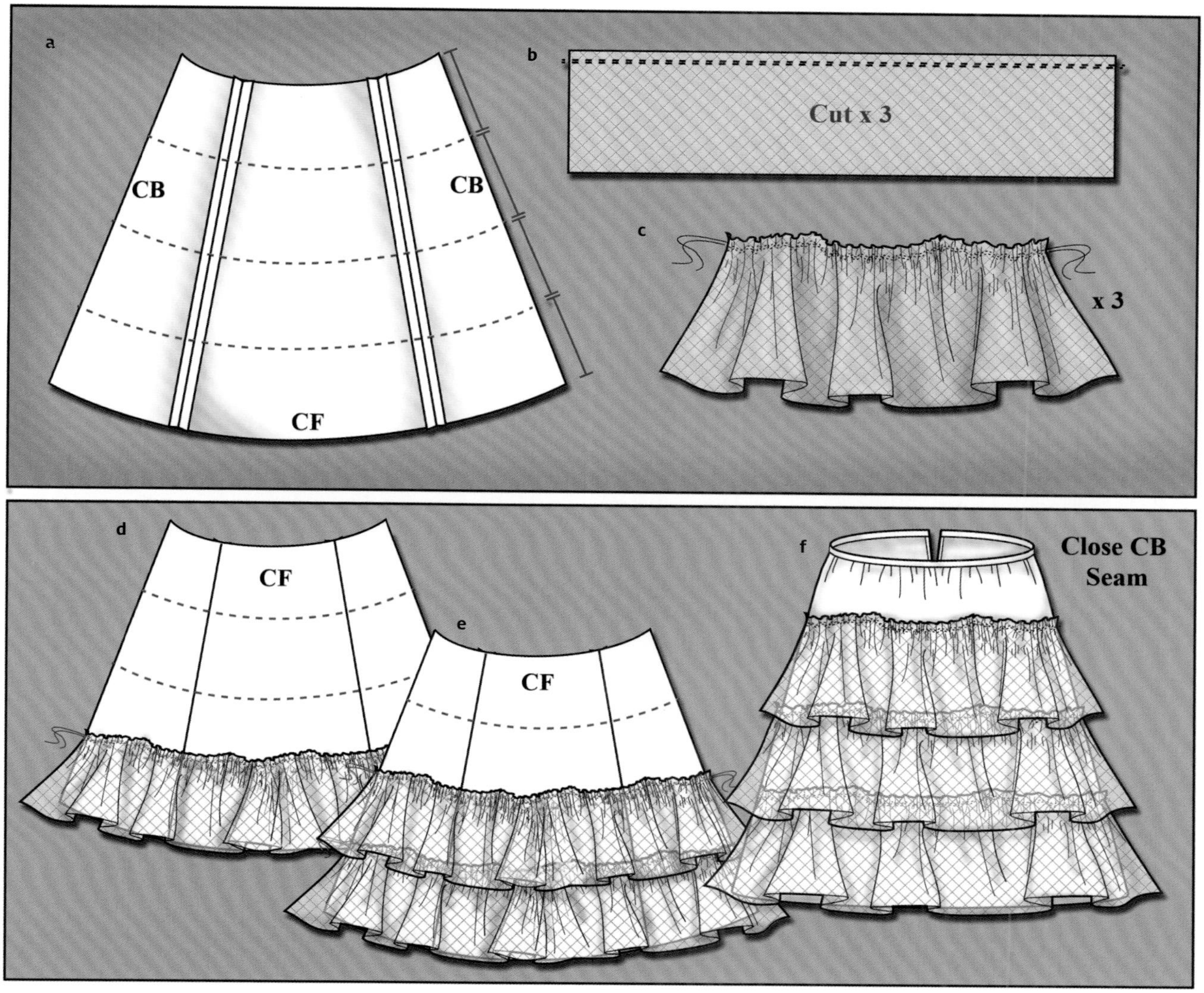
a
CB
CB
CF
b
Cut x 3
c
x 3
d
CF
e
CF
f
Close CB Seam

Figure 6.43a-f Petticoat assembly.

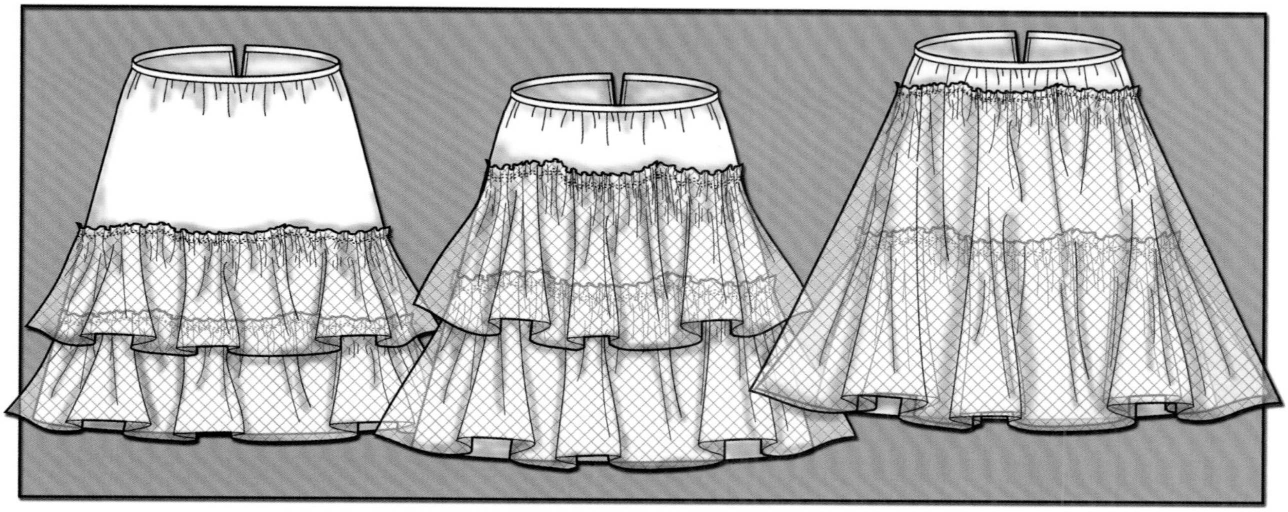

Figure 6.44 Petticoat examples.

PETTICOAT COVER

A petticoat cover is also often needed to protect the outer dress and keep the wearer warmer. Use cotton, taffeta, or wool for warmth.

1. To begin making the cover, you will need at least 4–5 yards of fabric. The cover needs to be wide enough to cover the petticoat without narrowing it with its weight.
2. It is important to place the crinoline petticoat or hoop skirt on the form and work on the cover on top of it.
3. Measure from the waist down to the hem level, at least 1–2 inches off the floor in the front. Dresses tend to be slightly longer in the back sometimes, but the Center Front (CF) has to be higher in order for the wearer to take steps forward without tripping.

4. Mark the level and add 2 inches for the hem allowance; rip or carefully cut with tailor's shears.
5. Hem the entire piece of cut fabric.
6. Close the open edges by folding your cover face-to-face. Stitch up from the hem toward the waist, stopping at least 7 inches from the waistline.
7. Place the petticoat cover over your crinoline petticoat, and pin the opening closed at either the side seam or the Center Back (CB) seam.
8. Begin pleating the large skirt. Make small, flat pleats (knife pleats) by folding a small amount of the fabric over the waistline.
9. It is best to devide your cylinder into quarters and pleat smaller sections.
10. Pleat and pin down flat until done around the entire skirt. (Figure 6.45a–e)

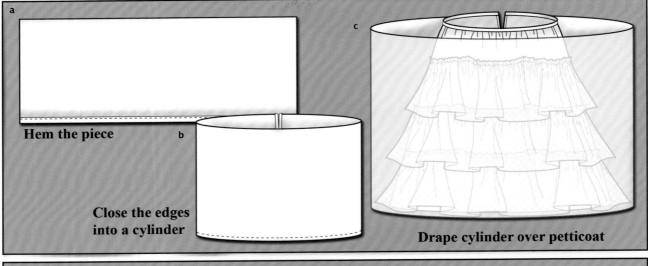

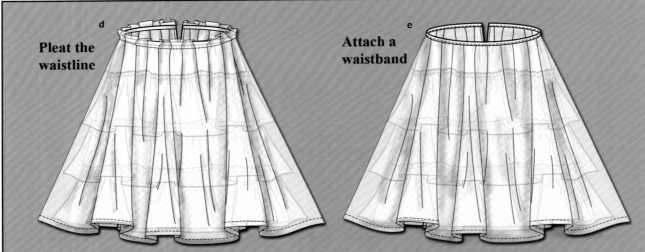

Figure 6.45a–e Petticoat cover.

11. Before removing the cover, hand baste the pleats in place to secure them from shifting.

12. Remove the cover, and run a straight stitch one more time, securing the pleats.

13. Add the waistband, a satin ribbon, twill tape, or gros-grain ribbon, leaving tails longer in order to tie the cover closed.

SEPARATE PETTICOAT OR SEWN-IN PETTICOAT?

A common question that comes up when someone is making evening or bridal gowns is do we add the petticoat to the dress or keep it separate? There is no right answer. The main purpose for a petticoat is to give fullness to the skirt when needed.

Therefore, the only issue arises in dress preservation or storage. It is easier to have a removable petticoat for closet storage flat in a garment bag. If the gown has a big petticoat attached, it will take up a lot more space in your closet; it may even take up the entire closet. Removable petticoats or hoop skirts can be rolled up into a smaller container and stored separately.

Today in the evening wear and bridal market, stores tend to like this idea. They can keep more dresses in stock and charge a little more money for the extra piece, the petticoat. A customer also has an option to wear a smaller petticoat if desired or no petticoat at all. The dress is shortened, and the customer can enjoy a gown that has no poof.

There is another known benefit for separating the petticoat from the dress, which is that it is easier to assemble a gown and keep the bulk out of the seams when a gathered or pleated waistline can be avoided from being sandwiched in between other layers of the waistline on the dress.

Remember, petticoat or not, it is up to the customer to decide about storage and the wear of the dress. That is why it may be more beneficial to design a gown with a removable petticoat.

Hoop Skirts

Historically, hoop skirts have been known as Farthingales, cages, hooped petticoats, and more. They were originally warn when women's waists were narrower as a result of the use of corsets; therefore the hips needed to look much wider to cinch the waitsline. Hoop skirts were used to keep wider skirts from falling in and kept them full and stiff.

Hoop skirts came in many shapes and sizes; for instance, in early 1850s, hoop skirts were as big as human cages. They were round, very wide, the same shape front to back and side to side, and shaped like a circle when held up vertically. At this time dresses were wider, and sometimes the women wearing them needed to enter rooms through double doors. During the time of Marie Antoinette's French Court, Farthingales grew in width at the hips, not all around the body. These hoop skirts were made of vertical bands of tape or leather holding up rows of steel and a bottom-pleated frill.

Caged hoop skirts (crinoline) were covered with layers of ruffled petticoats and decorated with lace hems and trims to add more décor. Around the time of the Civil War crinolines had to be covered in gutta-percha, a substance that protected them from wet weather conditions by making them waterproof. (Figure 6.46)

The hoop trend disappeared until Empress Eugenie of France created a new one, showing up in a dress with a flat front unsupported by a cage in the late 1850's. Charles Worth, a designer for Empress Eugenie at the time, decided to take this as an inspiration and turn heads with a new fashion trend for skirts with flat fronts and wider backs.

Later in 1860s, the idea of a cage crinoline became less favored as women took on more hard labor roles while men were away at war.

After the Civil War, toward the end of the 1800s, the back bustle of skirts grew in size as well. It began with the shift of the hoops to the back, not the front. The ruffled petticoats also took the same shape, adding ruffles at the back only. The first bustle came around 1868 with only a couple of half hoops added to the top back of the skirt petticoat and tied into a half-moon shape with ribbon inside the skirt. By the 1870s, the hoops were permanently added to the petticoats and were called the crinolettes. (Figure 6.47)

In 1877, the princess petticoat made of silk became a trend; it was white or colored and buttoned down in the back, from the knee level up to the waist, making it easier for self-dressing.

Figure 6.46 1850s hoop skirt.

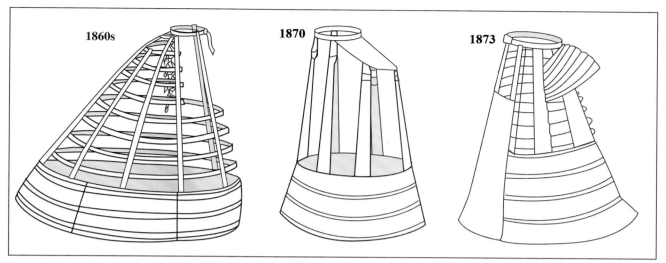

Figure 6.47 Hoop skirt.

DRAFTING A HOOP SKIRT

A hoop skirt can take on different shapes depending on the pattern used. When making a hoop skirt, it is important to decide the length, how wide you want it to be, the shape you want it to take, and how many hoops you want it to have.

Note: The more hoops, the stronger the petticoat and also the harder to sit or store.

- You can begin with an A-line skirt pattern, or you can use a wider pattern for a flared skirt; you can even use 4–5 yards of fabric and turn it into a cylinder.
- Remember to add the casing for the steel boning while the pattern is still flat for easier assembly.

Materials needed:

- 10–15 yards steel boning (regular steel or spiral boning). For spiral boning, get the larger size (½ inch); it is stronger and very flexible and easily returns back to its original shape after bending or sitting. Get the connectors as well in order to be able to close and connect the ends together.
- 4–5 yards of medium-weight cotton, muslin, or taffeta fabric for the hoop skirt lining. When using a cylinder to make a hoop skirt, consider using wider fabric to make the hoop skirt long enough with the hem and the waistline.

1. Cut your pattern pieces. Mark the hoop lines to follow for the casings.
2. Attach all of the pieces of the skirt together. Leave one side open; usually the backside is easier. Make sure your casing marking are lining up.

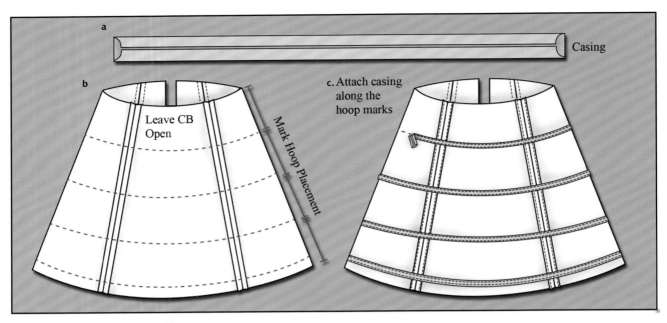

Figure 6.48a–c Hoop skirt assembly.

Note: If you are making a cylinder hoop skirt, you only have one piece, so there is no need to follow steps 3–4; instead move to step 5.

3. Press your seams open.
4. Pin your boning casing onto the inner side of the skirt. (Figure 6.48a–c)
5. Stitch the casings using your sewing machine.
6. Hem the petticoat to finish the raw edge, or attach a ruffle or lace trim.
7. Close the open side up from the hem to at least 7–8 inches from the waist to allow for the closure around the waistline if you decide to add a button closure, a hook and eye closure, or a ribbon.
8. Be careful not to close up your casings with your seam. Rip your seams away from the edge so you can avoid catching them in your closing seam.
9. If using elastic for the waistband, stitch the skirt closed all the way up to the waist. If not, pleat the waistline with flat knife pleats to reduce the bulk in the waist.
10. Push your steel boning into the casings.
11. When you get to the the correct width, use your pliers to cut the boning.

Note: If you are making a cylinder hoop skirt, you can alter the different hoop sizes by gathering the casing, slightly shortening the hoop circumference; tighten your hoop connectors directly on the dress form after the hoop skirt is complete.

12. Add boning hoop connectors on the cut side, place a boning tip back onto the cut edge, and connect the hoops together. To do this, slide the one end of the steel boning into the open end of the hoop connector on the other edge. (Figure 6.49a and b)
13. If needed, use a needle and thread to connect the casing down firmly around the connectors so the casing and hoops will not rip off from the skirts.

Bustles and Trains

To make a **train**, decide if your train will be long or short, attached to the gown, part of the skirt pattern, or detachable. Historically, only the royal families and the wealthy wore trains to show their status in society. The longer the train, the more important and wealthy the wearer.

TRAINS

1. Use your skirt blocks, and turn them into an a-line floor-length gown by closing your dart.
2. Add length to the Center Back (CB) seam by adding the desired length of the train to the pattern.
3. Connect the Center Back (CB) to the side seam by a straight hemline, making a sharp point, a curved line, or a rectangular shape.

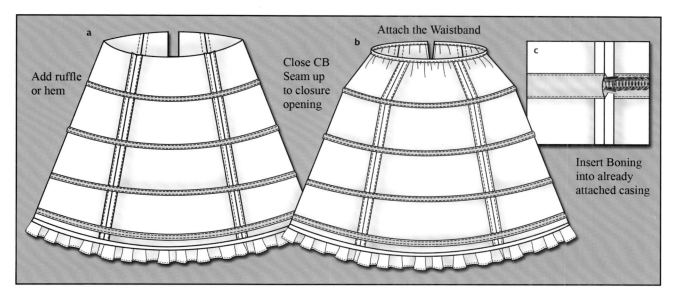

Add ruffle or hem

Close CB Seam up to closure opening

Attach the Waistband

Insert Boning into already attached casing

Figure 6.49a and b Hoop skirt assembly continued.

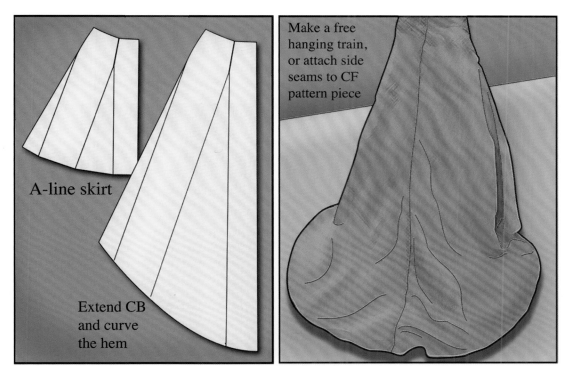

A-line skirt

Extend CB and curve the hem

Make a free hanging train, or attach side seams to CF pattern piece

Figure 6.50 Train.

4. Cut out your fabric, and finish your edges and hem. (You can also cut two panels, sew them together, finish all edges and add a contrast fabric or even color.)

5. Attach the train to the dress at the waistline, or close the waist of the train, decorate the top with embellishments, and attach it to the dress with large hooks or buttons to make it detachable.

6. Another way is to use a long rectangle fabric piece and pleat/gather up the waistline in order to attach it to the dress.

Note: If desired, decorate the train with embelishmnets, cut-outs, color blocking, appliqué, and trim. Add weights and insert them into the hem of the skirt to help the train open up and sit heavily on the ground when walking. (Figure 6.50)

PICKUP BUSTLE

The pickup **bustle** is used in modern bridal and evening gowns. The skirt is a simple six-panel skirt that is just missing the front three panels. However, when a full round skirt is desired, you can follow the same pickup steps and complete an entire skirt.

1. Start with making a gored A-line skirt pattern. Add seam allowances and hem allowance as well as grainline and notches.
2. Extend the pattern with the slash and spread technique. (Figure 6.51a–c)
3. Remember, you are making just a bustle; therefore, remove the front panels only, or you can also remove half of the front side panels as well.
4. Trace the panels on to your fabric and cut them out. Assemble these gores together to form a semi-circle skirt.
5. Finish the edges and hem the skirt.
6. Attach the waistband and get ready to bustle.
7. Place the skirt onto the dress form, and let it drape down smoothly on the floor, making a longer train.
8. Begin picking up fabric with your fingers and pinning it in place with safety pins.
9. Continue these pickups until you are ready with the bustle.
10. Pickups do not have to be even in width or length as long as the bottom hem will be even with the floor.
11. There is no need to stitch the pickups permanently until the look of the bustle is finished; then you can hand tack all the safety pin areas with a needle and thread or add ribbon inside the garment, bustling it when tied. (Figure 6.52a–c)

TWILL TAPE BUSTLE

For this bustle, you will need your fabric and twill tape.

1. Use a 60-inch wide fabric or attach two rectangles, adding to 60 inches.

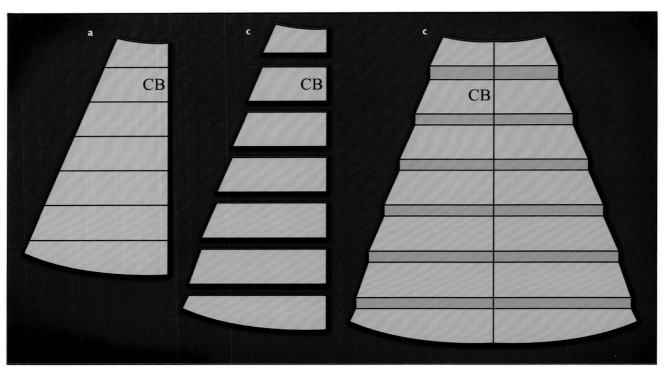

Figure 6.51a–c Pickup bustle.

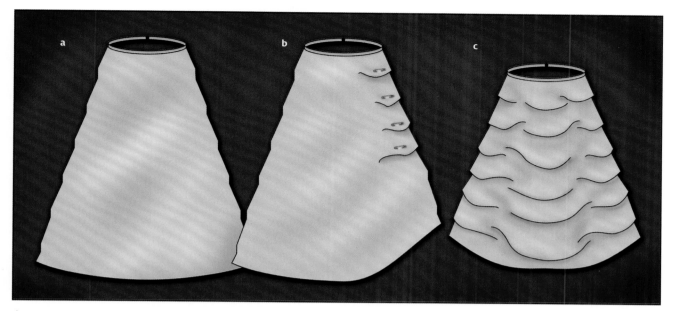

Figure 6.52a–c Pickup bustle continued.

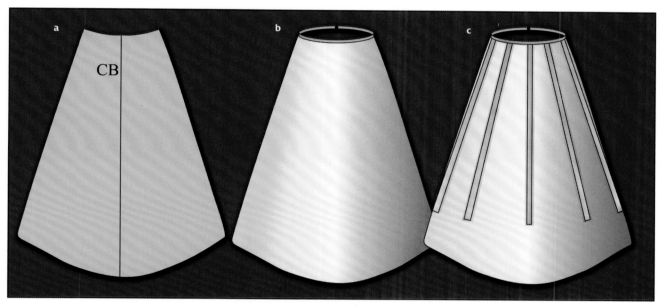

Figure 6.53a–c Twill tape bustle.

2. Cut these rectangles between 2 and 3 yards long, depending how much poof you need.
3. Finish the side edges.
4. Pleat or gather the top of the rectangle into the narrower waistband, but do not close the waistband completely.
5. Place the bustle onto the dress form inside out.
6. Cut five pieces of twill tape to the desired bustle length (waist to floor).

7. Attach them by tacking them under the open waistband, two tapes on the open sides, one on each princess line, and one in the Center Back (CB).
8. Flip the bustle right side onto the dress form with the tape under the fabric. (Figure 6.53a–c)
9. Begin picking up fabric with your fingers, pinning it in place to the twill tape with safety pins.

10. Continue these pickups on all areas of your bustle. It may look interesting to try alternating the pickup levels to show a flow direction.

11. Hand tack all the safety pin areas to the twill tape with a needle and thread.

12. Close the waistband and finish the bustle. You can also attach a lining piece to your bustle or permanently attach it to another skirt underneath. (Figure 6.54a–c)

FRENCH BUSTLE

A French bustle is used in eveningwear gowns and bridal wear with long trains, relieving the wearer of the stress and discomfort of wearing the long train and stepping on it all night long. (Figure 6.55)

Finish sewing your gown with a train.

1. Place gown on the dress form inside out. If your dress has a full skirt and requires a hoop skirt or petticoat, you need to place the petticoat under the dress for proper bustle placement.

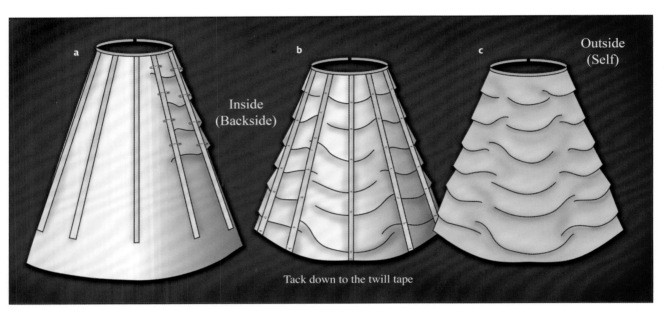

Figure 6.54a–c Twill tape bustle continued.

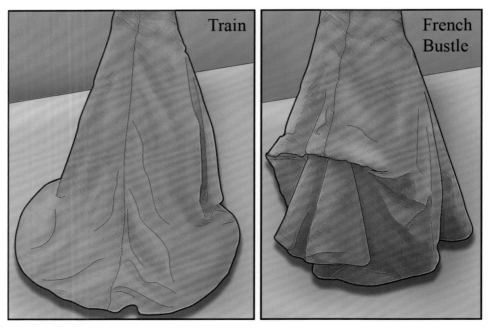

Figure 6.55 French bustle.

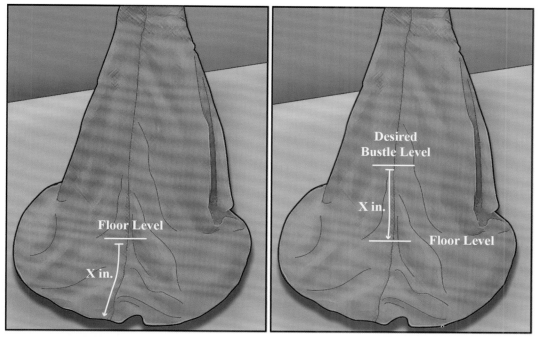

Figure 6.56 French bustle assembly.

2. Using the Center Back (CB) seam of your train, measure your train length from the floor intersection to the end of your train.

3. Decide where to begin the bustle drape. If you have no back zippers, then decide on the level below the hip area. Place a safety pin to mark it. (Figure 6.56)

4. Use the measurement of your train, and measure down from this area toward the floor; add another safety pin to mark the spot.

5. Attach ribbon similar in color to the dress on the inside of the dress to replace those two safety pins. Make sure to attach the ribbon securely. You can use a small square piece of lining fabric or even flannel to stitch over the ribbon to secure it and hide the raw edges.

6. Make sure to cut your ribbon diagonally to avoid fraying; even better would be to roll hem the edge. Tie the ribbon to check. (Figure 6.57)

Underlining the Skirts

Underlining has been used for centuries as an essential part of heavier gowns and long trains. All of the known luxury fabrics in the fashion industry today need good underlining support. The most common are silk velvet, dupioni, charmeuse, taffeta, crepe-de-chine, and wool.

Narrower and thinner fabrics can be underlined with thin cotton fabrics, and thicker fabrics such as velvet, velveteen, and taffeta can be underlined with silk organza.

Silk charmeuse is very often underlined with crepe-de-chine. It has a similar weight and drape but is sturdier than charmeuse. Before you start your skirt project, think about the underlining as well.

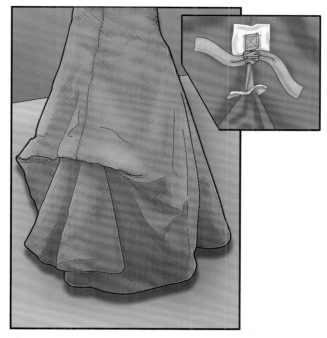

Figure 6.57 French bustle assembly continued.

CRISTOBAL BALENCIAGA

Cristobal Balenciaga was born in 1895 in Guetaria, a small fishing village in Spain. He began his creative career at an early age. When he turned thirteen, he met Marquise of Casa Torres and commented on her beautiful dresses. She was very interested in his vision and allowed him to make a copy of one of her haute couture gowns. She was so astounded by his work that she decided to wear the dress in public.

When Balenciaga turned fourteen, he went to Paris and visited the houses of Worth, Doucet, and many more. He was so inspired by what they were doing that he went home and opened his first couture workshop at age sixteen. This workshop opened its doors in San Sebastian, and his designs were inspired by Parisian style made for Spanish women.

Balenciaga was so successful that he opened his first couture shop and named it Balenciaga in 1915. In 1920, he opened his second house

Cristobal Balenciaga, 1927.

in Madrid. Unfortunately a civil war broke out, and he moved to Paris, where he opened another house.

In 1947, Balenciaga designed clothes that were very close-fitting in the waist and square in the shoulders. And in 1951, he designed clothes with open necks, looser waistlines, and wide shoulders. He also created coats with wider collars as well as sack and tunic dresses. He called his designs the Balenciaga Revolution.

Balenciaga believed that "a couturier must be an architect for design, a sculptor for shape, a painter for color, a musician for harmony, and a philosopher for temperance." He was known as "the Master of Couture." It has been said that when a woman wearing a Balenciaga gown walks into a room, there are no other women there. His gowns are so elegant and perfectly made that they become the center of attention.

In 1947, Balenciaga launched Le Dix, his first women's perfume.

He designed for the Queen of Belgium, the Duchess of Windsor, Princess Grace of Monaco, and the Queen of Spain. These ladies were fashion icons and known to be the best-dressed women in the world.

In 1958, Balenciaga was made Chevalier de la Legion d'Honneur and decided to retire after his thirty years working as a couturier. He closed his fashion house and moved back to Spain. His last public appearance was at Coco Chanel's funeral. She had once said that Balenciaga was the only couturier she knew who could design, cut, assemble, and sew a gown all by himself.

Evening dress and jacket, circa 1955.

Balenciaga died on March 24, 1972. He was and will always be an inspiration to many designers such as Ungaro, Givenchy, Courrèges, myself, and you—the future of design.

Nicolas Ghesquière became creative director of Balenciaga in 1997.

Evening dress with cape, 1961.

Chapter Review

This chapter is a great reference for skirts and skirt variations as well as a jump back into history with the discussions about petticoat and hoop skirts, bustles of historical descent and modern bustles, and the French bustle. In this chapter, the reader learned the concepts of draping, drafting, and shaping skirts of all shapes and sizes.

Projects

1. Drape a basic straight skirt. Make sure you true your pattern and pin it together to check the fit.
2. Design and construct a skirt with one of the bustles covered in this chapter.
3. Draft and assemble a hoop skirt.
4. Draft and assemble a crinoline petticoat.
5. Design and illustrate a board with three gowns showing three different trains or bustles covered in this chapter. Include fabric swatches and technical flats.

Key Terms

A-line skirt	Hip level	Train
Bustle	Hoop skirt	Trumpet skirt
Crinoline	Kick pleat	Waistband
Darts	Mermaid skirt	Yoke
Gored skirt	Peplum	
Flared skirt	Petticoat	

7

The Secret of the Corset

Objectives

- Learn the history of the corset

- Learn how to drape and/or draft a corset pattern

- Learn different items needed to build a corset

- Learn about different types of boning

- Learn how to build a two-layer corset

- Learn how to build a three-layer corset

- Learn about the life and work of Vera Wang

The **corset** (Figure 7.1) was introduced as early as the fifteenth century, when women wore them as undergarments. These corsets were boned with wood and **whalebone** to mold the body into an unnatural shape. In the sixteenth century, the wood and whalebone were replaced by iron or **steel strips**.

In the sixteenth through eighteenth centuries, corsets called **payres of bodies** were usually worn with a hoop skirt. The corsets turned the upper torso into a matching cone or cylinder. (Figure 7.2a) They had shoulder straps and flaps at the waist. This type of corset flattened the chest and pushed it up.

The corset later picked up a new name, **stays**, and became less constricting with the new high-waist Empire style in the eighteenth and nineteenth centuries. Some stays were still worn during this period, but these were often "short stays," which did not extend very far below the breasts. (Figure 7.2b)

During the Victorian era, the waistline returned to its natural position, and the corset returned. The new corset was shaped like an **hourglass** silhouette, which exaggerated the natural curves. Spiral steel stays curved with the figure. (Figure 7.2c) At this time many corsets were still sewn by hand to the customer's measurements, but with the invention of the sewing machine in the mid-nineteenth century, a thriving market developed for cheaper mass-produced corsets. (Figure 7.2d)

The straight-front corset, also known as the swan bill corset or the wool or health corset, was worn in the first years of the twentieth century. Its name derived from the very rigid, straight busk inserted in the center front of the corset, which forced the torso forward and made the hips protrude back, giving the torso an S shape. (Figure 7.2e)

In the years immediately before the World War I, corsets were long, straight, and not padded (as the 1890s corsets had been). This gave women a slimmer, less feminine figure, which carried over into the 1920s, when feminine curves were definitely out and even the breasts were flattened to produce a slender look.

Corsets were often made of rubber, but the invention of the Latex process by the Dunlop Rubber Company in the 1930s led to the invention of the modern two-way-stretch panty **girdle**. (Figure 7.2f)

Figure 7.1 Madonna in concert wearing a bustier designed by Jean Paul Gaultier.

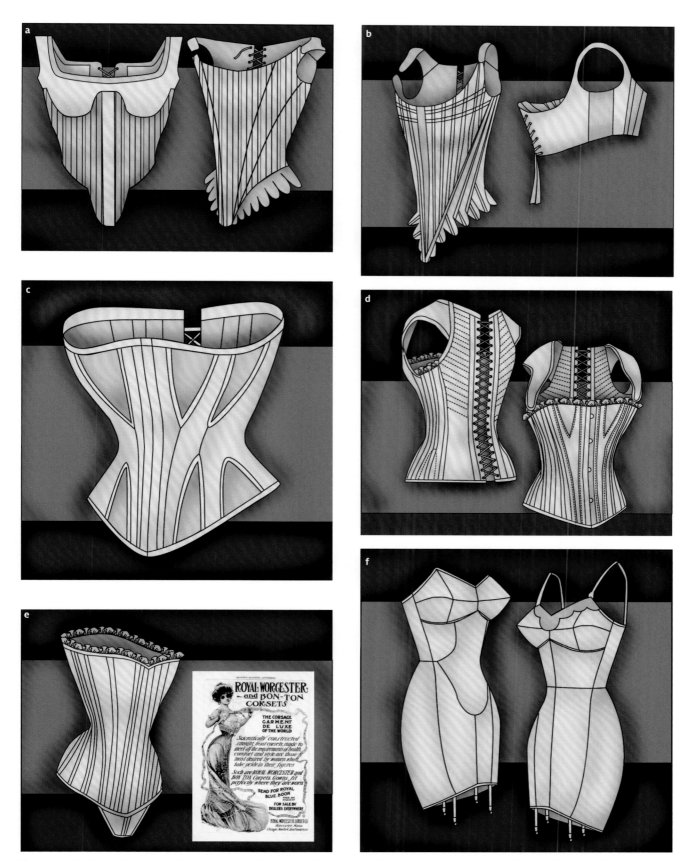

Figure 7.2 (a) Sixteenth and seventeenth centuries. (b) Early and late eighteenth century. (c) Victorian era. (d) 1890s. (e) Swan-bill corset, late 1800s/early 1900s. (f) Corset girdle, 1920s–1930s.

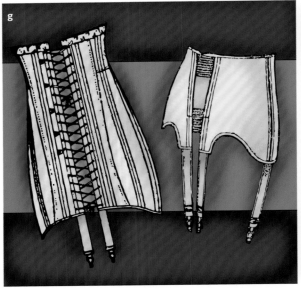

Figure 7.2 (continued) (g) and (h) Corset girdles, 1940s–1960s.

Related to the girdle was the liberty bodice, a fleecy vest reinforced with elastic, which was very snug and warm. It was well known to British women from the 1940s to the 1960s. (Figure 7.2g)

Using Draping to Pattern a Corset

As previously noted, a corset understructure (also called a boned bodice) serves as a foundation for strapless dresses, gowns, and tops. The boned bodice must be made out of tough and firm fabric and interfaced when additional support is necessary. The best way to make a great pattern for a boned bodice is to drape it.

The boned bodice can be patterned with eight pieces. (Figure 7.3a) It can be also be made with ten pattern pieces for a tighter fit. (Figure 7.3b) However, many corsets are patterned to have a bra top for better support and for design purposes. (Figure 7.3c–d)

A boned bodice can be made to provide a greater or lesser amount of support. For more support, use heavier fabric, stronger **boning**, more interfacing, and a lining.

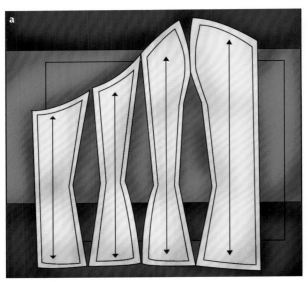
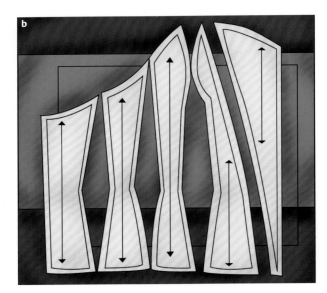

Figure 7.3 (a) Eight-piece corset patterns. (b) Ten-piece corset patterns.

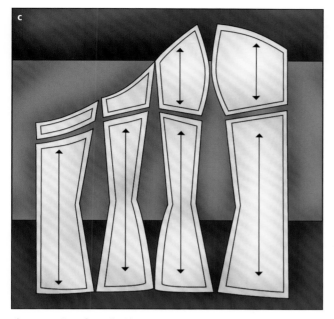

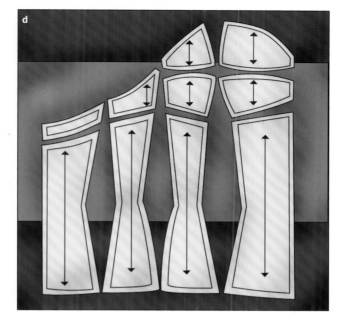

Figure 7.3 (continued) (c) Bra top corset. (d) Split bra top corset.

However, if such strong support is not needed—for example, when a boned bodice is constructed on the inside of the garment in order to keep the shape of the design or to shape the body better and not necessarily hold up the gown—then so many layers are not necessary.

To begin draping the corset style shown in Figure 7.4, get your muslin ready by cutting as many pieces as you have panels. You will need to measure the length and width of each panel and add 4 inches to each dimension. (Figure 7.5)

Before you start draping, use the style tape to mark a style line on the dress form. The style line should show the top and bottom of your design as well as any inside yokes, midriffs, bra tops, and so on. Make sure you mark around

Figure 7.4 Corset example.

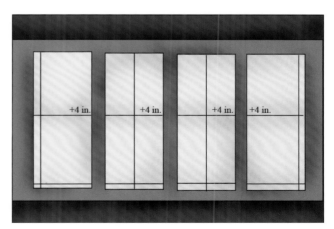

Figure 7.5 Preparing muslin.

to the back as well. You only need to drape half of the corset because it is symmetrical and the pattern can be cut twice for the other side. (Figure 7.6a)

FRONT CENTER PANEL

1. Start by folding and pressing the center front piece from which you have already cut 1 inch in the center front.
2. Pin the apex point along the bustline first with two pins pointing toward each other, forming an X. Then pin the fold against the center front line, with pins pointing toward the apex. Make sure the bustline is parallel to the floor.
3. Smooth the muslin with your right hand across the bust, and pin down the princess line on the dress from the apex point while shaping the bust. Feel the line with your fingers through the muslin. If you see tension at the waistline, clip a notch at the waist. (Figure 7.6b)
4. Mark the style along the style tape and the princess line to make the center front pattern piece of your bodice. (Figure 7.6c)
5. Remove the muslin from the form, and mark seam allowances. Pin back on the form. (Figure 7.6d)

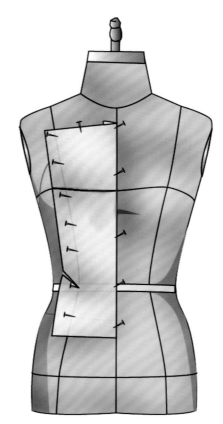

Figure 7.6b Drape the center front panel.

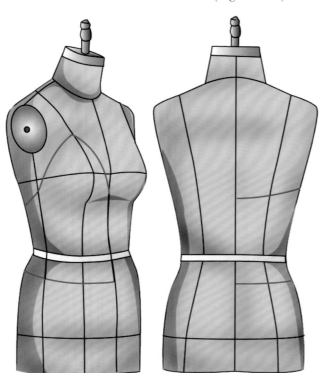

Figure 7.6a Style lines.

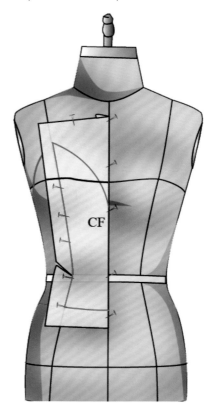

Figure 7.6c Mark the seam lines.

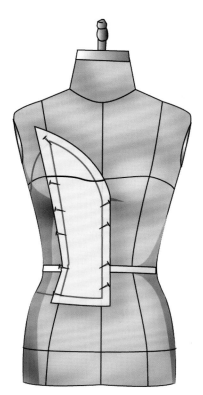

Figure 7.6d True the pattern.

FRONT SIDE PANEL

1. Pin the apex point along the bustline on the form, making sure it lines up with the bustline of the center front panel and is parallel to the floor.
2. With your left hand, smooth left toward the side seam, and pin down the side seam to the waist and then up above the bustline. Clip at the waist to reduce tension.
3. Smooth toward the princess line with your right hand, and pin along the princess line, smoothing the muslin up and down to shape around, under, and over the bust. Clip at the waist to reduce the tension. (Figure 7.7a)
4. Mark the lines all along the style tape, princess line, and side seam. (Figure 7.7b)
5. Take the pattern piece off the form, and add a seam allowance. Trim off the rest. Pin the two front patterns together to check the fit back on the form. (Figure 7.7c)

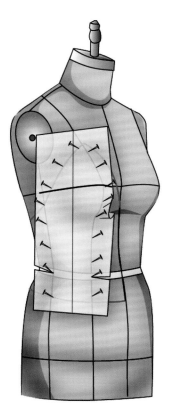

Figure 7.7a Drape the side panel.

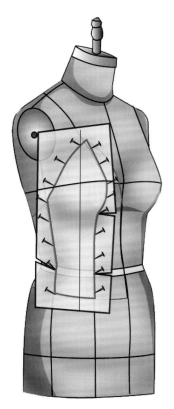

Figure 7.7b Mark the seam lines.

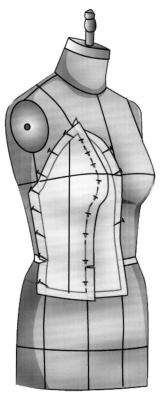

Figure 7.7c True the pattern.

BACK CENTER PANEL

1. Start by folding 1 inch from the center back along the longer side and press down.
2. Pin the fold against the center back line with pins pointing toward the side seam.
3. Smooth the muslin with your right hand across the waistline toward the princess line on the dress form while shaping the back.
4. Keep smoothing up the princess line and pinning the muslin at the princess line until you have pinned all around the style lines you have marked with tape. Clip a notch at the waist to remove tension. (Figure 7.8a)
5. Mark the style along the style tape and the princess line to make the center back pattern piece of your bodice. (Figure 7.8b)
6. Remove from the form, mark the seam allowances, trim, and pin back on the form. (Figure 7.8c)

BACK SIDE PANEL

1. To start draping the side piece, pin the straight grainline in the center of the side panel.

2. With your hand, smooth left toward the princess line and pin, smoothing the muslin up and down to shape around the back. Clip at the waist to remove tension.
3. Smooth right toward the side seam with your hand, and pin all along the side seam, smoothing the muslin up and down. Clip at the waist to reduce tension. (Figure 7.9a)
4. Mark the lines all along the style tape, the princess line, and the side seam. (Figure 7.9b)
5. Take the pattern piece off the form, and add the seam allowances. Trim.
6. Pin the two back patterns together to check the fit back on the form. Pin the back and front patterns together to make sure all the style lines align and the fit is good. (Figure 7.9c)

Hint: If you are making a corset with support in the bust, you will need to make another pattern for the inside **brassiere**.

1. First trace the corset patterns of your garment on paper.
2. Then construct the brassiere using the outside lines of the original pattern. Mark the measurement from the

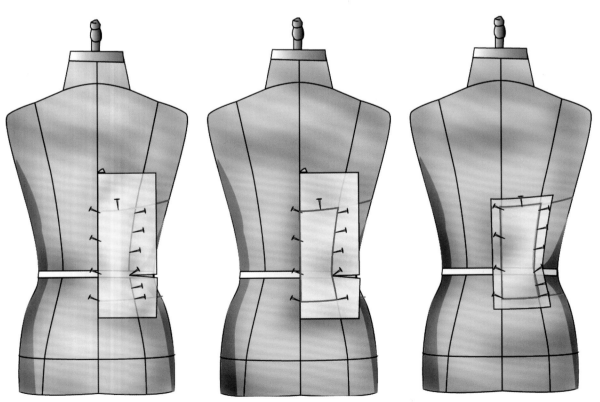

Figure 7.8a Drape the center back.   **Figure 7.8b** Mark the seam lines.   **Figure 7.8c** True the pattern.

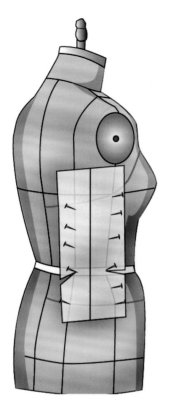
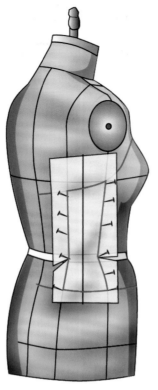
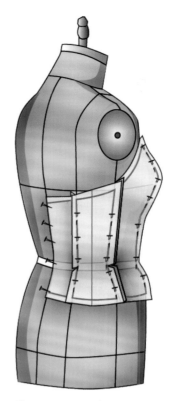

Figure 7.9a Drape back side panel.

Figure 7.9b Mark the seam lines.

Figure 7.9c True the pattern.

top of the corset to underneath the bust level. You will need to mark this level along the entire corset pattern, beginning at the center front and going around to the center back.

3. Cut out the patterns. If you want to reduce bulk in the corset, do not add any seam allowances to the brassiere. You will be butting the edges together to join them at the seam lines by wrapping stitches along both ends. (Figure 7.10)

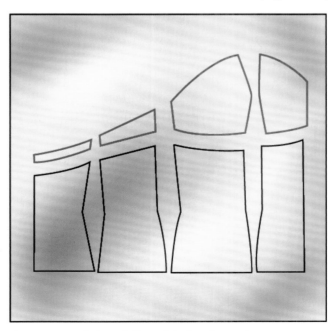

Figure 7.10 Mark the style lines of the brassiere and separate.

Using Your Pattern Blocks to Create a Corset Pattern

To begin, you will need to lay your front and back princess pattern blocks on a flat surface. Take another piece of paper, and lay it over the pattern blocks. Now trace the pattern. This way you can cut up the pattern without ruining the original. You can use waist-length blocks (Figure 7.11a) or hip-length blocks (Figure 7.11b), depending on the desired length of the corset.

1. When you are ready, start adding style lines to the pattern. Add style lines to the neckline of the corset and the hem as well. (Figure 7.11c)
2. Then you can take another piece of paper and trace the pattern pieces of the corset only.
3. Add seam allowances, and mark the pattern. Numbering the pattern pieces in order as they are sewn helps to avoid confusion.

If your pattern blocks already have ease, do not add any more to the corset or it will be too loose. When you are ready with your pattern, construct a muslin copy to test the pattern and add or take out ease where needed.

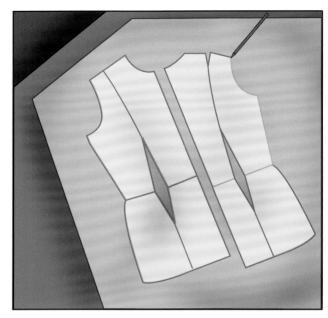

Figure 7.11b Hip length blocks (slopers).

Figure 7.11a Trace your front and back waist blocks (slopers).

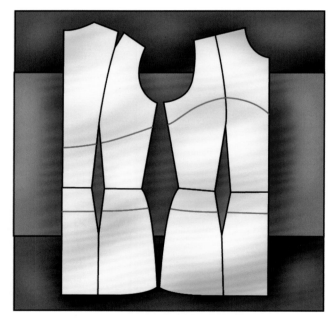

Figure 7.11c Mark your style lines and trace the corset patterns, seam allowances.

NEEDED ITEMS

Garment fabric (Figure 7.12a)

Canvas, horsehair interfacing, cotton twill, drill, or poplin (Figure 7.12b)—inside structure

Boning with casing—for the support of the garment. (Figure 7.12c) A **steel busk** will be needed for a center front opening.

Twill tape—for holding the eased pieces. (Figure 7.12d)

Grosgrain ribbon—for the waistband to keep the garment from shifting or sliding down on the body. (Figure 7.12e)

Figure 7.12a Garment fabric.

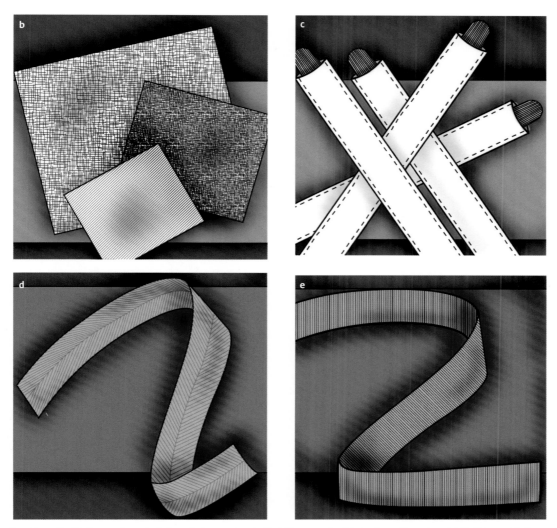

Figure 7.12 (continued) (b) Canvas, horsehair, interfacing, cotton twill, drill, or poplin. (c) Boning with casing. (d) Twill tape. (e) Grosgrain ribbon.

Cotton flannel or wool felt—for interlining the garment fabric so that the inside underlayers do not show through. (Figure 7.13a)

Thick batting—for the brassiere structure padding. (Figure 7.13b)

Lining fabric—for lining the garment. (Figure 7.13c)

Sewing supplies (Figure 7.13d)

Your design may also require hook and eyes, studs, and closures.

You may also need to use grommets, grommet pliers, a fabric hole punch, or fabric hole punch rotating pliers.

BONING TYPES

Choosing the right type of boning is important.

Ridgeline. This type of boning can be found in any fabric store and is not expensive. This boning is softer than most and can be easily sewn and cut. Smooth the ends with a nail file. (Figure 7.14a)

Spiral Steel Boning. This type of boning is made of small wires coiled together flat. This boning has to be cut with snips and cannot be cut with scissors. You can buy this boning by the yard and/or get it cut for you in specific lengths. If you get it professionally cut, measure every length of boning you will need for each seam. The professionals will also case the ends for you, which will keep the boning from damaging the fabric. This boning is very comfortable for the wearer because it bends easily backward, forward, and sideways. However, it does not come with a casing, so you will need to make one out of cotton. (Figure 7.14b)

Spring Steel Boning. This type of boning is made of strips of steel with blunt plastic-dipped ends. You can get these cut professionally. Unlike spiral steel, this type of boning is less comfortable for the wearer because it

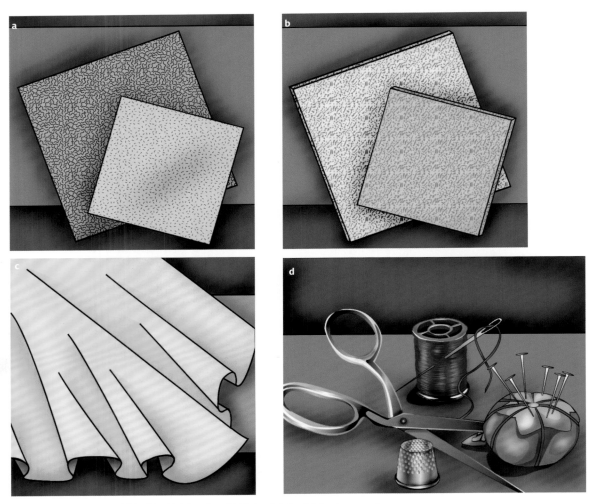

Figure 7.13 (a) Cotton flannel and wool felt. (b) Thick batting. (c) Lining fabric. (d) Sewing supplies.

bends easily backward and forward but not sideways. It does not come with a casing, so you will need to make one out of cotton. (Figure 7.14c)

Plastic Boning. This comes in different types and is sold in fabric stores; it is not expensive. It cannot be sewn through; however, it can be cut with scissors, and the edges can be rounded with scissors and/or a nail file. This type of boning is great to use in clothes that need washing because it tolerates water well. It comes in a cotton casing that makes it easier to attach to the garment. (Figure 7.14d)

Busk. Corset busks are usually made of steel or wood and most frequently utilize the traditional center front closure method. These come in a variety of lengths, shapes, thicknesses, and colors and may be lightweight or heavy-duty. Metal busks are a two-part closure made of a stainless steel and a black- or white-coated spring steel. One side of the busk features posts, and the other side has eyes for a solid fastening that can withstand the tension of corset lacing.

Lacing Bones. These are similar to the busk but used for the lacing, not closing a snap. They resemble a steel bone punched with holes to allow for the lacing. They support the fabric when a tight squeeze is needed for a shaping corset or even a costuming corset. They are usually placed in the center back of corsets to support the laces and hold the eyelets from popping out.

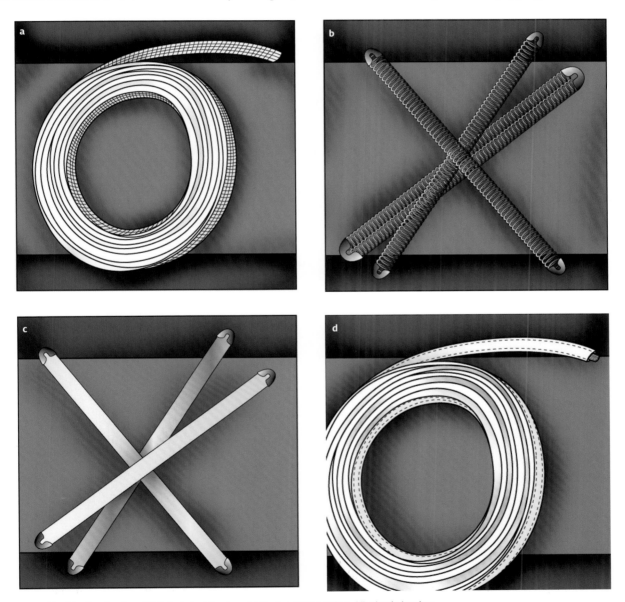

Figure 7.14 (a) Ridgeline boning. (b) Spiral steel boning. (c) Spring steel boning. (d) Plastic boning.

Construction of the Boned Corset Top

Now that you have draped your corset pattern, you can begin with the construction of the corset. Before you begin, make sure the pattern fits well on the body. You will also need to determine the waistline of your customer or the dress form and mark it on the patterns. The waistline can be marked ½ to ¾ inch below the original waistline to prevent the garment from sliding down. Also, make the waistline around ¾ inch narrower than the real waist measurement to make it sit tight at the waist and avoid sliding down to the hip. You will be using grosgrain ribbon at the waistline of your corset to hold the garment.

A well-structured corset is thick and has many layers; therefore, the garment outer layer has to be slightly larger than the inside pattern (¾ inch) to be able to wrap the entire structure. Divide ¾ inch by the number of panels you will be using for your corset. Count panels all around the body, not just half the body, or you will make it too wide. Add this amount to each panel.

INNER STRUCTURE OF THE CORSET

1. Cut the patterns out of the canvas, horsehair interfacing, or cotton twill.
2. Cut the brassiere out of thick batting fabric with no seam allowances. (Figure 7.15a)
3. Cut the grosgrain ribbon the length of the waistline minus ¾ inch.
4. Connect all of the pattern pieces in canvas. Press the seams open, and clip in the curved corners and waistline to avoid puckering. (Figure 7.15b)
5. The open seams should be stitched down with a catch stitch. (Figure 7.15c)
6. Next, connect the brassiere pieces by wrapping a hand-sewn seam along the edges. (Figure 7.15d)
7. Line up the brassiere on the inside of the canvas piece along the top seam line. Since the brassiere has no seam allowance, it should line up right at the top seam line; pin and baste the brassiere to the canvas. (Figure 7.15e)
8. Measure the seams minus the top and bottom seam allowance, and cut the boning to match the measurements.

Figure 7.15a Four-piece bra cup.

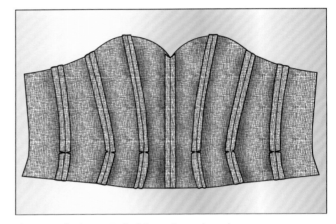

Figure 7.15b Connect all of the pattern pieces in canvas

Figure 7.15c Catch stitch seams.

9. If you are using boning with a casing, pull the boning out of the casing. Line up the casing with the seam lines along the princess seams. Make sure the center of the casing aligns with the seam line. (Figure 7.15f) Stitch on both ends of the casing.

10. If you are using steel boning with no casing, make the casing using bias strips of muslin. (Figure 7.15g)

11. Machine stitch the casing or hand stitch with whip-stitches. Insert the boning back into the casing. You will need to backstitch at the ends to close the boning and keep it from coming out. (Figure 7.15h)

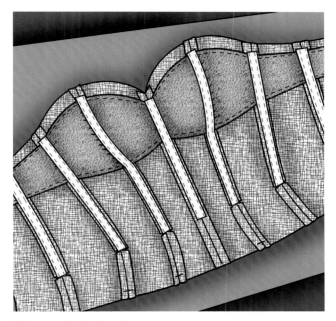

Figure 7.15f Attach casing.

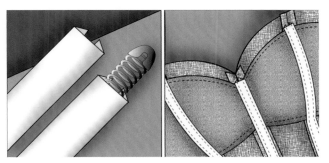

Figure 7.15g Bias casing.

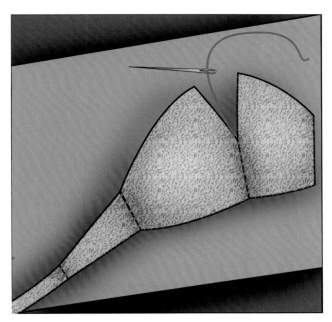

Figure 7.15d Connect the brassiere pieces

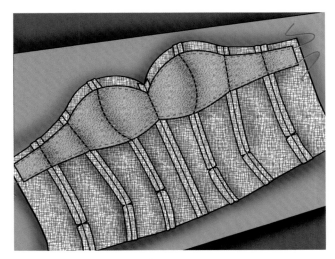

Figure 7.15e Attach the brassiere.

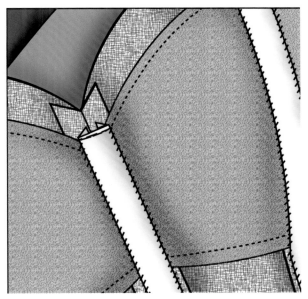

Figure 7.15h Casing by hand or machine.

12. Bones can also be added to the garment where there are no seams. Sew them in between seams for better support, (Figure 7.15i) even under the bust. (Figure 7.15j)

13. At the waistline, stitch the grosgrain ribbon through all the layers. (Figure 7.15k) Be very careful at the boning. End the grosgrain 1 inch from the closure on both sides.

CONSTRUCTING THE OUTER LAYER OF THE CORSET

1. Cut out the outer garment panels, and attach them together. Press the seams open. (Figure 7.16a)

2. Cut the interlining out of wool felt or flannel without seam allowances. (Figure 7.16b)

3. Line up the interlining pieces along the inside of the garment under the pressed-down seams. Baste the pieces in place.

4. Catch stitch the seam down to keep the interlining pieces in place while attaching the interlining to the outer garment. (Figure 7.16c) Make sure your stitching does not show through to the outside of the garment. Use matching thread.

5. Ease the top and bottom seam allowance by stitching a loose seam $\frac{1}{8}$ inch from the seam line to help the layers line up at the top and bottom. Pull on the bobbin thread, and then use twill tape to stitch it through the seam allowance to hold the ease in place. (Figure 7.16d)

6. Add any embellishments to the outside of the garment before you attach it to the boned bodice. (Figure 7.16e)

7. Attach the closure to the outer layer first, whether it is a zipper, buttons, or another type. (Figure 7.16f)

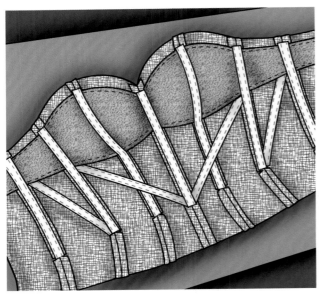

Figure 7.15i Boning in between seams.

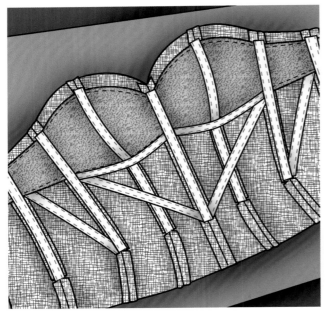

Figure 7.15j Boning under bust.

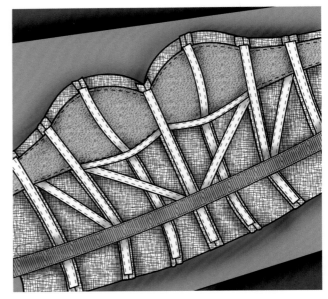

Figure 7.15k Grosgrain.

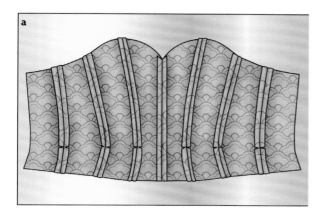

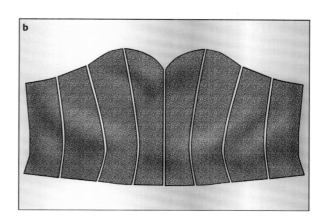

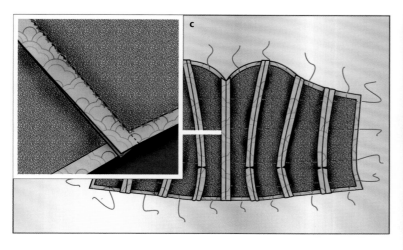

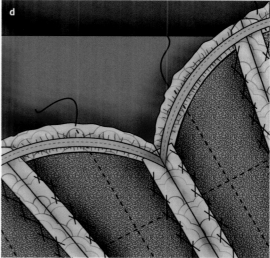

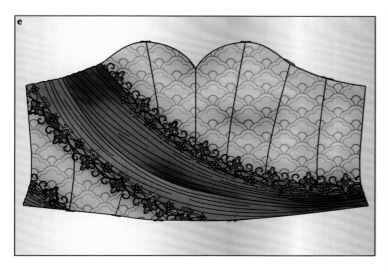

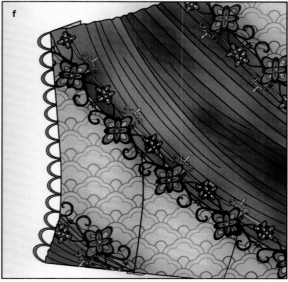

Figure 7.16 (a) Outer corset layer. (b) Cut felt or flannel, no seam allowances. (c) Fit flannel under seams, and catch stitch. (d) Ease the neckline with twill tape. (e) Decorate outer layer (f) Attach the closure.

INSIDE OF THE CORSET

The inside of the corset is the lining and/or lining with facing. You need to decide whether you will work with lining alone or with a facing attached to the lining. (Figure 7.17a)

If you are using a facing, cut the facing and lining pieces, and then attach them together. (Figure 7.17b)

ATTACHING ALL LAYERS TOGETHER

When you are ready to attach the layers together, you will need to decide where you will be leaving an opening. Boning bodices are very hard to flip inside out because they have the bones sewn on. Some of the places that work best are the bottom of the corset (make the opening large enough to get the longest piece of boning through), at the top of the corset in between two princess seams, and at one of the closure sides if it is long enough to get the longest piece of boning through.

1. Sandwich the layers correctly. Here is the order from the table upward:
   a. Lining, facing right side up
   b. Garment fabric layer, facing down (the lining and the garment should end up right sides together)
   c. Underlining structure, boning facing up (Figure 7.18a)
2. Make sure to pin the seams together and match them. (Figure 7.18b)
   a. Baste the pieces together.
   b. Stitch around with your sewing machine, leaving the opening to flip inside out and the closure area unstitched.

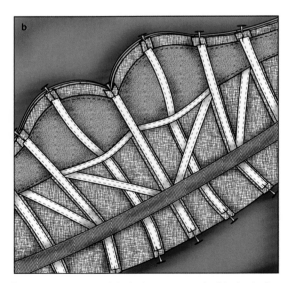

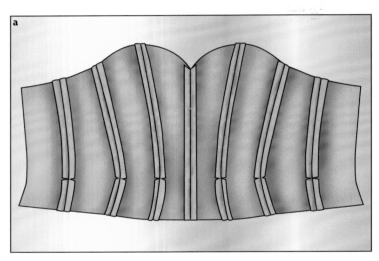

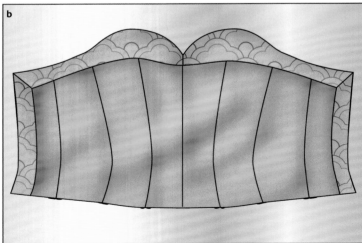

Figure 7.17 (a) Lining. (b) Lining with facing.

Figure 7.18 (a) Sandwich the layers correctly. (b) Pin the layers.

c. Press the seams flat, and clip the seam allowance, except for the opening for the flip. (Figure 7.18c)

d. Flip the garment inside out. (Figure 7.18d)

e. Close the opening by hand sewing it with invisible running stitches. (Figure 7.18e)

f. Attach the lining to the closure on the inside of the garment, and slip stitch by hand.

g. Press if you can. Be careful because the inside layers may show through after pressing.

h. The last thing you will need to do is hand tack the layers together at the top and bottom of the corset on the inside of the garment without catching the outer layer fabric. This way the lining will not roll out of the edge of the corset. (Figure 7.18f)

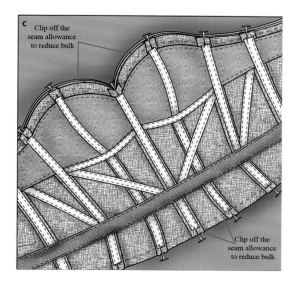

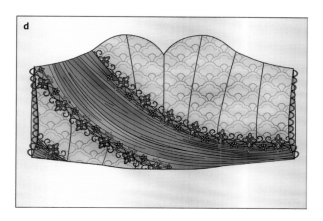

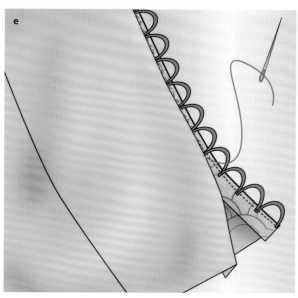

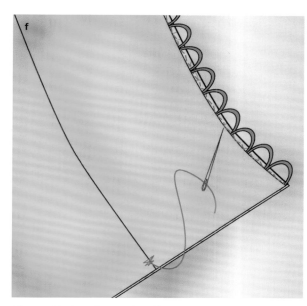

Figure 7.18 (continued) (c) Stitch the layers, and press. (d) Flip corset right side out. (e) Close the opening. (f) Hand tack the lining.

A BRIEF LOOK INTO THE LIFE OF

VERA WANG

Vera Wang was born on June 27, 1949, in New York City. A competitive figure skater in her teenage years, she studied art history at Sarah Lawrence and for her sophomore year went to the Sorbonne in Paris, where she discovered her love for design. She took a job with *Vogue* after graduation and soon became a senior fashion editor, a post she held until 1985, when she became design director for women's accessories at Ralph Lauren.

for her own wedding. The following year, with financial backing from her father, she opened her own bridal boutique in New York, initially selling wedding dresses from designers such as Guy Laroche, Arnold Scaasi, Carolina Herrera, and Christian Dior. Within a few years, Wang had launched her own signature collection of bridal wear.

Sharon Stone, Uma Thurman, and Holly Hunter. Wang soon expanded into elegant evening wear and couture gowns, as well as ready-to-wear, all offering a balance of classic elegance and modern sensibility.

Vera Wang 2014 Spring/Summer Bridal Collection.

Vera Wang 2012 Bridal Collection.

Vera Wang.

Wang married in 1989. Disappointed by the selection of wedding dresses available, she began sketching her own designs and eventually commissioned a dressmaker to produce one of them

Wang began receiving international attention in 1994, when she designed a beaded skating costume for Olympic skater Nancy Kerrigan. Her wedding dresses have been worn by numerous celebrities, including Mariah Carey, Jennifer Lopez, Victoria Beckham,

In 2001, Wang launched her first perfume and published a well-received wedding guide. She has since developed lines of jewelry, lingerie, and home products. In 2005, the Council of the Fashion Designers of America named Wang its Womenswear Designer of the Year. In 2006, she entered into an agreement to produce a less expensive line of ready-to-wear clothing for Kohl's.

Chapter Review

The corset was introduced as early as the fifteenth century, and we still wear it today. Corsets used to be boned with whalebone, wood, and different types of metal; however, today we wear corsets that are a bit more comfortable and boned with either plastic boning or **steel springs**, offering us the support we need without hurting our rib cage. In this chapter, you were introduced to corsets and how to make them. You learned how to pattern, drape, layer, construct, and tailor corsets inside and out. You also learned about the tools you need to make a corset and how to use them. Boning comes in four different types: ridgeline, spiral steel boning, spring steel boning, and plastic boning. You can choose any one of these types to create your corset today.

Projects

1. Design and sketch a garment inspired by each of the types of corsets discussed in the historical introduction to this chapter. Present it in a professional manner.

2. Make a boning sample for your book. Write down your steps, and insert them into one of your plastic cover sheets.

3. Create a page for your sample book with the items needed to make a corset. Include swatches and sketches. Write down all of the information you need to know for using each item. Insert it into one of your plastic cover sheets.

4. Design and construct a two-layer corset using the construction techniques covered in this chapter. Refer to Chapter 10 for closure ideas.

Key Terms

Boning	Horsehair interfacing	Steel busk
Brassiere	Hourglass	Steel springs
Canvas	Payres of bodies	Steel strips
Corset	Plastic boning	Thick batting
Cotton flannel	Poplin	Twill tape
Cotton twill	Ridgeline	Whalebone
Drill	Spiral steel boning	Wool felt
Girdle	Spring steel boning	
Grosgrain ribbon	Stays	

8

The Skill of Garment Embellishment

Objectives

- Learn different decorative skills to enhance your designs

- Learn embroidery techniques to decorate your garments

- Learn how to sew and decorate with lace

- Learn beading techniques to decorate garments

- Learn appliqué and cutwork techniques to enhance your garments

- Learn about the life and work of Elie Saab

Embroidery

Embroidery has been around for centuries in artwork and clothing and as a form of decoration. Embroidery was a popular way for women in the Victorian era to express their ideas and beliefs at embroidery circles, tea parties, or book readings or in the comfort of their own homes. Since hand embroidery was one of the simplest options, it was taught to younger girls in order to pass along the tradition, to grow their skills with age, and for mother/daughter bonding opportunities. The Victorian era widely popularized using embroidery in clothing, baby clothes, bedding, pillows, blankets, curtains, home décor, handkerchiefs, gloves, and so much more. (Figure 8.1)

Embroidery Tools

EMBROIDERY NEEDLES

Embroidery needles range in size and purpose and are measured in length of the needle, the shaft thickness, point sharp or blunt, size of the eye, and the shape of the eye. See Table 8.1 for types of needles you can use to avoid thread breakage.

EMBROIDERY THREAD/FLOSS

Embroidery thread (Figure 8.2) comes in cotton, silk, rayon, polyester, linen, and wool fiber content. See Table 8.2 for thread types.

EMBROIDERY HOOPS/FRAMES

Hoops and frames are used during the embroidery process. (Figure 8.3) They allow you to focus on a specific area of the garment or fabric and help to keep the fabric tight while you work, squeezing the fabric in between the hoops and stretching it tight.

Figure 8.1 Embroidery example.

Table 8.1 EMBROIDERY AND NEEDLECRAFT NEEDLES

Needle Type	Description	Usage
Embroidery (Crewel)	Embroidery Sizes 9–10 Smocking Sizes 7–9 General Sewing Sizes 3–8	Medium long needles with an oval eye. These needles are used for embroidery, ribbon embroidery, and smocking. The long oval eye helps several embroidery threads be threaded at the same time, such as three to six strands of silk, rayon, cotton, thicker perle cotton, wool thread, nondivisible cotton thread, and metallic thread. However, since the eye is too wide, some stitches such as bullion knots may be hard to pull through.
Sharps	Sizes 7–12	Medium long needles with small, round eyes that make the needles strong and prevent the thread from breaking. These needles have a size range to accommodate most weights of fabrics and can fit up to two strands of silk, cotton, or rayon thread. These needles are suitable for fine embroidery and hand appliqué as well as general sewing.
Milliner's	Sizes 1–11	Long shaft needles with tiny round eyes the same width as the shaft. These needles are used for beading and can be used bullion knots and French knots. Higher number needles can fit up to two strands of cotton, silk, or rayon thread, and the lower numbers can fit four to six strands.
Chenille	Sizes 18–24	Used for embroidery, ribbon embroidery, wool embroidery, and hand-worked buttonholes. These needles were originally used for chenille yarns and are thick and sharp. They have a large eye for thicker thread such as thick silk, six-strand cotton, tapestry wool, crewel wool, and heavy metallic thread.
Beading	Sizes 10–16	Long thin needles with a round eye and a fine point. These needles are used to make long stitches on fine fabrics and are thin for beading narrow beads and sequins.
Tapestry	Sizes 24–28	Medium-length needles with a thick shaft, a blunt point, and a long oval eye. They are used for needlework and as a substitute for bodkin. The blunt point is great to part the fabric threads instead of splitting, which can damage your fabric during use. You can use higher number needles (24–26) on decorative hem stitching on fine fabrics such as linens . Lower numbers (18–24) are great for counted thread embroidery such as crossstitch, shadow work, blackwork, needleweaving, pulled thread work, and wool embroidery.

Figure 8.2 Embroidery thread.

Table 8.2 EMBROIDERY THREAD AND FLOSS NEEDLECRAFT NEEDLES

Thread Type	Description and Usage
Cotton Embroidery Floss	This thread type is a soft six-strand (ply) floss made from Egyptian cotton mercerized to add shine. It is very often used for embroidery in many colors and allows adjustment in the thickness of the thread by using a different number of strands.
Pearl Cotton	This thread type is a finely twisted cotton thread that does not divide into strands and is only used for thicker applications. It has a shiny, silky, raised texture, and its lustrous finish makes it easy to use for a wide variety of fabrics and embroidery techniques. It comes in four sizes: 3, 5, 8, and 12. The lower the number, the thicker the thread.
Silk Floss	This thread type is made from 100 percent silk and has a lustrous shine texture that can add a beautiful embellishment and elegance to any embroidery. It is used in many projects, especially in crewel tapestry, smocking, and crossstitching.
Variegated Floss	This thread type is a blend of soft colors that flow into one another in a smooth transition and reveal the color change every few stitches. It can come in cotton, silk, or linen floss.
Metallic Floss	This thread type is 100 percent polyester or poly-blend floss with metallic shine. It works great as an embroidery floss with metallic shine.
Satin Floss/Rayon Floss	This thread type is a silky, six-strand (ply) shiny floss with lustrous threads that glide easily through fabrics. It comes in many vibrant colors that you can use to embroider satin stitches and long and short satin.
Heathway Wool Thread (Crewel Work)	This thread type is a soft, smooth, and silky wool that has a very nice sheen. It makes a beautiful satin stitch.
D'Aubusson Wool Thread (Crewel Work)	This thread type is a finer-sized wool with a slight sheen used for detail embroidery. It's easy to work with, and it retains the traditional look of wool thread without the scratchy texture.
Bella Lusso Wool	This thread type is a very fine, smooth Italian wool that's easy to work with. It makes a great satin stitch and feels like cotton embroidery floss or pearl cotton floss.

Figure 8.3 Embroidery hoops and frames.

STABILIZERS

A stabilizer is a form of interfacing that acts as a backing to prevent your fabric puckering when you are pulling the stitches tight; it is more commonly used with embroidery machines than in hand embroidery. However, if your fabric is very thin, slippery, or stretches when sewn, choose a stabilizer option from Table 8.3. These stabilizers are designed to be removed or trimmed after the embroidery design is finished. Some are designed to act as a permanent interfacing (fusible, non-fusible, sew-in).

Table 8.3 STABILIZER VARIATIONS AND USES FOR EMBROIDERY

Stabilizer Type	Fabric Uses	Description & Usage
Tearaway	Fleece, Faux Suede, Satin for small embroidery designs, Silk for thin and translucent silk embroidery	Prevents stitch distortion; versatile; use tearaway stabilizers for wovens. Can use one or more layers and then tear away layers separately to avoid pulled stitches. Weight ranges from 1.5 to 3 oz/yd^2. Good-quality tearaways should be strong and withstand multiple perforations. When choosing, consider ease of tear, good hoop stability, and perforation resistance options.
Peel and Stick Tearaway	All fabrics	**Sticky Stitch**™ is tearaway backing with a self-adhesive back. Use it when hooping is not an option. Examples: cuffs, collars, finished garments. Peel away after the embroidery is done.
Iron-on Tearaway		Iron-on tearaway is tearaway backing with a self-adhesive back. Use it when hooping is not an option. Examples: cuffs, collars, finished garments. Temporarily stabilize to avoid shifting and puckering. Peel away after the embroidery is done.
Tearaway/ Washaway		Tearaway/washaway stabilizer has similar properties to the previously mentioned regular tearaway. It dissolves easily in warm water and provides more support to the embroidery area.
Cutaway	Broadcloth, Burlap, Canvas, Charmeuse, Corduroy, Denim, Faux Leather, Faux Suede, Felt, Flannel, Fleece, Gabardine, Jersey Knit, Leather, Linen, Microfiber, Muslin, Neoprene, Nylon, Pique, Polyester Shantung, Satin, Heavier Silk, Spandex, Taffeta, Terry Cloth, Velour, Velvet, Vinyl, Wool	Cutaway stabilizers provide a stable base for delicate and stretchy fabrics during stitching and even afterwards. It's a permanent stabilizer. You can use cutaway stabilizers for knits and wovens. Weight ranges from 1.5 to 3.5 oz/yd^2. Helps maintain the crispness of details during the embroidery and retain its shape after wash. Do not cut too close to the design. When choosing a cutaway consider good hoop stability, ease of cutting, wash stability, and perforation resistance.
Washaway	Chiffon, Crinoline, Lace, Organza, Pashmina, Tulle	Water-soluble embroidery stabilizers (WSS) will dissolve completely when dipped in water, leaving no backing at all. They are a great option when a stabilizer is needed, but not wanted to be left inside the design. Used often for lace and sheer fabrics. **Water-soluble stabilizers companies.** Solvy is a fine water-soluble film. Badgemaster is heavier then the Solvy; can be hooped by itself and stitched on directly. Vilene WSS closely resembles other cutaway backings. Vilene Tacky is fibrous with a pressure-sensitive sticky coating for holding hard-to-hoop items in place while stitching.

(continued)

Table 8.3 STABILIZER VARIATIONS AND USES FOR EMBROIDERY *(continued)*

Stabilizer Type	Fabric Uses	Description & Usage
Heataway (Stitch-n-Heat)	All woven fabric types and pile fabrics	Company variations: Stitch-n-Heat, Heat N Gone—Embroidery Trick Film—Heat Away—Thermofilm Heataway is a transparent plastic meltaway film on fabrics with pile or on delicate fabrics. It can be torn away or melted away with heat using an iron at 120°C/240°F. Never iron with steam! Use brown paper during the melting process to protect your iron. Does not pucker, shrink, or change the color of your fabric.
No Show Fusible Mesh	Woven fabrics, sheers, and lightweight knits	No Show Nylon Mesh is a 1.5-ounce mesh stabilizer. It is made of soft, sheer nylon. Can be used in hooping embroidery. Works great with fabrics such as lightweight knits and woven fabrics, and is very comfortable for the wearer. It is invisible when viewed from the front of the garment. Iron it on using your iron at 250–260° only (to eliminate shrinking). When using on silk, wool, or polyester use the lowest temperature setting.
Liquid Stabilizer	Woven Fabrics	Regular Starch
Spray-on Fusible Adhesive	All fabric types	Spray-on fusible adhesive is a washable, dry-cleanable, acid-free stabilizer great for machine embroidery. It can make any fabric, paper, or batting into a fusible (iron-on) option. Has no odor and no CFCs.
Temporary Adhesive Spray	All fabric types	Temporary fabric adhesive used to temporarily bond fabric. Acid free and has no odor or color and is repositionable. Does not gum up sewing needles and eliminates sticky hands. Can be used for machine appliqué, quilting, basting, and hemming. It cleans up easily with soap and water or can be dry-cleaned.
Embroidery Stitch Covering	All fabric types	Polyester weave fusible backing used to cover finished embroidery stitches on the inside to prevent threads from coming in contact with skin and causing irritation.

Sources: www.embroiderysupplies.com, http://www.threadart.com/t-ChoosingStabilizer.aspx, http://www.allstitch.net, http://www.allbrands.com

EMBROIDERY SCISSORS

For embroidery and appliqué, use small, sharp scissors to move around and get into tight spaces, such as Gold Stork Embroidery Scissors (Figure 8.4) or small appliqué scissors with a duckbill side. Appliqué scissors are made with two different cutting blades. The bottom blade, shaped like a duckbill, pushes away the bottom layer of fabric for flawless, controlled cuts close to the stitching.

Figure 8.4 Embroidery scissors.

ORGANIZATION/STORAGE BOXES

Use thread organizers, needle organizers, and clear plastic storage box options with multiple compartments for all supplies.

Getting Started on Embroidery

- Prewash fabric before you begin to avoid shrinkage.
- Press out all gathers, creases, and wrinkles for smooth embroidery.
- Cut your fabric pattern piece, and secure the edges to avoid frayed ends.
- If needed, stabilize your fabric to avoid puckers and wrinkles in your fabric from tightly pulled stitches and thread bulk.
- Decide on a hoop/frame if your fabric is forgiving enough for one not to leave a permanent mark.
- To reduce the risk of these marks, remove the piece from the hoops when you are not working.
- Delicate fabrics that should never be used with a hoop include satin-faced silk, fine linens, velvet, corduroy, velour, terry cloth, and others. Pile fabrics are crushed inside the hoops. Test first.
- Covering hoops with a binding before use helps soften the corners and will not snag your fabrics.

USING THE HOOP

1. To set up the hoop, separate the two circular frame rings. Usually they have a side screw that you can twist and loosen.
2. Place the smaller ring on a table covered by your fabric. Smooth your fabric to flatten it, and center the design to ensure proper placement.

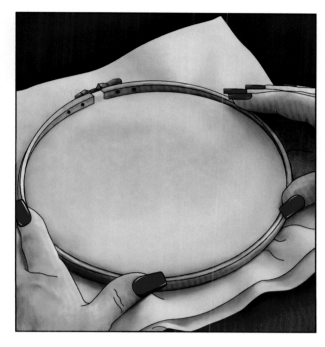

Figure 8.5 Using the hoop.

3. Place the larger ring, the one with the screw attached, on top of your fabric.
4. Push down, and snap the larger ring in place over the smaller ring with your fabric in between.
5. Check the fabric inside the hoops. It needs to feel tight when pressed and should not shake or wobble with waves.
6. To tighten, lightly pull on the fabric in various places around the hoop.
7. Tighten the screw. (Figure 8.5)

Securing Your Thread

To begin your stitching, you need to decide which method you will use to secure the thread. Keep it small and flat to reduce bulk and bumps. Making knots during embroidery is not recommended by professional embroiderers because knots add bulk and bumps to your work. However, if you are adding embroidery to a garment that will need to be worn and washed often, the embroidery needs to be permanently secured. In this case, make a small knot when you need to start and end your stitching.

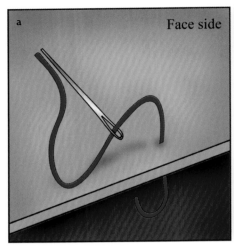
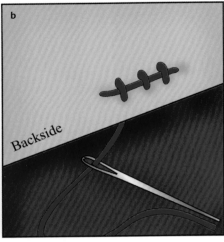

Figure 8.6 Stitch over.

STITCH OVER

1. Pull your needle and thread up from the backside, leaving a 1–1.5-inch tail of thread hanging from the backside.
2. Hold the tail flat against the backside of the fabric toward the direction of your design pattern.
3. As you continue the embroidery, the next five to eight embroidery stitches will catch the bottom tail and secure it down. (Figure 8.6)

AWAY KNOT

1. Make a regular knot at one end of the thread, and start on the right side of the fabric.
2. Begin pulling the needle through a couple of inches away from the design.
3. Continue embroidery until design is finished, and then you can clip the knot with small scissors.
4. From the backside, pull the thread out, and thread your needle with the end of this thread piece.
5. Begin weaving this piece through previously made stitches, threading loops until the thread ends. (Figure 8.7)
6. This is also an ending method for any embroidery technique. If you wish to secure the thread or to change colors, weave the leftover piece through previous stitches.

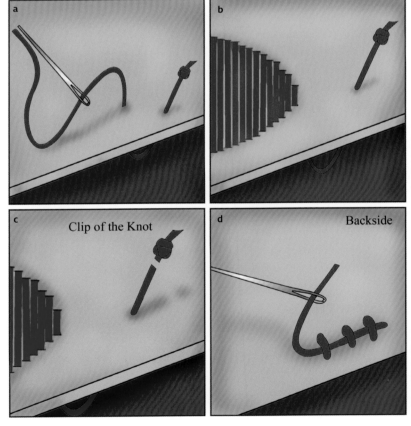

Figure 8.7 Away knot.

Embroidery Stitches

SATIN STITCH

The **satin stitch** is one of the oldest stitches worldwide. This stitch is flat and formed with equal stitches close together side by side. Make sure the stitches are tight, and then it will fill shapes.

1. Secure the thread, and insert the needle up into the fabric at one end of the motif.
2. Insert the needle down into the fabric on the other side of the design.
3. Pass the needle beneath the fabric back to the same side spot you started at, and insert the needle up into the fabric right next to the first stitch.
4. Insert the needle back down into the fabric right next to the second stitch you made.
5. Pass the needle beneath the fabric back to the same side spot you just made, and insert the needle up into the fabric right next to the third stitch. (Figure 8.8a and b)
6. Continue to repeat these steps until you get the entire shape filled.

LONG AND SHORT STITCH

Also known as the Kensington stitch, the long and short stitch is a very old stitch used for centuries. This method requires one long and one short stitch side by side close together. Stitch length needs to be alternated since the stitches should never be the same length.

This stitch is worked with a stitch direction (slant) to make it look 3-dimensional and follows the natural direction of the motif and its growth. Add padding for dimension.

1. Secure the thread, and insert the needle up into the fabric along the outline of your motif.
2. Use a chain stitch or a backstitch around the motif outline to achieve a great smooth edge and add some dimension to the edge from the surface of the fabric.
3. Begin the long and short stitch with the same color; you can continue with the same thread. If you need to change the thread, secure your outline thread in the back of the fabric.
4. Insert the needle down into the fabric one stitch lengthwise. Pass the needle beneath the fabric back to the same spot you started at, and insert the needle up into the fabric right next to the first stitch as close as possible to get a tight fill.
5. Insert the needle back down into the fabric right next to the second stitch you made, making it longer than the previous stitch. Pass the needle beneath the fabric back to the starting side, and insert the needle up into the fabric next to the third stitch as close as possible.

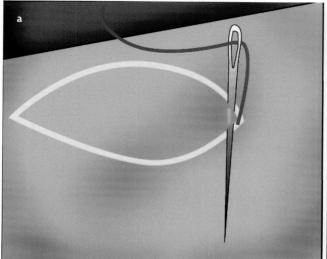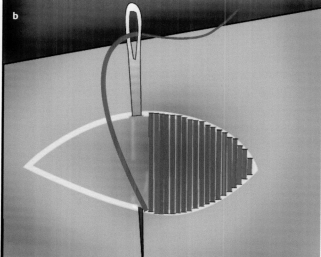

Figure 8.8a and b Satin stitch.

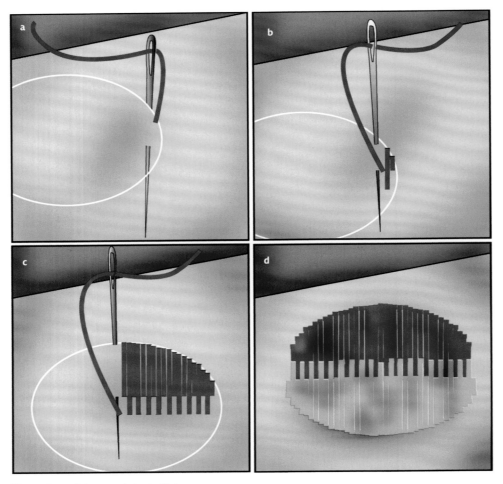

Figure 8.9a–d Long and short stitch.

6. Insert the needle back down into the fabric right next to the fourth stitch, making it shorter but not the same length as the first stitch. Pass the needle beneath the fabric back to the starting side, and insert the needle up into the fabric next to the last stitch as close as possible. (Figure 8.9a–d)

7. Continue these steps, filling the entire row.

8. To fill the rest of the shape, use same thread color or begin a slightly different shade of color for the second row. Keep adding more rows, stitching tightly through the ends of the first row and changing the color shades to get a better effect.

STEM STITCH

The **stem stitch** is a very versatile stitch used for flower stems, decorative lines, outline motifs, or even decorative edges because it behaves well with curved lines. To make the stem stitch wider, slope the angle direction of the stitch more.

1. Secure the thread, and insert the needle up into the fabric at one end of the motif.

2. Point the needle down diagonally, and take a diagonal stitch in and out of the fabric with the thread on the same side as the needle, making one diagonal stitch.

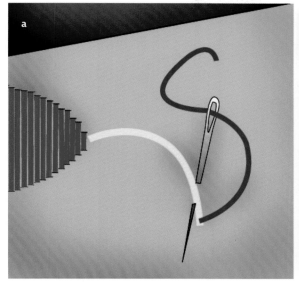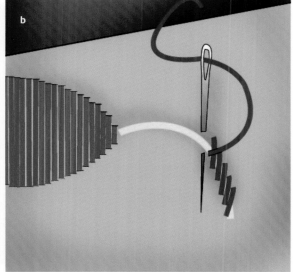

Figure 8.10a and b Stem stitch.

3. Make another same stitch in and out of the fabric right above the first stitch. Make sure your stitches are very close together. (Figure 8.10a and b)
4. Continue repeating these stitches until you get to the end of the line.

FISHBONE STITCH

This stitch is great to use for filling in shapes and making leaves and flower petals. Trace a leaf shape on your fabric, and mark a center line.

1. Secure the thread, and insert the needle up into the fabric at the top of the motif. Make a small satin stitch at the top of the center line of the leaf.
2. Insert the needle down into the fabric at the bottom of the first satin stitch, diagonally down along the center line. Pass the needle beneath the fabric. With your needle now facing upward, diagonally toward the other side of your leaf, bring the needle out right next to the first satin stitch you made, just on the other side of it.
3. With your needle facing downward diagonally, insert the needle through the center line again, passing your needle diagonally upward to the other side of your leaf. Bring the needle out right next to the second stitch you made.
4. Continue to repeat these steps until you get the entire shape filled. (Figure 8.11a–d)

COUCHING STITCH

The couching stitch, another old stitch popularized during the Middle Ages, is a method of attaching a thick thread in place with another thread. Couching is used widely with thicker thread, cord, trim, or yarn because it is too thick to pass through the fabric.

Couching uses two threads: one thicker thread (called the *laid thread*) and a second thinner thread (called the *couching thread*).

1. Secure the laid thread in the backside of your fabric, and bring it up to the right side of the fabric if possible. If it is too thick, make a couple of backstitches through the end of this thread to secure it in place. Leave the laid thread loose on the right side.
2. Secure the couching thread on the backside of your fabric, and bring it up to the right side at the starting point of your laid thread.
3. You should have two loose threads at your starting point.
4. To follow your motif, lay the laid thread on the fabric surface along the marked line.
5. Secure the laid thread in place with the couching thread by bringing the needle over and down into the backside of the fabric close to the other side of the laid thread. (Figure 8.12a–d)
6. From the backside of the fabric, ¼ inch to 1 inch away, make a small stitch up through the fabric on the opposite edge side, bringing the needle over and down into the backside of fabric close to the other side of the laid thread.
7. Repeat steps 5–7 to secure the laid thread to the fabric until you get to the end of your line.
8. If the laid thread is thin enough to go through a large needle eye and through the fabric, insert it into the

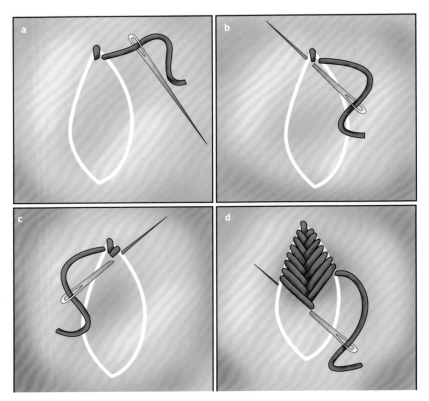

Figure 8.11a–d Fishbone stitch.

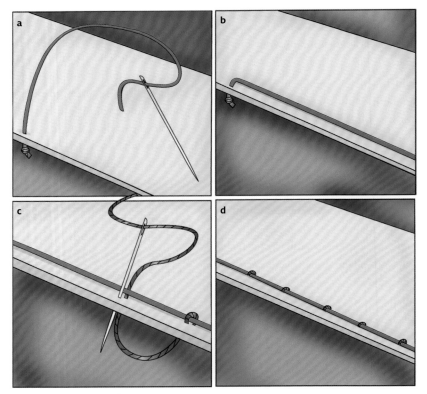

Figure 8.12a–d Couching stitch.

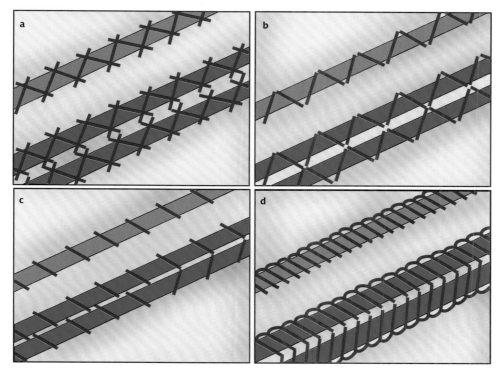

Figure 8.13a–d Couching stitch variations.

needle eye and bring it down through your fabric to secure it in the back.

9. The couching thread should also be secured in the backside alone or help secure the laid thread.

10. If the laid thread is thick, do the same steps you worked at the starting point by making extra couches in place before pulling it to the back. Trim off the extra laid thread but not too close to avoid fraying and loosening.

Hint: Different stitch variations for the couching thread include catch stitch, running catch stitch, detached chain stitch, blanket stitch, zigzag stitch, whipstitch, and many more embroidery and ornamental stitches. (Figure 8.13a–d)

MACHINE COUCHING

Couch with decorative stitches using your sewing machine. With your machine, you can use different thread colors and types of thread, such as metallic thread, ombre thread, silk thread, and cotton thread. (Figure 8.14)

Machine couching facts
- If you use a thicker top thread, it won't go through the needle; therefore wind it to your bobbin instead.

Then stitch with your garment facing down toward the bobbin plate.
- Presser feet such as a cording foot, a free-motion couching foot (which guides the thread as you sew),

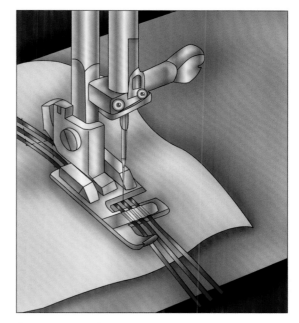

Figure 8.14 Machine couching.

an open-toe embroidery foot, and an appliqué presser foot help with the couching technique.

- For this method, use a larger eye needle, size 90/14, to give your thread type a little more room.

ZIGZAG COUCHING

1. Set your machine to a wide **zigzag stitch** with a medium or long stitch length.
2. Line up your laid thread along your motif, and pin or baste it in place.
3. Make a few backstitches to secure your laid thread with a straight stitch. Make sure you line up your laid thread so that the zigzag stitch catches it side to side.
4. Set to zigzag stitch slightly wider than the laid thread in order to catch along both sides of the trim and fabric. With the material centered under your foot, begin stitching toward the end of the laid thread.
5. Work in small sections for curved lines. At the end, make a few backstitches to secure it. (Figure 8.15a and b)

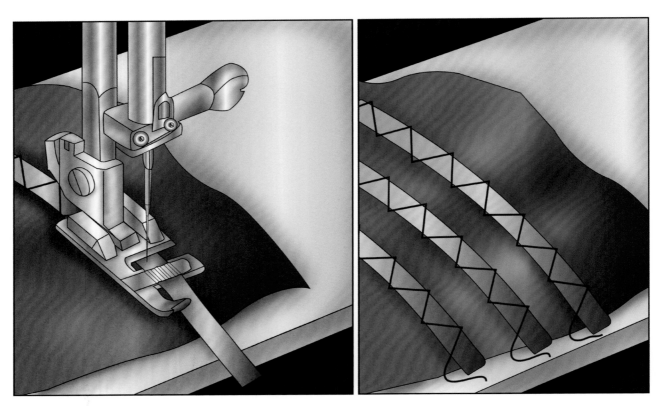

Figure 8.15a and b Zigzag couching.

EYELET STITCH

The eyelet stitch is used in both embroidery and cutwork. It looks like a small eye with a hollow cutout center. The eyelet takes on different shapes and sizes such as a circle, oval, drop, triangle, square, rectangle, or leaf. There are two methods used to make the eyelet stitch.

Satin Stitch Eyelet

1. To begin, mark your circle (shape) on your fabric, showing one guideline for the eyelet outline and another smaller one for the center.
2. Work a running stitch along the outer guideline, stitching around the outside of your shape ⅟₁₆ to ⅛ inches away from your marked line.
3. Use embroidery scissors to cut an X in the center of the smaller circle. Be careful when cutting to avoid cutting too far, and leave at least a ⅟₁₆- to ⅛-inch space from the cut to the guideline.

4. Start a new thread, secure it behind your fabric, and bring out your needle to the face side directly outside of the running stitch line mark #1. (Figure 8.16a–d)
5. To begin overcasting, take the needle into the hole and back out at mark #2. One satin stitch is now complete. The cut flaps of the inside fabric will fold back and act as an interfacing.
6. Repeat another satin stitch directly next to the first one to make the stitches tight together. Go into the hole and back out at mark #3.
7. Continue making satin stitches all the way around the raw edge of the eyelet.
8. Stop at the starting point; join the last and the first satin stitches together by stitching through them with a whipstitch. (Figure 8.17a–d)
9. Secure your thread behind the fabric, and trim off any fabric flap pieces.

Hint: You can also use the buttonhole stitch to finish the eyelet. (Figure 8.18a and b)

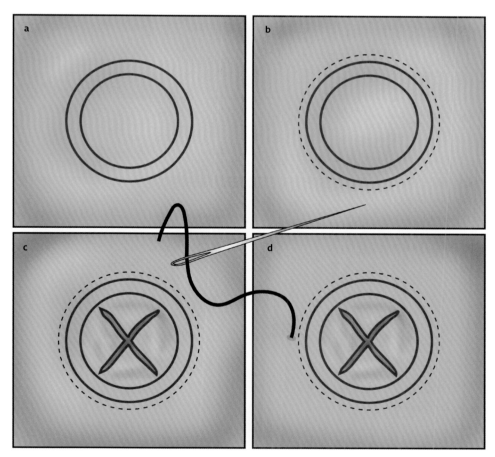

Figure 8.16a–d Eyelets.

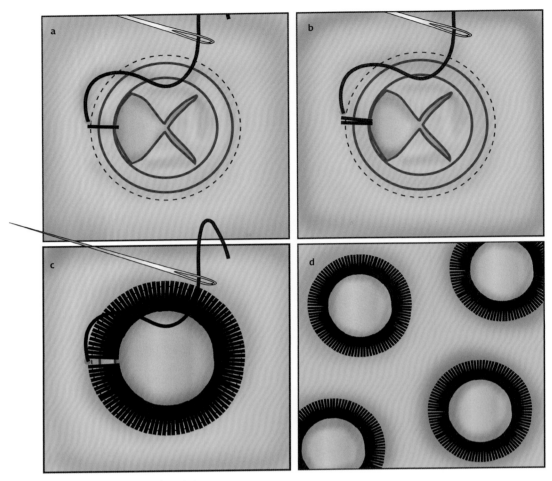

Figure 8.17a–d Satin eyelet stitch.

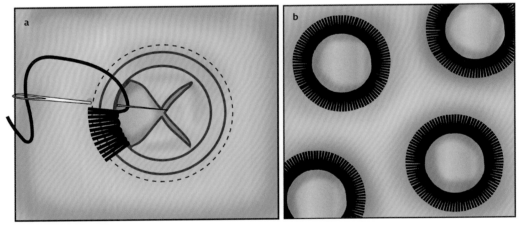

Figure 8.18a and b Buttonhole eyelet stitch.

Ribbon Embroidery

Back at the embroidery beginnings, ribbon embroidery was known as China ribbon embroidery; it later took on the name of Rococo and then became known as ribbon work.

Ribbon work has been around since ancient times when embroiderers used narrow pieces of cloth to weave creative designs. It began with hair decorations and headbands and then lead in the Middle Ages to decoration of royal clothing, clothes, chair covers, and even curtains.

By the fourteenth century, ribbon work expanded and slowly turned into silk ribbon embroidery. King Louis XI became king of France, and he loved he loved his clothes to be decorated with silk ribbon. He inspired his town of Lyon to start developing and manufacturing silk ribbon.

By 1660, King Louis XIV's reign influenced silk embroidery even more. His clothes were highly decorated and embroidered with silk and precious stones, starting a new fashion trend called Rococo style, which was characterized by massive embellishments. (Figure 8.19)

After both world wars and the Great Depression, people lost all interest in luxurious decorations as life had gotten darker and harder. However, since the 1990s, silk ribbon embroidery has been making a great comeback in many luxurious gowns made by famous couture designers.

Figure 8.19 Ribbon embroidery example.

SUPPLIES FOR RIBBON EMBROIDERY

Most embroidery tools can be used (hoops, needles, thread/floss, scissors, and more).

- **Awl.** A handheld tool that has a handle on one end and a metal shaft with a very sharp point on the other. (Figure 8.20a)
- **Cylinders.** Used as a ribbon holder underneath the ribbon loop stitch while working the stitch to hold it in place. Usually embroiderers have used chopsticks, drinking straws, or pencils. (Figure 8.20b)
- **Ribbon.** Ribbon used for silk embroidery is softer, narrow, drapes well, and is easy to pull through a small hole in the fabric to avoid damaging the fabric. Ribbon widths used are 2mm–7mm; the most common width used is 4mm. (Figure 8.21)
- **Needles.** Primarily large eye needles are necessary to fit the ribbon. The best needle to use for thread/floss is a tapestry needle. For ribbon embroidery, use a chenille needle or a Crewel needle with a sharp point to help bring the needle through the fabric.

Ribbon work tips:

- When cutting ribbon, cut shorter lengths in order to start new ribbon strips more often to avoid wear and tear as well as fraying.
- Cut your ribbon diagonally to avoid too much fraying of the ribbon threads as well as help you thread the ribbon into the needle eye with a cut tip. (Figure 8.22)
- When working ribbon stitches, make them bit looser than regular thread embroidery. Pulling too tight flattens the volume effect.
- It is helpful to puncture holes in tightly woven fabrics when using a wide ribbon.

STARTING KNOT

1. To thread the needle, use the diagonal cut end, and pull it through the eye.
2. Bring the needle up to the face side of the fabric, leaving a small tail ¼ to ½ inch in length still hanging on the backside. Hold it with your fingers to avoid pulling it out.
3. Make the first embroidery stitch on the face side a small one, and bring your needle back down to the backside of the fabric.

Figure 8.20 (a) Awl. (b) Cylinder (straw).

Figure 8.21 Embroidery ribbon.

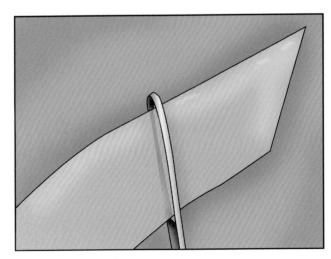

Figure 8.22 Cutting ribbon.

4. Pierce the small tail of ribbon on the backside with your needle at approximately ¼ to ½ inch from the diagonal end.

5. Pull the needle out, and tighten the small ribbon knot as you push the small knot down the ribbon to the surface of the fabric.

6. Continue stitching your embroidery. (Figure 8.23)

ENDING KNOT

1. When finished, bring the ribbon to the backside of the fabric.

2. To make a knot, insert the needle under a previously made stitch by pulling the thread to form a small loop.

3. Insert the needle through the loop and tighten; however, don't pull too tight or you may pull or flatten your embroidery.

4. Repeat steps 2–3 once more for a more secure knot.

5. Cut off the ribbon, leaving at least a ¼ to ½-inch long tail. Cutting too close may result in your knot coming loose. (Figure 8.24)

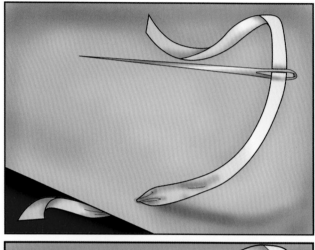

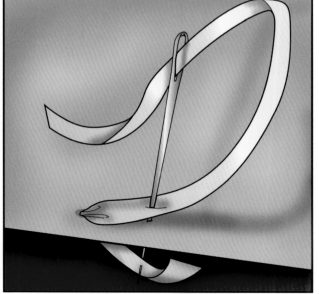

Figure 8.23 Ribbon starting knot.

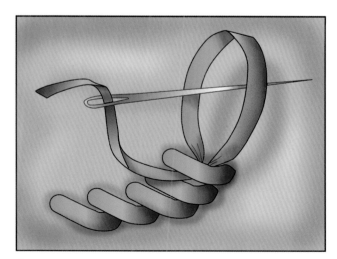

Figure 8.24 Ribbon ending knot.

Basic Ribbon Stitches

RIBBON STITCH

This stitch is good to use for flower petals, small leaves, and many more motifs. It looks like a 3-D rounded stitch with a permanent loop.

1. Secure your ribbon on the backside of the fabric, and bring your needle to the face fabric at mark #1.
2. Flatten the ribbon to the fabric surface with your finger, and hold it down.

3. Pierce the needle down through center of the ribbon and the fabric at mark #2 at least ¼ to ½ inch away from mark #1. Pull the needle through to the backside.
4. If only one stitch was required, secure your ribbon, but not too tight. For more stitches, pull the needle back through to the face side of the fabric, and repeat steps 2–4. (Figure 8.25a–c)
5. Secure the ribbon, and cut off the end, leaving a small tail.

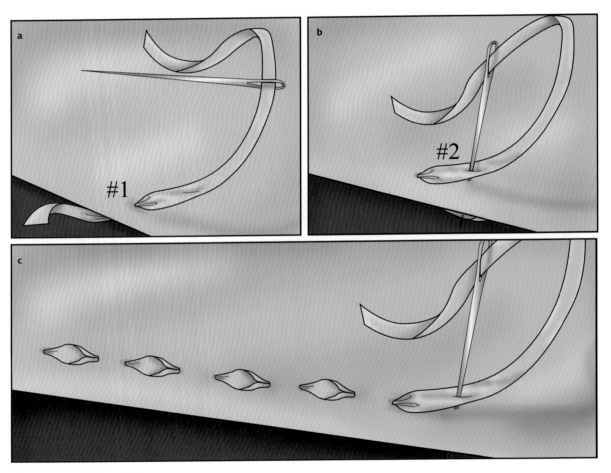

Figure 8.25a–c Ribbon stitch.

RIBBON STITCH PEONY

Using a ribbon stitch, work many loop stitches into a peony flower motif using one color ribbon or a mix or gradient of ribbon colors to make the peony change to a darker tone toward the center.

1. To begin, mark a circle shape on the fabric along with smaller radiating circles shrinking toward the center of the circle, creating rows. Number the rows depending on the size of the circle. You can have anywhere from three to ten rows. Our example will show three rows, with the third one being the center.

2. Secure your ribbon on the backside of the fabric, and bring your needle to the face fabric along the circle outline.

3. Work row #1 with ribbon stitches with their loops on the outside of the circle and the points facing the inside center of the circle. Stitch around the circle outline with the ribbon stitch. Secure the ribbon, and thread a new one.

4. After securing the new ribbon, directly under the first ribbon stitch of row #1, approximately $\frac{1}{16}$ to $\frac{1}{8}$ inch below, work row #2 around the circle to the starting point. Work these stitches with loops pointing to the outside of the circle and the points facing the inside of the circle. Secure the ribbon, and thread a new one.

5. Work row #3 repeating the previous step $\frac{1}{16}$ to $\frac{1}{8}$ inch below row #2. Make these ribbon stitches a bit longer in length. This will overlap them more and make them lift higher off the fabric surface. Secure your ribbon, and thread a new one.

6. To work the center, make one to three longer loop stitches or add a flat back crystal. Secure the ribbon and cut, leaving a small tail. (Figure 8.26a–d)

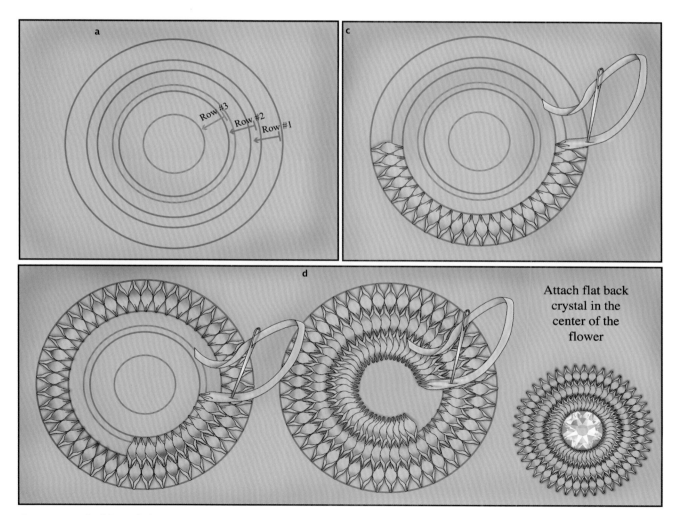

Figure 8.26a–d Ribbon stitch peony.

SIDE RIBBON STITCH

1. To begin, trace the motif.
2. Secure the ribbon on the backside, and bring the needle to the face side at mark #1.
3. Flatten the ribbon by smoothing it with your finger, and hold it down.
4. Pierce the needle down off-center to the farthest side edge of the ribbon at mark #2, ¼ to ½ inch away from mark #1. Pierce through the ribbon and the fabric, pulling the needle to the backside.

5. One side loop stitch slanting to one side is now complete. Secure the ribbon, but not too tight.
6. If you need more stitches, pull the needle back through to the face side of the fabric and repeat steps 2–4. (Figure 8.27a and b)

Ribbon stitch variations:

- 3–5 petal flowers
- Leaves and stems (Figure 8.28)

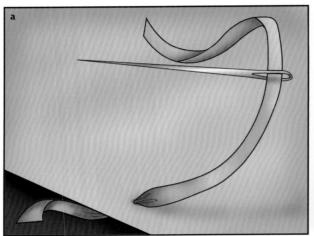

Figure 8.27a and b Side ribbon stitch.

Ribbon Stitch Flower Petals with a Flat Back Crystal in the Center

Ribbon Stitch Flower Petals with smaller Ribbon Stitches finished with a Loop Stitch for the Center

Stem- Couching Stitch with ribbon

Fern Leaves- Ribbon Stitches

Stems- Couching Stitch using ribbon

Figure 8.28 Flowers, leaves and stems.

TWISTED RIBBON STITCH

1. Secure the ribbon on the backside, and bring it up to the face fabric at mark #1.
2. Twist the ribbon only once, and hold it down with your finger. Pierce the needle centered at mark #2 down through your ribbon and the fabric, pulling the needle to the backside.

3. One twisted loop stitch is now complete. Secure the ribbon, but not too tight.
4. If you need more stitches, pull the needle back through to the face side of the fabric and repeat steps 2–4. (Figure 8.29a and b)

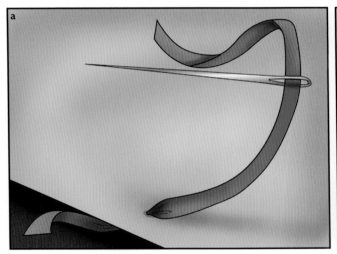 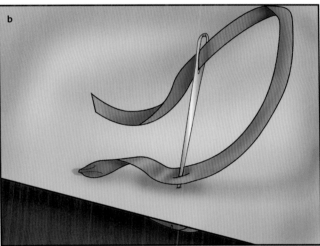

Figure 8.29a and b Twisted ribbon stitch.

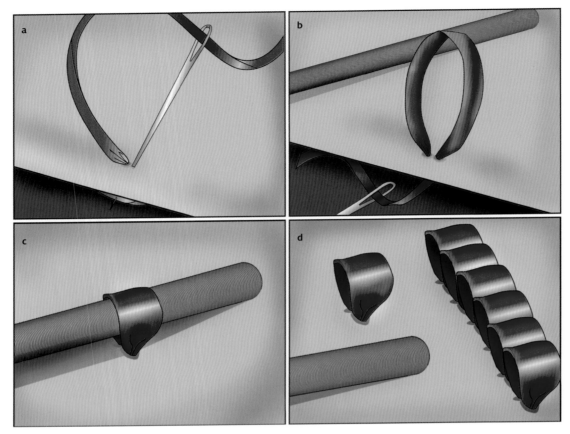

Figure 8.30a–d Loop stitch.

LOOP STITCH

This stitch is good to use for flower petals, small leaves, and many more looped motifs. It looks like a 3-D rounded stitch with a permanent loop. You can use a cylinder tool, drinking straw, pencil, or nail to hold your loop during the stitching. If worked around a circle from the center, this stitch forms a daisy flower motif. Mark your fabric with the desired motif.

1. To begin, secure the ribbon on the backside of the fabric, and bring it to the face side at mark #1.
2. Flatten down the ribbon backward, and place your cylinder against the ribbon, holding it down against the fabric surface.
3. Loop the ribbon around the cylinder, and pierce your needle down through the ribbon at mark #2 really close to the starting point through the ribbon or directly in front of the starting point through the fabric.
4. Pull the ribbon through to the backside until the ribbon is tight around the cylinder.
5. Secure the loop stitch behind the fabric with an ending knot, and pull your cylinder out from inside the loop.

6. If you need more stitches, pull the needle back through to the face side of the fabric, and repeat another loop. (Figure 8.30a-d)

Figure 8.31 shows the looped petal flower variation.

Figure 8.31 Loop stitch petal flower.

STRAIGHT STITCH

This stitch is good to use for flower petals, small leaves, and many more motifs. It looks like a short line. If worked around a circle from the center, it forms a flower motif.

Follow the same steps as a running stitch (basting stitch). (Figure 8.32a–c)

More straight stitch variations include:

- 5-petal flower (Figure 8.33)
- Fern stitch (Figure 8.33)

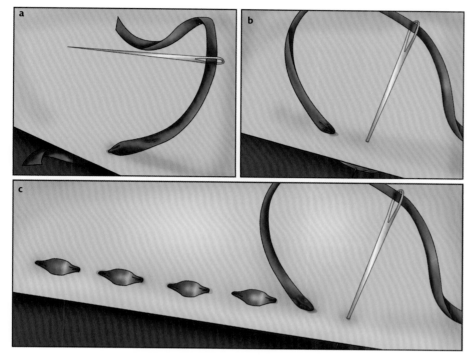

Figure 8.32a–c Straight stitch.

Straight Stitch Fern Leaves

Straight Stitch Flowers

Couching Stitch Stem

Figure 8.33 Petal flower and fern stitch.

FRENCH KNOT

1. To begin, bring the needle from the backside of the fabric to the face side through mark #1.
2. Now wrap the needle one time.
3. Hold the wrapped ribbon with your finger, and insert the needle back into the fabric at mark #2.

4. Secure your thread in the back of the fabric.

Hint: For a larger knot, wrap the ribbon more times around the needle before inserting it into mark #2. (Figure 8.34a–d)

French knot variations:

- Loop stitch with a French knot
- French knot flower blossoms (Figure 8.35a and b)

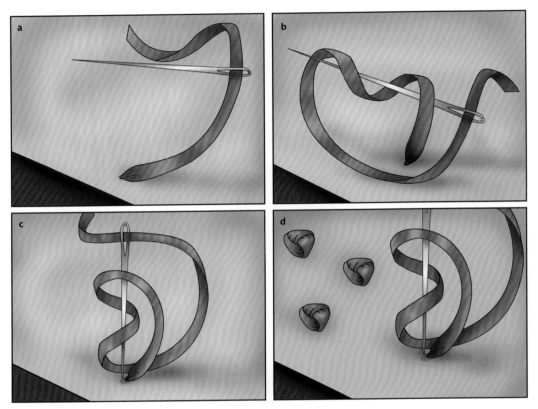

Figure 8.34a–d French knot.

Figure 8.35 (a) Loop/French knot. (b) Blossoms.

GATHERED RIBBON FLOWER

This ribbon uses a gathering technique and takes very little time to make. Use a ribbon strip between 4 and 8 inches in length.

1. To begin, thread your needle and make a small knot.
2. Along the edge of the ribbon, stitch a running stitch all the way from one end to the other.

3. Closer to the end, pull the thread to gather up your ribbon into a circle shape. Keep pulling and gathering until you can make a complete circle.
4. Fold a small amount of ribbon on one end, and overlap the other end.
5. Flip the flower to the backside, and whipstitch a narrow stitch, attaching the sides together. Secure the thread.
6. Add a center bead, pearl, crystal stone, or French knot. (Figure 8.36a–d)

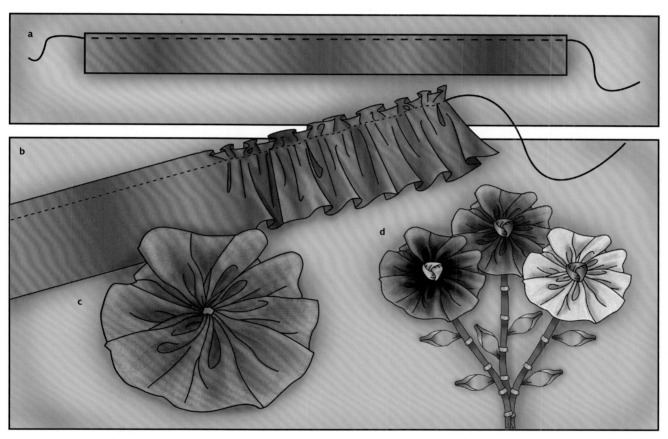

Figure 8.36a–d Gathered ribbon flower.

CORNER PETALS/LEAVES

1. To begin, measure your desired petal length, and cut your ribbon double the length plus ½ inch seam allowance.
2. Fold the cut piece in half to find the halfway point, and place a pin.
3. Open the ribbon flat on the table.
4. Fold both ends of the ribbon against the pin, making a corner.
5. Pull the pin out, and use it to pin down the folded ends.
6. Baste the ends making small basting stitches, and pull the thread to gather it up into a leaf/petal.
7. Secure your thread with a knot, and use the same thread to attach it to your fabric piece. Trim off the extra ribbon ends.
8. Attach to your garment, hiding the raw edge.
9. Continue making more leafs/petals. (Figure 8.37a–g)

Figure 8.37a–g Corner petals/leaves.

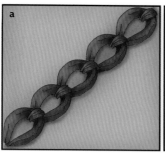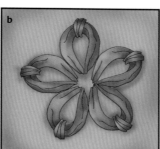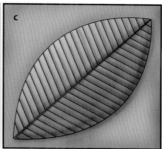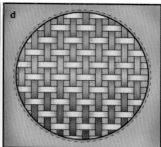

Figure 8.38 (a) Chain stitch. (b) Lazy daisy stitch. (c) Satin stitch. (d) Weaving stitch.

Ribbon work variations using embroidery stitches:

- Chain stitch (Figure 8.38a)
- Detached chain stitch (lazy daisy) (Figure 8.38b)
- Satin stitch (Figure 8.38c)
- Weaving stitch (two ribbon) (Figure 8.38d)

Goldwork

Goldwork is a very old skill and one of the most luxurious methods of embroidery using metallic threads, floss, plates, leather, and purl wire floss instead of the usual floss made for regular embroidery. (Figure 8.39)

Goldwork dates back to the times of Chinese textile expansion during the silk trade. The Chinese had their own traditions of clothing embellishments and had their own rules for specific textiles, colors, embroidery, and other materials for each of their social class levels. For their imperial attire and other ceremonial robes, they used gold threads and goldwork embroidery using a variety of different types and thicknesses of metallic threads. Using couching stitch techniques, they were able to decorate entire wardrobes with gold and jewels with inspirational religious images relating to their beliefs and stories.

Once the Silk Road opened trading of silk, goldwork traveled to the Middle East, influencing Babylonian, Assyrian, and Egyptian cultures. As the demand for gold thread grew, the Byzantine Empire began to produce and control gold embroidery and trades in order to raise its economic level. Goldwork then traveled to the Mediterranean, and by Renaissance times, it was even more popular for embellishing only the noble and the wealthy.

Goldwork reappeared with many embroideries and lavish garments made by famous couturiers in the

Figure 8.39 Modern goldwork (Dolce & Gabbana).

twentieth century. During the 1920s, which was know as the flapper age, women's dresses needed to be extra shiny; there was also a new gold décor trend that was influenced by the discovery of King Tut's tomb. This Egyptian trend brought more ideas, techniques, and methods of goldwork

Figure 8.41 (a) Tweezers. (b) Mellor.

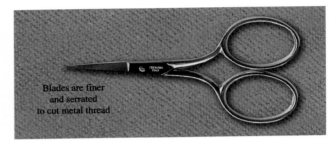

Blades are finer
and serrated
to cut metal thread

Figure 8.42 Metallic thread scissors.

Figure 8.40 1920s goldwork.

and helped it rise to a higher level of production and manufacturing. (Figure 8.40)

Today, we are very fortunate to have many varieties of threads, floss, purl, beads, and tools to use for metallic embroidery. As the age of Grand Couture is at its rise, needlework, embroidery, ribbon work, goldwork, and appliqué techniques have yet to reach their highest peaks.

Goldwork supplies:

Tweezers. Small handheld tools with one sharp leg and one regular. They are helpful when picking up or holding down threads while couching. Tweezers also help twist and warp the purl wire, metallic plates, or thicker threads into shape. (Figure 8.41a)

Mellor (stiletto). A metal tool with a paddle shape on one end and a pointed end on the other. The paddle end helps push metal threads down flat, which helps keep the surface flat. The sharp side helps puncture a hole in the fabric for the thicker metallic threads to enter the fabric. (Figure 8.41b)

Goldwork scissors or metallic thread scissors. Have a special blade that cuts metallic threads. The blades are fine and serrated, which helps the scissors hold their grip on the metallic threads and purl while cutting. (Figure 8.42)

Needles. A chenille needle is a good choice, as you need a needle with a sharp point and a large eye to work thicker metallic threads. A beading needle is also great to use when attaching small coil wire parts to the fabric, as you need a very skinny needle to go through the coil on the inside, which is similar to a bugle bead.

METALLIC THREAD

Metallic threads come in different types. Passing threads are regular solid threads similar to a thin wire. They are similar to the well-known embroidery floss made of four to six threads wrapped together. They can be unwrapped for a thinner thread as well as couched down.

Some metallic options also include a hollow coiled wire produced by winding plated wire that can be stitched through with a beading needle like a bead, purl, or **bullion**.

1. **Pearl purl (Jaceron).** This purl looks a lot like a string of very small metallic pearls and is a metal thread entirely. Pearl purl is used for the motif outline and is great on curved lines and sharp corners. It comes in length 3936 inches long. Stretch it slightly before couching it down. (Figure 8.43a)

2. **Smooth purl (Bullion).** This purl is used in India on decorative bridal or expensive sari scarves, dresses, pillow shams, or blankets. It is made with a hollow coil imitating a tiny spring that can be used as a long thread outlining the motif, or it can be cut into small pieces and stitched down through the center like a bead. It can be damaged easily and squeezed out of shape, so be careful with it. (Figure 8.43b)

3. **Rough purl.** This is similar to the smooth purl; however, it has a dull finish. (Figure 8.44a)

4. **Check purl (Frieze Brilliant).** This is made by wrapping the wire onto a square-shaped mold. This makes a spring with corners and adds some sparkle. This thread is approximately 2mm wide and 18 inches long and is made of metal. (Figure 8.44b)

5. **Crimped purl (Faconnee).** This purl is a round coil that has been crimped at small sections. This thread is approximately 32 inches in length. (Figure 8.45a)

6. **Passing thread** (Japan gold thread). Thinner and more flexible than purl thread, this metallic-looking thread is used for embroidery because it is thin enough to easily go through fabric. (Figure 8.45b)

7. **Grecian twist thread.** This is twisted with four threads: Two smooth strands and two crinkled strands. When authentic, the threads are made of real gold and silver-plated copper. It comes in 2.5mm width and is cut or sold by the yard. (Figure 8.46a)

8. **Glissen gloss thread.** This is an easy-to-use metallic thread. Thread it into a needle, and pull it through fabric. (Figure 8.46b)

9. **Single-ply metallic.** This high gloss thread is made to look like a wire attached to the fabric using the couching technique. It is wrapped around a filler when manufactured and comes in a variety of fiber contents, including: 3 to 5 percent silver, 22 to 25 percent polyester, and 70 to 75 percent viscose. (Figure 8.47a)

10. **Rococo thread.** This is real metal and is 39 inches in length. It is wider and shaped like a wavy hair strand, adding shine when waves hit the light. (Figure 8.47b)

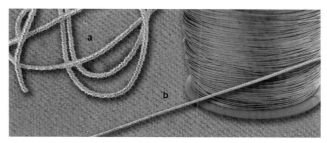

Figure 8.45 (a) Crimped purl. (b) Passing thread.

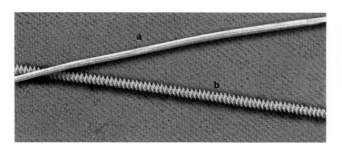

Figure 8.43 (a) Pearl purl. (b) Smooth purl (bullion).

Figure 8.46 (a) Grecian twist. (b) Glissen gloss.

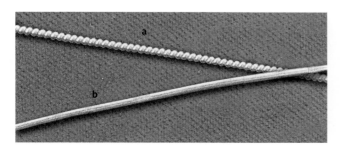

Figure 8.44 (a) Rough purl. (b) Check purl.

Figure 8.47 (a) Single ply metallic. (b) Rococo thread.

Figure 8.48 (a) Spangles/palettes. (b) Kid leather.

11. **Spangles/palettes.** These are known as metallic flat sequins that are made similar to the spangles of the Middle Ages. (Figure 8.48a)

12. **Metallic cords.** These are thicker, yarn-like cords woven or wrapped with metallic thread. These cords can be couched along the motif.

13. **Kid** (shiny leather). These are small pieces of metallic-colored leather, or faux leather, used during the embroidery process as an appliqué part of the motif. (Figure 8.48b)

ADDING FELT PADDING

When using felt padding, you can offer one or more layers of padding for a raised effect.

1. If you need more than one layer, cut out padding shapes using your pattern, and then cut out another layer smaller.

2. Keep radiating the size of more layers by cutting them smaller toward the center of the shape. Once you layer the pieces, the larger layer will fit right into the space offering a 3-D effect.

3. The smaller layer will be the first to be placed in the center of the motif followed by the larger shapes.

4. Secure the felt piece to your fabric, making small stab stitches/whipstitches through the felt and your fabric along the edge of the felt piece all the way around. (Figure 8.49a–f)

Hint: Try to use fusible felt for padding for attachment to fabric while stitching it around.

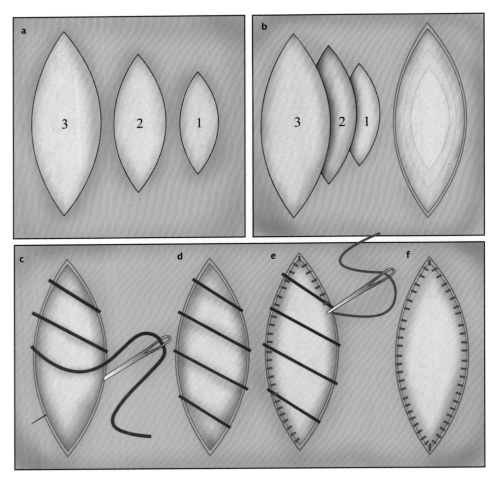

Figure 8.49a–f Adding felt padding.

GOLDWORK COUCHING TECHNIQUES

Goldwork uses many different ways to attach the gold threads—couching is one of the main techniques—and then the fabric is embellished further with beads, sequins, spangles, and even metallic-colored kid leather.

Purl Couching

Used for all types of purl: pearl purl, smooth purl, check purl, passing thread, and other threads and items.

1. To begin, decide on placement of the purl. If it is a segment, cut the purl into the length required before starting to couch, or leave a long purl for outlining.
2. Using the index and thumb fingers on both hands, gently stretch the purl to pull the coil slightly apart into its natural spring shape. This allows the couching stitches to go through the spring in between the coils and allows the purl to bend around the curves more smoothly.
3. Use two threads, one metallic purl and another silk thread, for the couching stitches.
4. Thread your needle with silk thread, line up the purl along your motif line, and begin making small couching stitches to secure the purl along the desired motif line. Each couching stitch goes between the coils of the purl.
5. For a corner, use small tweezers to bend the purl, and then couch it down.
6. Continue couching until the end of the motif, and cut the purl with metallic cutting scissors. (Figure 8.50a–d)

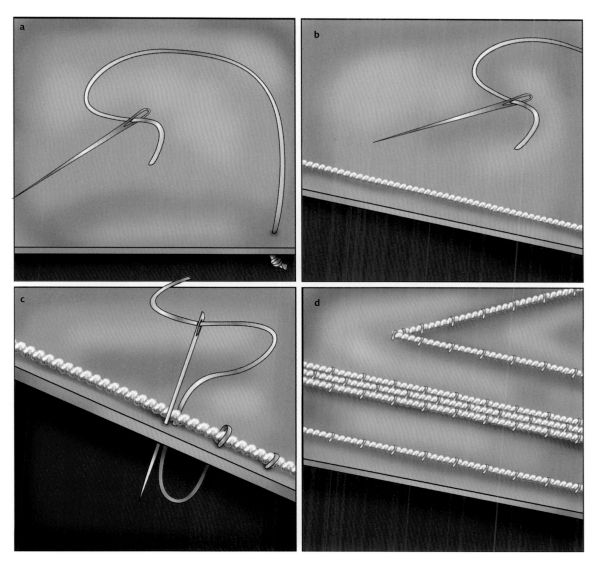

Figure 8.50a–d Purl couching.

Purl Rings and Flowers

With this type of couching, the outcome looks like a hollow ring. You can couch one ring alone or many close together, making a cluster fill or a circular flower motif.

1. Wrap the purl around a straw, a pen, or a pencil until it wraps around once completely.
2. Clip the purl 1/16 inch past the end of the ring.
3. Repeat steps 1–2 to make more rings if necessary.
4. Attach the two ends together by stitching through the hollow center with the needle and thread attaching the first and last coils. This will secure the ring and keep it in the desired shape longer as well as help couch it to your fabric.

5. Use a matching couching thread to make small couching stitches in at least four spots, A–D.
6. Add more rings for a flower motif, or add a bead inside the rings. (Figure 8.51a–c)

Purl Satin Stitch

If desired, add padding to the motif before adding the purl to offer levels of depth.

1. Measure the width of your shape following the same angle direction you will stitch.
2. Gently stretch the purl to pull the coil slightly apart into its natural spring shape.
3. Cut purl at the desired lengths to fill the motif. If shape width changes, cut several different lengths.

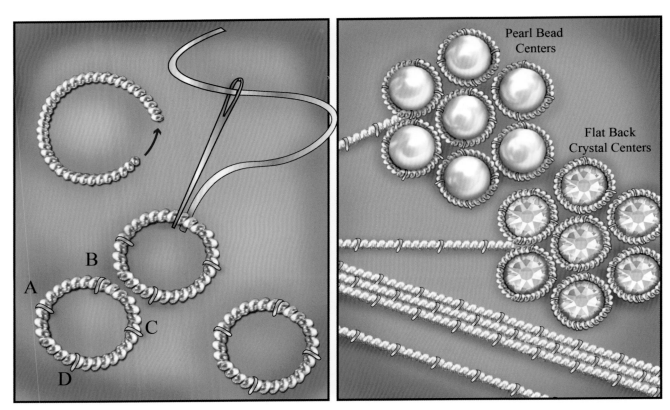

Figure 8.51a–c Purl rings and flowers.

4. Secure the couching thread, and bring it up at point #1.
5. Purl comes with hollow center; therefore thread the first purl piece onto your needle like a bead, pulling the purl down toward the fabric surface.
6. Then insert the needle down through the fabric at point #2.
7. Bring the needle back out at point #3.
8. Thread the next purl piece onto your needle, and insert the needle down at point #4.
9. Repeat steps 3–8 to fill the entire shape. (Figure 8.52a–d)

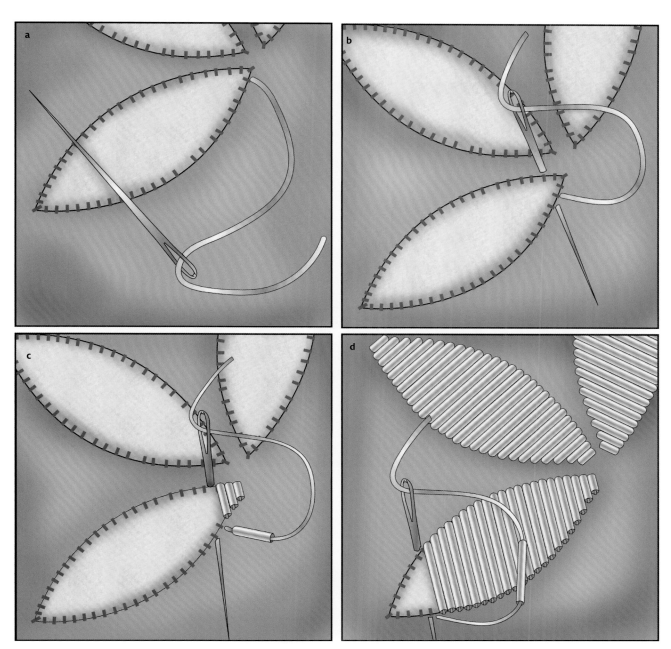

Figure 8.52a–d Purl satin stitch.

SINKING OR FINISHING A LOOSE THREAD

Sinking is a commonly used method to hide all the loose threads or tails in the backside of the fabric. Since some threads are thicker, there exists a method to help you achieve a neater piece of work without pulling out all of your beautiful stitches. Always leave 1–2 inches of loose thread hanging before couching and at the end.

1. Thread a loop of waxed sewing thread into your needle.

2. Catching one thread tail at a time, insert your needle down into the fabric at the endpoint of your motif line, catching the loose tail of purl inside the loop.

3. Once the tail is inside the loop, pull down on your needle. Be cautious with finer fabrics.

4. Once the threads are pulled behind the fabric, stitch it down with wrap stitches using sewing thread, and then trim the metallic thread. (Figure 8.53)

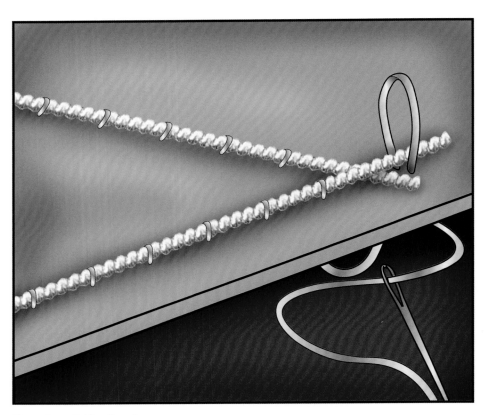

Figure 8.53 Sinking thread.

KID LEATHER

1. To stitch kid leather, transfer the motif shape onto the backside of the kid leather and cut it out.
2. Add padding on your fabric with a piece of felt before adding the leather.
3. Place the leather on fabric matching up the motif, but do not pin, as that will leave extra holes in the leather. You can use a piece of tape.
4. Hold it down with your finger, and run a couple of small stab stitches to couch down the leather.
5. Begin stitching around the outer edge to hold it in place. Stitches to use include a stab stitch, buttonhole stitch, and whipstitch. (Figure 8.54a–d)

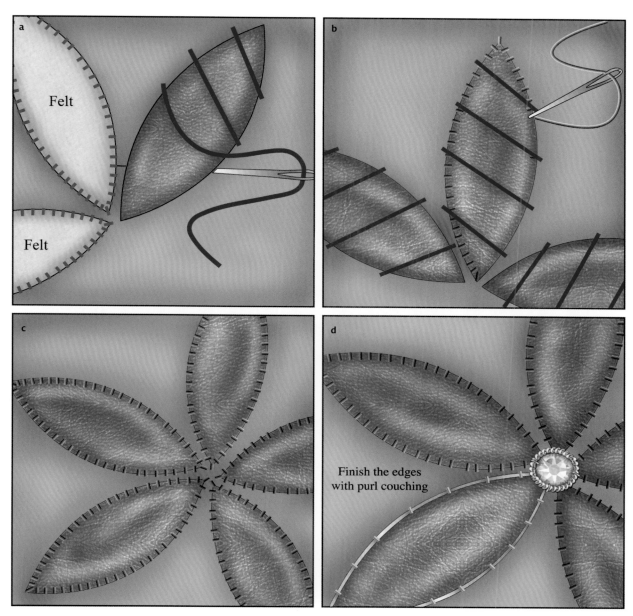

Finish the edges with purl couching

Figure 8.54a–d Kid leather.

Beadwork

Beadwork has been around for centuries. It can be made of wood, bone, rocks, shells, metal, crystal, jewels, glass, or plastic. In the early 1900s, Paul Poiret was one of the first designers to use embroidery with beads and sequins in his couture gowns.

Today beads come in an infinite number of colors, sizes, and shapes. The most common bead shapes include rocailles, bugles, sequins, rondelles, decorative beads, drops, pearls, and gemstones. Bead embroidery and decoration is one of the most important embellishments in couture gowns. Beadwork takes time and patience. Many designers spend hundreds of hours working on that one-of-a-kind dress. (Figure 8.55)

Figure 8.55 Beaded trim.

Beading Tools

THREAD

Polyester. Used most often. It is strong enough for beading on garment embroideries and even stronger with beeswax. Just pull it through the beeswax before beading, and press it down with an iron to melt the wax into the thread.

Silk. Is the choice among bead professionals; it does not twist while sewing and beading, makes the smoothest stitches, and is easy to use. This thread does not need beeswax; it is strong on its own and does not fray.

Nylon. Is pre-stretched, so it will not stretch and break while beading or after. Match thread and needle sizes so that you can get the thread through the needle eye. Thicker nylon thread is available and comes in a variety of different colors, but it may end up being too thick for delicate fabrics.

NEEDLES

You can use a variety of different needles: special beading needles, regular hand-sewing needles with small eyes, delica needles, and millinery needles. Make sure that all the beads you want to use will fit through the needle eye. Beads not only come in different sizes on the outside but also have different size holes. The needle most often used for beading is the beading needle. This needle is very long and narrow with a very narrow eye. The length is very helpful when you need to pick up several beads at a time. Beading needles come in different sizes: 10–16.

Delica needles are used primarily for delica seed beads, which come in very small sizes and require a very delicate needle. These needles come in a variety of different lengths, from 1 ¾ inches to 4 ¾ inches. (Figure 8.56)

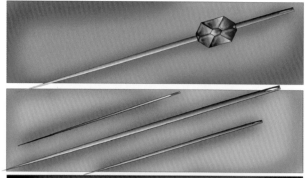

Figure 8.56 Needles.

TAMBOUR NEEDLE

Tambour beading is a different kind of beading done with a hook. This type of beading is used when the beaded garment will be worn often and needs the extra strength. (Figure 8.57)

The **tambour needle** hook is sold in two pieces: the holder and the tambour needle. The pieces come together to form a hook that looks like a crochet hook. This needle is changeable and sold separately as a spare. The needle is inserted into a shaft and then tightened by a small screw on the side of the holder. The holder comes in different materials and lengths. The needle end is very sharp so that it can easily penetrate through the fabric. Look for the size number on the package; the sizes range from 70 to 130. Lower numbers are better for fabrics that are more delicate.

BEAD BOXES

Most bead boxes offer multiple compartments to arrange the different beads. Keeping your beads neat and in order will make it much easier for you when you are working. (Figure 8.58)

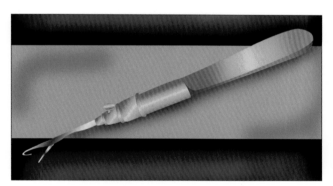

Figure 8.57 Tambour needle.

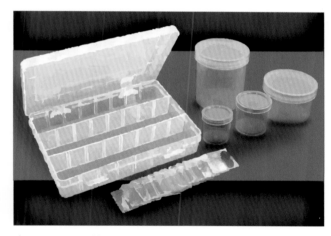

Figure 8.58 Bead boxes.

HOOPS AND FRAMES

Hoops and frames are often used when beading. They allow you to focus on a specific area of the garment or fabric and help to keep the fabric tight while you work.

Beads

ROCAILLES

These beads are the most common beads for fabric embroidery. (Figure 8.59a) They provide shine and color and come in various sizes. The higher the number, the smaller the bead. Rocailles are divided into several categories: seed beads, delica seed beads, charlotte beads. Seed beads are round beads with round holes. Delica seed beads are the most uniform of all seed beads and are square in shape with larger holes. Charlotte beads are seed beads with a coating that reflects light and makes them shine.

BUGLES

Bugles are shaped like a tube and made of glass or metal. (Figure 8.59b) Lengths vary between 2 mm and 35 mm. Bugles very often come in the same color and shape as rocailles.

DECORATIVE BEADS

These beads come in different shapes, sizes, colors, and cuts and can be made of glass, plastic, crystal, or even metal. These beads tend to be a bit more expensive and, due to their larger sizes, are most often used for trims, fringe, and beaded buttons. (Figure 8.59c)

SEQUINS

These beads are shiny, flat plastic or metallic beads that come in a variety of colors, shapes, and sizes. (Figure 8.59d) They have a hole in the center just like other beads. You can use them together with other beads.

RONDELLES

These beads are not as flat as sequins. Rondelles are shaped like a disk with a hole in the middle. They come in many sizes, colors, shapes, and materials. (Figure 8.59e)

Figure 8.59 (a) Rocailles. (b) Bugles. (c) Decorative. (d) Sequins. (e) Rondelles.

DROPS

Drops are designed to dangle when sewn. (Figure 8.60a) They have a hole on the top of the bead, which allows the bead to dangle. These beads come in many sizes, shapes, colors, and materials.

CRYSTAL, GEMSTONES, AND PEARLS

Crystal beads are more expensive then glass beads and most of the time come in small packages. Gemstones also come in smaller packages and cost more than regular plastic beads. Pearls are a bit harder to find and cost more than regular beads. You can find imitation pearl beads as well. (Figure 8.60b)

Figure 8.60 (a) Drops. (b) Crystals, gemstones, and pearls.

Beading Techniques

Beading is the one of the oldest embroidery techniques. Beaded fabrics have survived from the fifteenth and sixteenth centuries, when beads were made of gold, silver, and jewels and worn only by royalty and the richest individuals.

RUNNING STITCH

This stitch is the most commonly used beading stitch. It is fast and very flexible, accommodating curves and corners without stressing the fabric.

1. Secure the thread with a knot, and insert the needle up into the fabric at one end of the motif.

2. Place one bead through the needle, and pull it toward the fabric.

3. Insert the needle back down through the fabric on the other side of the bead.

4. Pull the needle out from the underside again in front of the bead.

5. Place another bead on the needle, and repeat all of the steps, beading the entire row. (Figure 8.61) For efficiency, you can pick up more than one bead at a time on the needle.

Hint: Any motif in beading embroidery, no matter the shape or size, should be started with the outline first. This will not only set you up for a correct shape or style, but it will also allow you to begin your beading in the desired direction adding different color changes, shadows, or pattern sequences.

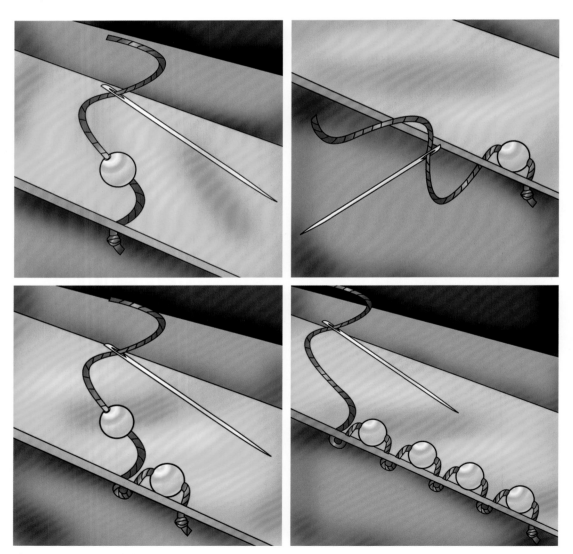

Figure 8.61 Running stitch.

SATIN STITCH

The satin stitch works the same way with beads as it does in embroidery. Secure the thread, and insert the needle up at the starting point.

1. Place beads on the needle, and pull them toward the fabric.
2. Insert the needle down into the fabric at a distance equal to the space taken up by the beads.

3. Pass the needle beneath the fabric back to the same side you started on, and insert the needle up into the fabric right next to the first stitch.
4. Place more beads on the needle again, and repeat steps 2 through 4. (Figure 8.62)

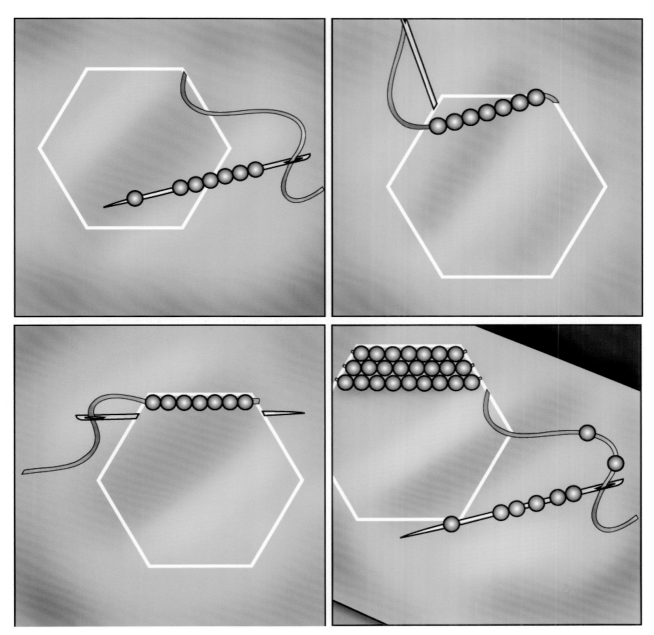

Figure 8.62 Satin stitch.

MOCK SATIN STITCH

The mock satin stitch with beads looks just like the regular satin stitch on the right side of the fabric; however, it is different on the underside.

1. Secure the thread, and insert the needle up at starting point.
2. Place beads on the needle, and pull them toward the fabric.

3. Insert the needle down into the fabric at a distance equal to the space taken up by the beads.
4. Pull the needle back out to the right of the beaded stitch you just made.
5. Place more beads on the needle again, and insert the needle into the fabric on the opposite side.
6. Repeat steps 2 through 5, and continue stitching parallel beaded rows. (Figure 8.63)

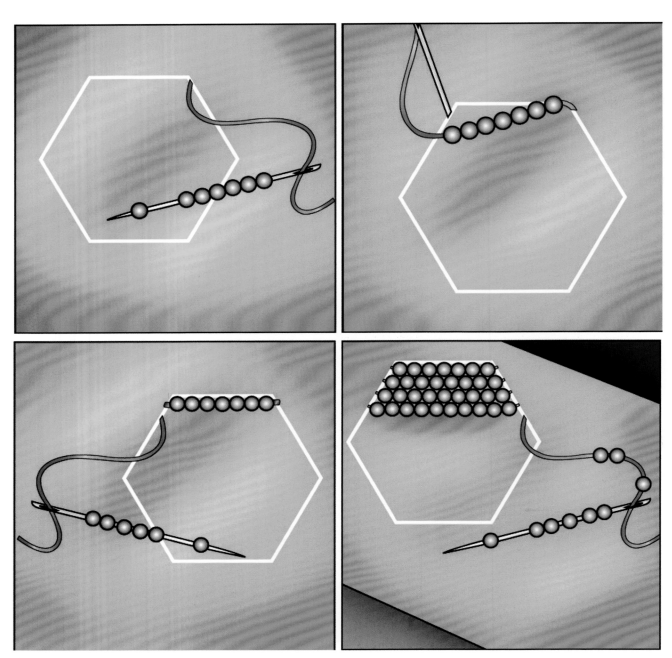

Figure 8.63 Mock satin stitch.

BACKSTITCH

This stitch works well with small beads, flat beads, bugles, and sequins. Choose thread that matches the color of the beads, or, even better, use clear thread.

1. Start working as you would with a plain backstitch. Secure the thread a short distance from the start, and pull the needle up through the fabric.

2. Insert one bead or several small beads on the needle, and pull it toward the fabric. Make one stitch the length of the bead(s) backward, bringing the needle two bead lengths under the fabric and up through the fabric again.

3. Place one more bead on the needle, and make another stitch backward along the line. (Figure 8.64)

4. Repeat steps 2 through 3 until you finish the entire row.

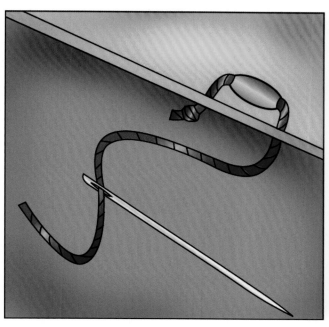 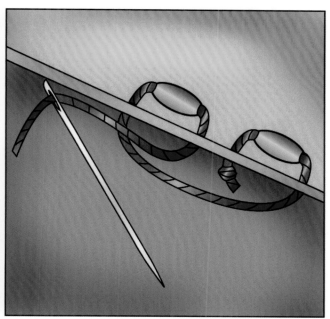

Figure 8.64 Backstitch.

CHAIN STITCH

1. Secure the thread, and pull the needle up through the fabric.
2. Place a bead through the needle, and pull it toward the fabric.
3. Reinsert the needle into the same bead from the same side it came from, and pull it through to the underside, leaving a small loop at the top of the bead.
4. Lay the bead sideways. Pull the needle up through the fabric to the right of the bead, pulling it through the fabric and the loop. Tighten your stitch. This forms the first chain stitch.
5. Repeat steps 2 through 4 until you have finished the strand. (Figure 8.65)

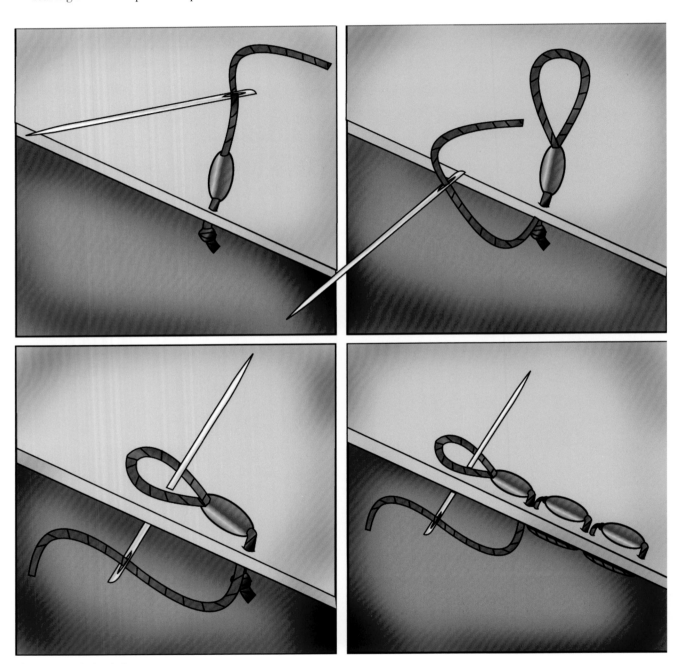

Figure 8.65 Chain stitch.

COUCHING

This stitch is a very nice way to follow curved lines or a specific design.

1. Secure the thread, and pull the needle up through the fabric.
2. Next measure the length of the line you wish to bead, and string a line of beads to that length.
3. Place the beaded strand along the line you wish to bead.
4. Using a new couching thread, make a small stitch up through the fabric and around the thread in between the beads.
5. Take the needle back down through the fabric, and repeat another small stitch a couple of beads over. Repeat. (Figure 8.66)

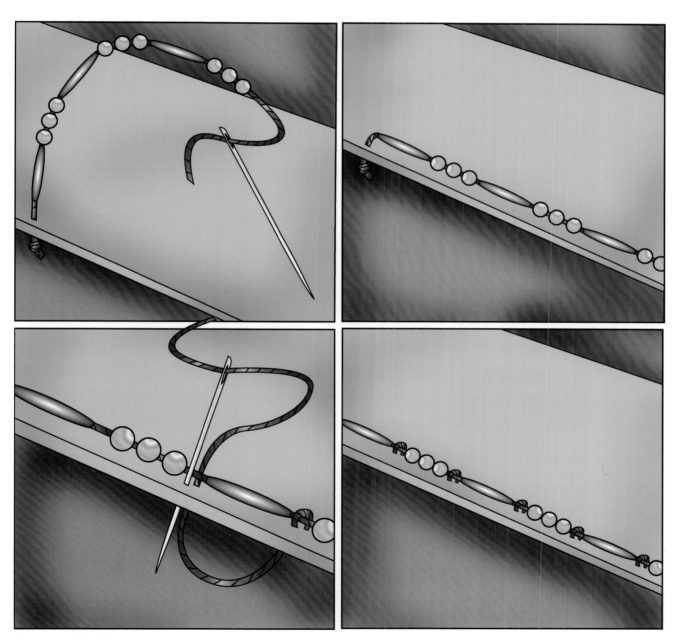

Figure 8.66 Couching.

ARC STITCH

Also called the lazy stitch, the arc stitch can be used to decorate motifs or outline edges, roses, leaves, and so much more. This stitch is similar to the running stitch.

1. Secure your thread, and bring your needle up at point #1.
2. Thread your beads to measure longer in length than your desired space. For example, if your space is four beads long, you thread will be six to seven beads long.
3. Take the needle back through the fabric toward the backside. Secure the thread with a small wrapped stitch before making another arc stitch.
4. On the right side of the fabric, you will see that the threaded beads form an arc. (Figure 8.67)
   More arc stitch variations:

   - Circular with a center pearl or crystal bead (Figure 8.68a)

- Fish scales pattern (Figure 8.68b)
- Flowers (lilies)
- Rose (Figure 8.68c)
- Fireworks or splash (Figure 8.68d)

LAZY DAISY

This stitch is used to make petals, leaves, drops, buds, and so on.

1. Secure the thread, and pull the needle up at point #1.
2. Thread the beads through the needle, and pull them down toward the fabric. You should have an even number of beads. The example shows the first bead in pink and the rest in green colors.
3. Reinsert the needle into the pink bead once more making a loop.
4. Then insert it down through to the fabric at point #2.
5. Bring your needle up through the fabric at point #3.

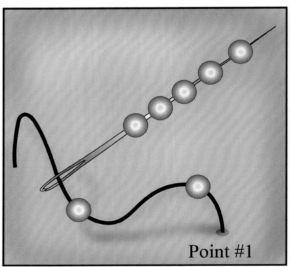

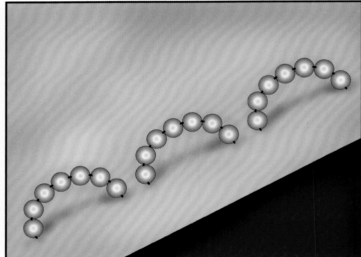

Figure 8.67 Arc stitch.

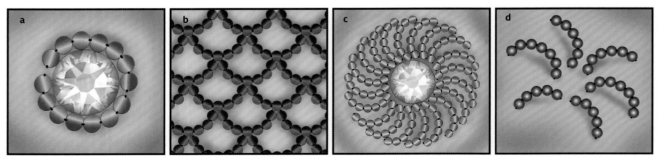

Figure 8.68a–d Arc stitch variations.

6. Pull the needle through the center of the rounded loop side.

7. Then insert the needle down into the fabric at point #4. Tighten your stitch. This last stitch acts like a couching stitch holding the loop down against the fabric.

8. Secure the thread, and continue making more loops.

9. Repeat steps 1 through 7 until you have finished the desired daisy motif, stitching the loops around a circle center. (Figure 8.69)

10. Add a pearl or a larger bead in the center to finish the daisy flower.

More lazy daisy variations:

- Three-petal flower (lily) (Figure 8.70a)
- Peony flower (Figure 8.70b)
- Flower leaves (Figure 8.70c)
- Bows (Figure 8.70d)

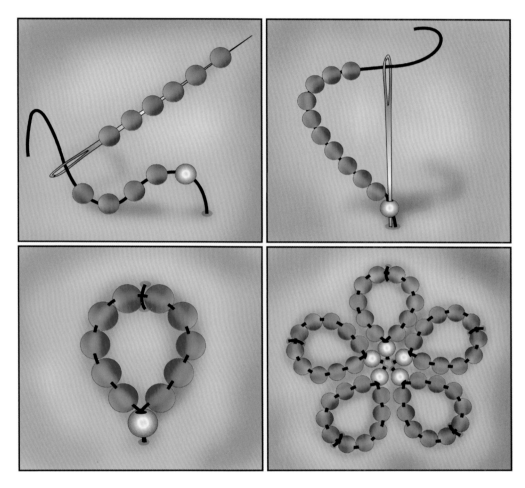

Figure 8.69 Lazy daisy.

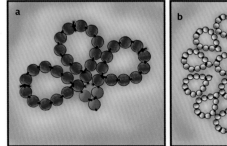
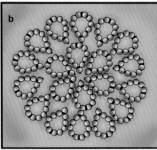
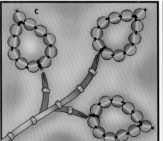
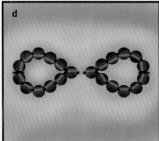

Figure 8.70a–d Lazy daisy variations.

BEAD LACE TRIM

Lace trim is a very neat and creative way to decorate your edges. This stitch forms a lace look made of beads. It can be worked in one layer or many layers.

1. Secure the thread in between the two layers of the turned-up edge or hem, and bring the needle up through the fabric to the outside.
2. Bead the needle with one bead, and again take a small stitch in the fabric.
3. Secure the bead to the fabric with a stitch by inserting the needle back through the single bead.
4. Bead the needle again with one or more beads, and stitch into the fabric to the right of the previous stitch, leaving some space in between stitches.
5. After taking the small stitch into the fabric, again insert the needle into the last bead.
6. Continue repeating the steps until you get to the end of your edge.
7. You can add more beads after finishing the row by going backward toward the beginning of the edge. (Figure 8.71)

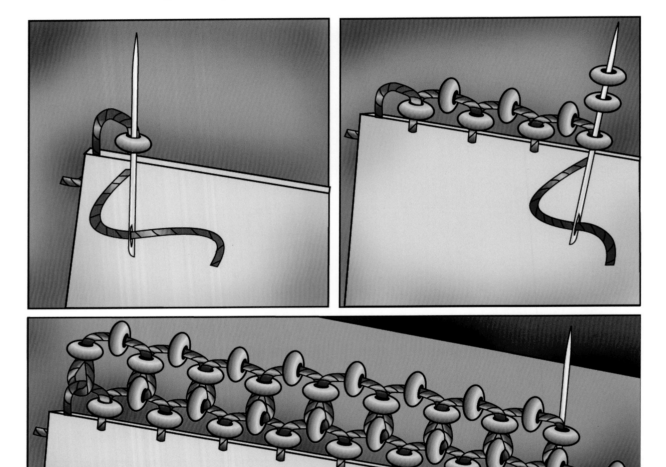

Figure 8.71 Bead lace trim.

LACE NET TRIM

This trim is the most decorative of all the trims mentioned in this chapter. It consists of two parts. The first part of the trim is closely beaded to the edge or hem horizontally, and the second part is beaded vertically and hangs down to form a fringe. The horizontal trim is worked with small beads, such as seed beads; bigger beads can be used as drops in the second, vertical part of the trim.

1. Secure the thread in between the two layers of the turned-up edge or hem, and bring the needle up through the fabric to the outside.
2. Bead the needle with one seed bead, and again secure it with a small backstitch through the fabric and the bead.
3. Pick up two more beads with your needle, and push them down toward the fabric.
4. Take another small stitch through the fabric edge, and insert the needle into the last bead once more, securing it.
5. Pick up two more beads and continue in this fashion until you get to the end of the edge.

6. You can add more rows if you desire a more decorative effect. Turn the fabric to the wrong side, and work the same direction as the previous row, right over the beaded row you have just created. However, instead of inserting the needle into the fabric, you will insert it into the top beads of the beaded row.
7. To work on the second part of the trim, secure the thread at the first bead of the horizontal trim.
8. Bead the needle with a number of seed beads. The number determines the length of your fringe trim. Use an odd number of beads in each group. Divide groups of beads with a bead of a different color. In the example, the thread is beaded with twenty-three beads. Every five beads, add an odd-color bead, and at the end of the twenty-third seed bead row, add a drop bead to dangle. Then the needle is pulled back through the last five beads and the odd-color bead. (Figure 8.72)
9. In the second vertical row from the odd-color bead you just beaded in step 8, put five new beads onto your needle and pull them through. Then add an odd-color bead and five more beads.

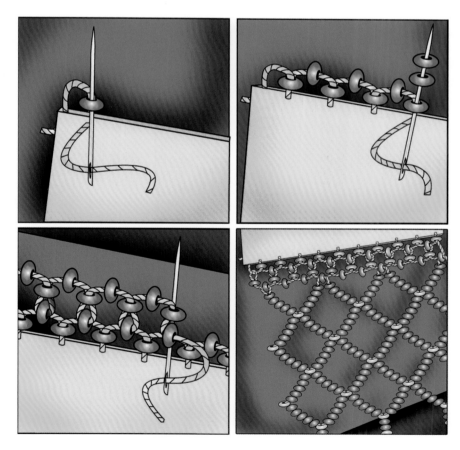

Figure 8.72 Lace net trim.

10. Pull your needle through the third odd-color bead from the bottom of the first row. Continue doing the same steps until you get to the top of the vertical trim. Bead five seed beads and one odd-color bead followed by another five seed beads. Then pull your needle through the first-row odd-color bead. Secure the thread at the third bead to the right of the first vertical row.

11. From the same bead along the horizontal row, begin a new thread and secure it. Bead another five seed beads to continue forming a fourth row.

12. Repeat all the steps until you get to the end of your edge or hem. (Figure 8.73)

BUGLE BEADS

Bugle beads are very sharp beads on the inside corner of the hole; therefore, use a double-waxed thread to avoid breakage during wear and tear of the garment. Bugle beads are longer than seed beads and can be as long as three to four seed beads in length. You can use various embroidery methods with bugle beads.

- Running stitch (Figure 8.74a)
- Backstitch (Figure 8.74b)
- Diagonal basting stitch (Figure 8.74c)
- Satin stitch (Figure 8.74d)
- Checkers sequence (Figure 8.74e)

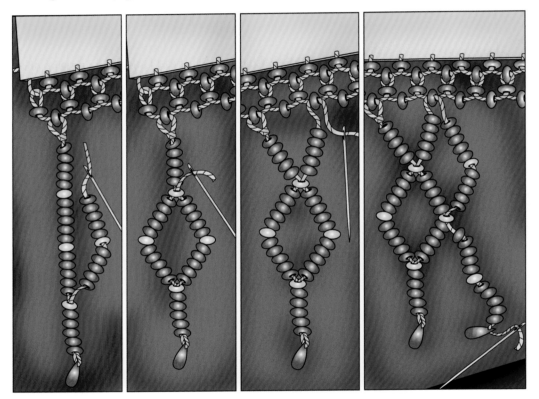

Figure 8.73 Lace net trim steps.

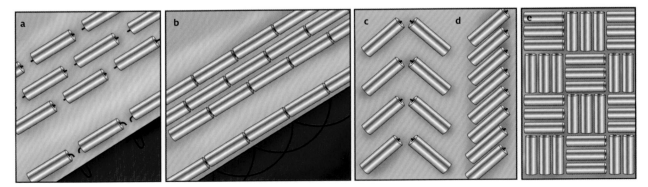

Figure 8.74a–e Bugle beading variations.

MOTIF BEADED EMBROIDERY

Leaf Motif Methods

Using Seed Beads

1. To work on this method, you will need to use two shades of seed beads, preferably one lighter and one darker.
2. Transfer your leaf motif to your fabric using marking tools, and mark a center line dividing two sides of the leaf.
3. Secure your thread and bring it up at the spine at the wider side.
4. Now, starting at the wider side of the leaf along the outline, make a slanted satin stitch using seed beads by threading three to four beads of one color at a time on to your needle. Begin the slant direction using the outline slant.

5. Continue making satin stitches of the same color to fill the same leaf side, threading a smaller amount of beads with each row in order to make the leaf get narrower toward the tip.
6. Fill the other side of the leaf as well. Using a different color, begin making similar satin stitches with a slant facing the opposite direction.
7. At the tip of the leaf, make one vertical stitch following the spine of the leaf along the center with a couple of beads. (Figure 8.75)
8. Secure your thread in the back.

Hint: You can also follow the same leaf motif with bugle beads. Use one or two shades of bugle beads, making slanted satin stitches on both sides of the leaf. (Figure 8.76)

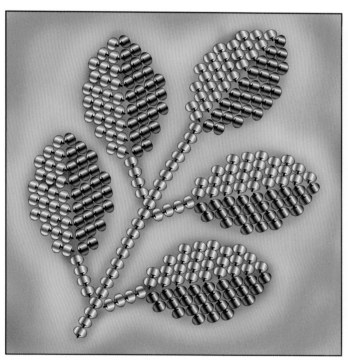

Figure 8.75 Satin stitch seed.

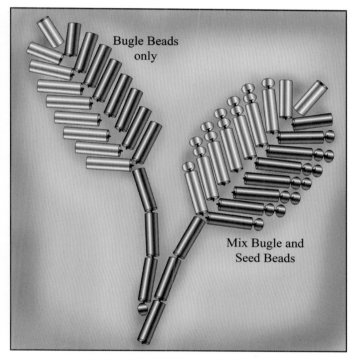

Figure 8.76 Bugle satin stitch.

Outline (Seed Beads or Bugle Beads)

1. Transfer your leaf motif to your fabric, and mark a center spine and the branches coming out of the spine of the leaf.
2. Secure your thread, and bring it up at point #1.
3. Make small running stitches with your seed beads outlining around the leaf, stitching two to three seed beads with each stitch until you reach back to point #1.
4. Bring your needle out at point #2 along the spine, and make beaded running stitches down the spine.
5. Stop at the first branch point #3. Make running stitches down the marked branch line toward the outline of the leaf.
6. At the end of the branch at point #4, bring your needle down into the fabric, and then bring it back up to the face fabric point #5.
7. Take your needle through one to three beads to add security and to bring your needle back to the center spine.
8. Before reaching the spine, take your needle back down into the fabric and back out to the face side at the spine point #6.
9. Continue running beads up the spine until you reach the next branch and the rest of the branches. (Figure 8.77)

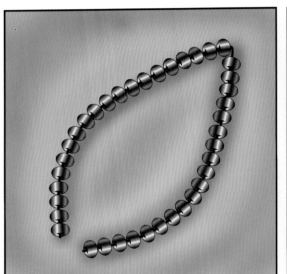

Figure 8.77 Leaf outlining.

TAMBOUR BEADING

Tambour beading is a great way to embellish garments and accessories. You will need to use a frame and a tambour needle. Place the fabric in the frame right side down. You will be working primarily on the underside of the fabric. Transfer the design you wish to bead to the underside of the fabric. (Figure 8.78)

Start by stringing, very loosely, an entire long chain of beads on a thread. Many professionals string all of their beads and re-spool the beaded thread onto another spool so that they can avoid spending time beading the thread later. (Figure 8.79)

Tambour beading is done using a tambour needle performing a chain stitch. The beaded strand is placed underneath the frame (on the right side of the fabric), and then the tambour needle pulls the thread in between each bead through the fabric to the top (the wrong side of the fabric) into a loop that makes up the chain stitch. Before you begin working on your garment, practice on scrap fabric to learn the technique.

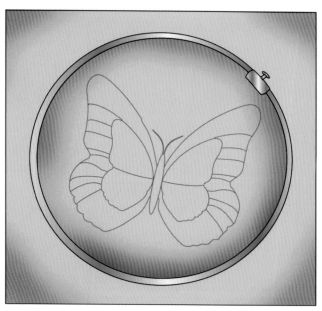

Figure 8.78 Tambour beading.

Figure 8.79 Beaded spool.

Tambour, Step-by-Step

1. Secure the thread on the underside of the fabric by threading a regular needle with the tip of the beaded strand, inserting it from underneath the frame to the top of the frame, making a knot, and backstitching a couple of times. This way the beaded strand is secure and hangs freely from the underside of the frame.

2. Now insert the tambour needle hook into the fabric along the bead to the underside of the frame, and, with the hook, grab the thread between the first two beads. After the thread is secure in the hook, pull the hook back up through the fabric, making the first loop. (Figure 8.80)

3. Keep the tambour needle in the loop; insert it into the motif, making the next stitch and grabbing the thread between the second and third beads. Hook it into the hook, and pull it back up through the fabric and the loop that was already on the hook. This will leave you with a new loop after you pull it tighter. This is very similar to crochet.

4. Continue steps 2 and 3 until you get to the end of your motif line. If your beaded thread ends, make another beaded thread and knot it to the end of the previous thread to continue with the stitch.

5. When you need to start a new line with a different color bead, repeat steps 1 through 4 to complete another tambour chain.

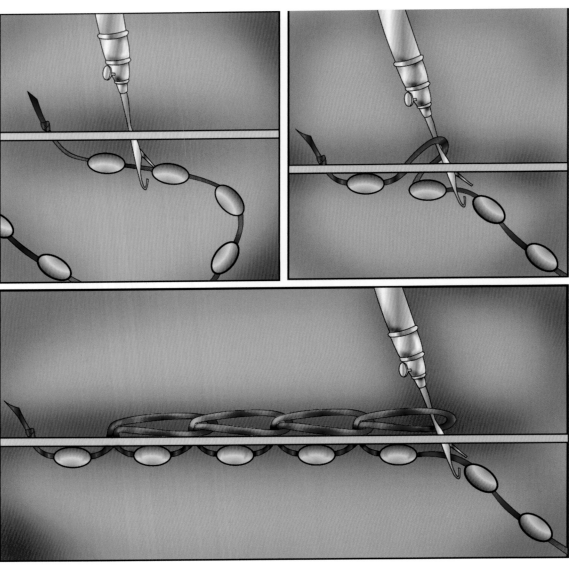

Figure 8.80 Tambour beading.

SEQUINS

Sequins are flat discs that have a metallic, shiny look and come in various colors, shapes, and textures. They also come with one or more punched holes for attachment purposes.

Before working your sequins, mark your motif on your fabric. Make sure to leave enough space in between lines if you are planning to make a parallel motif to fit your sequin width. (Figure 8.81)

To attach the sequins, use a sewing or a beading needle for smaller holes and matching or clear sewing thread/ floss. Clear thread is great for sequins because you can avoid matching the color of thread to your garment and to your sequins.

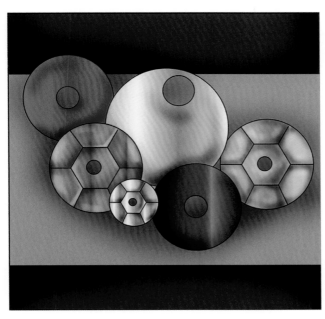

Figure 8.81 Sequins.

Running Stitch, Overlapping Sequins

1. Secure your thread in the back of the fabric, and bring the needle up at point #1.
2. Take the sequin, thread it on your needle, and pull the sequin down the thread to the fabric surface.
3. On the right or left side (depending on which direction you will be sewing) at point #2, insert your needle down into the fabric directly outside the sequin edge and back up at point #3, which is directly next to point #2.
4. Take another sequin and thread it on your needle, pulling it down the thread to the fabric surface. This sequin should half overlap the first sequin.
5. Continue the stitches in the same direction; insert your needle down into the fabric at point #4 directly outside the sequin edge and back up at point #3, which is directly next to point #5.
6. Continue repeating steps 2–5 until you are finished with your desired line.
7. Secure your thread behind the fabric. (Figure 8.82)

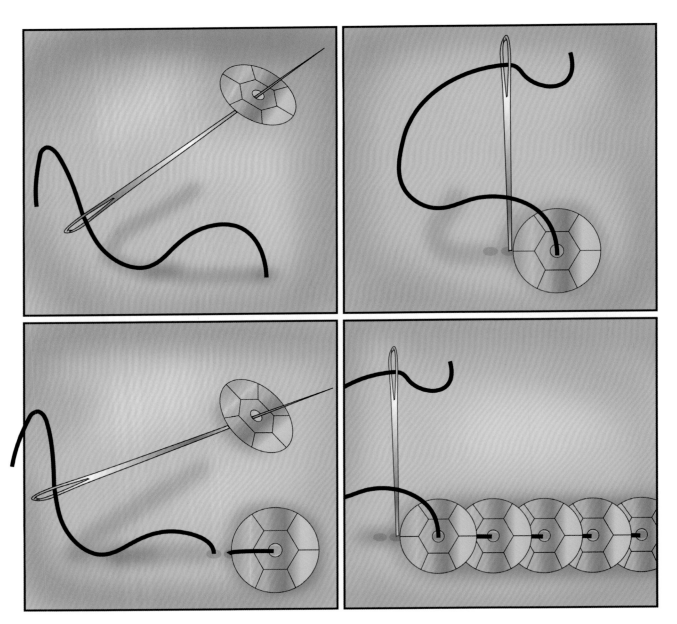

Figure 8.82 Overlapping running stitch.

Running Stitch, Side by Side

1. Secure your thread, and bring the needle up at point #1.
2. Thread a sequin on your needle, and pull it down to the fabric surface.
3. On the right or left side (depending on which direction you will be sewing) at point #2, insert your needle down into the fabric directly outside the sequin edge and back up at point #3. (The space from point #2 and point #3 is measured to be half the sequin width,)
4. Thread another sequin on your needle, pulling it down to the fabric surface.
5. Now continuing the stitches the same direction, insert your needle down into the fabric at point #4 directly outside the sequin edge and back up at point #5. The space from point #4 and point #5 is measured to be half the sequin width.
6. Continue repeating steps 2–7 until you are finished with your desired line.
7. Secure your thread. (Figure 8.83)

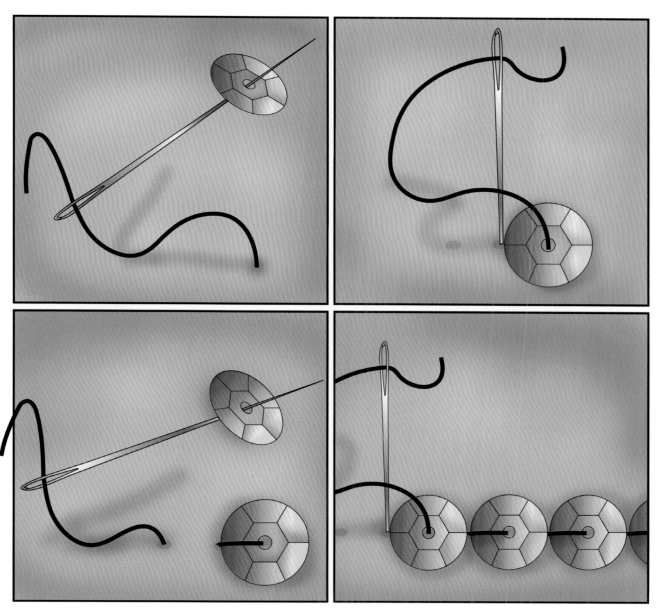

Figure 8.83 Side-by-side running stitch.

Double Stitch

1. Secure your thread, and bring the needle up at point #1.
2. Thread one sequin on your needle, pulling it down to the fabric surface.
3. On the right side at point #2, insert your needle down into the fabric directly outside the sequin edge.
4. Bring your needle back up directly through the center hole one more time.
5. Now taking your needle to the left side, insert your needle down into the fabric directly outside the sequin edge at point #3 and back up at point #4. (Now you have a choice to continue this sequence with your sequins side by side or overlap them. Point #4 can be directly next to point #3 or measured to be half the sequin width away from point #3)
6. You should now have a straight line sewn across your sequin.
7. Continue repeating steps 2–6 until you are finished with your desired line.
8. Secure your thread behind the fabric. (Figure 8.84)

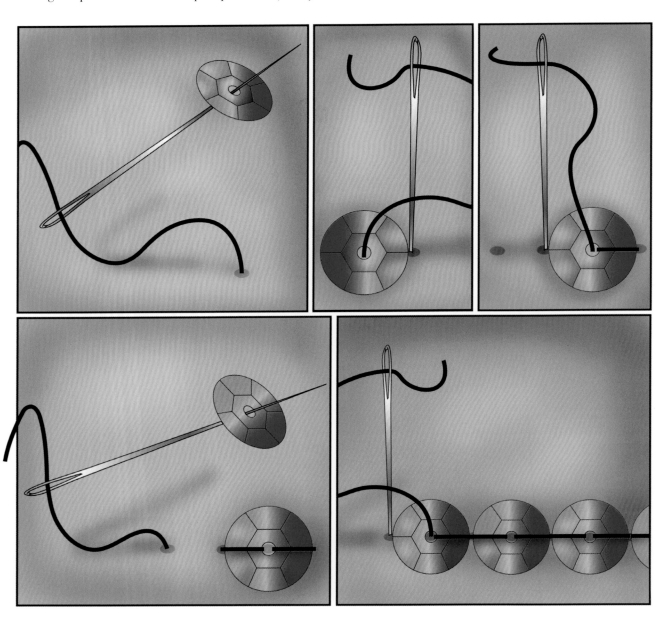

Figure 8.84 Double stitch.

RHINESTONES AND CRYSTALS

Today, we are very fortunate to be able to buy and use rhinestones and crystals to embellish our garments. There are many different variations of stones offered. Some rhinestones come with a flat back and holes for stitching, just like a button. Actually, many buttons come as a rhinestone option as well. (Figure 8.85)

Other crystals or rhinestones can also be added to your garment with a metallic clasp that is placed behind the fabric with sharp teeth that penetrate through the fabric and clasp the crystal in place with the help of jewelry pliers.

Sewing on the stones is the best option. It is the most secure and comfortable way to wear a garment with rhinestones, as otherwise the metallic piece rubs against the skin.

You may want to glue stones for craft decoration but not garment decoration, as that shows poor quality.

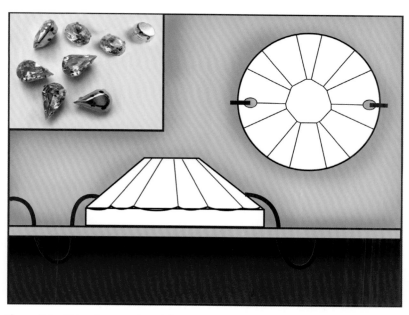

Figure 8.85 Rhinestones and crystals.

ELIE SAAB

Elie Saab was born in Lebanon in 1964. He was a self-taught designer who from an early age knew that he could be a great fashion talent. At age nine, he began his fashion career by making clothes for his sisters and expanded into selling his designs to his neighbors.

In 1981, at the age of seventeen, he decided to move to Paris to study fashion. Saab returned in 1982 to open up his first couture atelier in Beirut, as he was impatient to begin his career. He hired over a dozen employees to help him create his first collection, which debuted only a couple of months after the opening of his atelier. His designs showed a mix of inspiration from eastern and western styles.

Elie Saab designs are known for the use of richer fabrics, delicate lace, detailed embroidery, pearls, crystals, and silk threads.

His new collection was loved by the local women, and the word about it and his talent reached far beyond Beirut. He became the first non-Italian designer to become a member of the Italian Camera Nazionale della Moda and showed his collection in Rome.

In 1998, he held a fashion show in Monaco attended by the Princess Stephanie of Monaco. He launched his ready-to-wear collection in 1998 in Milan; it continues to be made in Italy to this day.

In 2000, he received an invitation from Chambre Syndicale De La Haute Couture in Paris to show his

Haute Couture Fall/Winter 2014–2015.

collection. After this, he began to show his collections in Paris every year—two shows a year for his couture line and two for his ready-to-wear line.

In 2002, Halle Berry wore one of his designs to the 2002 Academy Awards and won the Best Actress Award. His fame grew overnight after the awards. Saab became one of the most sought-after designers for red carpet appearances in Hollywood.

Today Elie Saab stores are located all over the world including boutiques in Beirut, Paris, and London. Saab headquarters are in Beirut, but the company also holds offices in New York and Paris. Saab has sixty retail outlets all over the world, eighteen of them in the United States.

All of Elie Saab's dresses have his signature sense of elegance, beauty, luxury, and romance.

Elie Saab, 2014.

Haute Couture Spring/Summer 2014.

Chapter Review

This chapter covered the skill of hand embroidery techniques, ribbon embroidery, goldwork, beadwork, and even cutwork, all of which are wonderful ways to add garment embellishments. This chapter shows many variations of similar skill used with different supplies.

Bead embroidery and decoration are some of the most important embellishments in couture gowns. By adding these intricate details to your garments, you produce designer, high-quality looks.

Projects

1. Make beadwork samples for your sample book. Work on all of the beading techniques covered in this chapter. Write down your steps, and insert them into one of your plastic cover sheets.

2. Make an embroidery sample for your book. Write down your steps, and insert them into one of your plastic cover sheets.

3. Make ribbon work samples for your sample book. Write down your steps, and insert them into one of your plastic cover sheets.

4. Make goldwork samples for your sample book. Write down your steps, and insert them into one of your plastic cover sheets.

5. Design and sketch a five-outfit collection utilizing three of the techniques covered in this chapter. Make sure each one of the outfits applies three of the techniques. Present them in a professional manner.

Key Terms

Beading	Goldwork	Rondelles
Beadwork	Kid leather	Satin stitch
Bugle beads	Metallic thread	Sequins
Bullion	Pearls	Tambour beading
Couch	Purl	Tambour needle
Drops	Ribbon work	Zigzag stitch
Embroidery	Rocailles	

9

The Skill of Fabric Manipulation

Objectives

- Learn decorative skills to enhance your designs

- Learn appliqué, cutwork, and lace techniques

- Learn smocking, shirring, and quilting

- Learn how to embellish with tucks, pleats, ruffles, and flounces

- Learn about the life and work of Yves Saint Laurent

Couture designs are known for delicate and extraordinary details. A detailed couture garment takes somewhere between two weeks and four months to make. Some have even taken longer, depending on the details. By adding these details to your garments, you produce designer, high-quality looks. (Figure 9.1a and b)

Appliqués

Appliqués are cutout fabric, lace, or cutwork shapes applied to the garment. They are attached on by hand, machine, or with heat.

Figure 9.1a and b Embellishment examples.

Figure 9.2 Appliqué is basted to keep it in place during attachment.

For iron-on appliqués, use a fusible adhesive between the fabric and the appliqué to keep it from shifting while stitching. Alternatively, you can baste an appliqué before securing. If you are applying it to a heavyweight fabric, basting is best to keep the motif in place. When you baste, make sure the garment fabric is flat on the table to prevent the appliqué from puckering. (Figure 9.2)

Before you begin, use fray glue to prevent the edges of your appliqué from fraying. You can use any fabric for appliqué; however, avoid fabrics that fray easily or turn the edges under.

OVERCAST STITCH

This stitch can be done loose or tight, almost like a satin stitch.

1. Secure your thread under the motif.
2. Start making diagonal stitches by taking the needle through the back of the fabric on both layers and out on the outside of the motif around the appliqué. (Figure 9.3)
3. Make sure the stitches are small. Do not pull the thread too tight.
4. Continue overcasting around the appliqué, and secure your thread.

RUNNING STITCH

The running stitch is generally used on children's clothing and is sewn around an appliqué with turned-up edges.

1. Secure the thread.
2. Make small running stitches in and out of the fabric around the entire motif close to the edge (⅛ inch). Secure the thread. (Figure 9.4)

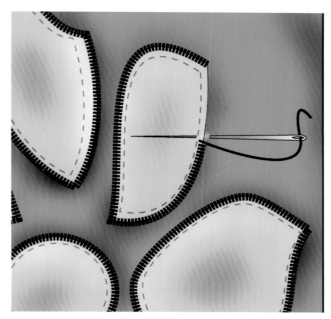

Figure 9.3 Overcast stitch.

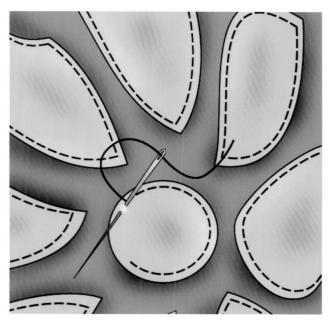

Figure 9.4 Running stitch.

BACKSTITCH

Used with turned-under edges and on raw edges that have been fray-checked. This is also a great way to outline your motif with a darker color.

1. Secure the thread.
2. Make small backstitches into the appliqué ⅛ inch from the edge around the motif, catching both layers of fabric. Secure the thread. (Figure 9.5)

CHAIN STITCH

1. Secure the thread.
2. Make a stitch forward into the fabric, loop the thread under the needle, and pull the needle out. This forms the chain stitch.
3. The next stitch is inserted back into the same hole it came out of. Make another stitch, looping the thread under the needle again. (Figure 9.6)
4. Continue chain stitches through both layers of fabric and appliqué. Secure the thread.

BUTTONHOLE STITCH

This stitch is a great way to connect the appliqué to the fabric and, at the same time, finish the raw edge of your appliqué.

1. Secure your thread, and pull it through at the edge of the appliqué.

2. With your needle facing down, make a stitch into both layers ⅛ to ¼ inch from the edge. Bring the needle out where the edge meets the fabric. Before you pull it out, make sure you place the thread under the needle. (Figure 9.7)
3. Repeat, making the same stitches around the entire appliqué. Secure the thread.

Figure 9.6 Chain stitch.

Figure 9.5 Backstitch.

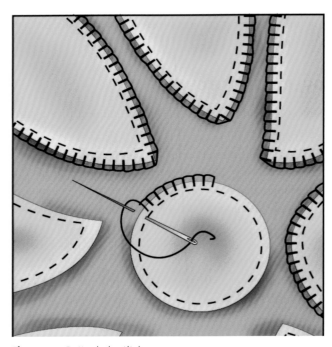

Figure 9.7 Buttonhole stitch.

CATCH STITCH

You can use this stitch with a raw-edge appliqué.

1. Secure the thread, and pull it through on the left side of your appliqué edge.
2. With your needle facing left, make a small stitch right to left on your appliqué, ⅛ to ¼ inch from the edge.
3. With needle facing left again, make the same stitch at the edge of the motif along the fabric. (Figure 9.8)
4. Continue around the appliqué; secure the thread.

SATIN STITCH

This is the most commonly used appliqué stitch. It gives a sleek finished edge.

1. Baste a couple of running stitches along the edge.
2. Secure a new thread.
3. Start making satin stitches, wrapping them around the edge. Continue around the appliqué. Secure the thread. (Figure 9.9)

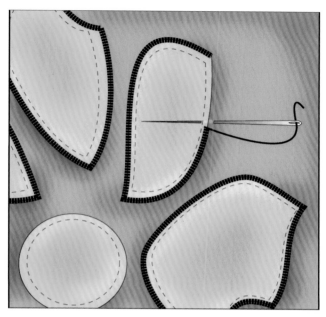

Figure 9.9 Satin stitch.

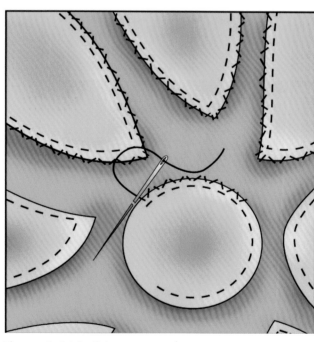

Figure 9.8 Catch stitch.

Appliqué Variations

INSERTION APPLIQUÉ

This appliqué is used with two methods.

Method 1

1. On paper, design a shape you would like to use as the insertion appliqué.
2. Transfer it to the back of your garment fabric, and cut it out.
3. Now transfer it to the insertion fabric, and cut it out as well. You should be able to fit the shape exactly into the cutout in the garment fabric.
4. Use any of these stitches to attach the pieces together: satin stitch, catch stitch, whipstitch, or even slip stitch.

Method 2

1. Make a shape on paper and another shape a bit larger (¼ inch larger all around).
2. Transfer the smaller shape to the garment fabric, and cut it out.
3. Now transfer the larger shape to the insertion fabric, and cut it out.

4. Place the bigger shape under the fabric opening, and baste in place.

5. Stitch around the opening. Possibilities include satin stitching, catching both layers of fabric; catch stitch, running catch stitch, whipstitch, and even machine stitch with a regular, decorative, or zigzag seam; or zigzagging your stitch around the appliqué motif, and then fraying the edge to make a fringe. (Figure 9.10)

APPLIQUÉ REVERSE

This appliqué is worked first from the back of the fabric and then stitched on the face side.

1. Fuse knit interfacing to the back of your fabric, and transfer your appliqué motif to the interfacing.

2. Place the fabric of the appliqué facedown underneath the garment fabric (back of the appliqué to the right side of the garment fabric). Pin in place.

3. Stitch a regular stitch with your sewing machine, through all the layers of fabric, and around the transferred motif from the wrong side of the fabric.

4. Turn the garment to the right side. With appliqué scissors, trim away the excess fabric around the stitch line you just made. (You are cutting around the appliqué motif close to the stitch line.) Make sure you are very careful, cutting close to the seam without cutting through it.

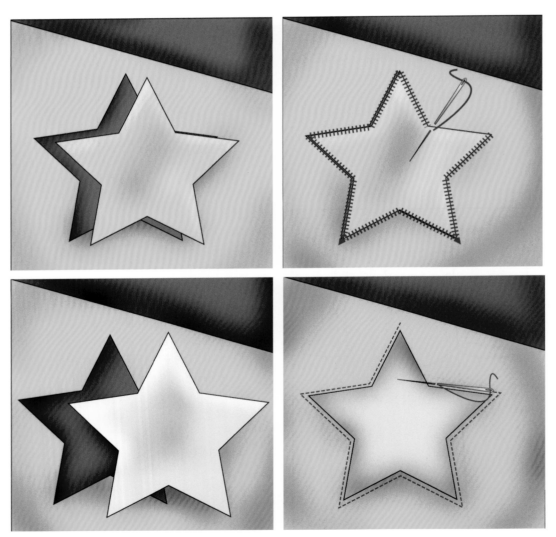

Figure 9.10 Insertion appliqué.

Figure 9.11 Appliqué reverse.

5. From the right side, you can either satin stitch by hand around the appliqué or use a tight zigzag stitch on your sewing machine. (Figure 9.11)

Sewing with Lace

When sewing with **lace**, make sure you choose lace that is very similar in thickness and weight to the fabric you will be using for the garment. Some laces have to be preshrunk just like garment fabric; read the care instructions on the label. You also need to determine which side is the right side of the fabric. With most lace, the smoothest side is the wrong side. When ready, cut out all of your patterns along the grain of the lace. Even though it is not visible in most laces, the bias of the lace will stretch a bit more, allowing you to determine the grainline.

You need to use different types of stitches and seams for different types of laces. For example, when you have a high-definition lace such as guipure, you will need to appliqué the seams. When working with less defined laces, you can use very narrow seams.

LACE APPLIQUÉ SEAMS

Lace appliqué seams are used for defined-motif laces. These laces have motifs embroidered with satin stitches.

1. Cut your patterns with extra motif overlaps and under-laps. (Figure 9.12a)
2. Match up your motifs in the seams, and stitch either by hand or on your sewing machine along the outline of your motif. (Figure 9.12b)
3. Cut off the excess lace close to the seam with embroidery scissors.

Hint: When sewing darts in lace, you can cut out the dart, leaving a little bit of seam allowance. Then lap the seam allowances and stitch. This makes an invisible dart. You would not want all the bulk of the dart to show through the top layer of the lace. (Figure 9.12c)

Finish lace hems with horsehair braid, rolled hems, or trim. You can use the scalloped edge of the lace as the bottom hem or trim on garments. (Figure 9.12d)

You can also cut these same scalloped edges off the lace clipping around the motif and sew them on regular fabric as a trim. This same technique is used when you need to finish your garment that is made of lace that has a curved hem or a hem that has been cut off the scallop during pattern cutting.

You can use an underlining of a different color or add an opaque color to eliminate garment sheer look. This also eliminates the seam showing through from the backside.

You can also work with lace using another method. You can try stay stitching the lace patterns to the underlining patterns and sewing them as one pattern into a seam. This method allows you to use regular seam allowances.

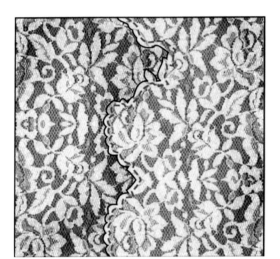
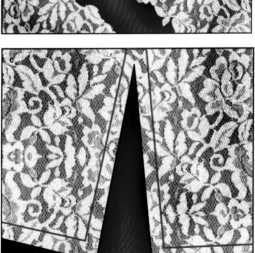

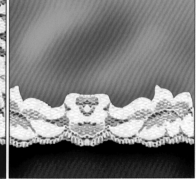

Figure 9.12 Lace appliqué seams. (a) Cut your lace around the motif. (b) Overlay one side over the other, stitch, and remove excess with embroidery scissors. (c) Darts should be cut out before sewing. (d) Lace hems.

Lace Insertions

You can sew a piece of lace into a cutout opening in any garment.

1. Cut out a shape in your garment with a ¼-inch seam allowance. Clip into the seam allowance, and fold under.
2. Place the lace underneath the opening.
3. Stitch through both of the layers, fabric and lace, all around the shape ⅛ inch from the fold. (Figure 9.13)

LACE APPLIQUÉ

This type of appliqué is cut out of netting fabric or lace and then stitched onto the garment fabric. You can either apply it on fabric, leaving it as is, or apply it on fabric and cut away the excess underneath the lace appliqué, making it sheer. Make sure you use a lace fabric that has a nice satin embroidery stitch around the motifs or cording to get a clean cut.

1. Find a lace motif you like and cut out the shape. Cut around the motif stitch or cord to avoid unraveling.
2. Mark placement of the lace appliqué on the fabric, and baste in position.
3. Secure a new thread, and begin making satin, buttonhole, whip, and/or catch stitches around the appliqué.
4. To finish, secure your thread.

Hint: Lace is also a great way to decorate any garment. It has even been appliquéd on sweaters, jeans, and warm wool coats. If you need to add more embellishment to your garment, add embroidery and beadwork on top of your appliqués.

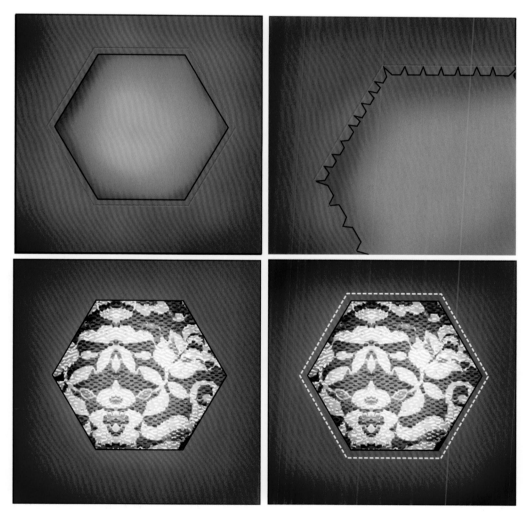

Figure 9.13 Lace insertions.

Shirring

Shirring is very commonly used on dresses, shirts, baby clothes, and often accessories. Shirring can be done with an elastic thread to provide stretch and help eliminate the need for darts in woven fabrics. (Figure 9.14)

Shirring can be done by hand or by machine. If you are using a machine, you can use the elastic thread in the bobbin and regular thread for the top machine stitch. You can also use a shirring foot so it will not be too stretchy.

Shirring is worked with multiple rows of parallel gathers. Before you begin, make sure your fabric is appropriate for shirring. By testing the fabric, you can determine how wide your pattern would have to be in order to gather into the width you will need for the garment. Test the shirring to calculate the proper width. To begin, mark parallel rows for the shirring. Shirring can also be made in a circular pattern.

1. Machine stitch or hand stitch a simple basting line over the marked lines.
2. After you have made all of the desired stitches, pull on the bobbin thread if you stitched with a sewing machine, or just pull on the stitched thread by hand to gather the stitches.
3. After you have tightened the gathered thread, make sure you secure the threads. You can tie the ends together. (Figure 9.15a and b)

In order to keep the shirring from stretching, sew a row perpendicular to the rows of stitching at both edges of the piece.

Hint #1: If you are using a sewing machine to create stretchy shirring, wind the elastic by hand, making sure to stretch the elastic as you wind. After you have finished the seam, the stitch will gather on its own when the elastic goes back to its original length.

Hint #2: If you want to keep the shirring from coming apart, you will need to attach a stay piece of fabric behind the shirring. (Figure 9.15c)

Figure 9.14 Shirring example.

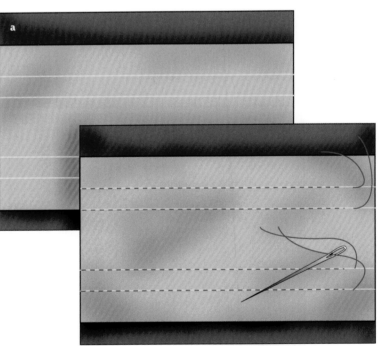

Figure 9.15 (a) and (b) Tighten the gathered threads, secure, and tie the ends together.

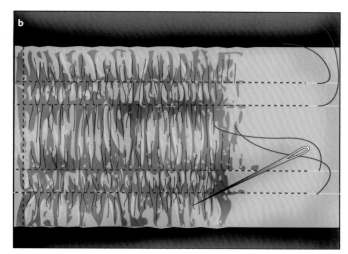

Gathering

Gathering is a very simple embellishment; however, it can be very creative.

1. To gather, make a basting seam.
2. Then pull on the bobbin thread and gather the fabric.
3. Stay stitch another seam over the gathering to hold it in place.
4. Now you can attach the gathering to your fabric. (Figure 9.16)

Gathering can serve as a ruffle or as a decoration for your garment embellishment.

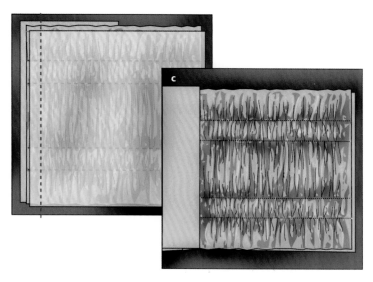

Figure 9.15 (c) Shirring stays.

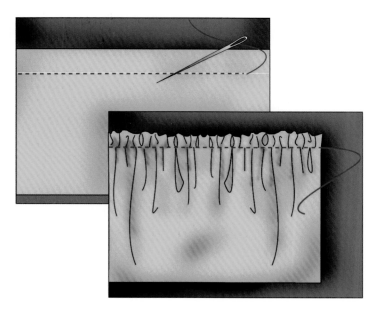

Figure 9.16 Gathering.

DRUNKARD'S PATH

To work on this gathering effect, decide how large your square pieces will be.

1. Once you have your square, mark a curved corner as shown on your pattern pieces of the square, and add seam allowances to both sides.

2. The corner side is ready, and the larger piece will need to be cut and spread to add extra fabric for gathering.

3. Gather the long side back to its original length by pulling on the basting stitch. You can stay stitch it to hold in place.

4. Pin the gathered side into the corner curve. Clip the curve in to fit and stitch. Hand stitch or machine stitch for a stronger seam.

5. Quilt many squares together to make a pattern. (Figure 9.17)

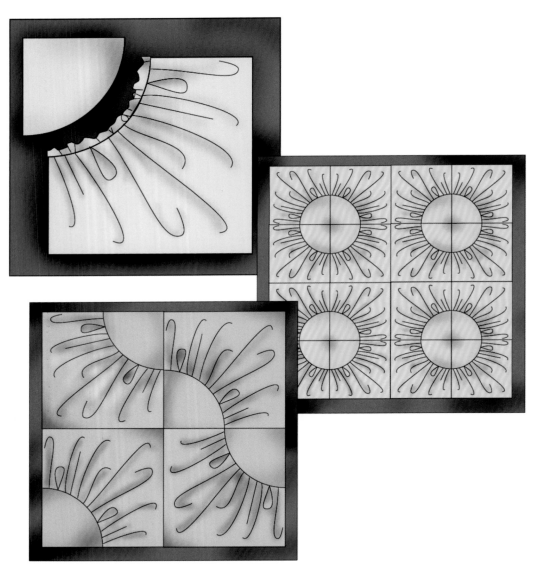

Figure 9.17 Drunkard's path.

DOUBLE-SIDED GATHERING

Double-sided gathering is a textured insert that is intended to be sewn in between more pattern pieces. Patterns can be straight gathered panels or can take a curved effect and become a **serpentine path**. (Figure 9.18)

You can make a ruffle and gather it on both sides for a decorative effect; then sew it in between other pieces of fabric or to another gathered piece.

1. Cut your rectangle to the correct length.
2. Sew a double seam on both sides of the rectangle. Do not backstitch.
3. Gather by pulling on the bobbin thread.
4. Keep gathering until you get the length you need.
5. Attach it to your garment in between two pieces of fabric or to another gathered piece.

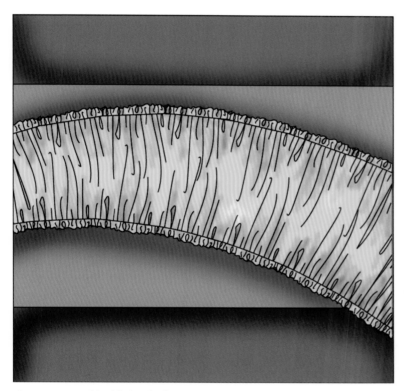

Figure 9.18 Double-sided gathering.

FLORAL GATHERING

These flowers are a great way to decorate your garment. Use one layer of fabric (preferably double-sided) or multiple layers by gathering up two or more circles at the same time. Make sure not to use too many layers, as your flower can become too heavy and bulky for the garment. Other options are to use two different fabrics and finish your edges at the same time. Pinking shears will add an edge texture.

1. Cut out your circle(s).
2. Baste a smaller circle inside your cut circle by hand or machine, and leave the thread lose at the end. No backstitching. If you have more layers, place them all together, and baste the inner circle through all of the layers.

Hint: The smaller the circle inside, the longer the flower petals.

3. Gather up your inner circle; it should turn into a shape that looks like a closed flower bud. Then wrap your thread around the bud and secure it.
4. Open your flower. You can press the flower bud to form a flat coin shape surface. Use the flat bud to attach it to your garment. (Figure 9.19)
5. Add more embellishments or beads to the flower center.

Figure 9.19 Floral gathering.

YO-YO GATHERING

Yo-yo gathering (Figure 9.20) is commonly used in clothing, furniture décor, curtains, pillows, handbags, and so much more.

Smocking

Smocking consists of fabric folds that are decoratively stitched at regular intervals to create a beautiful puckered pattern. Smocking can be done by hand or with a machine called a smocking pleater.

This type of decoration is done before the garment is constructed and can be used on yokes, bodices, pockets, sleeves, and waistlines. There are several different types of smocking, including gauging, **cable stitch**, **honeycomb stitch**, and **wave stitch**.

AMERICAN SMOCKING

American smocking is done by using a dotted grid as a guide, compared to **English smocking**, which is done using pre-pleated fabric.

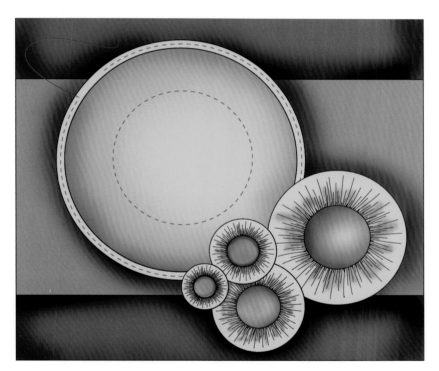

Figure 9.20 Yo-yo gathering.

HONEYCOMB SMOCKING

1. Using fabric marking pens or chalk pencils, mark the piece of fabric with a grid of dots. Make sure the points are measured evenly.

2. Start at the top on the right side of the fabric, and work your way down. Don't forget to secure the thread. Begin at the top corner point and stitch into the point right under the top point with your needle pointing upward, bringing it back out in the starting point. Pull to tighten the stitch. (Figure 9.21)

3. Insert the needle into the second point again, this time with your needle pointing left, and bring it out of the point to the left. When you work this stitch, the thread should be behind the fabric so that you can work the next row.

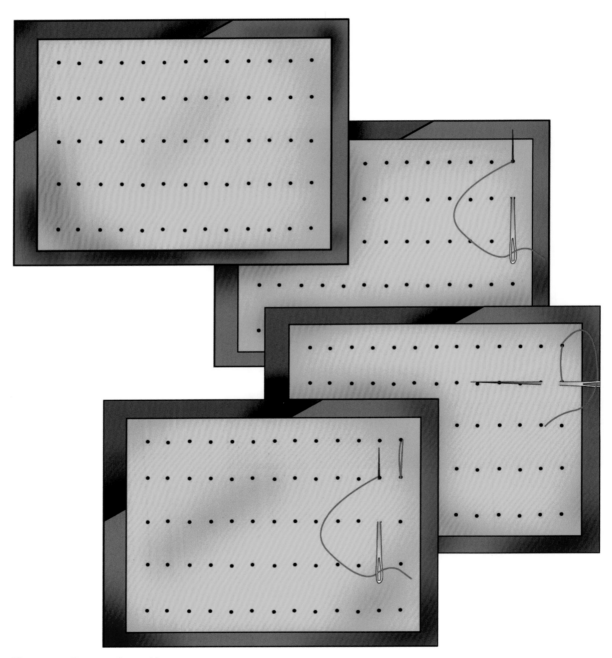

Figure 9.21 Honeycomb smocking.

4. Repeat step 2. Work your way down to the lower point with your needle pointing upward. Tighten.
5. Insert the needle in the fourth point, facing right, and out through the point on the right. (Figure 9.22)
6. Repeat steps 1–5 on all the rows until you get the entire piece of fabric smocked. Attach to a stay after the smocking is finished.

Hint: When marking your dots on the smocking guide, you can alternate different lengths for a more decorative effect.

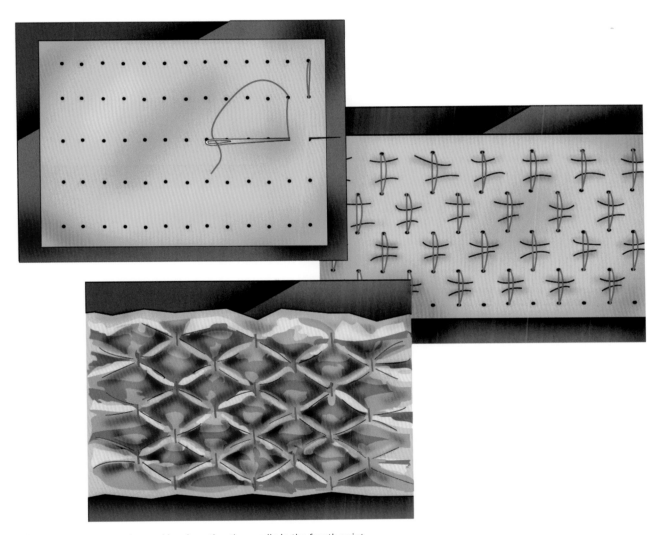

Figure 9.22 Honeycomb smocking, inserting the needle in the fourth point.

CABLE STITCH SMOCKING

Using fabric marking pens or chalk pencils, mark the piece of fabric with a grid of dots. Make sure the points are measured evenly.

1. Start on the top right side of the fabric and work your way down.
2. Begin at the top corner point holding the thread above the fabric on the left side of the needle. Stitch one small stitch at the second dot in and out of the fabric, with your needle pointing upward. Pull the thread out, and tighten the stitch. (Figure 9.23)
3. From the second point, hold the thread on the right side of the needle, making one small stitch at the third dot in and out of the fabric, with the needle pointing upward. Tighten.

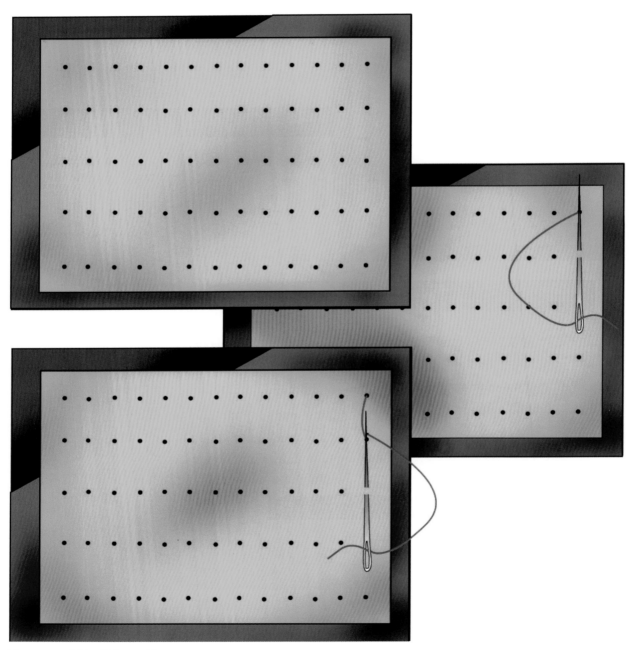

Figure 9.23 Cable stitch smocking.

4. From the third point, hold the thread on the left side of the needle, making one small stitch at the third dot in and out of the fabric, with your needle pointing upward. Tighten.
5. Continue these steps, making sure the gathering is even throughout. (Figure 9.24)

ENGLISH SMOCKING

English smocking is different from honeycomb and cable stitch smocking in that the fabric is pleated before smocking.

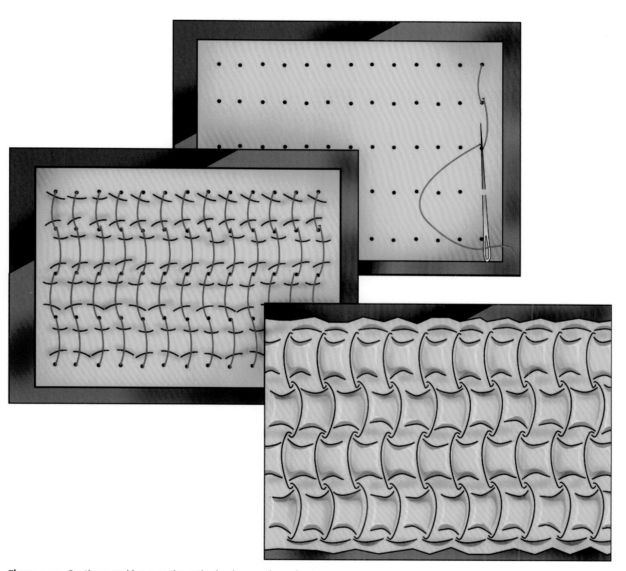

Figure 9.24 Continue, making sure the gathering is even throughout.

ENGLISH CABLE STITCH SMOCKING

Cable stitch is one of the simplest smocking stitches and can be used in conjunction with other smocking stitches and designs; it can also be beaded, wrapped with ribbon, or used as a border. It is not used on stretchy patterns because it does not stretch easily.

1. Begin by pleating the fabric, making sure the spacing is even. Press the pleats with an iron, or stitch them like tucks with a basting stitch. Take the basting seam out when finished with the smocking. With a marking tool, mark a guideline to follow. (Figure 9.25a)

2. Start stitching by bringing the needle up on the left side of the fabric piece, to the left of the first pleat.

3. With the needle facing left, insert it through the second pleat with the thread under the needle. Bring the needle out in between the two pleats. Pull the needle out to finish the stitch. This step is called an under cable. (Figure 9.25b)

4. With the needle facing left, make a stitch through the third pleat with the thread above the needle. Bring the needle up in between the second and third pleats. Pull the needle out to finish the stitch. This stitch is an over cable.

5. Repeat, alternating under cable and over cable stitching. Secure the thread.

Figure 9.25a and b English cable stitch smocking.

DOUBLE CABLE STITCH SMOCKING

The **double cable stitch smocking** is very similar to the regular cable stitch and is actually a set of two cable stitches stitched together, one higher than the other, with diagonal stitches in between. This stitch does not stretch.

1. After pleating the fabric, insert the needle and thread along the left side of the fabric.
2. Make one under cable, one over cable, and another under cable along the same row. (Figure 9.26)
3. When finished, make two diagonal under stitches.
4. Continue with another three stitches: overstitch, understitch, and overstitch.
5. When you are ready to stitch down, make two diagonal overstitches to match the two previous stitches.
6. Repeat steps 2–5.

Hint: You can make more than two diagonal stitches to create a deeper curve of the smocking stitch.

Figure 9.26 Double cable stitch smocking.

ALTERNATING CABLE STITCH SMOCKING

Alternating cable stitch smocking is very similar to regular cable stitch. It is more decorative and can be used with multiple colors of thread.

1. After pleating the fabric, from the left side of the fabric, make a row of cable stitches in one color thread. (Figure 9.27)

2. Using another color, make one understitch, one overstitch, and another understitch.

3. Make another three stitches below the row (overstitch, understitch, and overstitch).

4. Repeat steps 2–3 to finish.

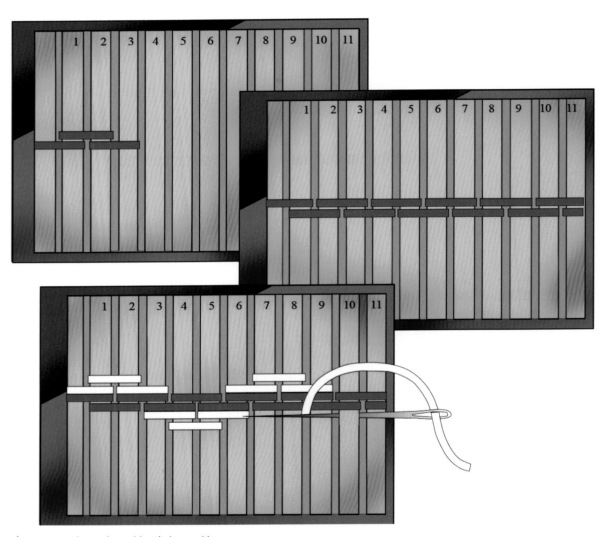

Figure 9.27 Alternating cable stitch smocking.

FLOWER STITCH SMOCKING

Flower stitch smocking is commonly used either alone or with other stitches. You can also use beads in the center of this stitch.

1. From the left side of the fabric, make three cable stitches: understitch, overstitch, and understitch. (Figure 9.28)
2. Mirror another three cable stitches right below the first three stitches.
3. Add a bead into the center of the flower if desired.

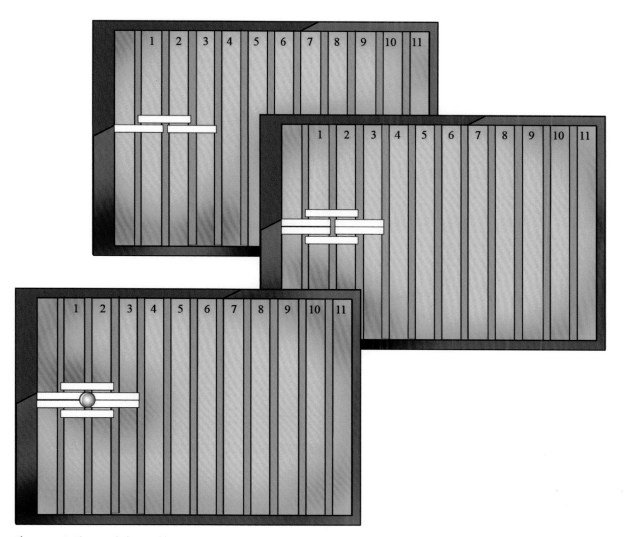

Figure 9.28 Flower stitch smocking.

Straight Stitch Smocking

STEM STITCH SMOCKING

Stem stitch smocking is often used for areas that do not need stretch, such as necklines, cuffs, and decoration.

1. Begin on the left side of the fabric. (Figure 9.29)
2. With the needle facing left in a slight diagonal slant and pointing upward, insert the needle through the second pleat with the thread under the needle.

Bring the needle out in between the first and second pleats.
3. Continue the same step for pleat three, and bring the needle out in between the second and third pleats.
4. Repeat steps 1–3. When you are done, tie off the thread in the back of the fabric.

Hint: Turn the stem stitch into a wheat stitch by making another row of stem stitches in the same or a different color and slanting the opposite direction. Make sure the stitches are close together.

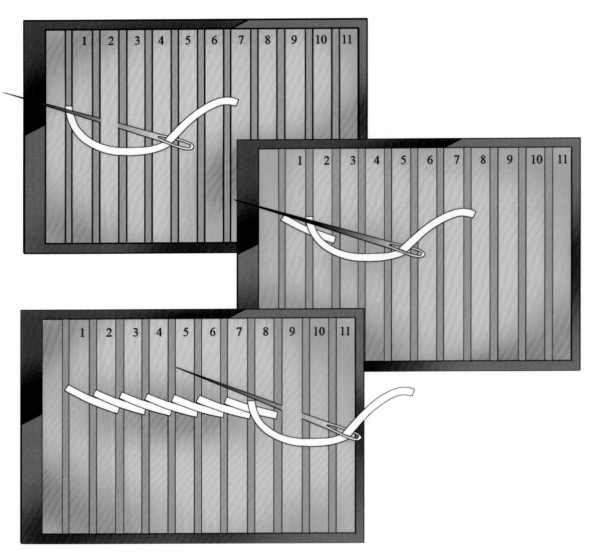

Figure 9.29 Stem stitch smocking.

CHEVRON STITCH SMOCKING

Chevron stitch (or **wave stitch**) **smocking** is a zigzag style with slight stretch. Use these smocking stitches on dresses, to eliminate darts, and on cuffs.

1. Start on the left side of the fabric. Begin along pleat one, and stitch one under cable through pleat two. (Figure 9.30a and b)

2. Keep your thread under the needle, and make one stitch through pleat three above the previous stitch.

3. With your thread over the needle, make an over cable through pleat four along the same line.

4. Next step is another long stitch facing downward. With the thread above the needle, stitch through pleat 5 along the bottom line of stitches.

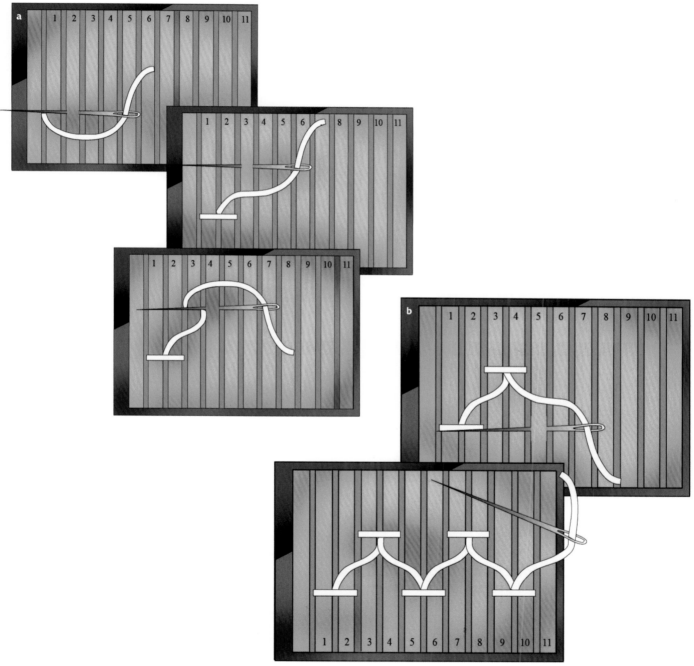

Figure 9.30a and b Chevron stitch smocking.

5. Keep the thread under the needle, and make an under cable stitch through the pleat.
6. Repeat steps 1–5 until you are finished with your row. Secure the thread.

Hint: Stitch another row of chevron stitches mirrored below the previous row forming a row of diamonds called the wave stitch diamond. (Figure 9.31)

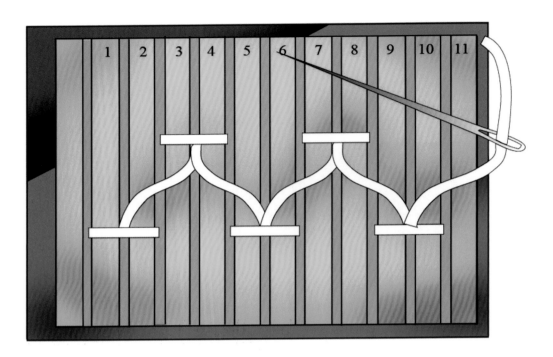

Figure 9.31 Wave stitch diamond smocking.

Decorative Quilting

There are two basic types of **decorative quilting**. In **English quilting**, two layers of fabric have a batting layer in between. All three layers are then stitched together and used for warm bedcovers and clothes. (Figure 9.32)

In **padded quilting** (Italian), only two layers are stitched. This quilting is used primarily for decorative purposes. This quilting can be done with cord or padding (also called Trapunto quilting) when added to the backside of the piece.

Quilting can be done freehand or by machine with/ without embroidery hoops.

Quilting interlining is often cotton or synthetic padding or batting. For **cord quilting**, the best choice is cotton cord, which comes in many different thicknesses.

Make sure to use strong thread when quilting. You can use cotton thread on natural fibers, such as cotton, linen, and wool. However, try to stick to the thread that most suits the fiber of the fabric used—polyester to polyester, silk to silk.

Figure 9.32 Decorative quilting.

ENGLISH QUILTING

1. Baste all the layers together—upper fabric, batting, underlining fabric—so that they do not come apart. (Figure 9.33a–c)
2. Think of the quilting design you want on your garment and then trace it onto the back layer.

3. If you have a pattern that needs to match up at the seams, make sure you design a motif and measure properly for it to line up. You can also leave 1–2 inches away from the edge of your pattern piece unstitched, sew up your garment seams, and then go back and quilt the unstitched part over your seams, allowing easy matching.
4. Begin sewing, following the lines. You can use your sewing machine or do the stitching by hand.

Hint: Keep it as is, or you can cut another lining to hide inside stitches or add warmth.

CORD QUILTING

If you are placing the quilting design on an already patterned garment piece, cut two of the same pattern in order to form two layers. Baste the wrong sides together to keep the two layers from separating.

The channels through which the cord is pulled can be either hand stitched or machine stitched and should be slightly wider than the cord.

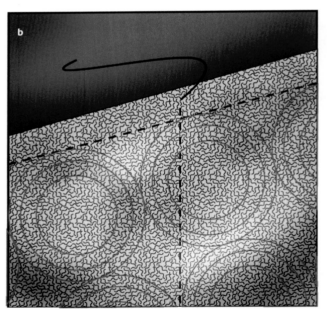
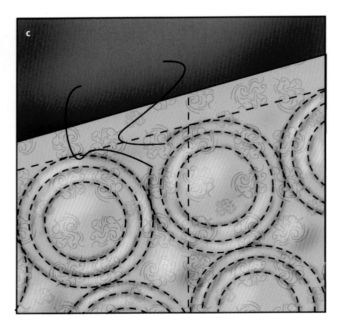

Figure 9.33a–c English quilting layers—underlining fabric, batting, and upper fabric.

Mark the design you wish to quilt on the backside of the fabric. (Figure 9.34)

1. Begin stitching through both layers along both lines on your design. You can do this by hand or with a sewing machine.

2. To insert the cord, use a needle with a big eye, and thread the cord. Working from the back fabric, insert the needle in between two stitch lines and in between the two layers of fabric, only picking up a little bit of the inner (backside) layer. Pull the needle out, and tighten the cord.

3. Insert the needle back through the same hole you pulled it out of and again pick up another small piece of the top layer. Always keep the needle in between your stitch lines.

Hint: If the cord you are using is too thick, use a small safety pin connected well to one end of the cord. Make small slits in the inner layer fabric with small embroidery scissors in between the channels. Catch only the one layer; do not cut through to the face layer of the garment.

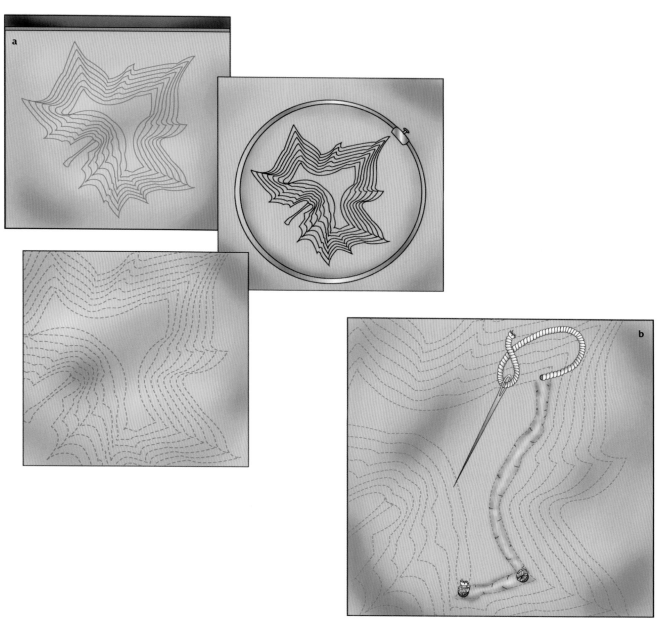

Figure 9.34a and b Cord quilting.

PADDED QUILTING (TRAPUNTO QUILTING)

You can use this quilting on its own or mix it up with other types of quilting to create a more decorative effect.

1. Baste the two layers of fabric together. Mark the motif on the back. (Figure 9.35a and b)
2. Working from the center of the design to the outside, stitch by hand or machine.
3. On the backside of the fabric, use small embroidery scissors to make a slit in between the stitch line motifs. Make sure you only clip the top layer.
4. Using a blunt needle or a crochet hook, stuff padding inside each motif, but not too much or it will start looking like a stuffed toy. One layer of batting or padding is fine. You can also use surgical cotton. (Figure 9.35c and d)
5. To finish, stitch the slits closed so that the padding does not come out. Stitch a backing panel of fabric to the quilted motif for extra support and lining.

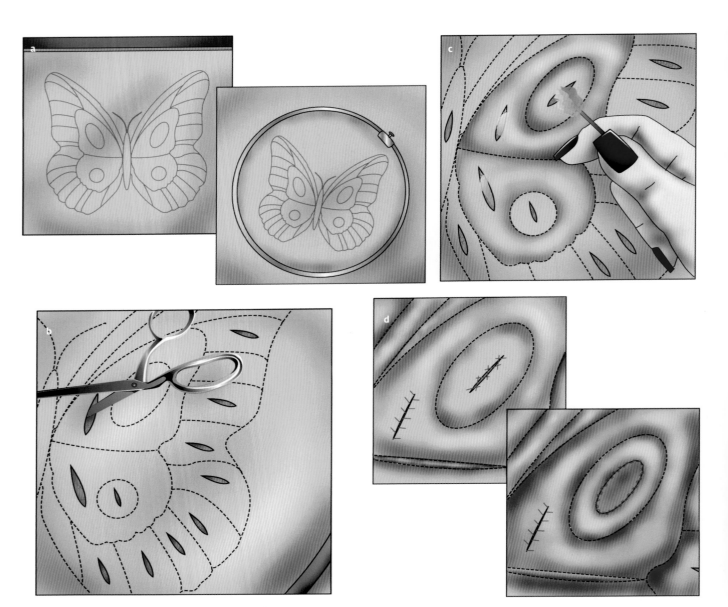

Figure 9.35a–d Padded quilting (Trapunto quilting).

Ruffles and Flounces

Ruffles can be used on collars, hems, center front décor, cuffs, necklines, and much more. A ruffle is a piece of fabric that is gathered on one side and is left loose on the other. A circular ruffle is a flounce; it is cut in a circular pattern and does not need to be gathered. It drapes on its own because of the circular cut.

STRAIGHT RUFFLE

A **straight ruffle** can be sewn onto any straight or curved edge. It is the simplest and most commonly used ruffle. Measure the proper edge needed for the ruffle.

1. First, hem one side of the rectangle you have cut with serging or with a rolled hem. (Figure 9.36a)
2. On the opposite side, sew two straight seams ¼ inch apart at the seam allowance. Do not backstitch. (Figure 9.36b)
3. Pull on the bobbin threads while gathering the fabric.
4. Gather until the length needed, and attach to the garment. (Figure 9.36c and d)

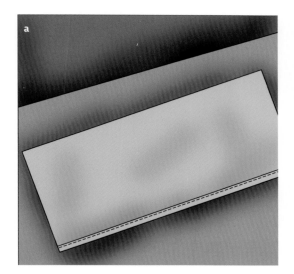
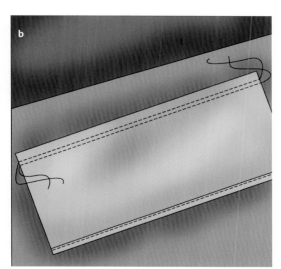
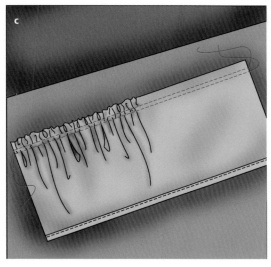

Figure 9.36a–d Straight ruffle.

DOUBLE RUFFLE

Double ruffles are gathered in the center of the rectangle with both sides hemmed. This ruffle can be made narrow or wide and topstitched to any surface of the garment. (Figure 9.37a)

1. First, hem both sides of the rectangle you have cut with serging or with a rolled hem. Or cut the strip on the bias of the fabric to avoid fray. (Figure 9.37b)

2. In the center of the rectangle, sew two straight seams ¼ inch apart. Do not backstitch at the end of the seams.

3. Pull on the bobbin threads while gathering the fabric. (Figure 9.37c)

4. Gather the length needed to attach it to the garment. (Figure 9.37d)

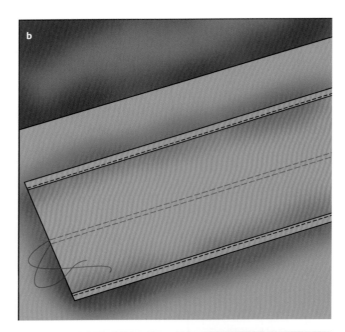

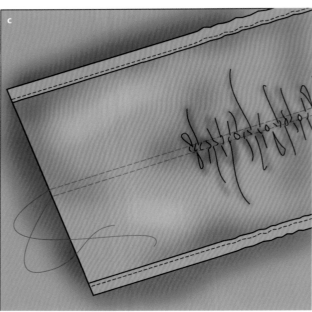

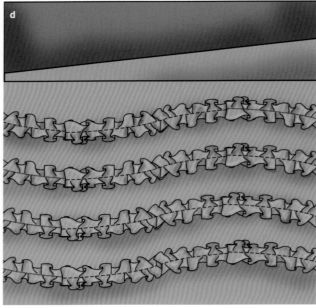

Figure 9.37a–d Double ruffle.

FOLDED RUFFLE

A **folded ruffle** is used as a thicker ruffle. You will not need to hem it, as it hems itself.

1. Cut the rectangle the length you need, and double the width you need.
2. Fold the rectangle in half along the lengthwise grain, wrong sides together. Press. (Figure 9.38a)

3. On the opposite side, sew two straight seams ¼ inch apart at the seam allowance through both layers. Do not backstitch. (Figure 9.38b)
4. Pull on the bobbin threads to gather. (Figure 9.38c)
5. Gather to get the length needed to attach to your garment. (Figure 9.38d)

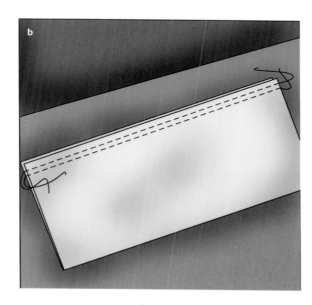

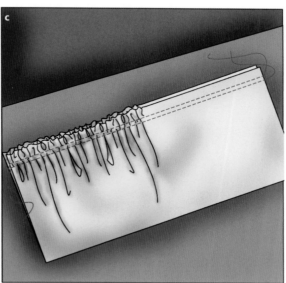

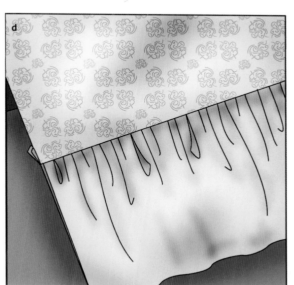

Figure 9.38a–d Folded ruffle.

DECORATIVE RUFFLE EXAMPLES

See ruffle examples. (Figures 9.39 and 9.40)

FLOUNCES

A **flounce** is a circular pattern with a circular center cut out. (Figure 9.41)

Figure 9.39 Decorative ruffle.

Figure 9.40 Decorative ruffle.

Figure 9.41 Flounces.

1. Fold your fabric in half and then in half again to make four quarters. (Figure 9.42a)
2. Along the closed corner, measure a curve with the length of the desired edge divided by four. Then draw the curve. (Figure 9.42b)
3. Along the corner sides, measure the width of the flounce and mark. (Figure 9.42c)
4. Now measure the same width along the curve every inch or so, and mark with a dot. (Figure 9.42d)
5. Connect the dots and you will get the hem level of the flounce.
6. Add seam allowances to the curves. (Figure 9.42e)
7. Cut along the seam allowance lines through all four layers of the fabric. (Figure 9.42f)
8. Open it and you will see you have created a circle. Cut a straight line through the circle along the grainline to open it up. Now you have a flounce. (Figure 9.42g)

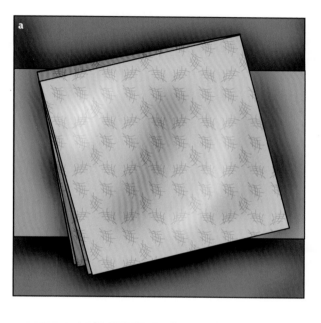

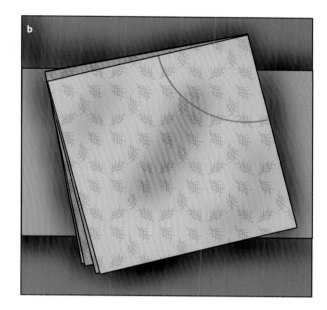

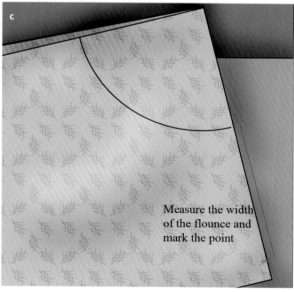

Measure the width of the flounce and mark the point

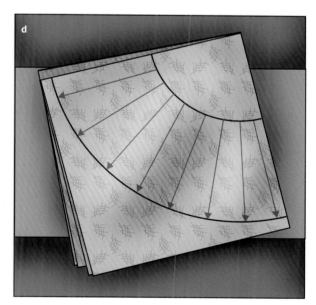

Figure 9.42a–d Flounce steps.

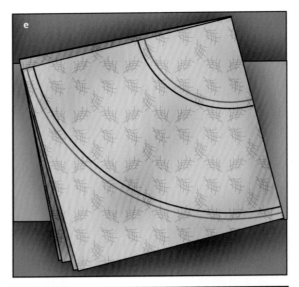

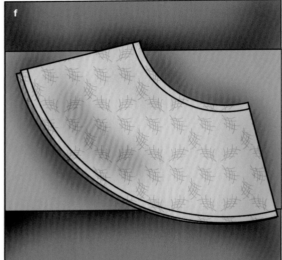

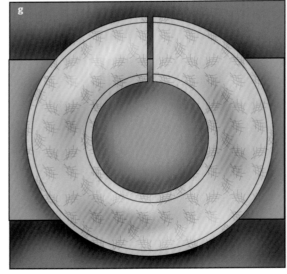

Figure 9.42e–g (continued)

To make longer flounces, you can make two flounces and connect them to each other with seams. (Figure 9.43a)

You can also cut a flounce in a spiral pattern. (Figure 9.43b)

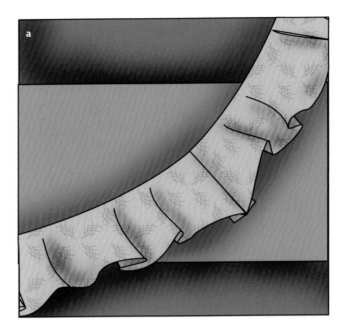

Figure 9.43 (a) Longer flounce with seam. (b) Spiral flounce, cut along the spiral line.

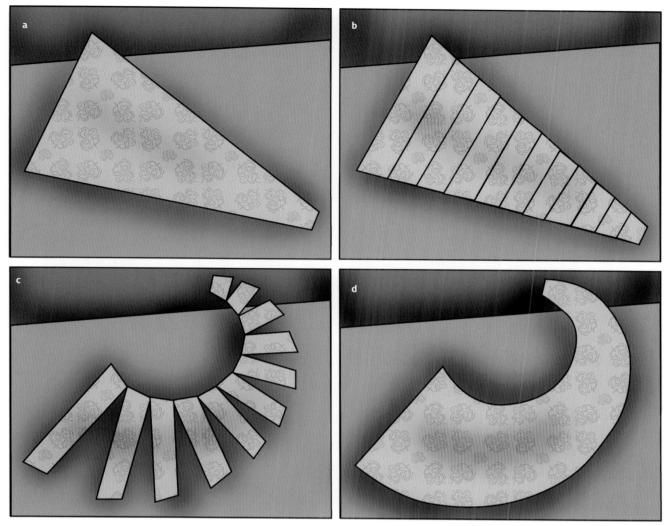

Figure 9.44a-d Controlled flounce.

You can make a controlled flounce by using a pattern and then slashing/spreading it. (Figure 9.44a–d)

Decorative Pleating and Pin Tucks

Pleats and tucks can be an integral element in the design of a garment, as with a pleated skirt or a shirt with tucks in the shoulders. However, you can also use tucks and pleats in a decorative way—on ruffles, cuffs, collars, and more.

To pleat, fold a piece of pattern paper the way you would like to pleat your garment. This will be your guide.

Fold your fabric into the paper pleats. Place a cloth over it and press. You can add steam if needed for the fabric. (Figure 9.45)

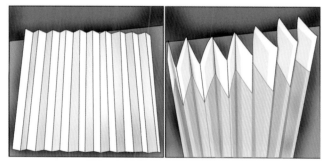

Figure 9.45 Use paper to help fold your pleats.

Box pleat (FIgure 9.46a)

Broomstick pleat (FIgure 9.46b)

Double box pleat (FIgure 9.46c)

Inverted pleat (Figure 9.46d)

Knife pleat (Figure 9.47a)

Accordion pleat (Figure 9.47b)

You can mix the following pleats for specific effects.

Knife pleats with box pleats (Figure 9.47c)

Box pleats with inverted pleats (Figure 9.47d)

Pleated Ruffles

A **pleated ruffle** is hemmed on both sides and stitched in the middle just like a double ruffle.

1. Hem both sides of the rectangle.
2. Pleat the rectangle. Press your pleats down to one side.
3. Stitch the pleats through the center of the pleated rectangle. (Figure 9.48)
4. Topstitch it to your garment.

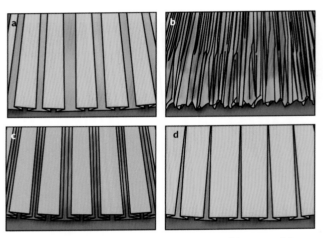

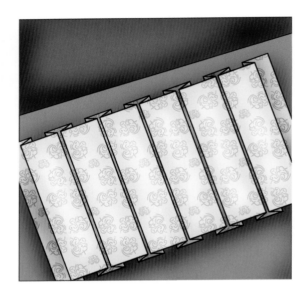

Figure 9.46 Box pleat variations. (a) Box pleats. (b) Broomstick pleats. (c) Double box pleats. (d) inverted pleats.

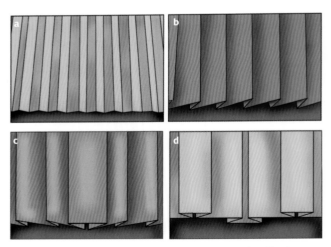

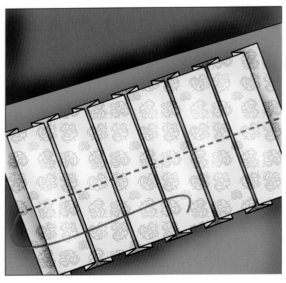

Figure 9.47 (a) Knife pleats. (b) Accordion pleats. (c) Knife pleats with box pleats. (d) Box pleats with inverted pleats.

Figure 9.48 Pleated ruffle.

Tucks

A tuck is very similar to a pleat except it is permanently stitched down to stay in place. Tuck widths can be small or large and are divided into three types: **spaced tucks**, **pin tucks**, and **blind tucks**. Some sewing machines come with a special foot for tucks that folds the fabric for you while you are stitching it down.

SPACED TUCKS

These tucks are made with space in between each tuck.

1. Mark your fabric on the grain with parallel tuck marks; leave space in between the tucks. There is no specific measurement for the space; your design will determine it.

2. Fold on the tuck marks, and stitch a seam to hold the tuck in place. (Figure 9.49)
3. Pick up the next fold, and stitch another tuck.
4. Continue these steps. Press the pleats down to one side.

PIN TUCKS

These are narrow tucks with space in between.

1. Mark your fabric on the grain with parallel tuck marks. There is no specific measurement for the space; your design will determine it. Mark very narrow tucks. (⅛ inch)

2. Fold one fold on the tuck marks, and stitch a seam to hold the tuck in place. (Figure 9.50)
3. Pick up the next fold, and stitch another tuck.
4. Continue these steps. Press the pleats down to one side.

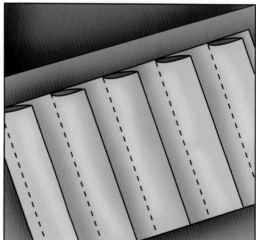

Figure 9.49 Spaced tucks.

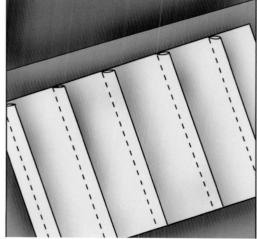

Figure 9.50 Pin tucks.

BLIND TUCKS

These tucks are made in a variety of widths and are very similar to regular knife pleats; however, they are stitched down.

1. Mark your fabric on the grain with parallel tuck marks. For this type of tuck, you will need to mark the tucks in even widths on both sides. The space in between the tucks should have the same width so that they overlap completely.
2. Fold on the tuck marks, and stitch a seam to hold the tuck in place. (Figure 9.51)
3. Pick up the next fold, and stitch another tuck.
4. Continue these steps. Press the pleats down to one side.

SCALLOPED TUCKS

Scalloped tucks are started as regular tucks and then scalloped with needle and thread.

1. Complete your tucks.
2. Pick up your needle and thread, and begin scalloping by wrapping your thread with whipstitches every inch or so. You can make the stitches closer if you desire. (Figure 9.52)

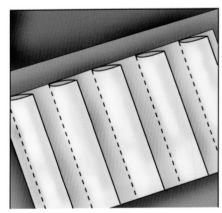

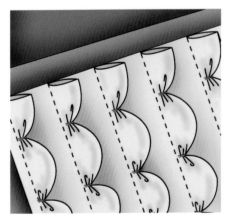

Figure 9.51 Blind tucks.

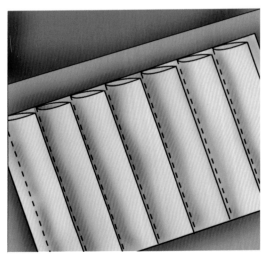

Figure 9.52 Scalloped tucks.

MEXICAN TUCKS

Mexican tucks are another very decorative way to tuck your garments. They look great on corsets, dresses, and even coats.

1. Make regular blind tucks.
2. From one side of the tucked piece, press all of your tucks in one direction, and stitch a regular seam with your sewing machine through them. Now press the tucks in a different direction, and stitch another seam with your sewing machine through all of them.
3. Keep doing this until you get through the entire piece. (Figure 9.53)

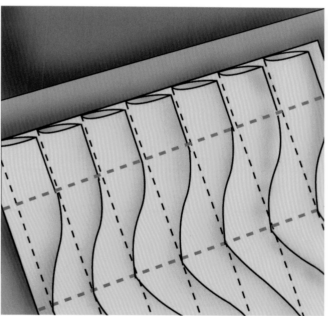

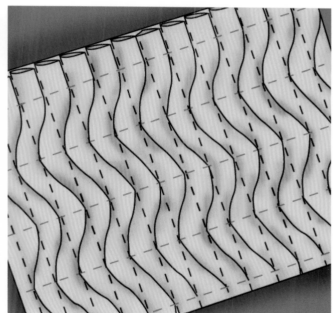

Figure 9.53 Mexican tucks.

SHARK TEETH

Shark teeth are a type of tuck that can be used for hems or garment decoration.

1. Make rows of regular blind tucks.
2. Clip your tucks up to the seams. Mark your lines to get straight cuts. You can mark them every inch, two inches, and so on.
3. Fold back through the center of each cut rectangle tuck. Make up a corner.
4. Do this to all of your cuts and press down. Make sure you fold the corners all the way back to the stitch.
5. Using a zigzag stitch, stitch over the seam of your tuck once more, catching the folded ends in the back. (Figure 9.54)

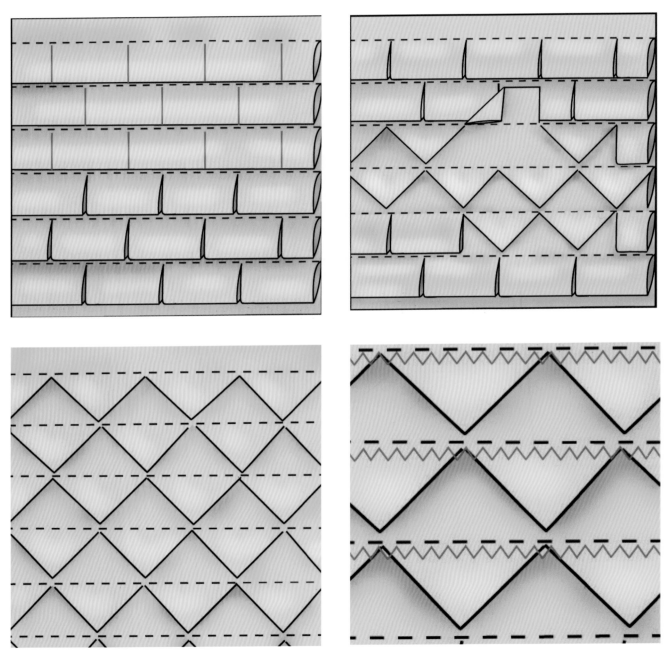

Figure 9.54 Shark teeth.

MORE DECORATIVE TUCKS

- Diagonal tucks (Figure 9.55a)
- Crossstitched tucks (Figure 9.55b)

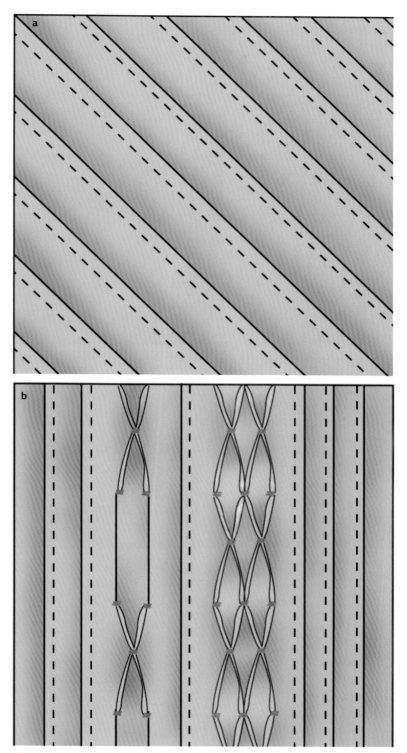

Figure 9.55 More decorative tucks. (a) Diagonal tucks. (b) Crossstitched tucks.

Rosettes

Rosettes are a great decoration for your garments, accessories, and even home design items. For a more decorative effect, you can bead them or use sheer ribbon.

1. Decide how high you want the rosette to be by measuring how much you would like your roses to stand out from the fabric surface. Cut a strip of fabric on the bias double the width.
2. The length of the strip should be approximately three times the diameter of the desired rosette.
3. Fold the strip in half and press.
4. Baste (by machine or hand) along the length of the strip ½ inch from the raw edge (Figure 9.56a), and gather by pulling on the bobbin thread while rolling up the rosette. (Figure 9.56b)
5. After the rosette has been rolled, use needle and thread to sew it in place. (Figure 9.56c)
6. Cut a small circle out of the same fabric, and hand-sew it to the bottom of the rosette, tucking in all of the frayed edges. (Figure 9.56d) This gives you a flat bottom to sew to your garment. (Figure 9.56e)

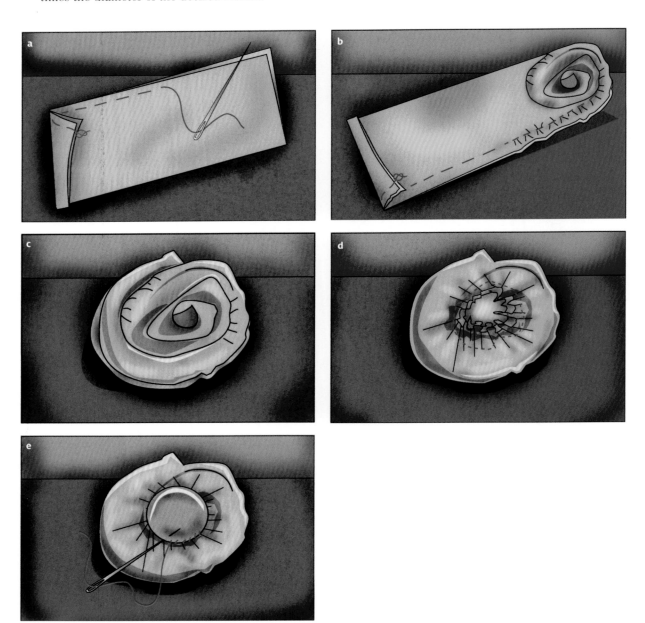

Figure 9.56a–e Rosettes.

Fabric Spirals

Fabric spirals are an excellent tone-on-tone embellishment for any garment (Figure 9.57a). Begin with bias strips of fabric 1–2 inches wide and 12–24 inches long. (Figure 9.57b) If you need them to be longer, they are cut on the bias and will stretch 10–30 percent.

1. Fold the strip in half, right sides together.
2. Stitch a line 1/16 to 1/4 inch from the raw edges. The distance depends on how thick you want the cords to be. As you sew, pull both sides of the strip to stretch it. (Figure 9.57c)
3. Thread a double thread on a hand-sewing needle, and make a double-thick knot at the end. Make sure the thread is longer than your strip.
4. On one end of your strip, insert the needle and pull it with the thread toward the other end of the strip so the tube turns right side out into a cord. (Figure 9.57d)
5. When you have successfully turned the cord to the right side, stretch it to eliminate gathers and folds, pin

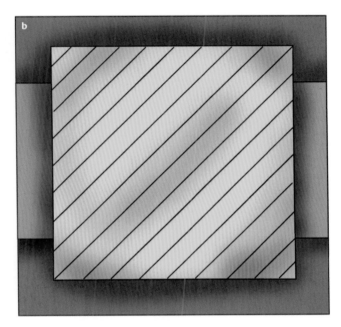

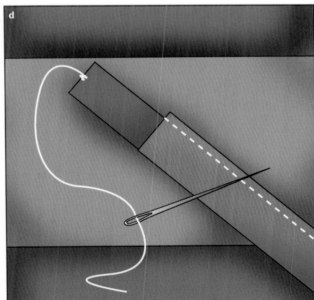

Figure 9.57a–d Fabric spirals.

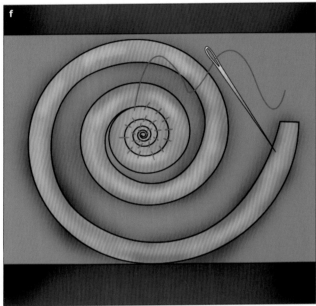

each end tightly to an ironing board, and let it stand overnight. (Figure 9.57e)

6. With your fingers, roll the cords into spirals. As you roll, stitch the spiral together on the wrong side. (Figure 9.57f)

7. When you have reached the desired diameter, cut off the rest of the cord. The raw edge of the cord will need to be tucked in and under toward the wrong side of the spiral and stitched down. (Figure 9.57g)

8. Keep making spirals until you have enough for a great design.

9. Sew the spirals directly to the garment with invisible stitches.

Fagotted Rouleau

A **fagotted rouleau** (Figure 9.58a) is a type of an application that has a lacelike appearance and works great to finish necklines, hems, and sleeves. You can even use your creativity and add it inside the garment as a design.

You will need to use heavy thread and bias-cut strips of fabric. If your design will be very structural and large, you will need to sew a couple of bias strips together before you begin. Turn your bias strips into long tubes.

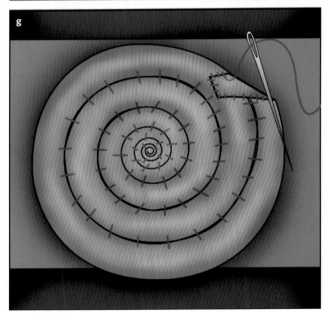

Figure 9.57e–g Fabric spirals

Figure 9.58a Faggoted rouleau.

1. To begin, lay your tubes in a design on paper, and pin in place. You can pin it directly to the garment and baste it in place as well. (Figure 9.58b)
2. Now you can make small stitches inside the design to hold the tubes in place by tacking a small stitch in the tubes, attaching both ends. (Figure 9.58c and d)
3. Once you are finished stitching, you can press the motif down using a pressing cloth.
4. If you are adding the Rouleau to an edge of the garment, make sure that your edge is also trimmed with the bias-edge finish so that you can attach the Rouleau with the same stitches. (Figure 9.58a)

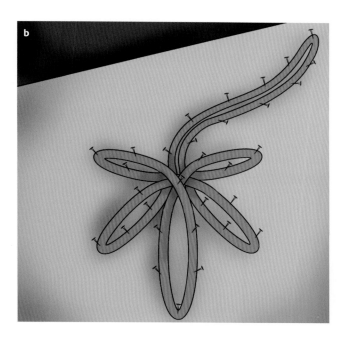

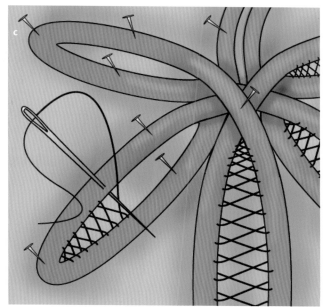

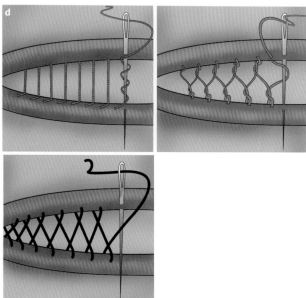

Figure 9.58b–d Fagotted rouleau.

YVES SAINT LAURENT

Yves Saint Laurent was born in Oran, Algeria, in 1936. He decided to leave home at seventeen to go to Paris, where he showed his illustrations and fashion sketches to Michel de Brunhoff, who, at the time, was the publisher of *Vogue* magazine. Brunholf published Saint Laurent's drawings in *Vogue* immediately. Saint Laurent went to fashion school and started working for Christian Dior after he won a contest with an asymmetrical cocktail dress in 1954.

After Dior died in 1957, Saint Laurent became the head haute couture designer for the house of Dior at the age of twenty-two. In his first collection for Dior in 1958, he introduced his famous trapeze dress.

Saint Laurent was drafted by the French army during the Algerian War of Independence, and while he was in the service, the House of Dior was led by Marc Bohan. Upon his return, Saint Laurent suffered a nervous breakdown and was hospitalized, leading Dior to release him.

Yves Saint Laurent.

Saint Laurent opened his own house, YSL, with his partner and companion, Pierre Berge, in 1962. Saint Laurent caught the imagination of the fashion world with his famous beatnik look in the late 1960s and early 1970s and with his well-known safari jackets for both men and women. YSL was also known for tight pants and high boots. In 1966, YSL produced the minimalist, androgynous tuxedo suit for women called Le Smoking.

Resort 2005.

YSL was the first design house to introduce a ready-to-wear line, bringing something new to the fashion industry. However, Saint Laurent believed that he was the last true couturier. He remained true to his styles and his well-known tailoring and classical cuts. Saint Laurent is a member of the Chambre Syndicale de la Haute Couture et du Prêt-à-Porter in Paris.

In 1971, YSL created a "40s" collection that brought him huge success. That same year, YSL launched its Rive Gauche Perfume and men's cologne Pour Hommes.

In 1983, Saint Laurent was honored by the Metropolitan Museum of Art.

Spring/Summer 1993.

In 2001, he was given an award and the rank of Commander of the Légion d'Honneur by French president Jacques Chirac. In 2002, he retired due to his disagreement with the fashion industry. He believed that the industry was more concerned about profit and money than about art. Saint Laurent died in 2008.

Chapter Review

This chapter focused on the skill of garment embellishments and how to work with them. Embellishments are a very important part of your couture garment, and learning the details can help you make a one-of-a-kind, high-quality sewn garment. You can work on each individually or mix them together. Shirring can be mixed with ruffles, and tucks can be mixed with flounces. You can get really creative by mixing different smocking techniques together. Quilting can be a great, creative way to add detail to your designs. You also learned how to make your own appliqués and decorative rosettes such as Madeleine Vionnet used on many of her designs. This chapter is full of great design embellishment ideas.

Projects

1. Make all of the appliqué samples for your sample book. Write down your steps, and insert them into one of your plastic cover sheets.
2. Make shirring samples for your sample book. Write down your steps, and insert them into one of your plastic cover sheets.
3. Make lace samples for your sample book. Write down your steps, and insert them into one of your plastic cover sheets.
4. Make ruffle samples for your sample book. Write down your steps, and insert them into plastic cover sheets.
5. Make flounce samples for your sample book. Write down your steps, and insert them into plastic cover sheets.
6. Make smocking samples for your sample book. Write down your steps, and insert them into your plastic cover sheets.
7. Make gathering samples for your book. Write down your steps, and insert them into plastic cover sheets.
8. Make pleat samples for your sample book. Write down your steps, and insert them into one of your plastic cover sheets.
9. Make tuck samples for your sample book. Write down your steps, and insert them into one of your plastic cover sheets.
10. Make a rosette sample for your sample book. Write down your steps, and insert them into one of your plastic cover sheets.
11. Make a fabric spiral and fagotted rouleu samples for your sample book. Write down your steps, and insert them into one of your plastic cover sheets.
12. Design and sketch a three-outfit collection utilizing three of the techniques covered in this chapter. Make sure each one of the outfits applies three techniques. Present them in a professional manner.

Key Terms

Accordion pleat	Double ruffle	Padded quilting
Alternating cable stitch smocking	English quilting	Pin tucks
American smocking	English smocking	Pleated ruffle
Appliqués	Fabric spirals	Rosettes
Blind tucks	Fagotted rouleau	Scalloped tucks
Box pleat	Flounces	Serpentine path
Broomstick pleat	Flower stitch smocking	Shark teeth
Cable stitch smocking	Folded ruffle	Shirring
Chevron stitch (wave stitch) smocking	Gathering	Smocking
Cord quilting	Honeycomb stitch smocking	Spaced tucks
Decorative quilting	Inverted pleat	Stem stitch smocking
Double box pleat	Knife pleat	Straight ruffle
Double cable stitch smocking	Lace	Straight stitch smocking
	Mexican tucks	

10

The Secret of Closures

Objectives

- Learn the history of zippers

- Learn how to insert zippers

- Learn how to use hooks and eyes

- Learn how to cover and apply snaps

- Learn how to make buttonholes and to sew on buttons

- Learn how to make button loops and frogs

- Learn about the life and work of Jean Paul Gaultier

Zippers

Metal slide fasteners were first introduced in 1891 by a Chicago inventor, Whitcomb Judson. However, the narrow woven-fabric zipper was not developed until 1912 by Gideon Sundback. In 1960, nylon **zippers** were introduced. The nylon zipper could be dyed different colors to match the garment and was lightweight.

Today we use three types of zippers: metal, polyester coil, and molded. Metal zippers are made by clamping interlocking metal teeth onto a narrow fabric tape. These are best for heavyweight fabrics, heavy-duty uses, or to add a metallic decoration to the garment.

Polyester coil zippers are manufactured from continuous polyester monofilament that is formed into a coil and then woven into the tape. These are used on most types of clothing, especially where an invisible zipper is used.

Molded zippers are made by injecting molded plastic teeth into the tape. It is used the same way as the polyester zipper.

Zippers come in different varieties: continuous chain zippers, closed-end zippers (both regular and invisible), and separating zippers. (Figure 10.1) Zippers also come in different thicknesses and lengths to match the fabric of the garment. Zipper tapes come in nylon, polyester, cotton, or a blend. Most tapes have a guideline woven into them for easier stitching.

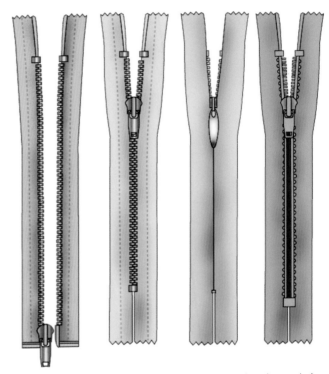

Figure 10.1 Zipper variations. Left to right: Separating zipper, chain zipper, invisible zipper, ladder zipper.

Hint: If the zipper is too long, shorten it before sewing. Whipstitch over the zipper teeth a couple of times in order to make a stopping point, and then cut off the longer part of the zipper.

Lapped Zippers

Lapped zippers are used on garments that require a side zipper, such as pants, skirts, and dresses and placed into plackets on a sleeve, purses, bags, or home items.

CENTER LAPPED

Center Lapped Zipper. Lapped zipper with even side flaps. It is first sewn into the face garment fabric, and then the facing or lining is attached to the zipper. (Figure 10.2)

Inspect the neckline or waistline where the zipper will start. Will you have a facing, a collar, or a waistline?

1. Measure ½ inch from the top seam line, mark it on the garment fabric, and line up your zipper to this mark. This ½-inch space allows you to turn down the seam allowance after facing attachment. For waistline or collar zippers, line them up to the top seam line.
2. Measure the zipper, and mark the length on the garment opening.
3. Stitch both ends right sides together with a regular seam from the bottom mark of the zipper length to the bottom of the garment. (Figure 10.3a)
4. Pin from the same point of the previous seam, and stitch a basting stitch up to the top of the garment or the top zipper mark. (Figure 10.3b) Press open.
5. Center the zipper over the open seam so that the top and the bottom of the zipper line up with your marks and the zipper chain lines up with the seam line. (Figure 10.3c)

6. Pin. Pull one of the seam allowances away from the garment together with one side of zipper tape.
7. Baste together. Sometimes the zipper tape already has a guideline for you to follow for the basting. Repeat on the other side of the seam allowance and zipper tape. (Figure 10.3d)

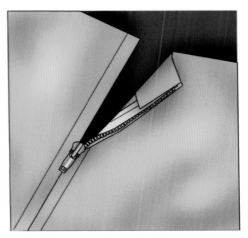

Figure 10.2 Center lapped zipper.

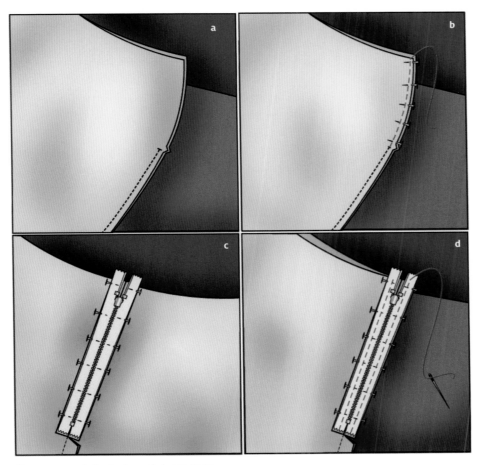

Figure 10.3a–d Center lapped zipper steps.

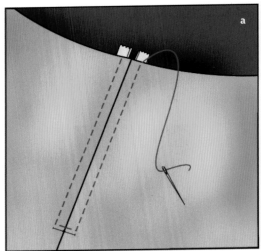
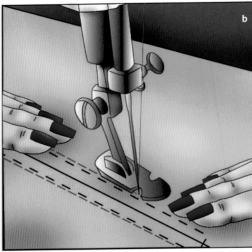

Figure 10.4a and b Center lapped zipper steps.

8. Keep the zipper closed; turn to the right side of the garment.

9. Baste ¼ inch from the center seam line, starting at the center seam at the bottom of the zipper and working up to the top through all of the layers. (Figure 10.4a)

10. Repeat on the other side back at the bottom and working up to the top.

11. Start stitching the zipper just outside the basting stitch using a regular stitch on your sewing machine, through all the layers from the bottom of the seam line working upward again, one side at a time. Backstitch. (Figure 10.4b)

12. Repeat on the other side back at the bottom and working up to the top. Backstitch.

13. Use a seam ripper to open the center seam basting stitch.

14. Test the zipper to make sure it is not too close to the chain.

Hint: When working with a centered separating zipper, sew it into the garment before you attach sides, sleeves, facings, or hems for easier attachment.

LAPPED ZIPPERS

Lapped Zippers. One lap over the zipper. (Figure 10.5) If you have a waistband or a collar at the end of the zipper, you can sew the zipper starting at the seam line at the top of the opening. If you have a facing, then you will need to begin the zipper ¼ to ½ inch below the seam line.

1. Mark the length of the zipper at your opening using your zipper measurement.

2. Stitch both ends right sides together with a basting seam from the bottom mark of the zipper length to the top of the zipper mark. (Figure 10.6a)

3. Press seams open. Line up the zipper to the seam. (Figure 10.6b)

4. Pull one of the seam allowances away from the garment so that you are holding one side of the seam allowance and one side of the zipper tape.

5. Baste them together along the mark on the zipper tape. (Figure 10.6c)

6. Turn the zipper face up so that the seam allowance folds under. Use a zipper foot along the left side of the zipper, and stitch a seam through the folded seam allowance. (Figure 10.6d)

Figure 10.5 Lapped zipper.

7. Turn your garment to the right side, and flatten the zipper and the other side of the seam allowance.

8. Baste the free seam allowance side and the garment fabric by hand from the bottom up, about ½ inch from the seam line. (Figure 10.7a)

9. With your sewing machine and a zipper foot, stitch right outside the baste line. (Figure 10.7b)

10. Rip out the basting in the zipper opening by taking out the first stitch you made to connect the two pieces together.

Hint: Follow the same steps for a separating zipper.

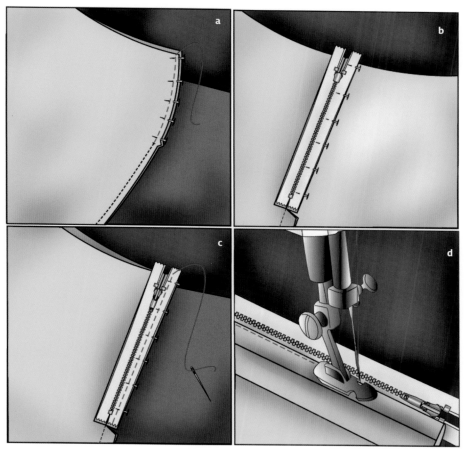

Figure 10.6a–d Lapped zipper steps.

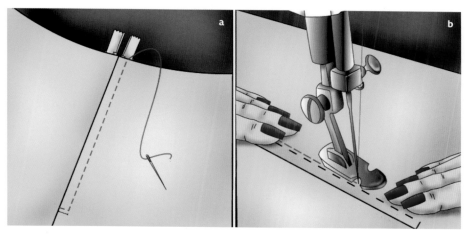

Figure 10.7a and b Lapped zipper steps.

Fly-Front Zippers

Fly-Front Zippers. Used in the center front of pants and skirts. They are one of the most common zipper applications for both men and women. The men's zipper fly flap is left over right side, and the women's fly is right over left. It is best to pattern the garment with the following pieces for the front of the pants: right front leg, left front leg, fly facing piece, and two identical fly underlay pieces. The zipper is inserted before both the inseams and the outseams are stitched. (Figure 10.8)

Mark all of your pattern pieces. On the front lap side, mark the curve to follow when topstitching in the center front. (Figure 10.9a)

1. Get your fly underlay ready by stitching the two pieces together face to face. Clip off the seam allowance to reduce bulk. (Figure 10.9b and c)

Figure 10.8 Fly-front zipper.

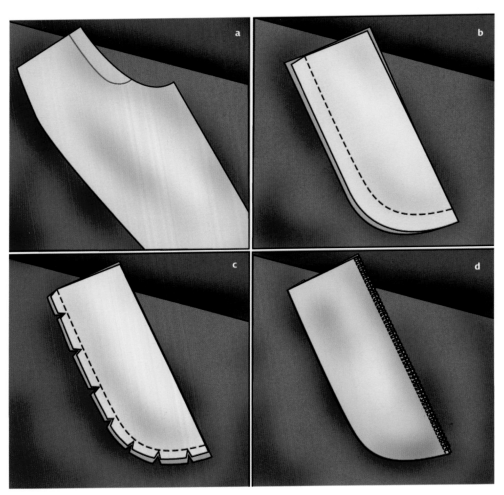

Figure 10.9a–d Fly-front zipper steps.

2. Turn right side out, and press. Finish the raw edge by serging or stitching a rolled hem. (Figure 10.9d)

3. Stitch up the front crotch 1½ inches from the crotch inside seam edge. (Figure 10.10a)

4. Fold it under lap side down, and pin the facing edge to the center front edge face-to-face from the placket bottom to the waist. Pin and stitch a regular seam along the seam line of the facing edge from the waist to the placket bottom. (Figure 10.10b)

5. Clip off the seam allowance.

6. Open the facing, and press both the facing and the seam allowance to the same side. (Figure 10.10c)

7. With the closed zipper facing down, line up the side of the zipper tape along the seam line connecting the pant side and the facing so that the other side of the zipper tape is about ¾ inch away from the facing edge. Pin/baste. (Figure 10.10d)

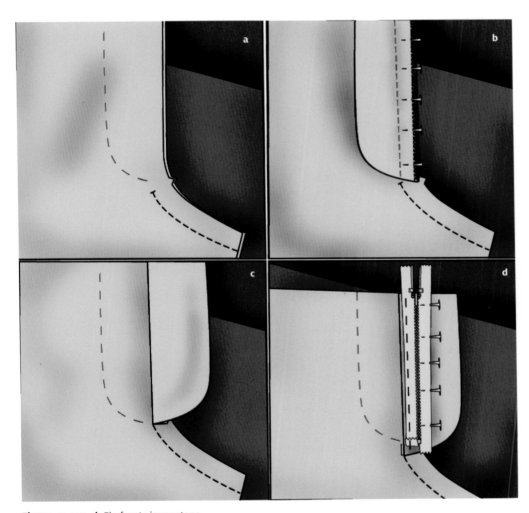

Figure 10.10a–d Fly-front zipper steps.

8. Using a zipper foot, stitch the side of the zipper closest to the edge of the facing close to the actual zipper chain. (Figure 10.11a)

9. Fold the facing along the seam, connecting it to the pant side and press. (Figure 10.11b)

10. Baste the facing in place right outside the marked curve line on the pant side. (Figure 10.11c)

11. Topstitch through all layers from the bottom of the placket along the marked curve line to the waist. (Figure 10.11d)

12. Stitch the other zipper side to the underlap.

13. On the other pant side, fold over the seam allowance in the center front of the open placket. (Figure 10.12a)

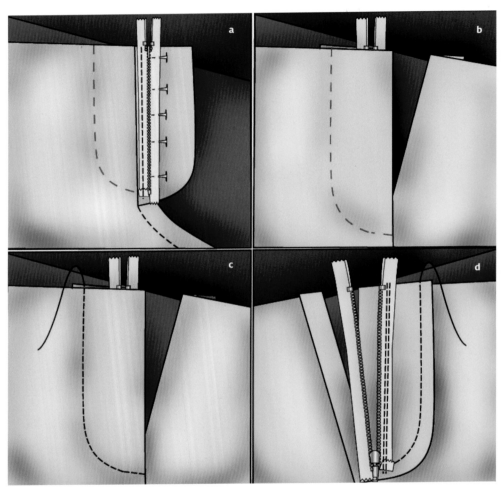

Figure 10.11a–d Fly-front zipper steps.

14. Open the zipper, and pin it to the unstitched side along the folded edge. (Figure 10.12b) Close the zipper, and make any corrections needed to avoid puckering. Open the zipper again, and baste the zipper side.

15. Line up the fly underlay so that the curved side is aligned with the curved topstitching on the wrong side of the garment and the other side of the underlay lines up with the edge of the stitched zipper side. (Figure 10.12c)

16. Baste through all of the layers.

17. Switch the zipper foot to the opposite side on your sewing machine.

18. Stitch through all of the layers close to the zipper chain from bottom of the placket to waist. (Figure 10.12d)

19. Remove all the basting.

20. Close the zipper, and press to flatten. Then stitch a few backstitches a couple of times along the bottom of placket.

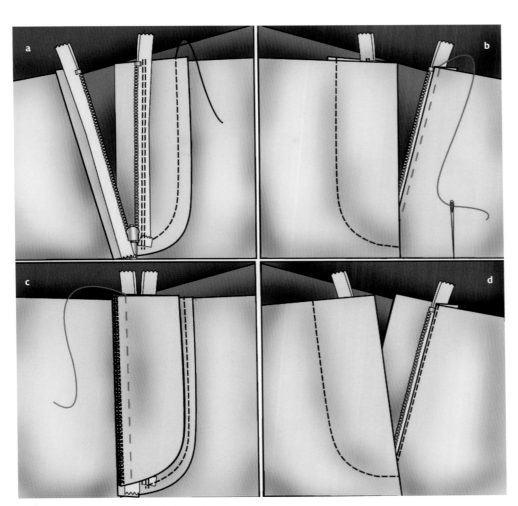

Figure 10.12a–d Finishing the fly-front zipper.

Invisible Zippers

Invisible Zippers. Used on any garment style and sewn into a regular seam attached to the seam allowance without any topstitching. Use an invisible-zipper foot with two grooves specifically designed to pull each one of the zipper chain sides through while stitching. (Some professionals can install an invisible zipper with a regular zipper foot.) (Figure 10.13a and b)

1. Press the zipper sides on an open zipper so that the zipper chain is pressed away from the tape. This makes it easier for the chain to fit through the zipper foot grooves. (Figure 10.14a)
2. Mark the zipper length on both sides of the opening.
3. Keep the zipper open, and line up the zipper tape edge with the right side of the garment opening edge while the zipper is facing down. Pin/baste the zipper in place. (Figure 10.14b)
4. Using the invisible-zipper foot, line it up so that the zipper side fits into the groove of the foot.

Stitch the zipper all the way down to the bottom of the opening. To reduce puckering, hold the fabric and the zipper firmly, but do not pull hard, as you can break the needle and/or mess up your stitch. (Figure 10.14c)
5. Line up the other side of the zipper tape edge with the other side of the opening edge of the garment, and pin in place. (Figure 10.14d)
6. Baste the second side of the zipper tape in place.
7. Line up the zipper chain with the second zipper foot groove, and stitch all the way down the zipper. Secure the stitch.
8. Close the zipper. If you need to stitch below the zipper, flip the garment to the wrong side and pin the seam allowances below the zipper face-to-face. Stitch a small seam, and secure the zipper. (Figure 10.15a)
9. To keep the zipper down, stitch the zipper tape to the seam allowance near the edge. (Figure 10.15b)

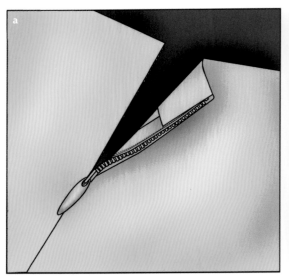
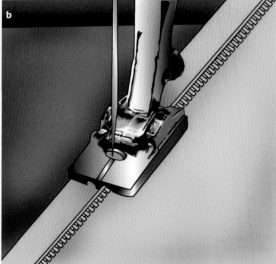

Figure 10.13a and b Invisible zipper and foot.

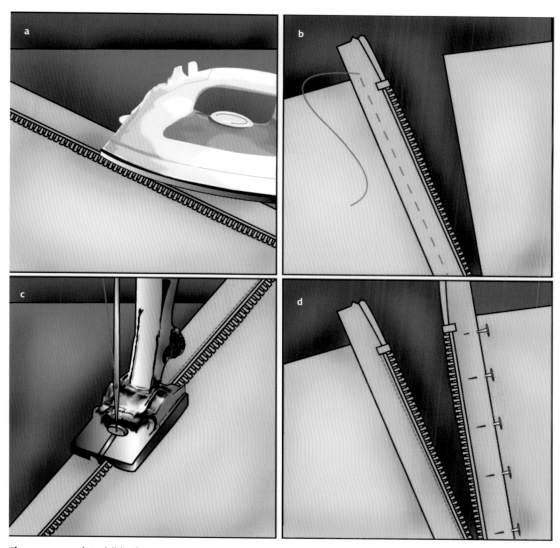

Figure 10.14a–d Invisible zipper steps.

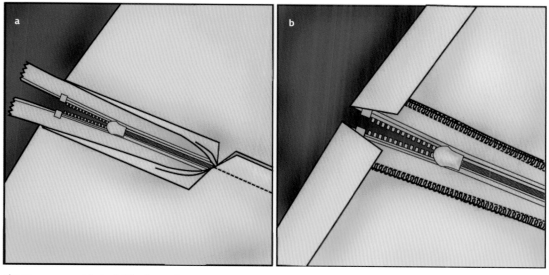

Figure 10.15a and b Invisible zipper steps.

Hand-Sewn Zippers

In couture sewing, zippers are sometimes sewn by hand. Some zippers need to be hand sewn if the garment is made of many structural layers, as in a couture gown, and the sewing machine is not able to sew the zipper without ruining the design. Examples include sequined or beaded garments. Many designers like to take off the sequins and beads around the seam allowance and about 1 inch from the seam line only to sew them back on after the garment seams are finished. However, sewing the zipper by hand may help you avoid the extra work of sewing the beads back on.

1. To start applying the zipper, press the zipper sides on an open zipper so that the zipper chain is away from the tape.
2. Then mark the zipper length evenly on both sides of the garment opening.
3. Line up the zipper tape edge with the right side of the garment opening edge while the zipper is facing down. Pin/baste in place. (Figure 10.16a)

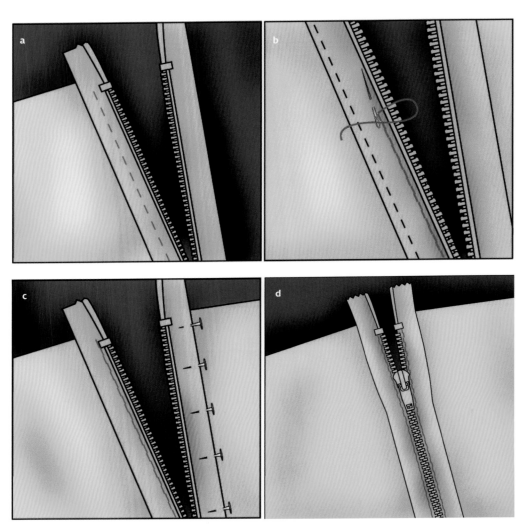

Figure 10.16a–d Hand sewn zipper.

4. Using a hand backstitch, carefully stitch the zipper tape all the way down to the bottom of the opening. (Figure 10.16b) For an invisible zipper, stitch along the marked line along the tape of the zipper. For a lapped or a centered zipper, stitch close to or along the line.

5. Line up the other side of the zipper tape edge with the other side of the opening edge of the garment, and pin in place. (Figure 10.16c) Baste the second side of the zipper tape in place.

6. Now backstitch this side all the way down the zipper. Check the zipper closure. (Figure 10.16d)

7. For a lapped zipper or a centered zipper, follow the same steps as a machine-sewn zipper. You can use any of the permanent stitches; however, the backstitch is best because it is the closest stitch to a machine stitch.

Hooks and Eyes

Hooks and eyes are another type of fastener for garments used in waistbands, necklines, and garment openings. They are very small and strong. (Figure 10.17)

Hooks and eyes come in various shapes and sizes. The smallest hook is used in fastening above a zipper in waistbands and necklines. This type of hook and eye can range in size between 0 and 3 and comes in black or silver. The regular eye is round in shape and looks like a loop.

Special-purpose hooks and eyes come in bigger sizes and can be metal or covered with a knit coat.

For casual pants/skirts, a flat hook and eye is used and is made to remain closed and not come open easily.

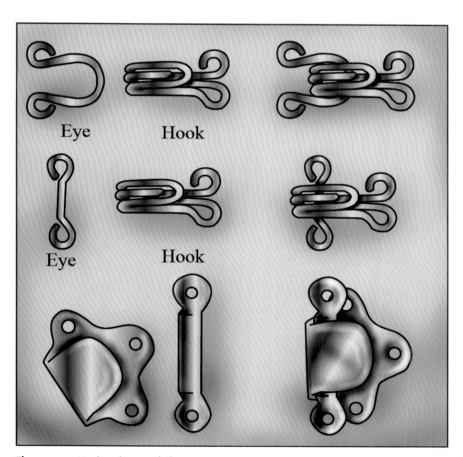

Figure 10.17 Hook-and-eye variations.

REGULAR HOOK AND EYE

Usually smaller in size and is connected to abutted edges inside the garment.

1. Mark two placement points on the inside of the garment. (Figure 10.18a)
2. Hold the hook with one hand and the needle with the other hand. Secure the thread through your mark, and insert the needle through the hook holes. (Figure 10.18b)
3. Begin regular whipstitches over and through each hole. When finished, pull the thread under and through one layer of fabric under the hook. Then bring it out close to the bent hook so you can whipstitch around the bottom of the hook to secure it to the fabric. (Figure 10.18c)
4. Make sure that the hook ends 2 mm from the edge to hide it when the fastener is closed.
5. Now hold the eye on the opposite side of the garment with one hand and the needle with the other. Whipstitch over and through the holes, and then secure both sides to the fabric. (Figure 10.18d) The eye should pass the edge 2 mm as well, so that the hook can fasten and leave a smooth closure.

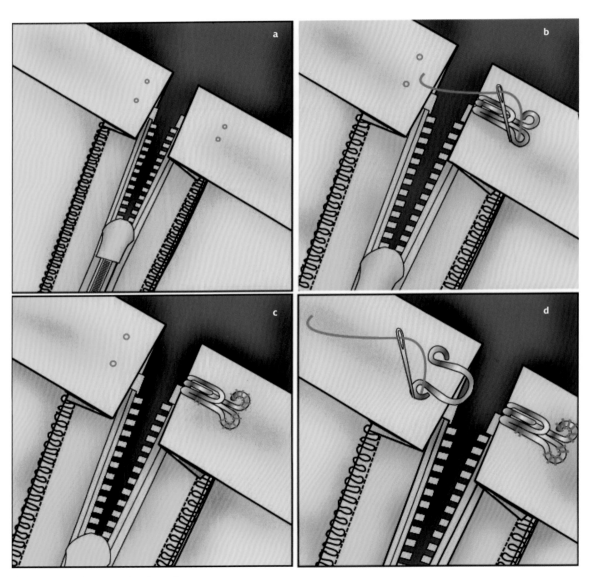

Figure 10.18a–d Regular hooks and eyes.

LAPPED HOOK AND EYE

Used with a lapped waistband sewn to the inside of the overlap and the straight eye sewn to the outside of the underlap.

1. Mark the holes placement of both the hook and the eye. Make sure they will overlap and close smoothly. The hook is sewn with the hook side ⅛ inch from the edge. (Figure 10.19a)
2. Secure your thread, and whipstitch the hook over and through each hole. Pull the thread under one layer of fabric under the hook, and bring it out close to the hook. (Figure 10.19b)

3. Whipstitch the eye through each hole. Because this eye is straight, only whipstitching the hole is necessary. (Figure 10.19c and d)

Hint: This technique works for the special-purpose flat hooks and eyes used for waistbands. Place the hook ⅛ inch from the edge on the inside of the overlap.

Hooks can also be accompanied by thread eyes or chains. Keep in mind that this type of chain should not be used on areas where a lot of strength is needed.

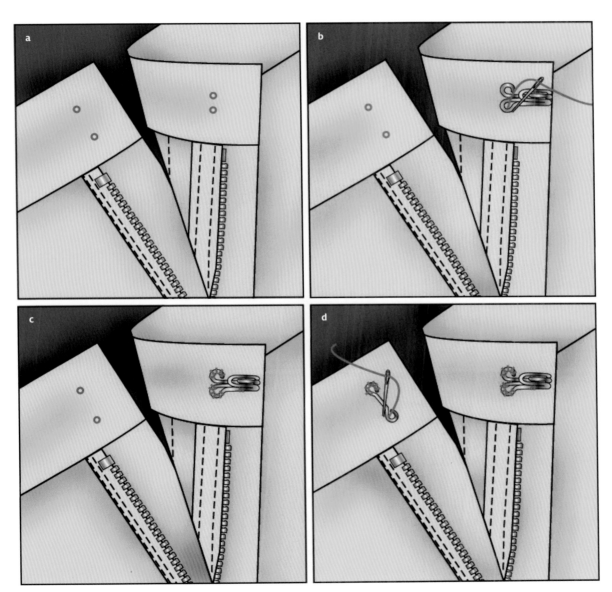

Figure 10.19a–d Lapped hooks and eyes.

Thread Chain Techniques

THREAD CHAIN

1. To begin, mark with dots where you will need to begin and end the chain.
2. Secure the thread under the fabric, and pull the needle through the dot you marked. (Figure 10.20)
3. Make a small stitch through the dot, and leave a big enough loop outside of the fabric to fit your fingers. (Figure 10.21a)
4. Let the needle hang down, or lay it on the table.
5. Hold the loop with your right index finger and thumb while holding the rest of the hanging thread with your other hand. (Figure 10.21b)
6. With the middle finger of your right hand, grab the hanging thread through the loop and pull while closing the previous loop. (Figure 10.21c)

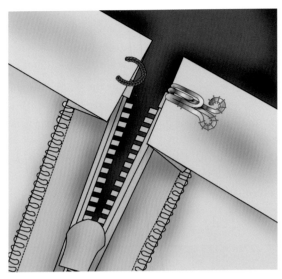

Figure 10.20 Hook and a thread chain.

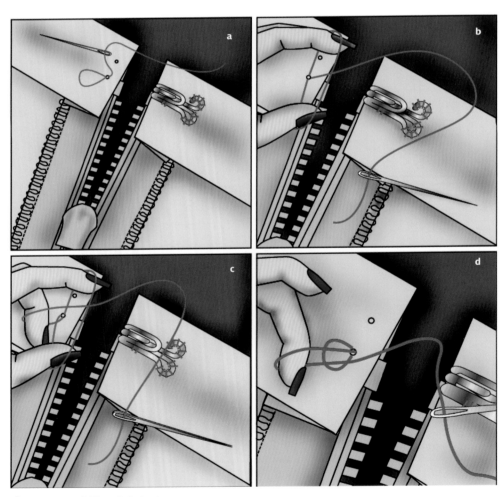

Figure 10.21a–d Thread chain steps.

7. Now you have made a new loop. Pull on the loop to make it big enough to fit three of your fingers. (Figure 10.21d)

8. Repeat steps 5 through 7 until you get a chain long enough to secure along your second dot or the finishing dot.

9. Pick up your needle at the end of the thread, and pull it through the last loop to finish the chain.

10. Insert the needle through the second marked dot in your fabric, and secure it behind the fabric. (Figure 10.22)

WRAPPED CHAIN

Wrap blanket stitches around the thread bars. Sew your hook to the inside of the overlap the same way you would a regular lapped hook. (Figure 10.23)

1. Secure the thread behind the fabric, and insert the needle into the first dot.

2. Take a stitch through the second dot with your needle facing up, and bring it out through the first dot again. This makes a thread bar from one dot to the other. Make another couple of bars using the same two holes. (Figure 10.24a)

3. End with your needle at the first dot. Without catching the fabric, just the thread bars, begin working your way down, wrapping blanket stitches around the threads to the other side. (Figure 10.24b)

4. Make sure that you make blanket stitches and not regular wrapping stitches because they make the **thread chain** stronger and keep it from unraveling while you work.

5. Insert the needle into the second dot, and secure the thread underneath.

Figure 10.22 Thread chain steps.

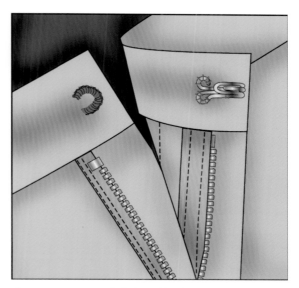

Figure 10.23 Wrapped chain and hook.

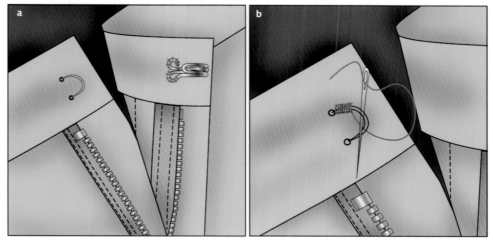

Figure 10.24 (a) Snap variations. (b) Snap press machine.

Snaps

Snaps are an easy fastener and quick to use. However, they are not always strong enough.

Snaps have two parts. The top ball part comes with an open groove in the center. The bottom socket piece gets inserted into the ball groove. (Figure 10.25a and b)

Snaps range in size and strength. The larger snaps are used in coats and jackets and are inserted with a snap press machine instead of being sewn on like the smaller snaps. These larger snaps are frequently made out of metal and come in different colors. Very often you will see decorative snaps in the fabric store, which can be covered with fabric and even come attached to a tape for easier application. Some come in different shapes as well. Sew-on snaps have holes for attachment just like hooks and eyes do. The application is also very similar.

HAND-SEWN SNAPS

1. Mark snaps placement on the garment. (Figure 10.26a)
2. Secure your thread, hold the ball with your left hand, and whipstitch every hole. Make sure the snap is no less than 4 mm from the edge or it will show. Secure your thread. (Figure 10.26b)
3. Close the lap to check the markings for the socket half of the snap.
4. Secure your thread underneath the fabric, and whipstitch the socket half in every hole. Secure the thread. (Figure 10.26c)

Hint: Snaps are also used in dresses and shirts to make lingerie strap guards, which lock the bra strap and the garment strap in place so that neither can shift. (Figure 10.26d) For this type of guard, the socket gets sewn onto the garment while the ball is attached to a thread chain.

Figure 10.25a and b Hand sewn snaps.

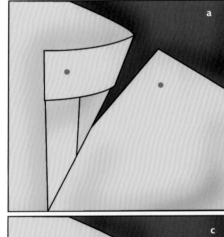

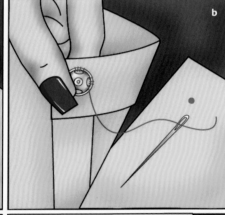

Figure 10.26a–d Hand sewn snaps.

SNAP COVERS

1. To cover your snaps, you will need to cut a circle out of your fabric twice the size of your snap side. (Figure 10.27a)
2. Stitch small basting stitches along the edge of the circle. Do not remove your needle or knot the end. (Figure 10.27b)
3. When ready, place your snap facedown on the circle and tighten the thread. It should wrap around the snap side. (Figure 10.27c)
4. Repeat the same steps to the other side of the snap.
5. Snap them together. This tightens the fabric inside the snap so that you can stitch on the backside of your snap to secure it. Trim off the extra fabric, and sew it on to your garment. (Figure 10.27d)

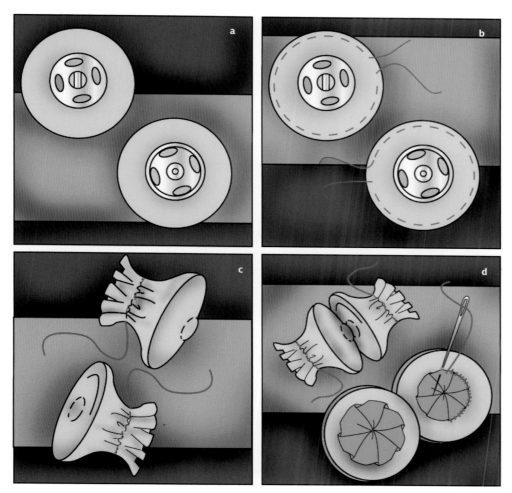

Figure 10.27a–d Snap covers.

Buttonholes

Bound buttonholes are made with a patch of fabric or two strips of fabric with two bound edge openings. (Figure 10.28) These buttonholes are very common in tailoring and coats.

Zigzag machine buttonholes are done with a zigzag stitch on a sewing machine. Most machines now come with a buttonhole setting. The buttonhole is cut open after it is sewn. Some sewing machines do not have the buttonhole setting. In that case, you can purchase a buttonhole attachment for your machine. This attachment clips on to the presser foot and the needle bar attachment. The buttonhole attachment moves the fabric right and left, allowing the needle to sew zigzag stitches around a measured buttonhole rectangle.

For handmade buttonholes, unlike machine-made buttonholes, the slit has to be cut open before you begin sewing the buttonhole stitches. You can stitch the buttonhole with a regular satin stitch along and around the slit opening, or you can whipstitch your buttonhole bars. Hand-made buttonholes are used on all types of clothing, such as sportswear, shirts, dresses, and so on.

It is very important that you test your planned buttonhole length on a scrap piece of garment fabric to make sure it is big enough for your button. Make sure you test with all of the fabric layers, including interfacing, facing, and lining. This way you can be sure that the button will fit the buttonhole. Buttonholes can be made vertical or horizontal.

HAND-STITCHED BUTTONHOLES

Before you begin, measure and mark the correct placement of all your buttonholes. (Figure 10.29)

1. Slash your marked buttonhole along the slash line with embroidery scissors.
2. Stitch around the buttonhole with a small basting stitch, keeping the same depth for all the stitches. It

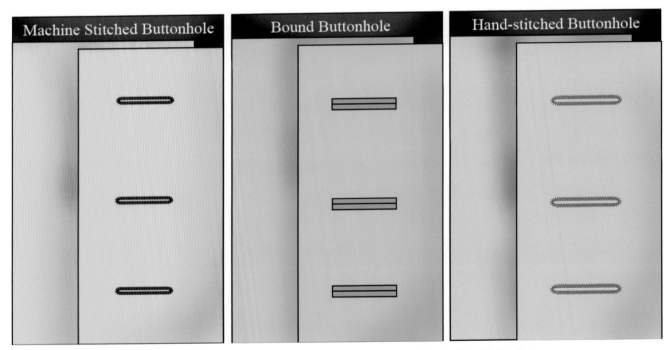

Figure 10.28 Buttonhole variations. Machine-stitched buttonhole, bound buttonhole, and hand-stitched buttonhole.

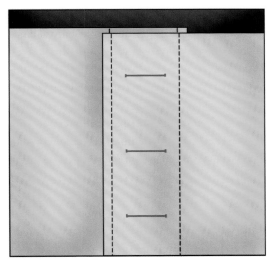

Figure 10.29 Hand-stitched buttonholes.

will work as a guide. The depth of the rectangle should be ⅛ inch from the slashed line. (Figure 10.30a)

3. Start a new thread, usually in the same color as the fabric, and secure it on the right side of the basted rectangle.

4. Begin whipstitching the bottom row of the buttonhole by inserting your needle from the slashed center to the bottom basted seam. Keep whipstitching until you get to the other side of the buttonhole rectangle, making sure you are stitching through all of the layers of the garment. (Figure 10.30b)

5. At the reached side, stitch around to the top row of the buttonhole, making your stitches form a fan shape. (Figure 10.30c) Continue into the second row of the buttonhole. Flip the fabric upside down for ease.

6. At the end of the row, make a couple of longer stitches connecting both rows. (Figure 10.30d)

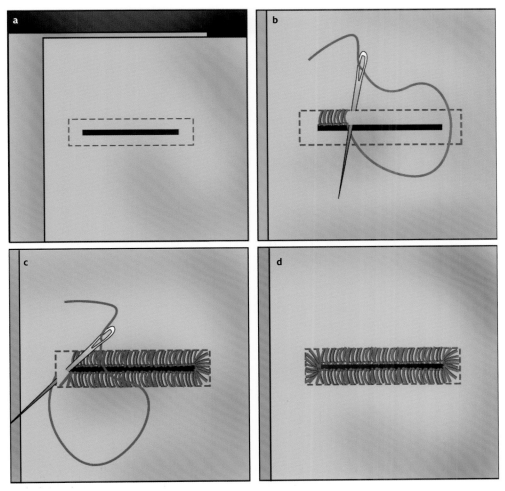

Figure 10.30a–d Machine-stitched buttonholes.

MACHINE-STITCHED BUTTONHOLES

Use a buttonhole stitch on your sewing machine or a buttonhole attachment.

If you are using a sewing machine setting, the size of stitches can be changed using the stitch size wheel; however, you may need to try a couple of different sizes to get the one you need. Practice on a piece of fabric before you begin, and test it with a button.

Sewing machine settings usually use a couple of steps on the wheel. It makes one side of the buttonhole, and then you turn the wheel to make the side stitches. You turn the wheel again to make the second bar of the buttonhole. Turn once more for the last set of side stitches. (Figure 10.31a)

Some sewing machines come with a buttonhole setting that makes the entire buttonhole from one turn of the wheel. In this case, input the size of the buttonhole.

Some buttonhole attachments come with a button-measuring tool that allows you to drop the button in the tool and the attachment makes the buttonholes to match the button. However, most buttonhole attachments do not come with this option. They do come with a sizing option, with screws that move the measurements to fit the button size. Test the buttonhole attachment on a scrap piece of fabric before you begin with your garment. (Figure 10.31b)

When the buttonholes are done, use embroidery scissors to cut the buttonholes open. This is usually done after the entire garment is finished.

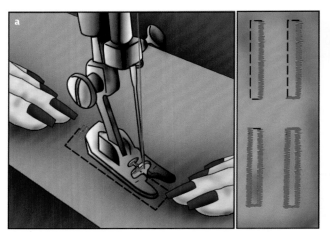

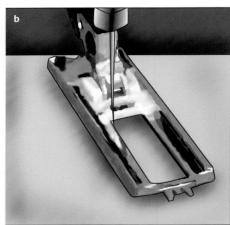

Figure 10.31a and b Regular machine buttonhole.

BOUND BUTTONHOLES

Patch Method

1. Cut a patch of fabric (use the garment fabric, unless you want the buttonholes to be a different color or fabric) 2 inches wider than the buttonhole and 1 to 1½ inches longer.
2. Mark the center of the patch by folding it in half. To stiffen the patch, use fusible interfacing. (Figure 10.32a)
3. Mark the buttonhole line on your garment.
4. Align the patch line with the line on your garment with the patch and the garment fabric right sides together. (Figure 10.32b)
5. Baste/pin the patch in place.
6. Mark the buttonhole rectangle on the wrong side of the patch. Remember, the buttonhole bound sides are usually ⅛ inch wide. The entire rectangle will be ¼ inch wide, and the center line of the patch will divide in half. (Figure 10.32c)
7. Stitch around the rectangle with a regular machine stitch, or make small backstitches by hand along the marked line. Press. (Figure 10.32d)
8. Remove the basting/pins from the patch.

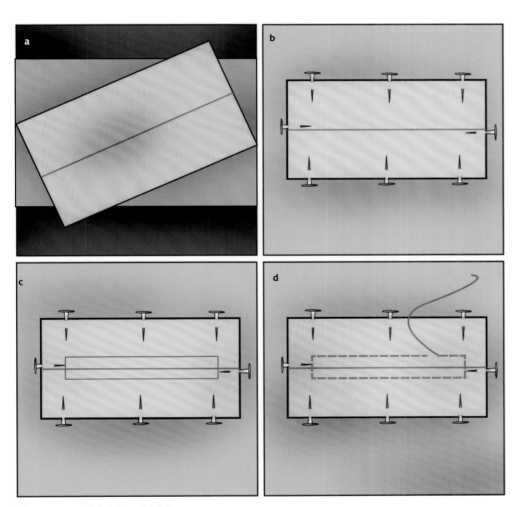

Figure 10.32a–d Patch method steps.

9. Using embroidery scissors, cut through all of your fabric layers corner to corner inside the rectangle without catching the stitch line. (Figure 10.33a)

10. Pick up the patch corners, and pull them through the cut opening toward the wrong side of the garment.

11. Straighten out the patch to make a clean open rectangle in the center. Press flat. (Figure 10.33b)

12. Fold the sides toward the center of the open rectangle.

13. If you fold each side to meet in the center, you will be forming the buttonhole sides from the right side. Press the folds. (Figure 10.33c)

14. Baste the folds. Turn to the right side of the garment, and baste the sides together with diagonal stitches. Press. (Figure 10.33d)

15. Fold over the garment fabric along the side of the buttonhole so that you see the sides of the folded patch and the triangular piece. Stitch along the fold through all of the folded patch layers and the triangle. Make sure you stitch next to the garment fold; do not catch it. Do the same thing all around the buttonhole along every side. (Figure 10.33e)

16. Keep the buttonhole basted closed until the garment is complete. (Figure 10.34a and b)

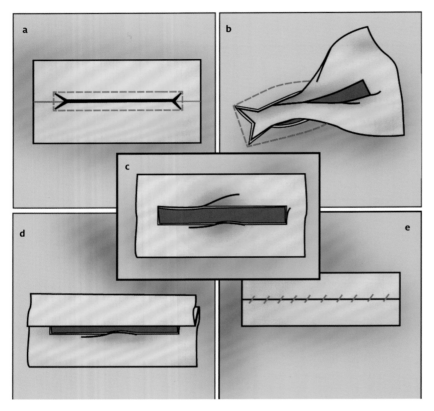

Figure 10.33a–e Patch method steps.

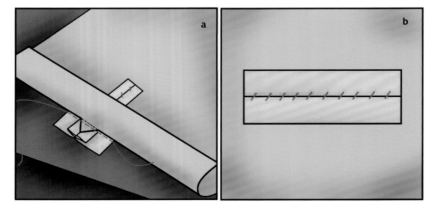

Figure 10.34a and b Bound buttonholes.

Strip Method

This technique is very similar to the patch technique except instead of a patch, you use two strips of fabric. The outcome looks the same on the right side.

1. Mark the buttonhole line on your garment fabric, and line up two strips of fabric, right sides together, one above the line and one below the line. (Figure 10.35a)
2. Baste/pin the strips to the fabric. (Figure 10.35b)

3. Mark the buttonhole rectangle on the strips, and stitch along the rectangle with a regular stitch. (Figure 10.35c)
4. Remove your basting and press. Buttonhole sides are usually ⅛ inch wide.
5. Using the embroidery scissors, cut through the garment fabric along the line you marked for the buttonhole slit in between the strips, but stop before the end of each side to cut a small triangle into the corners. (Figure 10.35d)

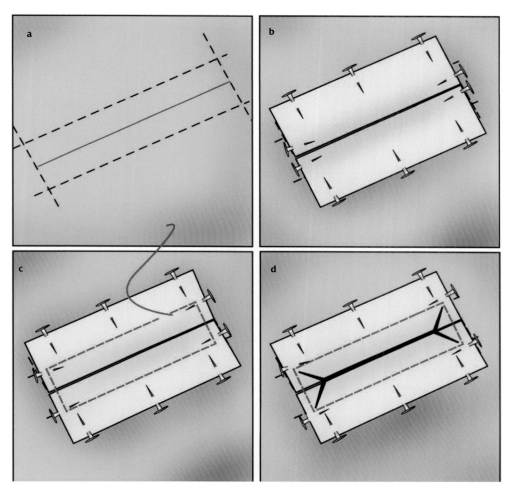

Figure 10.35a–d Strip method steps.

6. Pick up the strips, pull them through the cut opening toward the wrong side of the garment, and straighten them out. Make an open rectangle and press. (Figure 10.36a)

7. Fold each strip toward the center of the rectangle. Fold each side to meet in the center to form buttonhole sides from the right side. Press. (Figure 10.36b)

8. Baste the folds in place. Turn to the right side of the garment, and baste the sides together with diagonal stitches. Press. (Figure 10.36c)

9. Fold over the garment fabric along the side of the buttonhole so that you see the sides of the folded strips and the triangular piece. Stitch along the fold through all of the folded strip layers and the triangle. Make sure you stitch next to the garment fold; do not catch it. Do the same thing along every side. (Figure 10.36d)

10. Keep the buttonhole basted closed until the garment is complete.

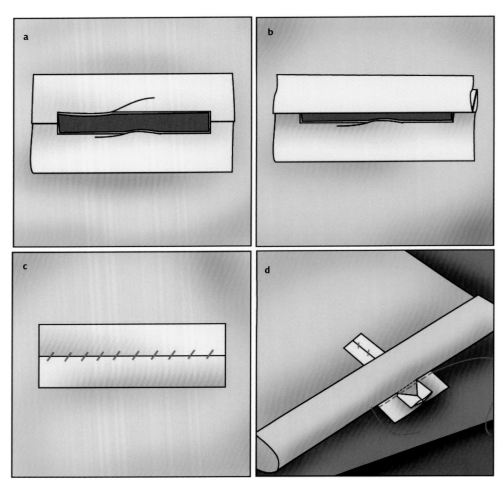

Figure 10.36a–d Strip method steps.

Buttons

Buttons come in many shapes and sizes. The most common type of button has two to four holes for attachment in the center. Other buttons are attached through one hole in the shank (back center of the button), which helps keep the button off the fabric surface for thicker fabrics. For extra-thick fabric, such as that used for coats, you may need to add an additional shank out of thread.

SEW-ON BUTTONS

1. Mark the button placement.
2. Secure the thread, and pull it through the marked spot.
3. Pull the needle through one of the holes in the button and down through another hole into the fabric. Make a couple of these stitches, keeping them loose. (Figure 10.37a)
4. Pull the needle through a new hole and then into another one, pulling through the fabric as well. Make a couple of these stitches, keeping them loose.
5. After you have sewn through all of the holes, pull the needle through one of the holes and then out in between the button and the fabric. (Figure 10.37b)
6. Pull the button away from the fabric. The loose stitches should leave some thread space in between the button and the fabric. (Figure 10.37c)
7. Wrap the thread a couple of times around the threads attaching the button. (Figure 10.37d)
8. Insert the needle into the fabric, and secure the thread.

Hint: For a longer shank, keep the stitches looser when sewing through the holes.

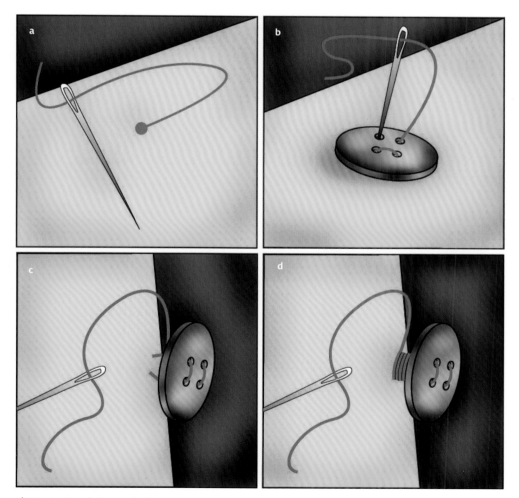

Figure 10.37a–d Sew-on buttons.

FOUR WAYS TO ATTACH SEW-ON BUTTONS

(Figure 10.38)

Hint: Some garments, such as outerwear or suits, need to offer more support in the button area so that the buttons don't tear off or leave holes in the garment. A reinforced button is sewn on the backside of the garment, and you sew the two buttons together, pulling from one button to the other. (Figure 10.39)

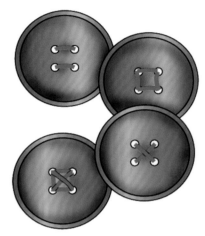

Figure 10.38 Four variations of buttonhole attachments.

Figure 10.39 Reinforcing the button.

SHANK BUTTONS

1. Secure the thread, and pull it through the marked spot.
2. Pull the needle through the hole at the shank. (Figure 10.40)
3. Take a couple of stitches in and out of the fabric and the shank.
4. Secure the thread.

Hint: If an extra shank is needed, leave your stitches looser so you can wrap around them just like in the sew-on shank.

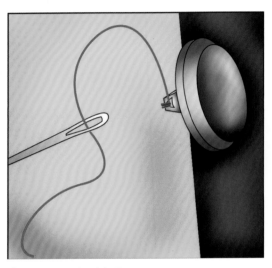

Figure 10.40 Shank button.

Button Loops

Button loops are a decorative way to add buttons to a garment. You can add buttons and loops to almost any design for decoration and/or practical closure.

Button loops are usually set into the opening between two layers of fabric. This way they stick out of the opening side in order to loop over the buttons.

You may want to test or practice with loops before you begin so that you know if your loops will work well with your fabric. If your fabric is very thin, you may want to add interfacing between the fabric and the facing piece.

Make button loops from scratch, or buy ready-made strips and cut them to the right size for the loops.

To make the fabric strips, cut a long bias strip of fabric, double the desired width, and add seam allowances. Fold in half, right sides together. Along the raw edge side, stitch the entire length of the strip. Now you can flip it inside out to the right side, and you get a long strip to use for your loops. Cut it into pieces.

To add cord, attach a safety pin to one end of the cord and pull it through the tube.

1. Measure the button. Take half of the button width, which will be the depth of the button loop. Mark it with two lines on your fabric. (Figure 10.41a)
2. Mark the seam allowance line away from the loop line toward the raw edge of the garment fabric. (Figure 10.41b)

3. Line up the loop strips so that the ends line up with the seam allowance line, and make sure the loop or the bend on the loop lines up with the loop line you marked for the bend. (Figure 10.41c)
4. Take the facing piece, and mark the same distance from the edge on the wrong side as you did from the edge to the seam allowance line. Mark the loop lines.
5. Place the facing piece on top of the garment piece, and line up the edge and the lines. Pin/baste.
   Stitch through all layers of fabric and the strips along the loop end line. Open up the facing and press down, and then fold it along the seam line toward the inside of the garment. The button loops should stand out of the opening seam line. Understitch the facing side with the seam allowances and loop ends. (Figure 10.41d)
6. Attach the buttons to the other end of the opening. Before sewing them on, make sure you mark the correct placement of the buttons using the loop side.

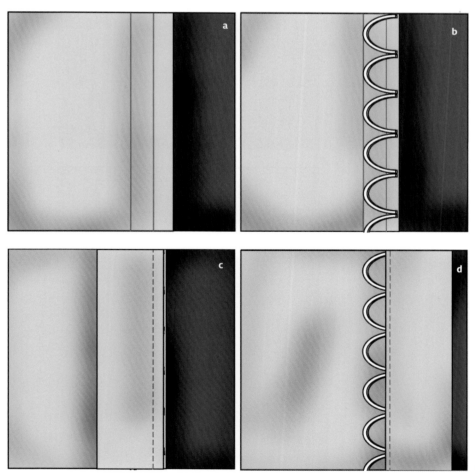

Figure 10.41a–d Button loops.

Frogs

Frogs are used as a practical or decorative button on any type of garment; however, try not to use them in places where there will be a lot of strain on the button.

Frogs are buttons and loops made of knotted cord attached on top of the garment instead of being placed into a seam.

FROG EXAMPLES

(Figure 10.42a–c)
To make a frog, make your own strap/cord or purchase premade cord.

1. Mark your frog shape motif on your fabric. (Figure 10.43a) You will need to pin into something to hold the frog in place; use a ham or ironing board by pinning a scrap piece of fabric on it. (Figure 10.43b)
2. Loop your frog so that the last weave goes through all the previous loops, and pin the cord to hold it in place. Here you can design your own frog.
3. When done, trim off the excess cord. Then you can secure the design by hand sewing small stitches along the underside of the frog. (Figure 10.43c)
4. To make your ball, loop another frog, and tighten it at the end. It should make a knot or a ball.
5. When making the ball, make sure that you make it big enough so that it can fit into the loop without coming out easily. (Figure 10.43d)
6. You can leave this a one-sided frog, or you can loop another duplicate of your frog motif to match on the other side.
7. Attach it to your garment.

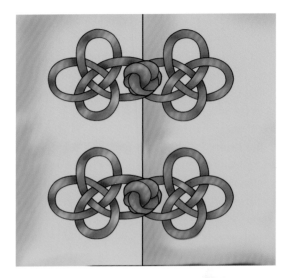

Figure 10.42 Frog examples.

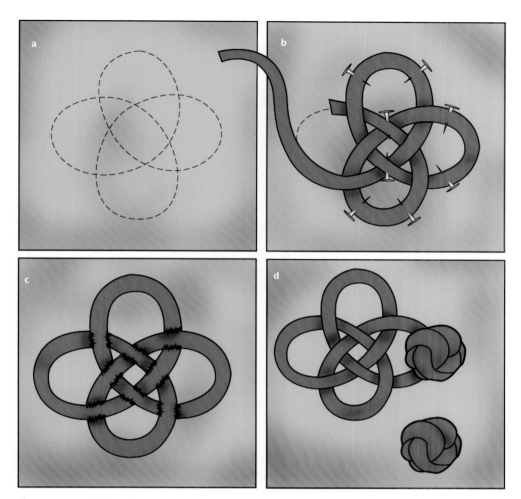

Figure 10.43a–d Frog steps.

JEAN PAUL GAULTIER

Jean Paul Gaultier was born in Arcueil, France, on April 24, 1952. He grew up in Paris, where he loved to skip school and go to his grandmother's house to sketch his designs. Though Gaultier never had any formal design training, he began sending his sketches to famous couture designers. One of these designers, Pierre Cardin, liked his work and hired him as an assistant in 1970. Over the next few years, Gaultier also worked for Jacques Esterel and for the house of Patou. Gaultier presented his first collection in 1976, although it was not until 1978 that he obtained sufficient backing to launch his own line.

Haute Couture Spring/Summer 2008.

Gaultier is often considered the "bad boy" of French fashion, and his designs are closely interwoven with pop culture. Gaultier himself did a stint as a host on the British television show *Eurotrash*. Street culture has been a strong influence on his collections, and his designs are often controversial, including skirts for men and a pointed basque and bra for women. The singer Madonna adopted that particular style and made it her trademark in the early 1990s. Gaultier also designed the costumes for Madonna's 2006 tour and for

rocker Marilyn Manson. Gaultier has designed wardrobes for many feature films, including Luc Besson's *The Fifth Element* and Peter Greenaway's *The Cook, the Thief, His Wife, and Her Lover*. He has also become known for his line of fragrances.

In 1997, Gaultier achieved a long-held dream when he released his own couture line. In addition to his couture and ready-to-wear lines, in 2003, Gaultier was named the chief designer for the house of Hermès.

Haute Couture Spring/Summer 2014.

Jean Paul Gaultier, 2014.

Chapter Review

This chapter covered all types of closures that can be used on your garments. Closures can be used for technical purposes in order to allow the garment to fit correctly. Zippers come in many types, lengths, and colors and are applied as a lapped zipper, centered zipper, or invisible zipper. Today we use three types of zippers: metal, polyester coil, and molded. Also covered in this chapter were applications of hooks and eyes, thread chains, snaps, and buttons. Buttons come in a variety of sizes and types; buttonhole variations covered in this chapter will help you along the garment process.

Projects

1. Make zipper samples for your book. Include all of the zippers covered in this chapter (lapped zipper, center lapped zipper, fly-front zipper, hand-sewn zipper, and invisible zipper). Write down your steps, and insert them into one of your plastic cover sheets.

2. Make hook and eye samples for your book (regular hook and eye and lapped hook and eye). Then make a sample of the thread chain and the wrapped chain for your book. Write down your steps, and insert them into one of your plastic cover sheets.

3. Make snap samples for your book, one with a regular snap and another with a self-covered snap. Write down your steps, and insert them into one of your plastic cover sheets.

4. Make buttonhole samples for your book. Write down your steps, and insert them into one of your plastic cover sheets.

5. Make button samples for your book (shank button and sew-on button). Write down your steps, and insert them into one of your plastic cover sheets.

6. Make frog samples for your book. Write down your steps, and insert them into one of your plastic cover sheets.

Key Terms

Bound buttonholes	Hooks and eyes	Shank buttons
Button loops	Invisible zippers	Snaps
Buttonholes	Lapped hook and eye	Strip method
Buttons	Lapped zippers	Thread chain
Center lapped zipper	Machine-stitched buttonholes	Wrapped chain
Fly-front zippers	Patch method	Zippers
Frogs	Regular hook and eye	
Hand-stitched buttonholes	Sew-on buttons	

11

The Skill of Hems and Other Edge Finishes

Objectives

- Learn how to hem garments

- Learn different types of hems

- Learn how to finish garment edges

- Learn variations of decorative hems

- Learn about the life and work of Valentino Garavani

Hems

Hems are finished edges of a garment. (Figure 11.1) Without hems, garments can look incomplete and unprofessional. However, hems are not always necessary. Some fabrics don't ravel and can be used for designs that purposely have a raw edge as a design element.

Hems are at the bottom of the garment, but you can use the same techniques to finish any edge, such as necklines, sleeves, and front closure areas on coats and shirts. Hems can be finished with hem seams, bias binding, or even facings. (Figure 11.2)

Facings are used to finish edges, such as necklines, armholes, waists, and even purses. Binding is used in place of serging to finish seam allowances inside the garment. Binding can also be used instead of facings to bind an edge at the bottom of the garment.

In couture, hems are usually left for last. At the last fitting, the hemline is marked with thread tracing, folded along the tracing, and basted, after which it is slip stitched by hand.

The hemline should be parallel to the floor unless it is part of your design to have a diagonal or uneven effect. (Figure 11.3)

One way to mark the hem is on a table with the garment laid out flat. You can use pins to mark the hem. From the bottom, measure the width of the hem and pin while turning the hem up to the inside of the garment. (Figure 11.4) Then try on the garment to ensure that the hem is straight and the length is correct.

Another way to get the hem parallel is to hang the garment on the form or fit it on your customer. By doing this, you can be sure the hem will be straight because the garment fits differently at the front and back of the body and will stretch differently all the way around. After the garment is fitted, use a ruler to mark the length from the floor to where you want the garment hem to fall. (Figure 11.5) Trace it, baste it folded, press it, and fit it again to make sure the hem is even all the way around.

The depth of the hem varies depending on the garment style and the weight of the fabric. In straight skirts and dresses, hems usually measure between 1 and 2 ½ inches. For full skirts or stretchy fabrics, hems measure 1 to 2 inches. With transparent fabrics, the hem is usually very narrow; a rolled hem is often used to finish the bottom edge.

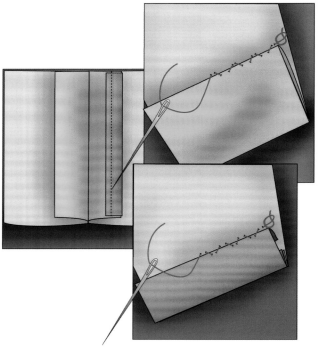

Figure 11.1 Hem examples.

Figure 11.2 The hem at the bottom of jacket.

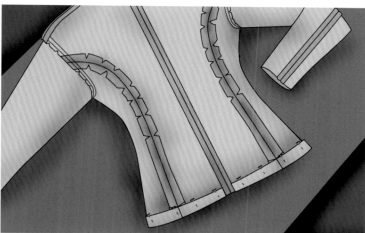

Figure 11.4 Hemming process.

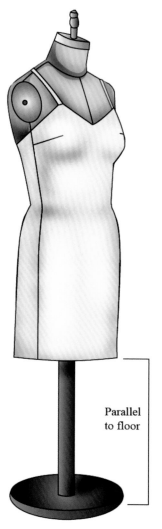

Figure 11.3 Hemline parallel to the floor.

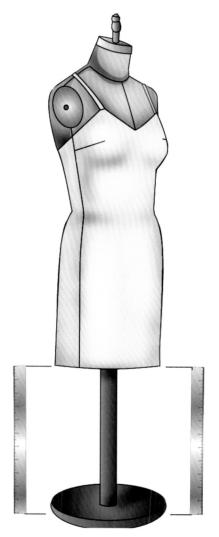

Figure 11.5 Measure evenly from the floor.

Hem Variations

SLIP HEM

Used to finish hems on skirts made of lighter fabrics, silks, cottons, and softer satins.

1. Secure the thread.
2. Start to hem by catching a couple of threads on the folded side and a couple on the garment side.
3. Keep alternating stitches up and down, catching a couple of threads each time. (Figure 11.6a)

Hint: Use on hems that are turned under, pinked, zigzag-edged (Figure 11.6b), or serged.

HONG KONG FINISH

Used to finish the seam allowance edge on the inside of the garment.

1. Make a straight seam, and press the seam allowance open. (Figure 11.7a)
2. Use a precut bias seam binding, or cut a bias strip of fabric. You can cut a bias strip out of chiffon, lightweight lining, organza, cotton, or even the same fabric that you used for the garment.
3. Stitch the binding to one side of the seam edge ¼ inch from the edge, right sides together. (Figure 11.7b)

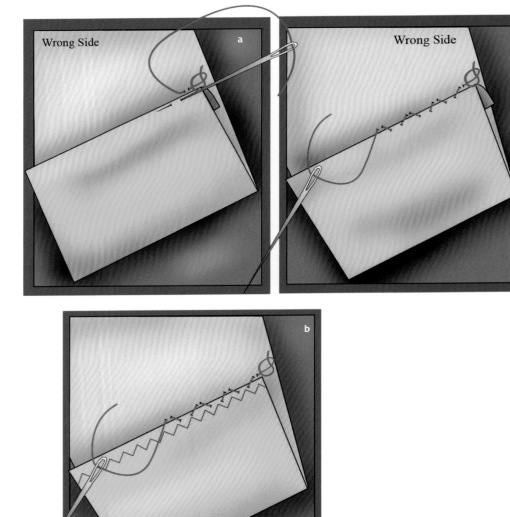

Figure 11.6a–b (a) Slip hem. (b) Slip with zigzag stitch.

4. Trim the binding and the seam allowance very close to the seam. (Figure 11.7c)

5. Fold the binding around the edge to the inside between the seam allowance and the upper garment fabric.

6. Topstitch through all layers of the seam allowance, not the garment. (Figure 11.7d)

Figure 11.7a–d Hong Kong finish.

HONG KONG HEM

Used to finish fabrics that ravel a lot. It uses the Hong Kong finish.

1. Follow steps 1–6 from Hong Kong Finish (previously mentioned).
2. Fold up the binded hem, and slip stitch the binding to the garment fabric. (Figure 11.8a–d)

SEAM TAPE HEM

Used as a seam finish on fabrics that fray after washing. Makes the garment look neat on the inside.

1. Fold the hem and baste.
2. Align the seam tape along the edge of the hem inside the garment and pin.

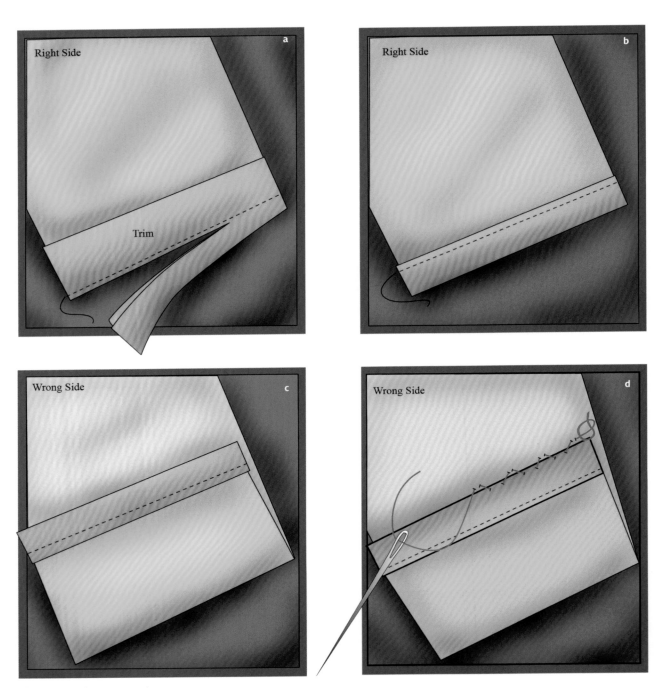

Figure 11.8a–d Hong Kong hem.

3. Edge stitch the seam tape in place. (Figure 11.9a)
4. Use the slip stitch to connect the seam tape to the garment fabric. (Figure 11.9b)

ROLLED HEM

Used on lightweight, light-colored, and transparent fabrics made narrow or wide (double hem). There are two methods: one has no guidelines, and the second, primarily used for curved edges, uses basted stitch guidelines for the folded edge.

1. Measure your guidelines along your hemline on your garment fabric and mark.
2. Fold the hem half the width of your hem seam allowance, and press it down. (Figure 11.10a)
3. Fold the edge again toward the inside another half of the width of your seam allowance. Fold it so that the edge meets the hemline. Press.
4. Slip stitch by hand, or topstitch with a sewing machine. (Figure 11.10b)

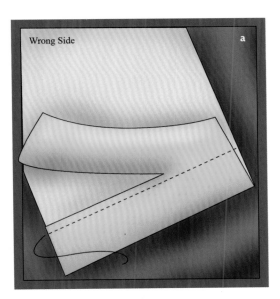

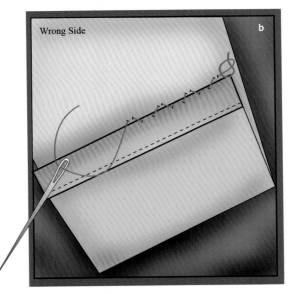

Figure 11.9a and b Seam tape hem.

Figure 11.10a and b Rolled hem.

FACED HEM

Used to finish shaped hemlines, increase comfort, add weight to the bottom, and reduce bulk.

Note: The facing for this hem needs to be the same shape as the bottom of the garment, and it should be cut slightly off grain so that it will lie smoothly inside a hem that is shaped, such as an A-line skirt.

1. Trim the hem to ¼ inch.
2. Measure the hem length. Cut a facing piece the same length/shape as the hem length and 2 inches wide.
3. Make a flat seam ¼ inch from the edge, right sides together. (Figure 11.11a)
4. Fold the facing along the seam line toward the wrong side. Press it down along the seam line. (Figure 11.11b)
5. To finish the hem, fold the edge of the facing in ¼ inch. (Figure 11.11c)
6. Then you can use the slip stitch to hand sew it down. (Figure 11.11d)

HORSEHAIR BRAID HEM

Used to finish hems on full skirts and to keep the hem away from the body by making it stiff on the end.

1. Trim the hem to ¼ inch.

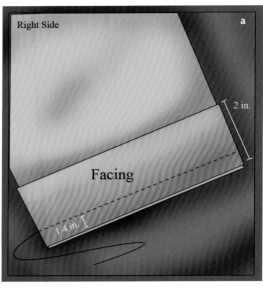

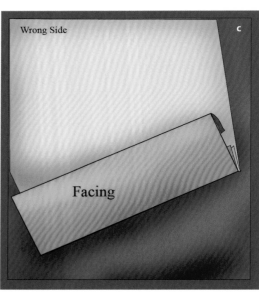

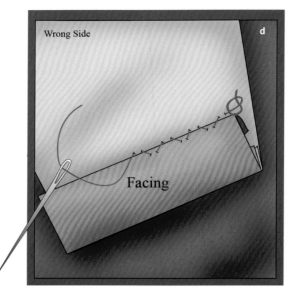

Figure 11.11a–d Faced hem.

2. Line up the horsehair braid along the edge. (Figure 11.12a)

3. Make a flat seam ¼ inch from the edge, right sides together. (Figure 11.12b)

4. Fold the horsehair braid toward the wrong side of the garment. (Figure 11.12c)

5. To finish the hem, use the catch stitch to hand sew it down. (Figure 11.12d)

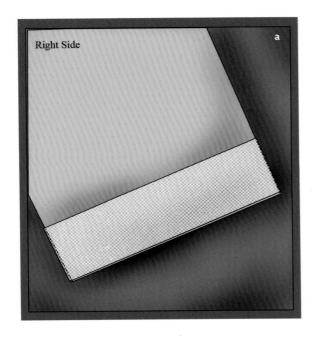

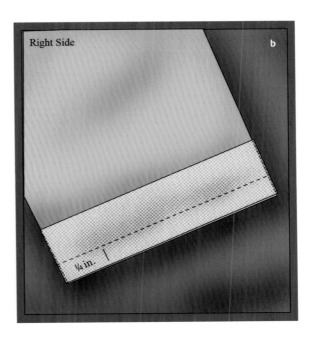

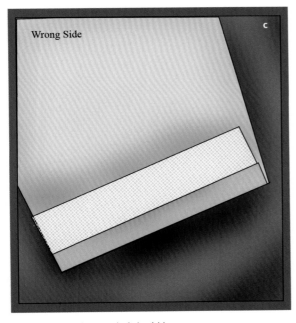

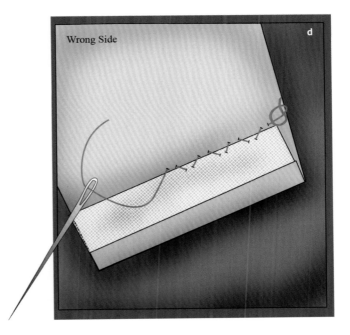

Figure 11.12a–d Horsehair braid hem.

Decorative Hems

(Figure 11.13a)

PLEATED HEM

1. Cut a strip of fabric at least twice the length of your hem as wide as you like.
2. Mark the halfway point so that when you pleat, you do not use up more fabric on one side than the other.
3. Pleat as desired. Measure to make sure it fits the hem. (Figure 11.13b)
4. Baste the pleats along the top edge. (Figure 11.13c)
5. Pin the pleated strip along the bottom hem of your garment, right sides together, followed by the facing hem piece on top of the **pleated hem**. Sandwich all three layers together. (11.13d)
6. Stitch all the way around the hemline. Press the facing toward the inside of the garment, and press the pleats so that they hang down. (Figure 11.13e)
7. Slip stitch the facing on the inside of the garment to finish neatly. Then stitch the lining over the facing to completely close off the inside of the garment so it looks clean. (Figure 11.13f)

Figure 11.13a Pleated hem.

Figure 11.13b–f Pleated hem steps.

FLOUNCE HEM

This is a great decorative way to finish your hems.

1. Cut a flounce long enough to stretch around the entire hem as wide as you like.
2. Finish the **flounce hem** with a rolled or serged rolled hem before attaching it to the garment. (Figure 11.14a)
3. Pin the flounce along the bottom hem of your garment, right sides together, followed by the facing hem piece on top of the flounce. Sandwich all three layers together. (Figure 11.14b)
4. Stitch all the way around the hemline. Press the facing toward the inside of the garment, and press the flounce so that it drapes down. (Figure 11.14c)
5. Slip stitch the facing on the inside of the garment. Then stitch the lining over the facing to completely close off the inside of the garment so it looks neat and clean. (Figure 11.14d)

RUFFLE HEM

(Figure 11.15a)

1. Cut a ruffle long enough to stretch around the entire hem as wide as you like.
2. Finish the **ruffle hem** with a rolled or serged rolled hem. (Figure 11.15b)

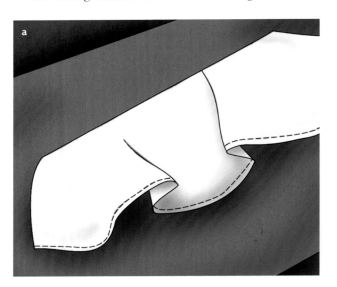

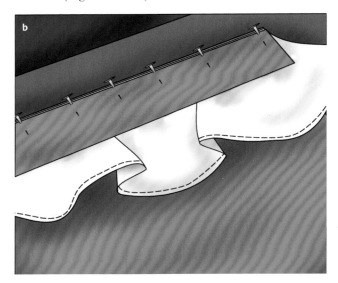

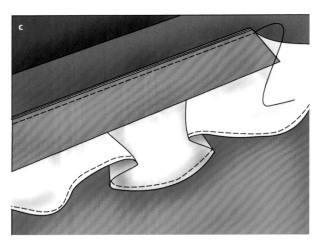

Figure 11.14a–d Flounce hem.

3. Pin the ruffle along the bottom hem of your garment, right sides together, followed by the facing hem piece on top of the ruffle. Sandwich all three layers together. (Figure 11.15c)
4. Stitch all the way around the hemline. Press the facing toward the inside of the garment, and press the ruffle so that it drapes down. (Figure 11.15d)
5. Slip stitch the facing on the inside of the garment. (Figure 11.15e)

Figure 11.15a Ruffle hem.

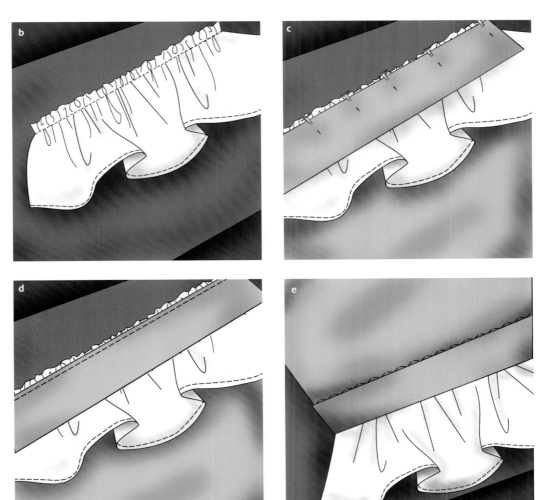

Figure 11.15b–e Ruffle hem steps.

SCALLOPED HEM

Used to decorate garments. It is very important to keep the scallops symmetrical and the corners sharp. (Figure 11.16a)

1. Decide how big and wide you want your scallops. Mark the scallops along your hemline on your pattern, using a compass, a drinking glass, or even a plate. (Figure 11.16b)
2. When you are making your pattern, your facing/lining scallop hem should be the same shape as the outer garment. (Figure 11.16c)
3. When your patterns are complete, attach the outer garment pieces together, leaving only the hem to finish.
4. Then put the lining together and attach the facing to the lining, leaving only the hem to finish. (Figure 11.16d)
5. Attach the facing to the outer garment piece, right sides together, along the edge of the scallops. (Figure 11.16e)
6. Flip the scallops right side out, and press down neatly.

Figure 11.16a Scalloped hem.

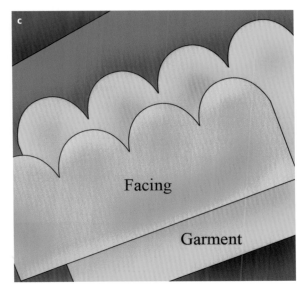

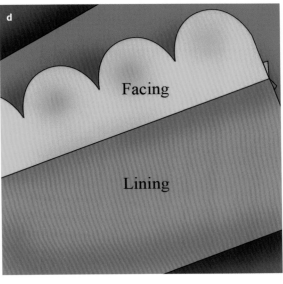

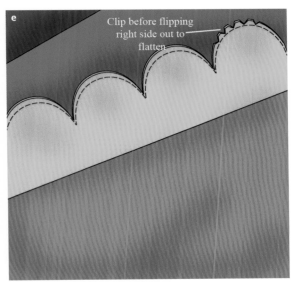

Figure 11.16b–e Scalloped hem steps.

FRINGED FRAYED HEM

Used to decorate a woven fabric garment. Seen on denim and on a variety of woven cotton fabrics. (Figure 11.17a)

1. Stitch a zigzag seam along the hem 1 inch from the edge. This seam will keep the fringe from fraying farther into the garment. (Figure 11.17b)
2. Begin to pull crosswise threads out, leaving the lengthwise grain hanging to form a fringe. (Figure 11.17c)

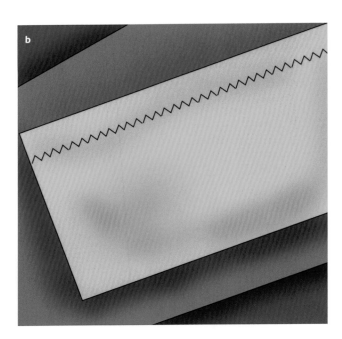

Figure 11.17a Fringed frayed hem.

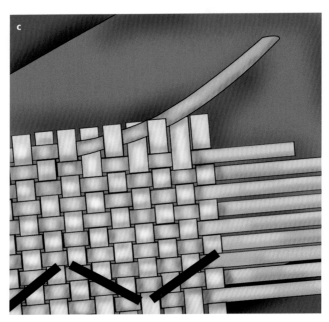

Figure 11.17b and c Fringed frayed hem steps.

FEATHERS AND FEATHER TRIM

When you design with **feathers**, use different types: peacock, duck, ostrich, pheasant, vulture, and so on. (Figure 11.18a) Feathers are great for any season and can withstand any weather.

When sewing with feathers, you need to consider the importance of securing the feathers well so they do not fall off.

1. Sew through the stem of the feather to attach it to the fabric; however, you need to make sure you wrap the stitches over a couple of times. The best way to attach feathers individually is to sew through both the stem and larger stitches to cover the feathers inside as well. (Figure 11.18b)

2. Making loops and threading the stem through them before you run the needle and thread through the stem will make the feather hold better. (Figure 11.18c)

3. If you are attaching feathers as a trim, attach the feathers to a braid by sewing the stems in place, and then attach the braid to the hem of the garment.

4. Purchasing a ready-to-sew feather trim that is already attached to a ribbon makes it easier to attach it to the hem edge or sandwich the ribbon in between the facing and the outer shell of the fabric. (Figure 11.18d)

Figure 11.18a Feathers.

Figure 11.18b–d Feathers attachment steps.

HOW TO HEM A FACED OPENING

When you are hemming a jacket opening, a slit opening, or even a clipped edge on a garment, you can follow the opening hem method. After hemming the rest of the garment you are ready to hem the opening.

1. Mark and turn up the hem of the garment. (Figure 11.19a)
2. Fold the side of the opening over the hem. (Figure 11.19b)
3. To reduce the bulk, cut off the inside corner diagonally from the edge to the corner of the opening. (Figure 11.19c)
4. Fold over the top corner diagonally to make a nice, sharp point. Press it and stitch it with a slip stitch. (Figure 11.19d)

Lining Hem

Two methods of lining attachment are (1) lining completely attached to the garment or (2) free hanging.

ATTACHED LINING HEM

(Figure 11.20a)

1. Place the garment flat on the table inside out, and mark where you would like the lining to end. (Figure 11.20b)
2. Fold up the hem on the lining, and pin to the garment hem. (Figure 11.20c)

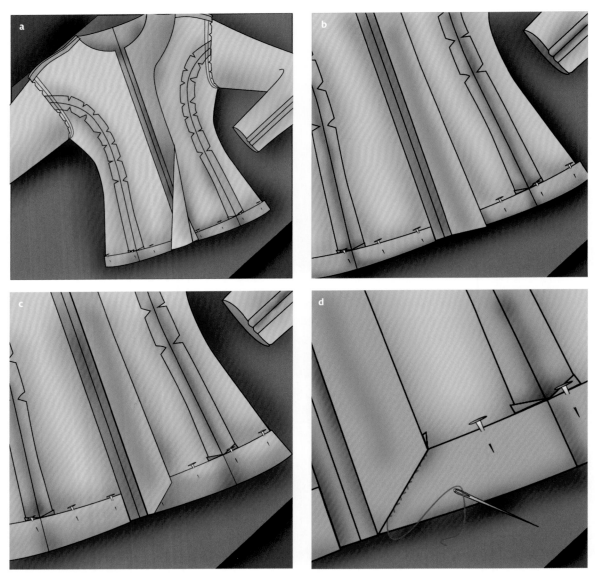

Figure 11.19a–d Hemming a faced hem.

a

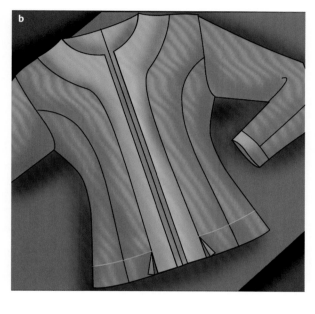

b

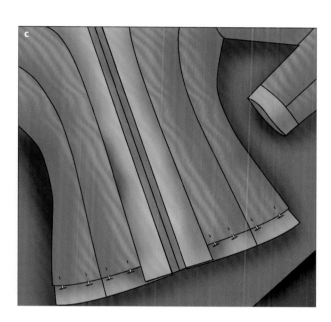

c

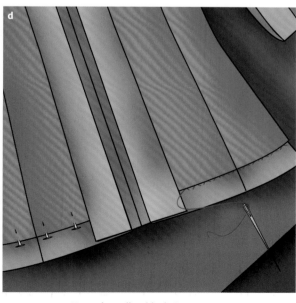

d

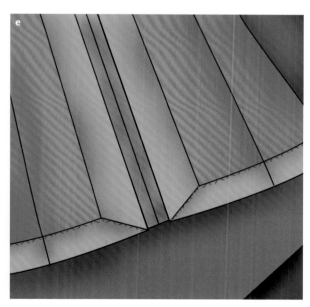

e

3. Slip stitch the lining fold to the garment hem to finish the hem, and attach the lining to the garment. (Figure 11.20d)

4. For corner opening, turn it under along the hem and also along the facing of the corner. Slip stitch along the side opening and the corner to the hem. (Figure 11.20e)

Figure 11.20a–e Hemming a lined jacket.

FREE-HANGING LINING HEM

Used in a skirts (Figure 11.21a). The lining does not get attached to the garment fabric; it hangs loose and is hemmed separately. A thread chain attaches the lining hem to the skirt hem.

1. Fold the lining under so that the lining is about 1 inch from the bottom of the garment hem. Pin/baste in place. (Figure 11.21b)
2. Slip stitch or machine stitch the hem just underneath the lining inside the garment. (Figure 11.21c)

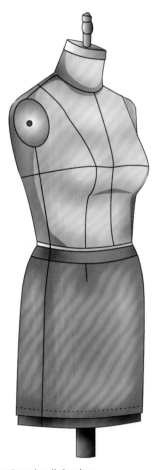

Figure 11.21a Free hanging lining hem.

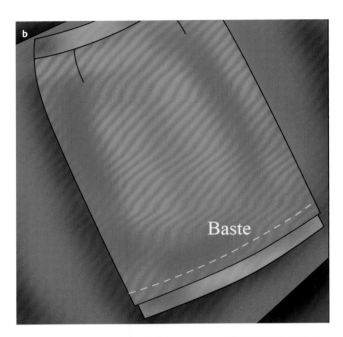

Figure 11.21b–c Free hanging lining hem steps.

3. At each seam, sew French tacks to connect the lining to the garment. Make the tacks measuring anywhere from ½ inch to ¾ inch long. (Figure 11.21d)

4. Near the opening or corner edge, slip stitch the facing after you have stitched the lining hem to keep the lining in place so it won't move into the opening. (Figure 11.21e)

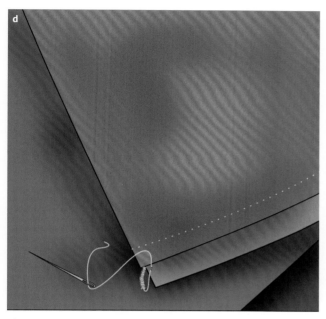
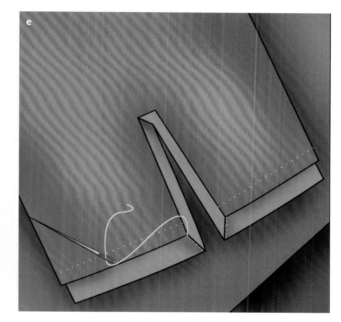

Figure 11.21d–e Free hanging lining hem steps.

A BRIEF LOOK INTO THE LIFE OF
VALENTINO GARAVANI

Valentino Garavani was born in Voghera, Italy, on May 11, 1932. His artistic talent became evident when he was in high school, and at the age of seventeen he moved to Paris to study at the École des Beaux-Arts and the Chambre Syndicale de la Couture Parisienne. He worked as an apprentice at the fashion houses of Guy Laroche and Jean Desses for a number of years. Then he moved back to Italy in 1959 where, with the support of his father, he opened his own atelier on the Via Condotti. His designs were successful from the start, with women such as Elizabeth Taylor, Jackie Kennedy, and Jacqueline de Ribes buying his couture dresses and the press making him known around the world.

In 1968, Valentino had a breakthrough with his legendary all-white

Fall/Winter collection 2015.

collection, which included garments made from the most luxurious fabrics, some costing as much as $2,000 a yard. He became known as the designer of the beautiful, influential, well-dressed women of the international jet set. Valentino was never interested in the fashion avant-garde. He designed clothes that women wanted to wear and made his name with dresses that were elegant, feminine, and exceptionally well made—the essence of glamour. It is no surprise that Valentino's designs are so often found on the red carpet at Hollywood premieres and award galas.

In the 1970s, Valentino began to spend more time in New York, where he became well acquainted with the famed fashion editor Diana Vreeland and the artist Andy Warhol. It was around this time, too, that Valentino,

at the suggestion of his partner, Giancarlo Giammetti, became one of the first designers to move into the licensing of many types of products. He opened boutiques all over the world and currently has thirty-five stores in sixteen countries. He also branched out into a line aimed at younger women, R.E.D., named after his trademark color, rosso Valentino.

In 2006, Valentino had a cameo in the film *The Devil Wears Prada*, which starred Meryl Streep. An interview with the fashion designer is included as an extra on the DVD of the film.

Valentino announced his retirement in fall 2007, and the spring/summer couture collection he presented at the Musée Rodin in Paris in January 2008 was the last of his forty-five years in the fashion world.

Fall/Winter collection 2006.

Valentino Garavani, 2011.

Chapter Review

This chapter covered different ways you can hem your garment. Hemming a garment is very important because if it is not done correctly, the garment will not look finished and neat no matter how neat the rest of the garment is. In this chapter, you learned about hems that are used often, such as the **slip hem, rolled hem, faced hem, Hong Kong hem**, and more. You also learned about **decorative hems** that offer you a chance to get creative with your garment. Adding a flounce or a ruffle at the bottom of a skirt can add a creative touch.

Projects

1. Make hem samples for your book. (Hong Kong hem, **Hong Kong finish**, double hem, **seam tape hem**, rolled hem, faced hem, and **horsehair braid hem**). Write down your steps, and insert them into your plastic cover sheets.
2. Make lining hem samples for your book (**lining hem** and free-hanging lining hem). Write down your steps, and insert them into your plastic cover sheets.
3. Make decorative hem samples for your book (pleated hem, flounce hem, ruffle hem, **fringed frayed hem**, and **scalloped hem**). Write down your steps, and insert them into your plastic cover sheets.

Key Terms

Decorative hems	Hong Kong finish	Ruffle hem
Faced hem	Hong Kong hem	Scalloped hem
Feathers	Horsehair braid hem	Seam tape hem
Flounce hem	Lining hem	Slip hem
Fringed frayed hem	Pleated hem	
Hems	Rolled hem	

12

The Skill of Basic Tailoring

Objectives

- Learn tailoring techniques used in high-class dressmaking

- Learn to stay stitch and understitch

- Learn different varieties of pocket techniques

- Learn about the life and work of Alexander McQueen

Pockets

PATCH POCKETS

Patch pockets are applied on the outside of the garment and can be decorative or plain and boxy.

1. Make a patch pocket pattern, and cut it out of the desired fabric on the lengthwise grain.

2. Interface the pocket.
   - You can use sew-in interfacing cut from the pocket pattern. Stay stitch the interfacing to the pocket on the wrong side of the pocket, and trim off the seam allowances.
   - Or use iron-on interfacing before applying the pocket.

3. For a square pocket, you will need to fold the hem of the pocket 1 inch on the right side of the fabric. Stitch a horizontal line from side to side at ⅝ inch. (Figure 12.1a)

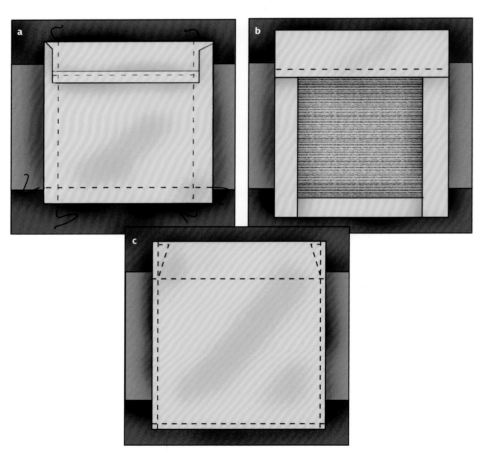

Figure 12.1a–c Patch pockets.

4. Stitch vertically from top to bottom along the seam line. In addition, stitch a horizontal seam from side to side along the seam line at the bottom of the pocket.

5. Clip off the seam allowances along the hemline ⅛ inch from the seam only at the hemline. Flip the hem right side out, and press down. (Figure 12.1b)

6. Miter the corners by folding them along the corner or clipping off the corner ⅛ inch away from the corner. Continue folding in the seam allowances, and press them down. (Figure 12.1c)

7. Place the pocket on the garment, and topstitch it in place. To do so, you need to begin stitching at the bottom center of the pocket and work your way down and up on one side and then begin at the same point and stitch toward the other side. Doing this will eliminate pocket stretching and shifting.

8. To reinforce your pockets, stitch a triangle along the corners of the pockets in order to avoid the fabric ripping if the pocket is carrying a heavy load.

9. For rounded corners, your pattern will have rounded corners at the bottom. Instead of stitching horizontal and vertical lines along the seam line, sew a seam along ⅝ inch, and then sew a row of gathering stitches along ⅜ inch from the edge around the bottom corners of the pocket. (Figure 12.2a and b)

10. Clip off the seam allowance close to the gathering. Pull a little bit, and gather enough to shape the pocket curve along ⅝-inch stitching. (Figure 12.2c)

11. Press the pocket flat, and topstitch it on the garment again, beginning the stitch at the bottom center of the pocket.

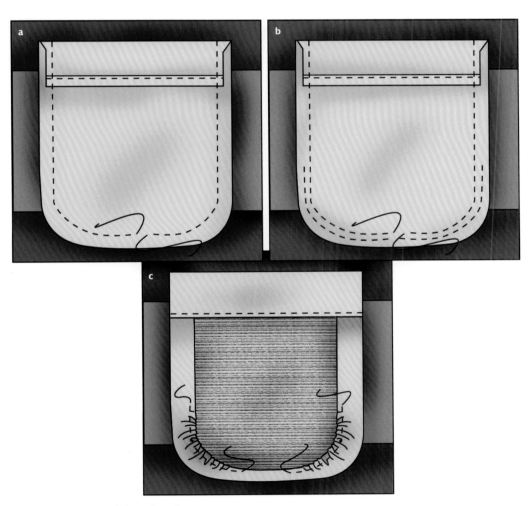

Figure 12.2a–c Rounded patch pockets.

Hint #1: You can make patch pockets of any shape. You can also add details and embellishments to the pockets. You can make pleats, tucks, gathering, smocking, appliqué, embroidery, and beading embellishments. (Figure 12.3)

Hint #2: When pocket shapes get very stylized, line the pocket by cutting two patterns and sewing them together face-to-face or right sides together. Leave a small opening in the seam so that you can flip it right side out. Now slip stitch the opening closed. Press the seams flat, and then topstitch it to your garment. (Figure 12.4a–c)

12. To add a **flap** to your patch pocket, measure the width of the patch pocket and make a pattern for the flap at the same width. You can make it any length you want. You can even make the flap almost cover the patch pocket completely.

Figure 12.3 Decorative patch pockets.

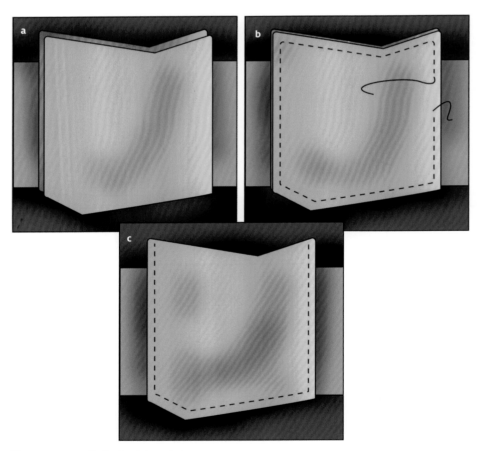

Figure 12.4a–c Stylized patch pockets.

13. Now cut two of the same flap pattern. Line them up right sides together and pin. (Figure 12.5a)

14. Stitch a seam along the seam line around the flap, leaving a 1-inch opening unsewn. Cut off two of your corners with a diagonal seam line on the top of the flap. This will give you diagonal corners so that when you attach the flap above the pocket, your corners will not be seen under the flap. (Figure 12.5b)

15. Flip it right side out through the opening, and slip stitch the opening closed. Press flat, and mark a new seam line along the top of the flap on the inside.

16. Pin the flap to the garment right above the patch pocket, not more than ¼ inch away. Pin it as if the flap is open, away from the pocket.

17. Stitch a seam along the flap seam line. Stitch another seam along the edge of the flap to flatten it. Press. (Figure 12.5c)

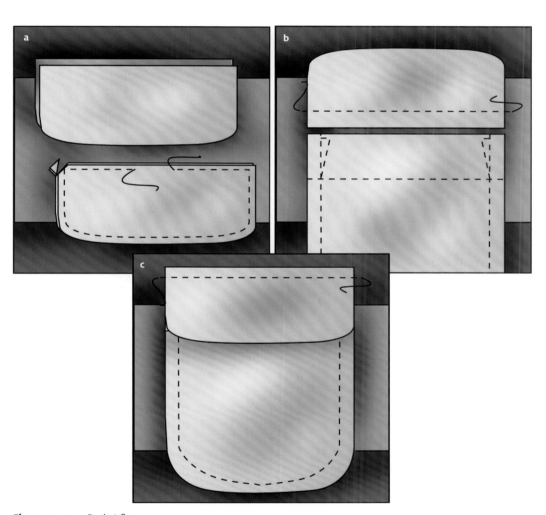

Figure 12.5a–c Pocket flap.

WELT POCKETS

Welt pockets are similar to bound buttonholes, just larger in size.

1. Cut a patch of fabric (use the garment fabric, unless you want the welt pocket to be a different color or fabric) 2 inches wider than the desired pocket width and 4 inches longer. Mark the center of the patch by folding the patch in half. If you need to stiffen the patch, iron on some fusible interfacing.
2. Mark the pocket slash line on your garment.
3. Align the patch line with the line on your garment. Make sure you are placing the patch and the garment fabric right sides together.
4. Baste or pin the patch so that it will not shift while you sew. (Figure 12.6a)
5. Mark the welt rectangle on the wrong side of the patch around the slash line. (Figure 12.6b)
6. Now that you have the rectangle marked, stitch around it with a regular machine stitch, or if you are sewing by hand, make small backstitches along the marked line. Press after you finish. (Figure 12.6c)
7. Remove the basting stitches from the patch, or remove the pins holding it in place.
8. Using embroidery scissors, cut through all of your fabric layers, corner to corner, inside the rectangle. (Figure 12.6d)

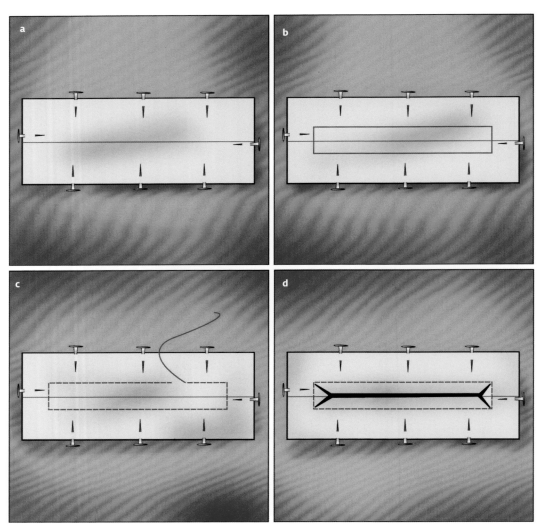

Figure 12.6a–d Welt pocket steps.

9. Pick up the patch corners, and pull them through the cut opening toward the wrong side of the garment. (Figure 12.7a)

10. Straighten out the patch to make a clean open rectangle in the center, and press so that the seam lies flat. (Figure 12.7b)

11. Fold the sides toward the center of the open rectangle. If you fold each side to meet in the center, you will be forming the pocket sides from the right side. Press the folds. If you fold only one side to cover the entire opening, you will have a single welt pocket. (Figure 12.7c)

12. Baste the folds to keep from shifting. Turn to the right side of the garment, and baste the sides together with diagonal stitches. Press. (Figure 12.7d)

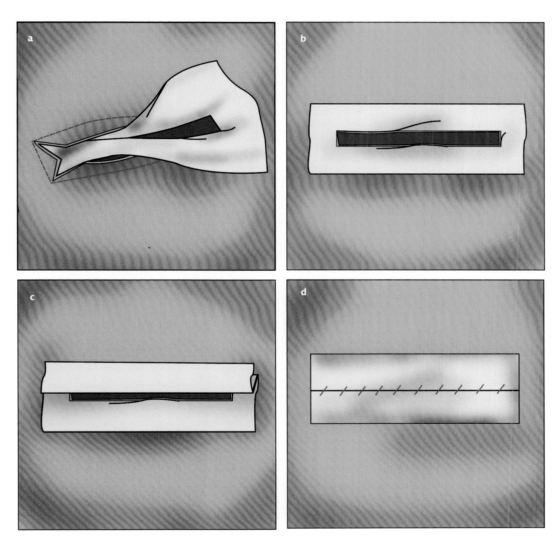

Figure 12.7a–d Welt pocket steps.

13. Fold over the garment fabric along the side of the pocket so that you see the sides of the folded patch and the triangular piece. Stitch along the fold through all of the folded patch layers and the triangle. Make sure you stitch next to the garment fold; do not catch it. Do the same thing along every side of the welt pocket. (Figure 12.8a)

14. Keep the welt basted closed until the garment is complete. Then you can pull the stitches out. Press.

15. Now take two rectangles the same length as the patch. One should be one patch width longer than the other plus seam allowance. The bottoms should be shaped like a pocket curved at the angles. Now cut them out of the lining fabric.

16. Line up one of them to the top of the patch and pin. Align the second one with the bottom of the patch and pin. (Figure 12.8b)

17. Now stitch them in place. You can stitch them together and form a pocket, and then serge or whip-stitch the seam allowances. (Figure 12.8c)

18. Press the pocket. (Figure 12.8d)

Figure 12.8a–d Welt pocket steps.

IN-SEAM POCKETS

In-seam pockets are sewn inside a seam. You can place them anywhere you have a seam. Usually they appear along the hip, inside the side seam.

Method #1

1. Pattern your pants or skirt, and mark the area where you want your pockets to be.
2. Make your pocket patterns to fit in the space you marked. (Figure 12.9a)
3. Before sewing your pockets, you need to add pocket seam support. This support keeps the pocket from stretching and ripping down the seam. To add the support, you can stitch a seam binding or a bias strip of fabric along the seam line between your marked points for the pocket. Do this on both sides of the side seam.
4. Stitch the pocket sides in place. Line up the garment and the pocket side right sides together, and make a seam along the seam line. Do this on the front and back pieces of your garment. (Figure 12.9b)
5. Stitch up your side seams from the hem to the first marked point or right at the beginning of the pocket. Then stitch from the second marked point to the waist. This way you will leave the pocket open. (Figure 12.9c)
6. Sew up your pocket around the seam line. This will close the pocket lining and form the pocket. (Figure 12.9d)
7. Understitch ¼ inch from the seam line on the inside of the pocket. This will flatten the seam and keep the pocket lining inside the pocket.
8. To hide lining, use the same fabric for the lining of the pocket as you use for the garment, or you can face your pockets with a face fabric. To do so, attach the pocket lining to the pocket facing before you attach it to the side seam.

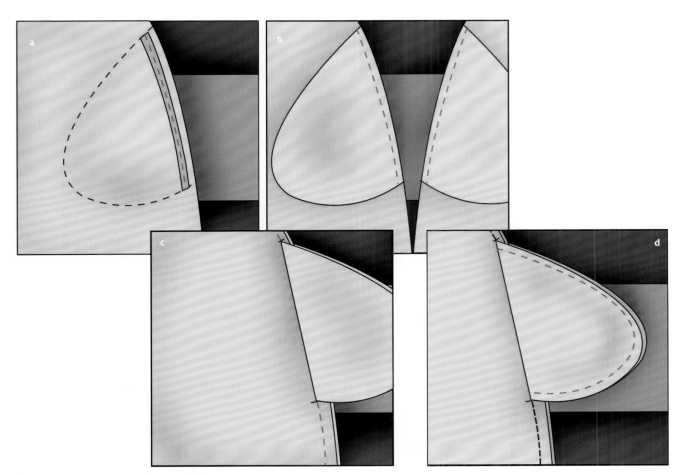

Figure 12.9a–d In-seam pockets, method 1.

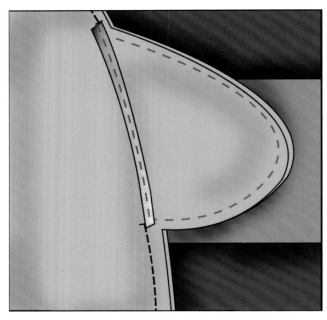

Figure 12.10 In-seam pockets, method 2.

Method #2

1. Pattern your pants or skirt with the pocket attached.
2. Add pocket seam support. To add the support, you can stitch a seam binding or a bias strip of fabric vertically along the seam line from the beginning of the pocket to the top of the pocket. (Figure 12.10)
3. Start stitching up the side seam on your garment. When you get to the pocket, stitch around the pocket seam line as well. Press.

4. Flip the garment to the right side, and check your pockets. To reinforce the pocket, backstitch a couple of stitches at the bottom of the pocket at the side seam. Press.

Method #3

1. Pattern your pants or skirt with the pocket facing attached. Then pattern the pocket lining minus the facing. Make sure you add a seam allowance on both the facing side and the lining so that they can be stitched together. (Figure 12.11a)
2. Before sewing your pockets, you need to add pocket seam support. To add the support, you can stitch a seam binding or a bias strip of fabric vertically along the seam line from the beginning of the pocket to the top of the pocket on the facing. (Figure 12.11b)
3. Stitch the pocket sides in place. Line up the facing piece on the garment and the pocket side right sides together, and make a seam along the seam line. Now you have attached the lining to the facing. Do this on the front and back pieces of your garment.
4. Start stitching up the side seam on your garment. When you get to the pocket, stitch around the pocket seam line as well. Press.
5. Flip the garment to the right side, and check your pockets. Press.

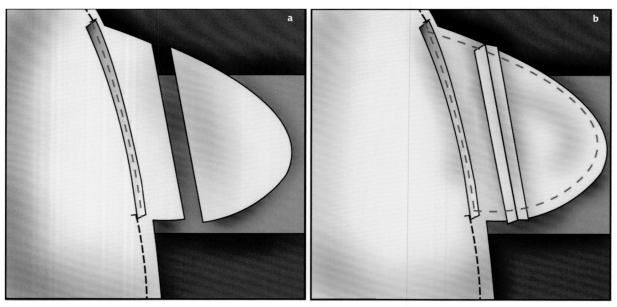

Figure 12.11a and b In-seam pockets, method 3.

HIP POCKETS

1. To begin, you need to pattern your garment minus the pockets. Then pattern your **hip pockets** so that when sewn to the garment pattern, they will complete the garment. (Figure 12.12)
2. Line up the interfacing to the pocket opening on the garment, and baste in place half the width of your seam allowance. If you are using fusible interfacing, now is the time to use it.
3. Line up the pocket edge facing to the garment, right sides together. Pin and stitch a seam through all of the layers at the marked seam line.
4. Clip off the seam line close to the seam to reduce bulk, and press the seam toward the facing. Understitch ¼ inch from the seam to flatten the facing.

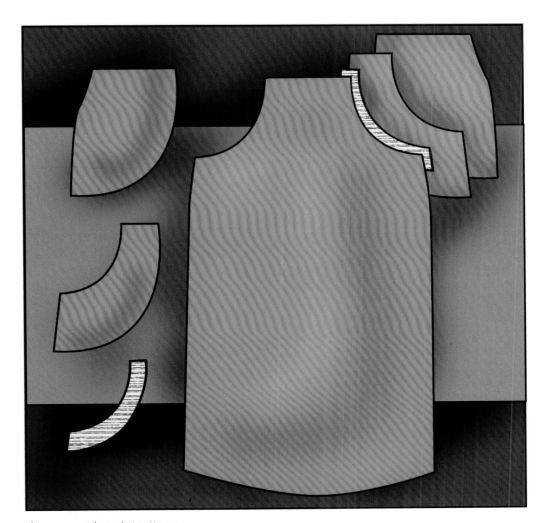

Figure 12.12 Hip pocket patterns.

5. Flip the facing to the inside of the garment, and baste it flat so that it can stay in place while you sew the rest of the pocket. (Figure 12.13a)

6. Line up the pocket to the garment line and the facing bottom edge right sides together. Pin in place, and stitch along the marked seam line. Then you can either whipstitch or serge the edges. (Figure 12.13b)

7. Stay stitch along the top of the pocket through all of the layers to keep the pocket in place. You can also stay stitch along the side seam in the hip area. Press the pocket, and remove the basting stitch. (Figure 12.13c and d)

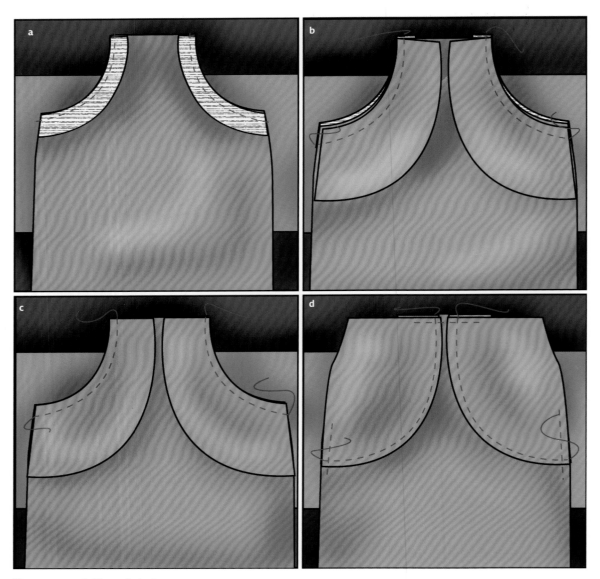

Figure 12.13a–d Hip pockets steps.

Tailoring

Tailoring has been around for hundreds of years, having begun during the Middle Ages. Tailoring has always been referred to as suit construction; however, when we refer to couture tailoring, we can also discuss tailoring techniques that are used in couture garments. These techniques include pockets, collars, sleeves, and cuffs. For example, a simple patch pocket can be designed to fit a couture gown, yet you can concentrate on careful tailoring of the pockets. Tailoring steps have also been used inside corset construction. The layering of the interlining, padding, interfacing, canvas, and lining are very similar to careful tailoring construction. Today in the United States, tailoring is not commonly used because suits are sold in department stores and altered to fit the customer. These suits are ready to wear. They do not have the layering and quality of old-fashioned tailored suits made by professional tailors. However, you may still find very successful tailors in Europe, especially in Milan, Paris, Rome, and London. Today we see couture tailoring taking on a bigger role. Many designers create couture coat collections and couture suits. These suits have high-quality tailored sewing, and these designers hire professional tailors to do the job. (Figure 12.14)

To begin making your tailored jacket, you will need to purchase the supplies. You will need good quality fabric. You can use wool, cotton, linen, or even certain silks. (Figure 12.15) Choose a weave that does not ravel easily. For the interfacing and collar, you will

Figure 12.14 Chanel suit.

Figure 12.15 Suit fabric.

need **hair canvas** or horsehair interfacing, organdy, or fine cotton muslin. You will also need to purchase padding fabric (cotton flannel works well for this purpose). You may also need **silk organza** or lightweight cotton fabric for the backing of your face fabric if you choose a lightweight face fabric. Your needles need to be small and short because you will be sewing most of the details by hand.

When you are working with a regular fabric for your tailoring jacket, use either muslin or even face fabric itself as an interfacing for the body of the jacket. The rest is all about the grainline. When you cut your patterns, it is ideal to cut them on a specific grainline in order to give your jacket a better fit and wear.

Ready to begin your jacket, you will need to make a pattern. You can drape the pattern, or you can use measurements to pattern it. Keep in consideration the extra fit rules, like extra darts at the neckline to make the collar **roll** better, and the fit of the darts. Some darts become princess lines that start in the armhole on the side of the bust in order to offer a good fit for a female body. You will need to add ease to your jacket in order to give the jacket some room to be worn over another layer of clothing, sometimes even two layers of clothing in the cool weather. See Figure 12.16 for the patterns you should have in place.

When you are done with the fitting, lay the jacket on a flat surface, take the basting apart, and make the needed changes.

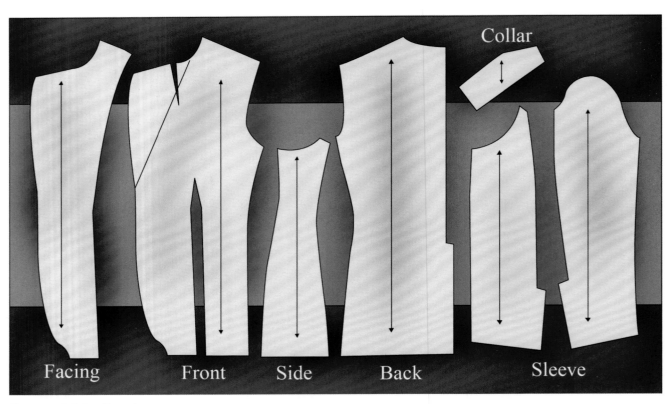

Figure 12.16 Suit pattern pieces.

JACKET TAILORING

1. Begin preshrinking fabric, then pressing it, and laying it out on a flat surface neatly with no folds or wrinkles. Fold your fabric in half to cut two of each pattern piece. (Figure 12.17a)
2. Lay out the pattern pieces you have already corrected after the fitting on your fabric, and pin them in place. Line up your patterns to follow the grainline. (Figure 12.17b)

- Some patterns, like the **under collar**, need to be cut off grain in order to allow the collar to fit and roll around the neck and the shoulders. By cutting it on the bias, it stretches to take its shape and rolls better. Stick to the same grainline when you line up your interfacing patterns on your interfacing fabric.

3. Cut out patterns.
4. Instead of marking your patterns with chalk, you will need to use your needle and thread to thread trace

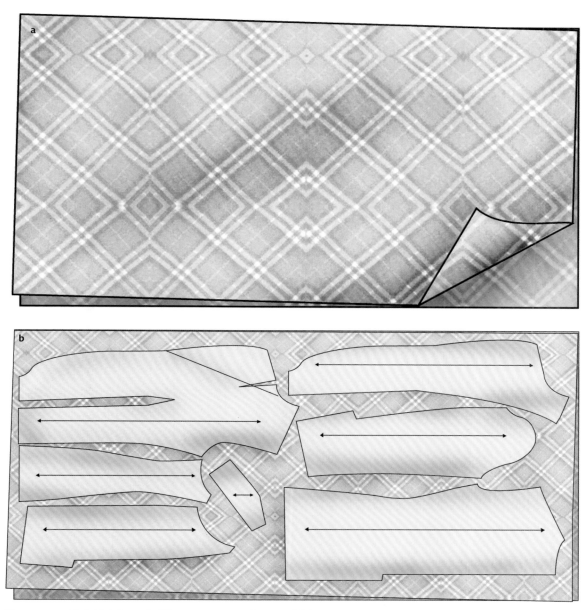

Figure 12.17 (a) Get fabric ready. (b) Lay out pattern pieces on fabric.

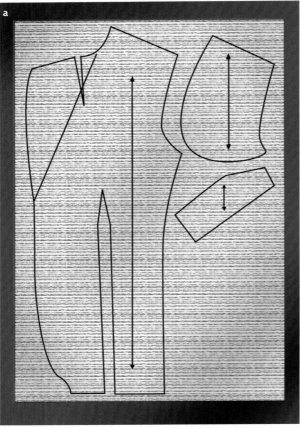
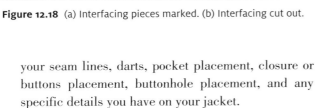
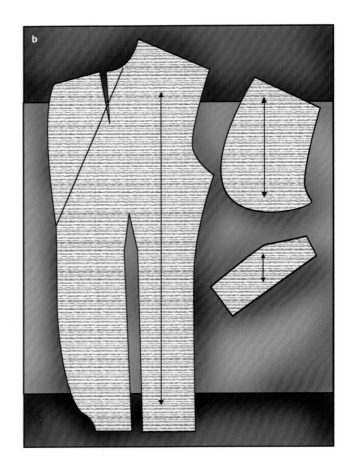

Figure 12.18 (a) Interfacing pieces marked. (b) Interfacing cut out.

your seam lines, darts, pocket placement, closure or buttons placement, buttonhole placement, and any specific details you have on your jacket.

5. Cut your interfacing pieces out of your interfacing fabric. Whether it is hair canvas, muslin, horsehair, or linen, make sure your grainline matches the garment fabric pieces you have already cut. For example, the body patterns should be cut on grain, while the under collar should be cut on the bias. (Figure 12.18a)

6. When you cut your interfacing, cut out your darts and your seam allowances to reduce bulk in the darts and the seams. (Figure 12.18b)

7. If you are making a warmer, thicker jacket, you will need to add another layer to your jacket: cotton flannel padding. Flannel is usually added to the chest area and the upper back area to add warmth and stiffness. You will need to cut double-layered flannel pieces on grain for each area of application. (Figure 12.19) For lighter jackets, cut these out of your interfacing fabric just to add stiffness but not too much warmth.

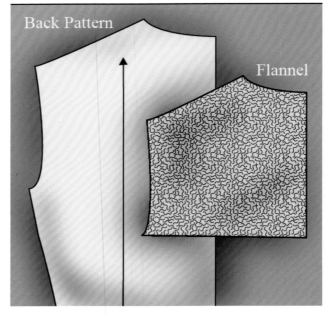

Figure 12.19 Cotton flannel for warmth.

8. If your garment fabric is lightweight, you will also need to add a backing layer, which is usually made of cotton muslin, soft cotton, silk organza, **silk muslin**, or even another layer of interfacing. You will need to cut your backing patterns either for the entire jacket or for just the body of the jacket. The backing will make your fabric stronger, it will wrinkle less, and it will help your jacket drape better. The backing patterns are usually lined up with the underside of the jacket face fabric patterns before the seams are stitched. Then these stay-stitched patterns are treated as one pattern.

JACKET BODY SEWING STEPS

1. Stitch up your darts in the face fabric only. If you want welt pockets and bound buttonholes on this jacket, you will need to do them now. (Figure 12.20a)

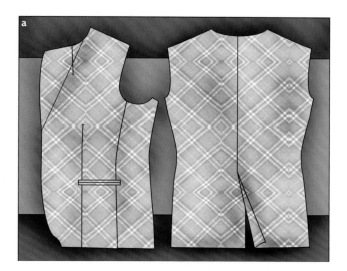

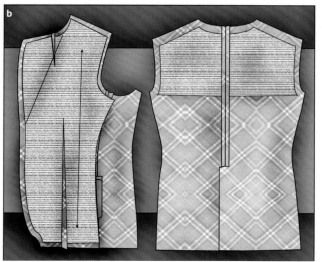

2. Line up your interfacing with the underside of the face fabric. Make sure your edges line up with the seam line of the face fabric as well. Make sure your cutout darts fit tightly around your face fabric darts. Do this for both the front and back of the fabric. (Figure 12.20b) If your jacket has bound pockets and buttonholes, you will need to cut the opening out of your interfacing.

3. Catch stitch by hand along your interfacing dart legs, seams, and bound pockets, if you have them, attaching them to the face fabric dart seam. (Figure 12.20c)

4. Next, using a different thread color than your garment, baste large stitches throughout your pattern in a grid, beginning in the center of the pattern and working your way out from the center. These stitches are made to keep the pieces from shifting. (Figure 12.20d) Start again in the center, and work your way up and down, following the horizontal direction at least three times along the pattern and then cross baste vertically in at least three places. Do this for both the front and back patterns.

5. Next you will need to take your cotton flannel double-layer pieces and quilt a grid on them for both

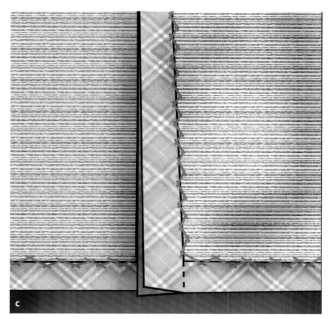

Figure 12.20 (a) Body sewing, add pockets and buttonholes. (b) Line up interfacing. (c) Catch stitch interfacing.

the front and back of the jacket. (Figure 12.20e) You can then line up the flannel pieces on top of the interfacing in the chest area in the front and the upper back area in the back. Baste it in place, and catch stitch the edges to the (a) **lapel** fold line, (b) seam lines in the shoulder, and (c) armhole and some of the upper body side seam. Do this for both sides of the front and back. (Figure 12.20f)

6. Take your style tape and line it up along the lapel roll/ fold line in the front pattern. Your roll line should have been marked on your pattern when you were fitting the muslin sample. Line it up so that the tape is actually on the front pattern side and the edge lines up with the fold line. (Figure 12.20g) The tape holds the lapel from

stretching because it ends up on the bias of the fabric when you cut the front patterns on grain. The tape should be ¼ inch shorter than the fold line of the lapel. This way you can ease the fold line into the tape and prevent it from stretching during wear. Catch stitch the tape to the interfacing to both front sides.

7. Next you will need to make small diagonal basting stitches up and down the lapel. This is called **pad stitching**. (Figure 12.20h) Make sure you use thread that matches the color of your jacket. You will be basting through both the interfacing and the face fabric; you will not want the thread to show. These stitches will be permanent. When you are making the small diagonal basting stitches, make sure you only catch a

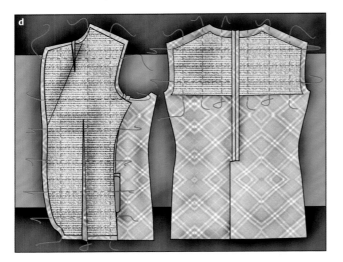

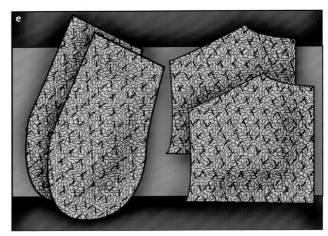

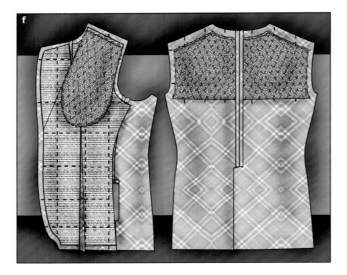

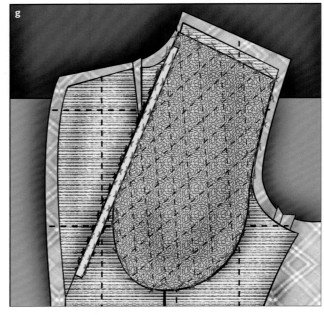

Figure 12.20 (continued) (d) Baste up, down, right, and left. (e) Quilt the flannel. (f) Attach flannel to the front and back. (g) Twill tape attachment.

couple of threads of the face fabric when you take your stitch so you will barely see the thread coming through to the face side. If you keep your finger under the fabric, you can feel how many threads you are picking up with the needle. At the corners, pad stitch a bit tighter, so that your corners will be stiffer and stronger. If you want your lapels to be soft, make those stitches longer and looser. Do this to both front sides.

8. Trim off ⅛ inch from the center front edge of the interfacing. Use the same style tape, and line it up beginning 1 inch from the shoulder around the lapel seam line down toward the hemline. (Figure 12.20i) Cut the tape ⅛ inch shorter, and ease it in the lapel curve area. Make sure you line up the tape edge with the seam line on the pattern side, not on the seam allowance. Catch stitch it in place. Do this to both front sides.

9. Press the lapel to flatten all of the stitches. Use a damp cheesecloth or cotton cloth, and then take it out and press again in order to steam dry. Then use the edge of the ironing board to line up the lapel fold line and press. Do not press too hard, as you want the lapel to look like it rolls a bit when it is folded over the chest. Press the rest of the jacket fronts.

10. Stitch your back pieces to the front pieces at the side seams.

11. Stitch your back panels together at the center back seam line. Press seams open. (Figure 12.20j) Now catch stitch your interfacing at the seam lines.

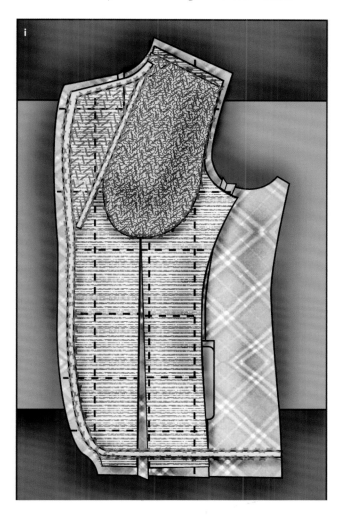

Figure 12.20 (continued) (h) Pad stitch the lapel. (i) Line up the style tape along the center front and down to the hem. (j) Attach the front and back.

COLLAR-TAILORING TECHNIQUES

1. Now that the jacket body is complete, begin working on the collar. Stitch a center back seam on the under collar. Then baseball stitch the sides of the interfacing together as well. (Figure 12.21a)

2. Place the under collar and the under collar interfacing wrong sides together, and baste them in place. Make sure you line up the edge of the interfacing with the under collar seam line.

3. Pad stitch both layers together. Pad stitch the corners of the under collar tighter than the rest of the collar because these corners need to stay stiff and hard. (Figure 12.21b) Some tailors like to pad stitch the roll line and under the roll line to the inside edge of the collar the same shape as the roll line. The diagonal lines follow along the roll line horizontally. Press the collar down with a hot iron so that it will flatten the collar and make it stiff.

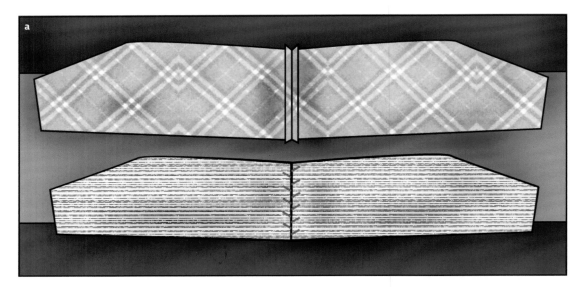

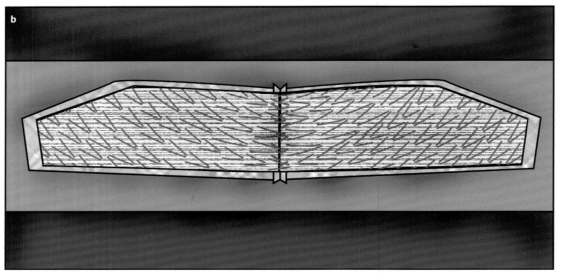

Figure 12.21 (a) Stitch the center back seam. (b) Pad stitch the under collar.

4. Lay your under collar facedown, and fold along the roll line on the ironing board. Press. Use a pressing ham to roll the collar over. (Figure 12.21c)
5. Line up the center back seam on the body of the jacket with the center back seam of the collar, and baste the collar to the neckline of the jacket. Do not make any permanent stitches yet. Make sure that the collar is in the right place and fits well by fitting the jacket. (Figure 12.21d)

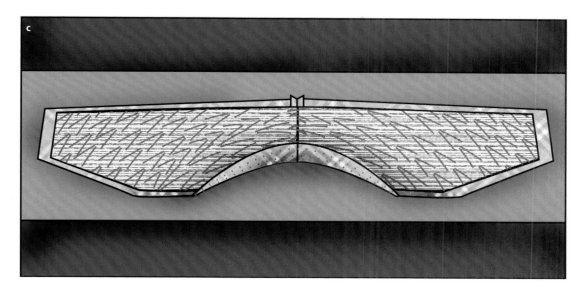

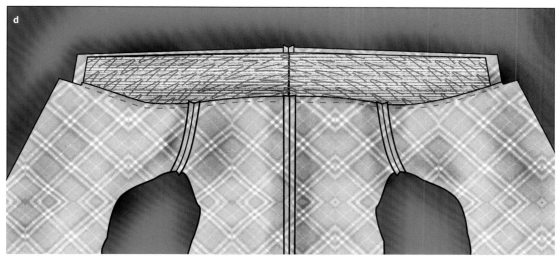

Figure 12.21 *(continued)* (c) Press down the roll line. (d) Baste collar to the center back.

JACKET FACING AND LINING

Fit the jacket. Make sure you pin the jacket closed in the button area. Does the jacket fit the body? Is there enough room to move around, and will the sleeves fit in the armhole? Make adjustments if necessary.

1. Begin work on the sleeves. Stitch up the seams on two-piece sleeves. Then baste them in place for the fitting. (Figure 12.22a)

2. During the fitting, it is very important to check the sleeves. Check the length, the drape, and the shoulder. Does the jacket need **shoulder pads**? Mark any corrections that need to be made.

3. When ready, attach the jacket facing. Line it up with the center front of the garment, right sides together.

Make sure you use your markings to match up the facing correctly. Baste along the seam line. Flip it right side out to check the fit. If it fits well, flip it back and stitch a permanent seam. (Figure 12.22b)

4. Clip the seam allowance to ⅛ inch from the seam line to reduce bulk. Make sure you only clip it to your notches. (Figure 12.22c)

5. Flip it right side out again, and understitch the facing on the facing side ¼ inch from the edge. Make sure you only catch the facing and the seam allowances on the inside, not the face fabric of the lapel. You can sew the understitch by hand, making small backstitches. Mark a seam line 1 inch from the inside edge of the facing so that you can line up the lining later. (Figure 12.22d)

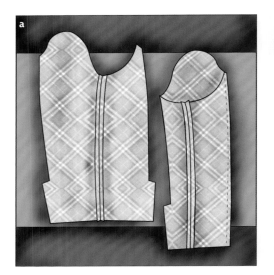
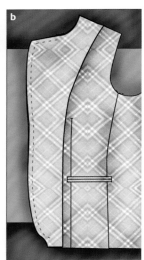
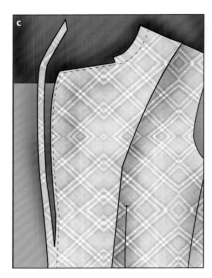
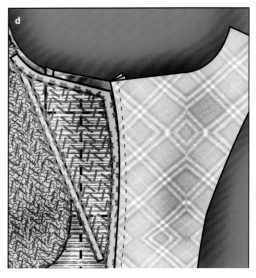

Figure 12.22 (a) Stitch up the sleeves in the seams. (b) Attach the facing, and flip it right side out. (c) Trim off seam allowances. (d) Understitch the facing.

6. To finish the hem, turn it in by folding along the hem-line. Press to flatten in place. (Figure 12.22e)

7. Then stitch a catch stitch or a running stitch along the edge of the hem allowance. Catch only the inter-facing. (Figure 12.22f)

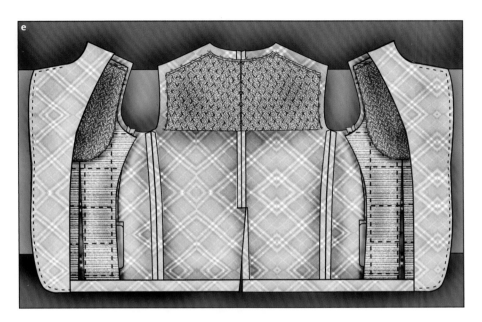

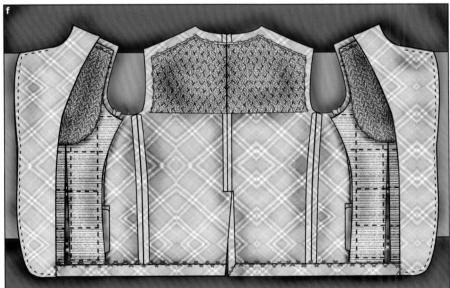

Figure 12.22 *(continued)* (e) Turn up the hem. (f) Catch stitch along the edge.

8. Attach the lining. It will cover all of your stitches and pieces and make the jacket look very neat. It will also make it easier to wear.

9. The lining will be sewn slightly bigger than the face side because it needs to fit the body well and because it does not stretch due to the weave of the lining fabric.

10. Use your lining patterns to cut your lining pieces out of the lining fabric. Keep seam allowances 1 inch wide, leaving room for error. Keep the hem the same width as you have on the jacket. Cut the center front to fit and attach to the facing pieces; however, give yourself a good 1 to 1.5 inches for seam allowance. Back lining needs extra fabric in the center back seam for a pleat down the center back. (Figure 12.22g)

11. You will begin by sewing a lining that will be a bit larger than the face jacket. Your seams will be ⅛ inch from the marked seam line. This way your lining will end up a bit larger than the face jacket. (Figure 12.22h)

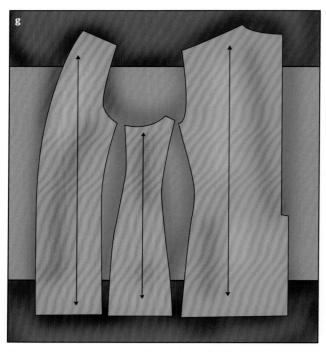

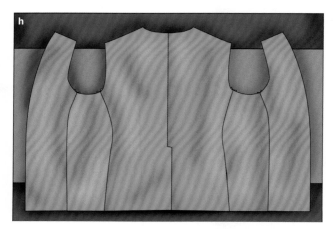

Figure 12.22 *(continued)* (g) Lining pieces. (h) Attach the lining together.

12. Lay the jacket facedown on a flat surface. Catch stitch the facing edge to the interfacing. Make sure you leave at least 1 inch unsewn from the neckline. (Figure 12.22i)

13. Next line up the lining on top of the jacket wrong side down. Make sure you line up all of the seams and pin. This way the lining will be uniformly larger between each seam. When pinning the back, make a 1-inch pleat along the center back, and pin it in place. (Figure 12.22j)

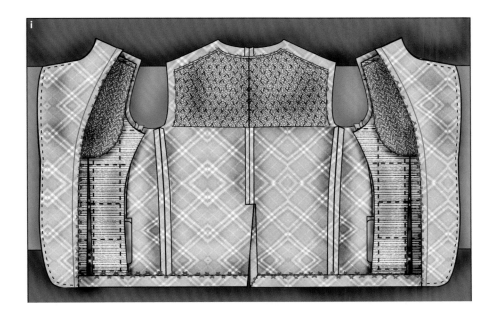

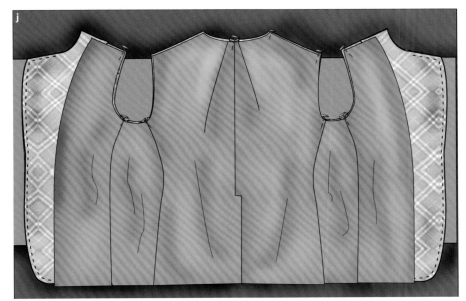

Figure 12.22 (continued) (i) Catch stitch the facing. (j) Lining facedown. Pin.

14. Align the center front panels to the facing. To do so, fold the lining under along the lining seam line, and pin it along the marked seam line along the facing. For extra fabric in the shoulder, the best thing to do is to make a pleat with it along the shoulder near the seam line of the armhole. (Figure 12.22k)

15. Pin and baste the lining and the jacket 2 to 3 inches below the seam lines along the top of the jacket and about 4 to 5 inches from the hem. This way the lining can be easily connected to the hem. Make sure you leave ¾ to 1 inch of the face fabric hem. Turn your lining under, and blind stitch in place. (Figure 12.22l) Press.

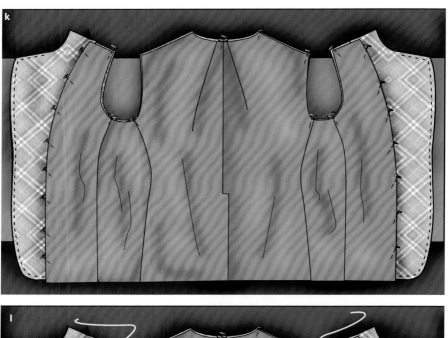

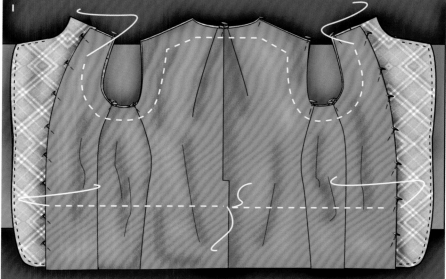

Figure 12.22 *(continued)* (k) Align the lining and facing. (l) Baste the lining.

16. Sew up your shoulder seams. To do so, move the lin-
    ing out of the way, and stitch the jacket closed at the
    shoulder seams. (Figure 12.22m) Catch-stitch to the
    interfacing. Press. Make sure to catch the lining and
    hem, not the interfacing and face fabric.

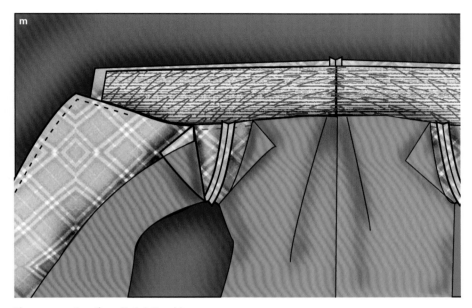

Figure 12.22 *(continued)* (m) Shoulder seams.

FINISHING TOUCHES

1. To attach a shoulder pad, you can sew it in place with catch stitches along the shoulder seam. The shoulder pad should end at the armholes seam line, not at the end of the seam allowance. (Figure 12.23a)

2. Attach a sleeve to the jacket. Some jackets need another shoulder pad piece called the roll. Sewn in between the sleeve and the shoulder pad, it gives the sleeve a stronger shoulder that curves out a bit without draping down right away. (Figure 12.23b)

3. Place the jacket on the form inside out. Fold over one side of the lining seam allowance at the shoulder seam, and overlap it over another side of the shoulder seam. Stitch in place by backstitching. (Figure 12.23c)

4. Place the lining sleeve on the jacket sleeve, and pin it in place. Fold the seam allowance in, and stitch the sleeve lining in place. (Figure 12.23d)

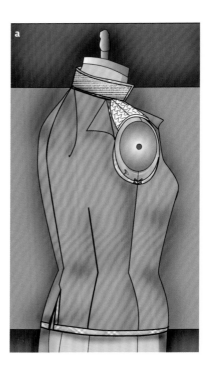 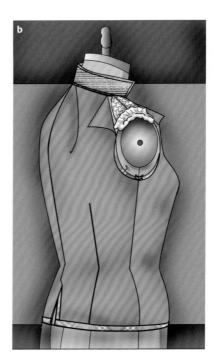 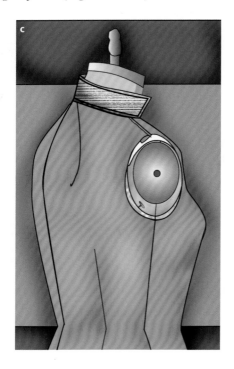

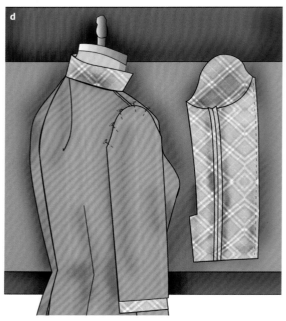

Figure 12.23 (a) Attach the shoulder pad. (b) Attach the roll. (c) Close the shoulder seam. (d) Stitch the sleeve lining in place.

5. Your jacket is almost complete. You need to have another fitting to make sure everything fits well and the lining is not too small or too large.

6. To finish the jacket, attach the **top collar** pattern piece. To do so, you can line up the collar piece to check whether it still matches up with the under collar. If it does, you can pin the top collar and the under collar right sides together. Pin only on the outer edges and the corners. (Figure 12.23e) Baste along the seam line, and then flip it right side out to see how the collar looks.

7. Flip it back inside out, and stitch a permanent seam along the outer seam line.

8. Clip the corners so that your corners will be sharp when you flip it out. Press.

9. Flip the collar right side out again. Use a point turner to help push out the corners and get them to be as sharp as you want them to be. Press the collar flat using a damp cloth. Do not press too much or you will get shiny marks on your collar.

10. When ready, baste ¼ inch from the edge of the collar, and add another basting stitch to attach the lower edge of the collar to the under collar and the jacket. (Figure 12.23f)

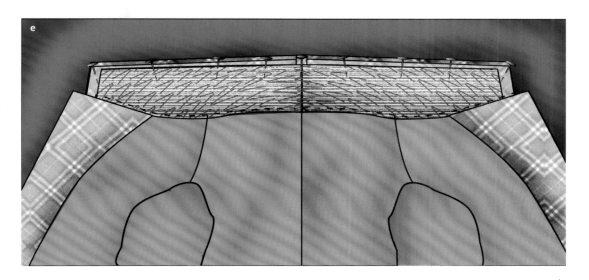

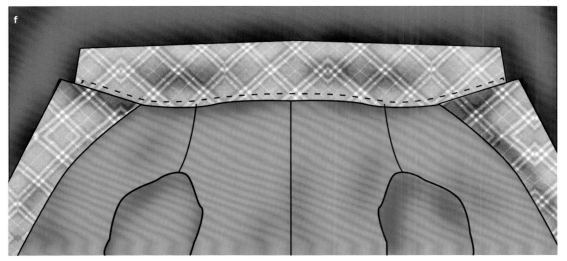

Figure 12.23 (continued) (e) Attach the top collar. (f) Fold the collar edge and baste.

11. Fold the seam allowance of your lapel facing, and overlap the collar along the seam line. Pin in place. (Figure 12.23g) Do so for both sides of the jacket. Then use a fell stitch to stitch it to the collar and finish. (Figure 12.23h) Sometimes the collar and lapel are topstitched through for design purposes and also to flatten the edge if it is too thick.

12. For the sleeve cuff, you can use your creative ideas to either finish it with buttons like a regular suit or trim it with delicate trims and embroidery. It is important, though, to keep your lining straight. If it twists, it will be very uncomfortable to wear the jacket. To make sure you are doing everything right, flip the jacket inside out and place on the form. The sleeve hem

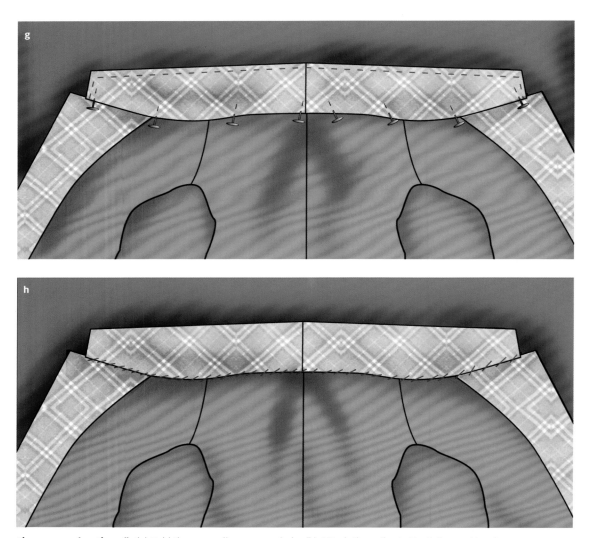

Figure 12.23 (continued) (g) Fold the seam allowance and pin. (h) Attach the collar to the lining and lapel.

should be pressed inside the jacket, and the lining should overlap the seam allowance and be stitched on. You can use a blind stitch or a fell stitch to attach the lining sleeve to the sleeve. (Figure 12.23i)

13. For the finishing touches, sew on your buttons and make buttonholes. If you have bound buttonholes, you can slash an opening along the buttonhole opening in the front facing. (Figure 12.23j) If you wanted bound buttonholes, they should have been done before you put the jacket together. Whipstitch the opening around the buttonhole area on the facing side.

14. Some finishing touches may include embellishments on the jacket such as beading, trim, topstitching, embroidery, and so on.

15. Now that your jacket is complete, you can remove the large basting stitches from the jacket, shown in red on Figure 12.23k, and steam the jacket on the form to finalize the tailoring process.

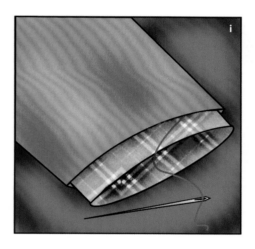

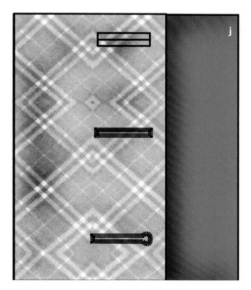

Figure 12.23 *(continued)* (i) Finish the cuff. (j) Buttons and buttonholes. (k) Remove the large basting stitches.

A BRIEF LOOK INTO THE LIFE OF

ALEXANDER McQUEEN

Alexander McQueen was born on March 17, 1969, in Lewisham, London, where his family lived in public housing. He was one of six children supported by a very low income his parents were able to earn. His father worked as a cab driver, and his mother taught social science.

McQueen was teased tremendously at school, and at the age of 16, he dropped out and went to work on Savile Row, in London's Mayfair district. There, he worked at the Anderson and Shephard tailor shop and then moved to Gieves and Hawkes. He learned many skills from these two jobs and decided to advance his skills beyond tailoring. McQueen moved on to theatrical design and began making costumes with Angels and Bermans. His theatrical style always inspired his designs.

After the theater, McQueen moved to Milan where he found work as a design assistant to Italian fashion designer Romeo Gigli. Being around a designer inspired Alexander to come back to London and enroll at Central Saint Martin's College of Art & Design. In 1992, he graduated with an M.A. in fashion design. His final graduating collection was inspired by Jack the Ripper and was so adored by famous London stylist Isabella Blow that she bought the entire collection.

Only four years after graduation, McQueen became Chief Designer of Givenchy (under LVMH) from 1996 to 2001, one of the most prestigious French haute couture fashion houses. However, McQueen felt stifled at this job, as he desired more creative freedom. Even with this feeling of constraint, he won British Designer of the Year in 1996, 1997, and 2001 for his work at Givenchy.

In 2000, Gucci bought 51 percent of McQueen's company, Alexander McQueen, and helped him with enough capital to grow larger. McQueen left Givenchy and in 2003 was named International Designer of the Year by the Council of Fashion Designers of America and a Most Excellent Commander of the British Empire by the Queen of England. He also won another British Designer of the Year honor.

McQueen opened his stores in Milan, New York, London, Las Vegas, and LA. He became a worldwide success.

Unfortunately, McQueen had to live through multiple tragedies that proved insurmountable to him. First was the death of his longtime friend and benefactor, Isabella Blow, in 2007, to whom he dedicated his 2008 Spring/Summer line. And second was the passing of his lifetime muse, his mother, on February 2, 2010. On February 11, 2010, just one day before his mother's funeral, McQueen was found dead in his Mayfair, London, apartment, of an apparent suicide.

Despite his relatively short career, McQueen cemented his place as one of the most talented avant-garde designers in the history of fashion. Following his death, his company was taken over by a longtime co-designer, Sarah Burton.

Alexander McQueen, 2003.

Alexander McQueen designs on display at the Savage Beauty exhibition at the Victoria & Albert Museum in London, England, 2015.

Alexander McQueen designs on display at the Savage Beauty exhibition at the Metropolitan Museum of Art, New York City, 2011.

Chapter Review

Stay stitching will help you sew the perfect garment by preventing the fabric pattern from stretching and/or changing shape before and during construction. In order to protect your pattern from distortion, stay stitch as soon as you cut your pattern and then remove the paper pattern. You followed the steps to make a great tailored jacket. You also learned how to make great pockets, whether they were placed on a tailored suit or on a couture gown.

Projects

1. Make a stay stitching sample for your book. Write down your steps, and insert it into one of your plastic cover sheets.
2. Design and tailor a jacket. Use your creativity. Design, tailor, and construct a matching corset top to the jacket. You can design a top using a boned bodice as a stay instead.
3. Design and construct a couture garment using ten techniques covered in this book.

Key Terms

Flap	Patch pocket	Tailoring
Hair canvas	Roll	Top collar
Hip pocket	Shoulder pad	Under collar
In-seam pocket	Silk muslin	Welt pocket
Lapel	Silk organza	
Pad stitching	Stay stitching	

GLOSSARY

Alencon lace. A fine French-made lace with filled-in motifs outlined with a heavy silk cord, called cordonette, that creates a raised outer edge on a sheer net background.

A-line skirt. A skirt that narrows at the waistline and forms an A-shape flare down to the hem.

American smocking. Smocking made by hand-sewing using a dotted grid as a guide.

Apex. A point located along the bustline in the center of the bust on the dress form, body, and garment patterns. Used to line up the garments and also to line up the bustline during draping and pattern.

Appliqués. Cutout fabric shapes applied to the garment fabric. Other types of appliqués include embroidery, lace appliqué, cutwork appliqué, and reverse appliqué.

Applique scissors. Used for working and cutting appliqués, cutwork, and embroidery.

Armscye. An armhole term used in garment construction, draping, and pattern blocks.

Atelier. Also known as a room or couture house in which an artist or couturier creates his or her designs.

Backstitch. A very commonly used stitch. It is the strongest permanent hand stitch. There are two types of backstitches: one is referred to as a full backstitch, and the other is a half backstitch.

Basting. Temporary stitches used to hold the garment pieces together before the seams can become permanent.

Beadwork. Also known as bead embroidery, one of the most important embellishments in couture gowns. The decoration is done by threading beads through decorative embroidery stitches.

Bias. The diagonal stretch across the lengthwise and crosswise grainline of the fabric. A garment cut along the bias of the fabric is called being cut on the bias; it fits the body closer. It also offers a great drape to the fabric.

Bustle. A wonderful technique to shorten a long train temporarily to allow easier wear of the long skirt. Also used as a gown decoration in the back design of the skirt.

Buttonhole scissors. Used to cut open buttonholes and for cutwork.

Buttonhole stitch. Used for a variety of different stitches in many widths and tightness in embroidery, cutwork, buttonholes, hems, appliqués, and much more.

Canvas. Strong and rough cotton used as an inner structure in corsets and tailoring.

Catch-stitch. Looks like a stitch shaped as a letter X, catching a small amount of threads on one side of the fabric and then a couple of threads along the edge of the hem, forming a crossing diagonal line.

Center back. A term used to describe the center back of the body on the pattern piece and the dress form.

Center front. A term used to describe the center front of the body on the pattern piece and the dress form.

Chambre Syndicale. The organization located in Paris, France, dictating and governing French haute couture. To become a member of this organization, a couture house is required to have a minimum of fifteen staff members and present a collection of at least fifty designs, both day and evening garments, in January and July of each year.

Charmeuse. A light, soft fabric with a satin front and dull back known as the luxury and lingerie fabric. Great for draping.

Chiffon. Transparent, fluid, soft fabric made of fine twisted silk or manufactured yarns. Great for draping with a feminine touch.

Cord quilting. Quilting technique used to decorate clothing by pulling a cord in between two layers of fabric.

Cotton. A soft, comfortable, strong, and easy-to-use fabric. Comes from the cotton plant's seedpod.

Couching. Stitch technique used to bead a curved or a straight line along a specific motif.

Cowl. A draped fabric forming layers of drapes that can be added to a neckline, a center low back, sleeves, peg skirt sides, and so on.

Crinoline. Nylon netting used for petticoats and underskirts made with many layers of tulle to hold a dress away from the body and keep it from being tangled between legs during wear.

Cutwork. Also known as needlepoint lace. A motif is embroidered on fabric and then the negative part of the motif gets cut out with embroidery scissors or is burned out.

Darts. A triangular shape along the waistline or around the bust area. Added to allow a great fit around the waistline or bust in order to allow a wider cylinder fit tighter around the waist. Dart sides, called dart legs, should always be equal in length. Dart point, called the drill hole.

Double needles. A sewing machine needle that is formed with two needles attached at the top shaft. This needle can stitch a seam with two parallel stitches at the same time.

Draping. A technique to pattern a garment using pinning, trimming, and stretching of the fabric directly on the dress form.

Ease. Added to the garment pattern to allow movement and also added when a larger pattern piece needs to be sewn onto a smaller pattern piece.

Embroidery. A decorative technique where ornamental and decorative raised stitches are used to make a design or motif on fabric using a needle.

English quilting. Used to make warm coats and bed covers. In this type of quilting, two layers of fabric have a layer of batting in between. All three layers are then stitched together.

English smocking. This type of smocking is different from American smocking in that the fabric is pleated and does not use a dotted grid as a guide.

European knot. Used to secure the thread underneath the fabric before the hand sewing begins.

Facing. Used to finish edges on necklines, armholes, hems, pockets, zipper flaps, collars, cuffs, and so on and to strengthen the edges so that they do not stretch when the garment is worn or washed.

Fédération Française de la Couture. An organization dictating the rules of French couture. Membership in this federation is based on high standards of excellence.

Fibers. Threadlike strands spun into yarns that in turn are woven or knitted.

Flared skirt. A skirt that is narrow at the waist and flared out at the hem in various widths.

Flou. A person in charge of the second workroom in a couture house, where the soft pieces are made by the dressmakers.

French seam. Common used seam for joining sheer and silky fabrics. It does not show raw edges.

Gathers. Fabric width pulled and gathered together with thread to allow the width to narrow as well as form more volume. Used in ruffles, skirts, sleeves, embellishments, and so on.

Girdle. A type of corset that was modernized with elastic latex fabric and worn as underwear for women around the waist and bottom to shape the body.

Godets. A triangular pattern piece inserted in between the seams or to the edges of cutout areas.

Goldwork. A very old skill and one of the most luxurious methods of embroidery using metallic threads, floss, plates, leather, and purl wire floss instead of the usual floss made for regular embroidery.

Gored skirt. Gored skirts allow the skirt to follow the grainline for a proper fit using panels without the use of darts.

Grainline. Refers to the orientation of the yarns in a woven fabric. The lengthwise grains run along the length of the fabric and are called the warp yarns. The yarns that are woven in and out perpendicularly to the warp yarns are called the weft yarns. These run side to side forming the cross grain of the fabric.

Hair canvas. Used as interfacing inside the corset, jackets, collars, and so on.

Hairline seam. Narrow version of the flat fell seam used for sheer and lightweight fabrics.

Hoop skirt. A cage petticoat, also called the farthingale, made of rows of steel hoops held by leather strips. Today the hoops are also inserted into channels sewn into an A-line skirt petticoat.

Hourglass. Refers to a narrow waist, wider chest, and wider hips silhouette on a woman's body.

Interfacing. Used to describe the fabric used to support the garment, making it stronger for certain areas that need support.

Interlining. Very similar to underlining; however, its main purpose is to effectively add warmth to your garment without adding bulk.

Kick pleat. Help women take a step and walk in a tight skirt, long jacket, shirt, or coat.

Lace. Dates far back into fashion history and was crocheted and embroidered by hand. Most laces have a floral motif, and sometimes you can find a geometric motif with circles and triangles.

Lapel. A part of a tailored jacket that is located between the collar and the buttons. The lapel is folded along a roll line and is faced before the collar is attached to it.

Leather. Attractive, smooth, soft, tear-resistant animal skins used for clothing and industrial wear.

Linen. The second oldest natural fiber used. It comes from the flax plant, which has a natural luster due to its wax content.

Lining. Fabric used to cover the inside of the garment to make the inside more attractive and to make it easier to wear the garment. Durable luxury fabric three times stronger than cotton.

Loop turner. A tool used to flip straps right side out.

Man-made fiber. Consists of filaments extruded in a liquid form into various fibers. These fibers are usually colored and dyed while they are in the liquid form before the fibers become the filaments.

Mermaid skirt. Got its name for the silhouette shape it takes when the straight gored skirt begins to flare out toward the bottom hem, turning into a mermaid-shaped skirt.

Mock french seam. Used the same way as the French seam when you are unsure of the fit of the garment. Since it is very difficult sometimes to get a nice French seam on a curved edge, you can use this method.

Muslin. Cotton fabric used for draping and the construction of toiles and samples. Also a term describing toile in the United States.

Natural fibers. Fibers that come from natural plants.

Padstitching. Diagonal stitches used in tailoring to make the lapel, shoulder pads, and the collar stronger. This type of stitching is always used in couture to make two layers of fabric stronger.

Peplum. Worn as a short overskirt and attached to the skirt at the waist or the jacket. Keeping the length of the peplum 2 to 3 inches below the waist will help keep the body looking slim.

Petticoat. Made of crinoline netting, cotton, fleece, flannel, or hoops to hold the dress skirt away from the body and from falling in.

Plastic boning. Affordable boning that comes in different types and is sold in fabric stores. It cannot be sewn through; however, it can be cut with scissors, and the edges can be rounded with scissors or a nail file. It comes in a cotton casing, which makes it easier to attach to the garment.

Première de l'atelier. The head of the tailoring workroom in a couture house. This person cuts the first pattern, makes and fits the toiles, prepares cuts and fits the garments, and oversees the garments' completion.

Purl. A hollow coiled wire produced by winding plated wire and stitched through with a beading needle like a bead. Used for goldwork embroidery.

Ribbonwork. Embroidery techniques stitched with the use of ribbon to make flower- and petal-like motifs.

Ridgeline. Inexpensive boning that can be found in any fabric store. This boning is softer than most and can be easily sewn through and cut.

S-bend corset. Also known as the swan bill corset, straight front corset, and the health corset. It was worn in the first years of the twentieth century. This corset forced the torso forward and made the hips protrude back, giving a torso an S shape.

Schiffli lace. A sheer net fabric lace that is embroidered and decorated on a Schiffli machine. A Schiffli machine should be used when embroidery that looks like it is done by hand is needed.

Seconde de l'atelier. The second in command to the premiere de l'atelier. This person is in charge of all the tailleurs.

Sharps. Very sharp needles used for delicate fabrics.

Shirring. Very commonly used technique worked with multiple rows of gathers to decorate clothing. Shirring can be done by hand or machine.

Shoulder pad. A pad sewn on along the shoulder seam inside a jacket to raise the shoulder level on a body. It also helps keep the shoulders nice and stiff in a tailored jacket.

Silk. A natural fiber used to make soft, drapable woven or knitted fabrics. Silk fiber comes from a cocoon of a silkworm. The silkworm produces the natural glue sericin, removed during the silk manufacturing.

Simple knot. Also called the waste knot. It temporarily holds the thread in the fabric until you can secure it with backstitches; then you can cut the knot off.

Smocking. Consists of fabric folds that are decoratively stitched at regular intervals to create a beautiful puckered pattern. Smocking can be done by hand or a smocking pleater.

Spiral steel boning. Made of small wires coiled together. This boning has to be cut with snips and cannot be cut with scissors. It is sold by the yard or cut for you in specific lengths. The edges are then covered with a special casing that keeps the boning from damaging the garment fabric.

Spring steel boning. This type of boning is made of strips of steel with blunt plastic-dipped ends. It can be cut professionally or with pliers and snips.

Tailleur. Responsible for the actual production of the garments in a couture house.

Tailor's tacks. Used to mark patterns, darts, pleats, and tucks on double layers of fabric when you do not wish to mark fabric with chalk. Used on thicker fabrics.

Tambour needle. Type of needle used to perform tambour beading on garments that are worn often and where the beading needs to have extra strength. The needle is made up of two parts: the needle hook and the holder.

Thread tracing. Used to mark thinner fabrics and muslin toiles.

Toile. Known as a mock-up garment of the design ready to be made. It could be patterned, draped, or both, and then sewn or pinned together to check accuracy of fit to the body or the form.

Trains. Historically, trains were only worn by the royal families. Today trains are a wonderful way to add luxury and status to a gown with a longer skirt in the back than in the front.

Trumpet skirt. See Mermaid skirt.

Underlining. Used for support and reinforcement of delicate, knit, stretchy, and loosely woven fabric. It adds stability and strength to lightweight fabrics, reduces wrinkling, reduces transparency in light-colored fabrics, and provides a layer of fabric to connect to hems.

Vendeuse. A very important person to the couture house, as he or she oversees the whole experience of the client, from selection of styles to delivery of the finished garment. He or she assists the client with advice on which collection pieces would suit the client and books fittings.

Venice lace. A type of openwork embroidery made from unique crochet stitches and wrapped satin stitch embroidery over the crochet that forms a 3-D motif with a crochet net background or no net, just creative crochet stitches.

Waistbands. Add strength to skirts and pants during wear and help them stay up along the waistline.

Whalebone. Inserted down the center front of a stay (fifteenth-century corset) to mold the body into an unnatural shape.

Wool. A natural fiber that comes from sheep, goat, alpaca, rabbit, or camel fur.

Yoke. Another way to be able to add a nice fit at the waist without using darts.

FIGURE CREDITS

2.25	Doug Kanter/AFP/Getty Images	**B3.2**	Loomis Dean/The LIFE Picture Collection/Getty Images
2.26a	Karl Prouse/Catwalking/Getty Images	**4.0**	Mark Sullivan/WireImage
2.26b	Antonov/WWD/© Condé Nast	**B4.1**	Marice Cohn Band/Miami Herald/MCT via Getty Images
2.27	Fairchild Books/Bloomsbury Publishing	**B4.2**	Daniel SIMON/Gamma-Rapho via Getty Images
2.28	WWD/© Condé Nast	**B4.3**	Daniel SIMON/Gamma-Rapho via Getty Images
2.29	Karl Prouse/Catwalking/Getty Images	**5.0**	Pascal Le Segretain/Getty Images
2.30	Katzman/WWD/© Condé Nast	**5.31a**	Aquino/WWD/© Condé Nast
2.31	Mark Mainz/Getty Images	**5.31b**	Centano/WWD/© Condé Nast
2.32	Centeno/WWD/© Condé Nast	**5.31c**	Dan/WWD/© Condé Nast
2.33	ThomasVogel/iStock	**5.39**	Antonov/WWD/© Condé Nast
2.34	Fernanda Calfat/Getty Images	**5.42a**	Mitra/WWD/© Condé Nast
2.35	Frazer Harrison/Getty Images	**5.42b**	Luca Teuchmann/WireImage/Getty Images
2.36	Fernanda Calfat/Getty Images	**5.45a**	STRDEL/AFP/Getty Images
2.37	DOUG KANTER/AFP/Getty Images	**5.45b**	Richard Bord/Getty Images
2.38	Fairchild Books/Bloomsbury Publishing	**B5.1**	Apic/Getty Images
2.39	Art Resource	**B5.2**	Chicago History Museum/Getty Images
2.40	JEAN-PIERRE MULLER/AFP/Getty Images	**6.0**	Pascal Le Segretain/Getty Images
2.41	WWD/© Condé Nast	**6.1**	Dominique Charriau/WireImage/Getty Images
2.42	Maria Teijeiro/Getty Images	**6.23**	Catwalking/Getty Images
2.43	Francois G. Durand/WireImage/Getty Images	**6.38**	Willy Maywald/Gamma-Keystone via Getty Images
2.44	Frazer Harrison/Getty Images	**6.42**	John Parra/Getty Images
2.45	Aquino/WWD/© Condé Nast	**6.46**	Hulton Archive/Getty Images
2.46	WWD/© Condé Nast	**B6.1**	Lipnitzki/Roger Viollet/Getty Images
2.47	M. Caulfield/WireImage/Getty Images	**B6.2**	Chicago History Museum/Getty Images
2.48	Andreas Rentz/Getty Images	**B6.3**	Chicago History Museum/Getty Images
2.49	WWD/© Condé Nast	**7.0**	Liz McAulay/Getty Images
2.50	Robin Platzer/FilmMagic Getty Images	**7.1**	The LIFE Picture Collection/Getty Images
2.51	Mondadori Portfolio via Getty Images	**B7.1**	Perry Hagopian/Contour by Getty Images
2.52	Steve Granitz/WireImage/Getty	**B7.2**	David Livingston/Getty Images
2.53	Iannaccone/WWD/© Condé Nast	**B7.3**	Fernanda Calfat/Getty Images
2.54	WWD/© Condé Nast	**8.0**	Pascal Le Segretain/Getty Images
2.55	Larry Busacca/Getty Images	**8.1**	Victor VIRGILE/Gamma-Rapho via Getty Images
2.56	Graham Denholm/Getty Images	**8.19**	Imagno/Getty Images
2.57	WWD/© Condé Nast	**8.39**	Venturelli/WireImage/Getty Images
2.58	WWD/© Condé Nast	**8.40**	Bert/Mansell/The LIFE Picture Collection/Getty Images
2.59	Fairchild Books/Bloomsbury Publishing	**8.55**	ROBYN BECK/AFP/Getty Images
2.60	Evan Agostini/Getty Images	**B8.1**	Foc Kan/WireImage
2.61	Karl Prouse/Catwalking/Getty Images	**B8.2**	Catwalking/Getty Images
2.62	Mark Mainz/Getty Images	**B8.3**	Victor VIRGILE/Gamma-Rapho via Getty Images
2.63	Chris Moore/Catwalking/Getty Images	**9.0**	Jason Merritt/Getty Images
2.64	Nancy Nehring/Getty Images	**9.1a**	Giannoni/WWD/© Condé Nast
2.65	Tony Barson/WireImage for amfAR/Getty Images	**9.1b**	Giannoni/WWD/© Condé Nast
B2.1	Sasha/Getty Images	**9.32**	Maitre/WWD/© Condé Nast
B2.2	Photo12/UIG/Getty Images		
B2.3	Library of Congress		
3.0	WWD/© Condé Nast		
B3.1	Edward Miller/Keystone/Getty Images		

9.40 Karwai Tang/Getty Images for Vogue and The Dubai Mall

9.41 Andreas Rentz/Getty Images for IMG

B9.1 WWD/© Condé Nast

B9.2 Giannoni/WWD/© Condé Nast

B9.3 PIERRE GUILLAUD/AFP/Getty Images

10.0 David H. Wells/Getty Images

B10.1 Pascal Le Segretain/Getty Images

B10.2 FRANCOIS GUILLOT/AFP/Getty Images

B10.3 Catwalking/Getty Images

11.0 Catwalking/Getty Images

11.17a Catwalking/Getty Images

B11.1 Giannoni/WWD/© Condé Nast

B11.2 Pascal Le Segretain/Getty Images

B11.3 Elisabetta A. Villa/WireImage

12.0 Erin Combs/Toronto Star via Getty Images

12.14 Pascal Le Segretain/Getty Images

12.15 Tim Graham/Getty Images

B12.1 Evan Agostini/Getty Images

B12.2 Anthony Harvey/Getty Images

B12.3 Paul Zimmerman/Getty Images

INDEX